OFFA'S DYKE

SILVER PENNY OF OFFA
STRUCK AT CANTERBURY

(See cover, front and back)

The coin was struck at Canterbury by the moneyer Ibba in the course of the penultimate decade of the eighth century. It marks the second of the three stages by which Offa was feeling his way towards the *novus denarius* of the Carolingians, and may fairly be called a *penny* though the weight and diameter have still certain affinities with the obsolete *sceat*. The beardless, diademed, profile portrait is imitated from Roman coins of the fourth century, and was to be characteristic of the English portrait penny for the next two and a half centuries. The reverse type is basically an elaborate cross fleury with voided centre and with the letters of the moneyer's name disposed symmetrically in the angles. It is peculiar to the reign.

The reproduction on the covers is enlarged to three diameters. Acknowledgement is due to the Trustees of the British Museum.

PLATE I

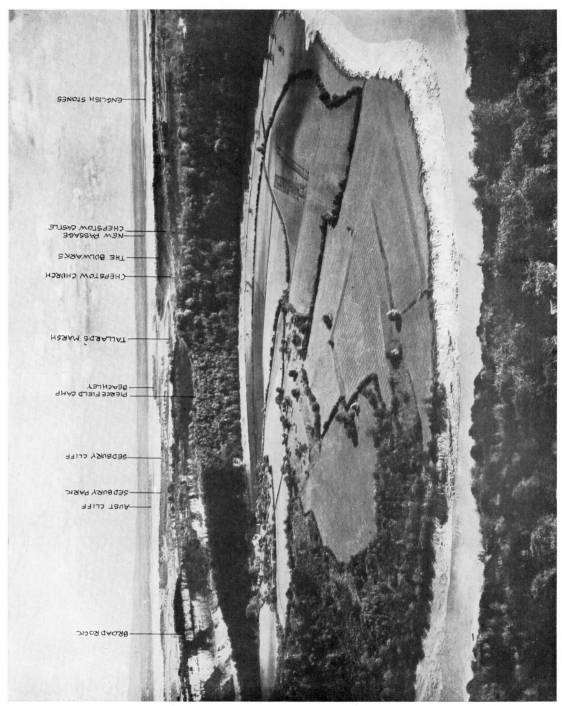

ENGLISH STONES

NEW PASSAGE
CHEPSTOW CASTLE

THE BULWARKS

CHEPSTOW CHURCH

TALLARDS MARSH

PIERCE FIELD CAMP
BEACHLEY

SEDBURY CLIFF

SEDBURY PARK

AUST CLIFF

BROAD ROCK

The Lower Wye valley from the Wyndcliff (700 ft.): showing the Mercian frontier at Broadrock, and Beachley peninsula. The cultivated land in the foreground, encircled by the river Wye, is Lancaut. Broken lines extending S. and SE. from Point N2, Fig. 94, indicate the area included in the photograph. Beyond the Severn the English coast—Gloucestershire and Somersetshire—is visible.

OFFA'S DYKE

A FIELD SURVEY OF THE
WESTERN FRONTIER-WORKS OF MERCIA
IN THE SEVENTH
AND EIGHTH CENTURIES A.D.

BY

SIR CYRIL FOX, F.B.A.

WITH A FOREWORD BY
SIR FRANK STENTON, F.B.A.

London: Published for
THE BRITISH ACADEMY
by GEOFFREY CUMBERLEGE
OXFORD UNIVERSITY PRESS, AMEN HOUSE, E.C. 4
1955

Oxford University Press, Amen House, London E.C.4

GLASGOW NEW YORK TORONTO MELBOURNE WELLINGTON
BOMBAY CALCUTTA MADRAS KARACHI CAPE TOWN IBADAN

Geoffrey Cumberlege, Publisher to the University

———

PRINTED IN GREAT BRITAIN

CONTENTS

CONTENTS

PART II. WAT'S DYKE

VIII. WAT'S DYKE: FROM THE DEE ESTUARY NEAR HOLY-WELL, FLINTSHIRE, TO MAESBURY, SHROPSHIRE, IN THE BASIN OF THE MIDDLE SEVERN

PART III

IX. THE MERCIAN ACHIEVEMENT: A COMMENTARY

APPENDIXES

PLATES

FIGURES

(All these are Maps, 6 in. to 1 mile reduced, unless otherwise indicated)

FOREWORD

THE investigation of Offa's Dyke, which is described in detail in this book, has demonstrated that it is a unitary work, inspired by a single purpose and controlled by a single mind. It must therefore have a definite historical setting. One major result of the present survey is the confirmation of its traditional attribution to the age of Mercian ascendancy in south Britain, and in particular to the reign of Offa (757–96), the most powerful of the Mercian kings. That it is post-Roman has been proved by excavation at a critical point of its northern sector. The scale of the work, which can now for the first time be clearly seen, reflects the power of a ruler whose authority throughout the Midlands was unchallenged. The mastery of a broken terrain displayed by its builders can only have been acquired through generations of experience. Here and there, as, notably, in its spectacular course up and around the mountain bastion of Herrock Hill, it seems to pass beyond its essential purpose of defining a frontier to positive defiance of the peoples beyond its line. A work of this type presupposes the political stability of the Mercian peoples who carried it through, and the previous development of their economic life to a point at which it could support the burden of a great public undertaking. The early history of the Mercian kingdom is very obscure, but so far as can be seen, it was not until the eighth century that these conditions were satisfied.

That the building of the Dyke was ordered by Offa is stated categorically in Asser's *Life of King Alfred*, written, to judge from internal signs, within a century of Offa's death. The individual character of this work and the problems of interpretation which it raises have exposed it to much criticism, but no critic has yet shaken the massive arguments for its genuineness set out by W. H. Stevenson in the edition which he published in 1904.[1] When Stevenson wrote the notes to this edition he was unable to point to any early evidence that the Dyke was attributed to Offa on the English side of the border. The discovery of medieval forms such as *Offedich* for the central portions of the Dyke[2] prove that a compound *Offan dic* had long been current locally among an English-speaking people. These pieces of direct evidence agree with all that is known about Offa's position in the insular world of his day. He was the strongest ruler who had so far appeared among the English peoples in Britain, and the supremacy which he established between the Humber and the Channel marks an important stage in the political unification of England. The emphasis which he himself laid on his royal authority is strikingly illustrated by the copious and varied signed currency which he issued, and in particular by the brilliant series of silver pieces which bear his portrait[3] or that of Cynethryth his queen. He claimed descent from the ancient rulers of the continental Angel, and among them from an ancestral Offa, commemorated in heroic verse as a king who had established a permanent boundary against a rival power. It has been suggested with high probability that in drawing

---

[1] *Asser's Life of King Alfred* (Oxford, 1904) and p. 281 below.
[2] Examples are quoted by E. Ekwall, *The Concise Oxford Dictionary of English Place-Names*, p. 332.
[3] See cover, front and back.

a boundary-line along his western border Offa of Mercia was consciously emulating his ancestor's achievement.[1]

Before the present survey was completed the most anomalous feature of the Dyke, regarded as a frontier-line, was its reduction to a series of discontinuous fragments in the plain of north-west Herefordshire, and its replacement as a boundary by the river Wye between Bridge Sollers in Herefordshire and Redbrook in Gloucestershire. It can now be seen that in west Herefordshire an expanse of ancient woodland made the construction of a continuous line of earthwork unnecessary and often impracticable. There is no such convincing physical reason for the absence of any artificial definition of the boundary in the Hereford section of the frontier. It is on the whole most probable that already in the eighth as in the eleventh century the Welsh district of Erging between the Worm, the Wye, and the Monnow was attached, though in virtual autonomy, to the English territory north of the Wye.[2] Something of its condition in the early tenth century is revealed by an enigmatical document in which the English *witan* and 'the councillors of the Welsh people' agree upon regulations for intercourse between the Englishmen and Welshmen forming a people described collectively as the Dunsæte.[3] The latter name never appears again, but the geographical details given in the treaty show that the Welshmen whom it covers are the men of Erging, and that they are separated from the Englishmen who with them comprise the Dunsæte by a river which can only be the Wye.[4] The wording of the treaty suggests an attempt to define a relationship which was already of long standing, and may well be as ancient as the age of Offa. It is probably significant that the Dyke reappears on the left bank of the Wye close to the point at which the river begins to form the eastern boundary of the kingdom of Gwent, which in Offa's time was undoubtedly subject to its own independent dynasty.[5]

The contemporary materials for Offa's reign throw little direct light on the making of the Dyke. So far as can be seen, it was only by slow degrees that Offa rose to the unchallengeable supremacy in the south which permitted the undertaking of a great public work affecting many private interests and demanding sustained control.[6] The *Anglo-Saxon Chronicle* and the charters of the period suggest that Offa's ascendancy cannot have been finally established until 784, at the earliest. On the Welsh side, the ancient *Annales Cambriae* record a battle between Welshmen and Englishmen at Hereford in 760, a harrying of the south Welsh by Offa in 778, a harrying of the Welsh by Offa in the summer of 784, and a harrying of 'Rienuch'[7]—apparently an alternative name for Dyfed—in 795. This tale of harryings is probably complete, and, if so, it allows a peaceful interval of eleven

---

[1] Sir Cyril Fox, 'The Boundary Line of Cymru' (*Proceedings of the British Academy*, xxvi, pp. 291–4) and below, pp. 288–90. The suggestion has been reinforced by K. Sisam, *Studies in the History of Old English Literature* (Oxford, 1953), p. 135.

[2] On the district known as Erging in Welsh and Ircingafeld in Old English see J. E. Lloyd, *History of Wales* (1911), i, pp. 279–80.

[3] The document is printed in F. Liebermann, *Die Gesetze der Angelsachsen*, i, pp. 374–9 and discussed

ibid. iii, pp. 214–19.

[4] *Royal Commission on Historical Monuments, Herefordshire*, iii, pp. lviii–lix.

[5] J. E. Lloyd, op. cit. i, pp. 274–5.

[6] The making of the Dyke is discussed from this angle in F. M. Stenton, *Anglo-Saxon England* (ed. 2, 1947), pp. 212–13.

[7] On this, and other British district-names of the same type, see J. E. Lloyd, op. cit. i, pp. 281–2.

years towards the close of Offa's reign for the building of the Dyke. Nothing is known of the reason for Offa's devastation of Rienuch in 795, and it is hard to imagine any connexion between a raid into this remote country and his defensive works along the Anglo-Welsh frontier-line. On the other hand, it is not improbable that a battle at Rhuddlan entered by the *Annales Cambriae* at the end of the annal recording Offa's death in 796 may have been an episode in an unrecorded war provoked by the closing of the frontier on the Dee at Prestatyn.

No people could have carried through an undertaking on the scale of Offa's Dyke without previous experience in similar types of construction. There are many short dykes in the central march of Wales, most of which control ancient trackways. Some at least of these dykes must be older than Offa's crowning work. But the chief historical problem connected with Offa's frontier-line is its relationship to the formidable barrier known as Wat's Dyke which runs from Basingwerk on the Dee to the Morda brook in Shropshire. In a sense, the problem has been made more acute than ever by the present survey, which has shown that throughout its demonstrable length Wat's Dyke is a work of the same order of magnitude as Offa's Dyke itself. The geographical relationship between the Dykes is clear. As Sir Cyril Fox has said, 'Wat's Dyke presents a visible barrier to the highlanders when they have reached the Lowlands; but Offa's Dyke here controls access to the Lowlands'.[1] On all grounds it is improbable that Wat's Dyke represents a withdrawal of the frontier to the Lowlands. The Mercian kings retained the initiative in their dealings with the Welsh for a generation after Offa's death,[2] and in the later history of the Mercian kingdom there is no hint of the energy needed for the construction of an earthen barrier on the scale of Wat's Dyke.[3] Historically, the problem of the Dykes centres around the conditions under which the Mercians passed from the conception of the short dyke impeding one or two lines of passage to the conception of a racial frontier.

The problem is made peculiarly difficult by the fragmentary nature of the evidence for early Mercian history. The Mercian kingdom hardly comes into view before the year 632, when Penda, the first of its kings who is more than a name, appears as the ally of Cadwallon king of Gwynedd in a devastating invasion of Northumbria.[4] It is probable that Penda remained in alliance with the line of Gwynedd, for there were Welsh princes—the king of Gwynedd among them—in the army which Penda was leading when Oswiu of Northumbria overthrew him in 654.[5] A Mercian king who was on these terms with the Welsh rulers is unlikely to have defined his own territory against them. In the next generation, Wulfhere, Penda's eldest surviving son, became the overlord of all the southern English peoples,[6] but he was heavily defeated in an attack upon Northumbria,[7] and it may be doubted whether he was ever secure enough in his overlordship to concentrate

---

[1] Below, p. 271.

[2] For the situation on the March in this period see Sir Ifor Williams, 'The Poems of Llywarch Hên, *Proceedings of the British Academy*, xviii (1932), p. 298.

[3] The significance of the name Wat's Dyke is discussed by Sir Cyril Fox below, pp. 287–9.

[4] Bede, *Historia Ecclesiastica*, ii. 20.

[5] *Historia Brittonum*, ed. T. Mommsen, *Mon. Germ. Hist.*, *Auctores Antiquissimi*, xiii. i, p. 208.

[6] Eddius, *Vita Wilfridi Episcopi*, c. xx.

[7] Dated to 674 by P. Hunter Blair in *The Early Cultures of North-West Europe* (H. M. Chadwick Memorial Studies), pp. 254–5.

a major effort on the western border of his own kingdom. For half a century after his death in 674 no king of Mercia or any other region was accepted as overlord throughout southern England. The internal history of Mercia under its kings Æthelred (674–704), Cenred (704–9), and Ceolred (709–16) is obscure, but offers no suggestion of power in reserve for great public enterprises. The little that is known of it gives the impression that the consolidation of the kingdom must have been imperfect. For nine years in Æthelred's reign, his remote kinsman Guthlac was able to maintain a band of military companions with which he harried the lands of his enemies.[1] Another band, which must have resembled that of Guthlac, was brought together a few years later by Æthelbald, another member of the royal house, in opposition to Ceolred the reigning king.[2] Its exploits are unrecorded, but its existence must have seriously embarrassed the responsible governors of the Midlands.

It is with Æthelbald himself, who succeeded Ceolred in 716 and reigned until 757, that the Mercian kingdom re-emerges from obscurity. In 731, in the last chapter of his Ecclesiastical History, Bede states without qualification that all the southern 'provinces' of the English, as far as the Humber, were subject with their kings to Æthelbald king of the Mercians.[3] In 736, in a charter of which a contemporary text has fortunately survived, Æthelbald claims this position for himself, and combines his claim with a title which in its literal sense conveyed a direct challenge to the princes of Wales. In the words of gift, he styles himself *Rex non solum Marcersium sed et omnium provinciarum quae generale nomine Sutangli dicuntur*: in the attestation clause he styles himself *Rex Britanniae*.[4] In 746 or 747, Boniface, the legate of the Roman Church in Germany, congratulates him on the settled peace which he has in his kingdom.[5] It should be emphasized that no ancient authority connects Æthelbald's name with the building of Wat's Dyke. But it can at least be said that there is no other king to whom the first of the great Mercian earthworks can be attributed with so high a degree of historic probability.

There remains one piece of direct evidence pointing conclusively in the same direction which has long been familiar but has often been misinterpreted. Writing before the year 749 Felix, the biographer of St. Guthlac, describes one of his hero's visions in a passage which is of crucial importance for the early history of the Midlands.[6] It reads:

Contigit itaque in diebus Coenredi Merciorum regis, cum Brittones infesti hostes Saxonici generis bellis predis puplicisque vastationibus Anglorum gentem deturbarent, quadam nocte gallicinii tempore cum more solito vir beatae memoriae Guthlac orationum vigiliis incumberet, extimplo cum velud imaginato sopore opprimeretur visum est sibi tumultuantis turbae audisse clamores. Tunc dicto citius levi somno expergefactus, extra cellulam qua sedebat egressus est et erectis auribus adstans verba loquentis vulgi Brettonicaque agmina tectis succedere cognoscit. Nam ille aliorum temporum preteritis voluminibus inter illos exulabat quoadusque eorum strimulentes loquelas intelligere valuit. Nec mora, per palustria tectis subvenire certans, eodem pene momento omnes domos suas flamma superante

---

[1] *Memorials of Saint Guthlac*, ed. W. de Gray Birch, p. 13.

[2] Æthelbald and his *comites*, or military companions, while in exile figure prominently in the Life of Guthlac by Felix.   [3] *Historia Ecclesiastica*, v. 23.

[4] *Cartularium Saxonicum*, no. 154, *Facsimiles of Ancient Charters in the British Museum*, i. 7.

[5] *Sancti Bonifatii et Lulli Epistolæ*, ed. M. Tangl (1916), p. 147. 'Audivimus quoque quod . . . pacem stabilitam in regno tuo habeas.'

[6] *Memorials of Saint Guthlac*, ed. W. de Gray Birch (1881), pp. 29–30.

conspicit, illum vero intercipientes acutis hastarum spiculis in auras levare coeperunt. Tum vero vir dei tandem hostis pellacis millenis artibus millenas formas persentiens, velut prophetico ore sexagesimi septimi psalmi primum versum psallebat 'Exurgat Deus'. Quo audito, dicto velocius eodem momento omnes demoniorum turbae velud fumus a facie eius evanuerunt.

This passage has often been taken to imply that a British population was surviving in the fens around Crowland as late as the middle of the eighth century. What it really proves is that in the reign of King Cenred, that is, between 705 and 709, the Welsh were carrying out a series of devastating raids over Mercia. The singular precision with which these raids are dated is itself a testimony to their formidable character. They show that in the age-long conflict for the domination of the marchlands the initiative in these years was with the Welsh.[1] They imply that no effective barrier had as yet been interposed anywhere between Wales and the English Midlands. Under these conditions, the creation of an artificial line of defence for the protection of the Mercian lowlands becomes a natural response to an intolerable situation. Wat's Dyke falls into place as a defensive work covering the heart of the historic Mercia, and more particularly as an attempt to close the dangerous gap between the middle Dee and the upper Severn which presented no major obstacle to movement from the west. The attribution of Wat's Dyke to Æthelbald, the first Mercian king who can have been in a position to deal with the situation described by Felix, becomes something more than a theory based on a balance of probabilities.[2] Offa's Dyke, in its turn, will then appear as the completion on a grandiose scale of a work of frontier defence begun by Æthelbald with a limited objective and an immediate purpose in view. It cannot be through mere coincidence that the meagre authorities for the early history of the Midlands provide a pattern into which the making of the two great dykes falls so neatly into place.

The practical achievements of the Anglo-Saxons have often been denied the recognition which they deserve. The military disaster in which their kingdom perished, and the efficiency of the Norman genius which founded a new order upon its ruins have created a perspective which has unfairly dwarfed the men of an earlier age. Time has dealt hardly with their public works, such as the numerous fortresses which they built for the defence of the land in the ninth and tenth centuries. But the greatest of all their public works survives. Through the years of labour which Sir Cyril Fox has spent upon the present survey, Offa's Dyke can now be followed for all but a few miles in its northern sector, in the assurance that what is visible upon the ground is of eighth-century construction, and that in the stretches where no earthwork can now be traced, its place was taken from the first by forest or river. The frontier-line which Offa drew from the estuary of the Dee at Prestatyn to the Severn Sea at Sedbury Cliffs can now be seen for what it is—a work of the Dark Ages which in the strength of its conception and the intelligence of its planning is comparable with Hadrian's Wall itself. The outstanding memorial of its type and period in north-western Europe now at last comes fairly into view.   F. M. STENTON

---

[1] They may, in fact, have formed part of a more general Welsh revival, for which there is some evidence in this period. The *Annales Cambriæ* record Welsh victories in 722, and the inscription once legible on 'Eliseg's Pillar' near the upper Dee attributed the recovery of Welsh territory from the English to Elise King of Powys, whose grandson died in 808.

[2] Below, pp. 271–3.

AUTHOR'S PREFACE (1953)

THIS book presents a detailed record of archaeological fieldwork on the western frontier of Mercia—Offa's Dyke, the 'Short Dykes', and Wat's Dyke, first published year by year in *Archaeologia Cambrensis* between 1926 and 1934 inclusive, followed by the relevant portion of the Sir John Rhŷs Memorial Lecture for 1940, in which a broader treatment of the theme of the Mercian frontier in the seventh and eighth centuries was attempted. I am very sensible of the honour done to me by the Council of the British Academy in thus providing at its own cost a definitive edition, in a format so spacious and handsome, of a piece of work which, though carried out with care and alertness of mind, has recognizable defects, because it was a pioneer effort in which a suitable technique of survey and record had to be evolved. I learnt, however, from experience, and the narrative gains breadth and significance as it proceeds; each of the original six reports occupies a chapter of the book.[1] Since I know its imperfections, I am highly appreciative of the distinction given to the record by the foreword written for it by Sir Frank Stenton, F.B.A.

It will, I think, assist the reader if some account of the genesis of the work—since it belongs to the past rather than the present—and the reason for its original publication in parts, is included in this preface.

It is, in brief, a detailed account of a series of journeys, with notebook and camera, level and staff, along the borderlands of north and central Wales, across Herefordshire and down the Wye valley, following the line of Offa's Dyke; and of a return to the north when this was done, to follow the line of its precursor, Wat's Dyke. A significant counter-attraction was provided by 'Short Dykes'—little barriers across ridges or valleys—met with here and there in the central zone in the course of the survey. These journeys occupied eight successive summers from 1925 to 1932. The fieldwork then stopped, for personal reasons, and the projected definitive work on the Short Dykes was never carried out. This is well worth doing, by a younger man suitably equipped for the task.[2]

The idea of undertaking the Survey was not my own, though I entered on it with enthusiasm, and with some appreciation of the problems involved, as the Introduction (Chapter I) may show.[3] My previous work on the Dykes of Cambridgeshire was known to the Director of the National Museum of Wales, Dr. (now Sir Mortimer) Wheeler, Secretary of the Academy, and I was greeted by him on taking up my post as Keeper of Archaeology there in January 1925 with the news that the Council of the Museum had

[1] Changes made (other than verbal) are noted in the text, and dated 1953.

[2] A summary of the problems of Linear Earthworks will be found in *Antiquity*, 1929, pp. 135–54; and on the methods of Field Survey in general, and of the Dykes in particular, in a paper by three authors in *Antiquaries Journal*, 1946, pp. 175–9. On pages 214 ff. of this book the considerations on which my acceptance or rejection of banks or ditches as part of a running earthwork were

based are set out.

[3] The cost of the fieldwork was mainly covered by annual grants from the National Museum of Wales and the Board of Celtic Studies of the University of Wales. Personal friends, gratefully remembered by the author, also helped. Tribute was paid to them, and to those who furthered the work in the field, in the original reports.

approved of sufficient annual leave of absence for the fieldwork involved in the research. Nothing could have been better devised: it provided the finest possible introduction to Wales and the Welsh, and largely accounts for the affection I have for both. Many a good friend, many a remembered acquaintance, did I make in manor houses and farms, in the fields and on the moors—for the follower of the line of any ancient 'running earthwork' must be trespassing all the time—and, when the day's work was done, in inns and country hotels. I, a lowlander born and bred, learnt in this undertaking the profound physical and cultural significance of a Border where highland and lowland meet, visually, and by talking to men and women who had always lived in the 'debatable land'.

The character of the original record was due to one of these Welsh friends of nearly thirty years ago, the Reverend Ellis Davies, M.A., F.S.A., Vicar of Whitford, local Secretary for Flintshire of the Cambrian Archaeological Association, and Joint Editor of *Archaeologia Cambrensis*, who met me on the Dyke, and then and there offered to publish the survey section by section as I produced it. The offer was in due course confirmed by the Council of the Association, with which body I was afterwards long and happily connected.

This mode of publication, which was carried on for five years,[1] gave a quality of immediacy and freshness to the Survey of Offa's Dyke, since it was, year by year, a primary record of experience; moreover, as I wrote in 1931 at the end of the fifth report, the detailed writing-up, as a winter's task, clarified ideas and indicated possibilities which might be followed up in the next season's work.[2]

The record of the survey, viewed in this aspect, thus represents the gradual growth of comprehension of the range of information—technical, military, political and economic —which can be obtained from the study of a running earthwork, and increasing understanding of the best way to set it out; it is the history of a pilgrimage, mental as well as physical, and that is, I hope, part of its interest. It shows how the author, grappling with unexpected and baffling problems in the first year (Chapter II), thereafter improved his methods and increased his understanding of the way the Dykes were laid out and constructed, the part likely to have been played by the Mercian State organization, and so forth. Thus the reader interested in field research can learn something more than facts gathered and marshalled; why the Dykes were aligned thus and not otherwise, why they are large here and small there, and why gaps occur; and can share, I hope, the excitement of discovery of the mind behind the work, and the varying quality of the human material through which shape was given to the concept.

The survey was started at the N. end of Offa's Dyke, in Flintshire, because the barrier was being studied from the Welsh side, and *in preparing a 'map ribbon' one should work from left to right*. This immediately involved me in difficulties; I could not find the course of the Dyke—or approve the line of my predecessor in research—from its apparent fade-

---

[1] The Council of the Cambrian Archaeological Association and the present Editor, Dr. V. E. Nash-Williams, have kindly approved of this definitive publication, and have lent to the Academy the very large number of blocks used for the original papers.

[2] The first season's work on Wat's Dyke was 'held' and a single report produced after the second season.

out near Newmarket, Flintshire, to the sea 3 miles away; and as Bishop Asser, writing in the ninth century, affirmed that King Offa built it *mari usque ad mare*, this represented a real frustration at the outset. On the other hand, looking at the matter in the perspective of the years, I think that had I started at the S. end, I should have failed to provide the solutions for the problems there met with, that came easily to a mind fortified by five years' experience of the methods employed by the Offan engineers. I now consider it likely that the work was begun in the centre, completed in the S., and in the N. left incomplete. As for the northern portion, I gratefully draw attention to pages 13–20 of this book wherein my friend Mr. Arnold Taylor, F.S.A., Inspector of Ancient Monuments for Wales, who has long been interested in the Dyke, carries the inquiry a stage farther, extending the line of the Dyke another mile, and giving reasons for supposing the traditional view that it ended at Prestatyn, a small coastal town in Flintshire, to be almost certainly correct.

In such an undertaking as this, a companion was essential. Mr. Dudley W. Phillips, who in 1925 was a student at the University College of South Wales, Cardiff, and attended my course of lectures in archaeology, offered to accompany me. He took a keen interest in the work, and in the fourth year, 1928, when he had taken his degree, I offered him partnership in recognition and appreciation of his services, and in furtherance of his career; his name, then, appears with my own on the title-page of the fourth Offa's Dyke report in *Archaeologia Cambrensis* (1929), and thereafter down to the sixth report (1931). Almost immediately after this new arrangement had been agreed upon, however, Mr. Phillips accepted an overseas appointment; and though he came back to England for the long vacations, and so was able, to my satisfaction, to maintain his part in the fieldwork, the preparation of the reports remained as before, entirely in my hands.[1] He was a 'good companion'; his fiddle always accompanied him on these expeditions, and his talk, interlarded with appropriate music (either invented or drawn from memory) will be remembered, I am sure, in many an inn parlour on the Welsh border till our generation passes away.

A feature of the scheme of the research laid down at the beginning and carefully maintained throughout, which is, of course, the most important part of the survey, is the detailed description of the character of the work, and the provision of a 6-in. O.S. map record of every yard of earthwork, Offa's and Wat's, that was visible:[2] and a series of Profiles all to the same scale amounting in all to fifty-seven (Offa) and fourteen (Wat); particularly important, because the destruction of ancient banks and ditches of all kinds which our generation is witnessing throughout Britain, owing to the overmastering need for extending arable and ley farming and to the power of the machines now available for these purposes, is likely seriously to reduce in height and breadth, or even completely remove, hundreds of yards of each of these earthworks. Having such a record, these losses are not here so catastrophic as elsewhere.

---

[1] Mr. Phillips helped me down to the end of the work on Offa's Dyke, and to a limited extent on that of Wat's Dyke. See *Arch. Camb.*, 1929, p. 1; 1930, p. 1; 1931, p. 1; 1934, p. 205.

[2] Only at one point did we fail to make our way along the earthwork itself from end to end of each sector studied. This was on the Highbury, Gloucestershire, plateau (p. 187).

A great improvement on the original work is the provision of a new series of eight key maps embodying references to all the large-scale 'strip' maps referred to in the previous paragraph. These new maps are portions of the 'quarter-inch to the mile' of the Survey showing the relief of the country-side in colour, in relation to the courses of Offa's and Wat's Dykes (which are here accentuated); these have been specially prepared by the Ordnance Survey for this work. I am greatly indebted to the British Academy for meeting the extra cost involved.

Year by year the map record of the more interesting, or best preserved, portions of the two great Dykes was, in the 6-in. form, submitted, by request of the Chief Inspector of Ancient Monuments, to the Ministry of Works, for scheduling as 'Ancient Monuments' under the appropriate Act. I gratefully acknowledge his interest in the survey. The complete List is here included as an appendix, since it provides the reader with information as to where, on any part of the Border, he should find good examples of Mercian layout, scale, and technique, in this field of military (and political) effort. It may be pointed out that in many of the long series of strips of the O.S. map, which are the framework of the survey and are all reproduced here, extensions of the portions of the Dyke hitherto known and recorded thereon are by me frequently added. In due course these additions will be printed in the new 6-in. maps, when revision of rural districts is undertaken; I am now informed, however, that further delay in production of these is inevitable.

The dates given at the heads of the chapters are those of the original publications, and should be borne in mind, for many reasons, by a reader. In Chapters II, IV, and VII there is much rewriting and in Chapter IX, the Commentary, I have in places modified the original text of the Rhŷs Lecture to suit its new function; in the others few significant changes have been made in the descriptive text, but paragraphs now seen to be irrelevant have been deleted, and comments have been modified here and there. The paragraphs on parish and county boundaries, a familiar part of the original sectional publication, have been grouped in another appendix.

The historical aspect of the research is of course of great interest, and the student coming fresh to these frontier problems should read, in Sir Frank Stenton's *Anglo-Saxon England*, the history of Mercia; and in the late Sir John E. Lloyd's *History of Wales*, that of the Welsh kingdoms; and should look at the relevant maps in the *Historical Atlas of Wales* by Professor William Rees. On this Welsh side there was, of course, no such unity of control as the Mercians, after their absorption of semi-independent tribes such as the Hwicce of Gloucestershire, Warwickshire, and Worcestershire, possessed along the 120 miles from the Dee estuary to the Severn estuary.

The kingdoms or principalities, then, which 'ran' with the western frontier of Mercia in the eighth century were, firstly, in the centre and north from the borders of modern Flintshire to the upper reaches of the river Wye near Hereford, *Powys*. The holders of power at the time when King Offa was active in the Mountain Zone will have been Brochwel and his son and successor Cadell.

Secondly, in the south, *Gwent*, with which was associated 'an outlying member of the older Morgannwg, *Erging*'—Ircingafeld, or Archenfield the Anglo-Saxons called it—the boundary between the two peoples here being, in the main, the river Wye from Hereford to the Severn.

Thirdly, in the north, *Gwynedd*, whose princes probably claimed, but often lost to Powys, the coastal strip bordering the estuary of the river Dee and flanked by the estuary of the river Clwyd. This was part of the 'Middle Country', Y Berfeddwlad, so called from its politically precarious position in relation to its powerful neighbours:[1] its eastern cantref, Tegeingl, formed the greater part of the modern Flintshire, and through it the surviving portions of Offa's Dyke in this county are aligned.

As for the dates of these great works: Sir Frank Stenton considers that Offa's Dyke may confidently be assigned to the last 12 years of Offa's long reign of 40 years, 757–96,[2] I have suggested that the 'Short Dykes' cover a hundred years or more from the mid-seventh century onwards, and that Wat's Dyke is likely to be the work of King Æthelbald (716–56), King Offa's predecessor. These matters are discussed in the course of the Survey.

---

[1] Sir John E. Lloyd, *History of Wales*, i. 239.   [2] *Anglo-Saxon England*, 1943, pp. 211–13.

I. INTRODUCTION (1926)

THE travelling earthwork known as Offa's Dyke, between Wales and Mercia, is generally believed to have extended from the estuary of the Dee near Prestatyn in the N. to the estuary of the Severn near Chepstow in the S. The distance between these two points as the crow flies is 120 miles. This belief is based on a passage in Bishop Asser's *De rebus Gestis Ælfredi*, written in the last decade of the ninth century; Offa reigned from 757 to 796. It represents the Welsh tradition: 'Rex nomine Offa qui vallum magnum inter Britanniam atque Merciam de mari usque ad mare facere imperavit.' The significance of 'usque' here will not escape the reader: the 'whole way' from sea to sea.[1]

The English tradition is represented by a thirteenth century deed in the Public Record Office wherein is a reference to 'Offediche' in a grant of land at 'Riston'—Rhiston near Chirbury, Salop (my Figs. 42–43).[2]

Throughout the greater part of its sinuous course the trace is apparent, and local tradition confirms the topographer who identifies the bank and ditch which are its material evidences as Offa's Dyke. There are, however, broad stretches of country whereon its alignment is uncertain, and others where its course is entirely unknown, and its former existence in doubt.

It should be possible to determine from a study of the character of the Dyke in various sectors of its long course, and from its behaviour in relation to recurring obstacles of like type, such as rivers, whether it bears the impress of one mind or several. If the latter, it may be the work of more than one period. That its function, in its final phase, was to define a political boundary may be taken for granted; but its alignment and its constructional features in certain sections may have been dictated by military considerations.

I am well aware that the Dyke has been studied by others, but I suggest that, excavation apart, the need for a complete and careful survey is urgent. There is no adequate or dependable record of its alignment, none of its form or exact dimensions at various points; the essential bases for a consideration of the major problems which it presents are thus at present lacking. Valuable reports by H. L. Jones (1856), E. Guest (1858), and others on the topography of the Dyke will be found in the literature;[3] they are inadequate because the writers, providing neither maps nor plans, necessarily fail to record with sufficient exactitude the character and alignment of the earthwork in the sectors they are dealing with. Their method did not allow for the possibility that the Dyke might be destroyed by later generations; but destruction has been going on more or less continuously. Of certain portions of the Dyke referred to by Guest and others, as being manifest to all observers,

---

[1] See W. H. Stevenson, *Life of King Alfred*, Oxford, 1904, p. 14 and note, p. 204.

[2] Note (1953). On this see Sir Frank Stenton in *Anglo-Saxon England* (1943), p. 211.

[3] See Bibliography, p. 295. I have found only one paper illustrated by a *map*, that by G. Ormerod, which includes a reproduction of the 1-in. O.S. map of the Chepstow district; Hartshorne includes a generic profile *plan* of the Dyke in his *Salopia Antiqua*.

B

no visible trace survives, and the dimensions and alignment of such portions is therefore unknown. Had the Dyke been mapped, field by field, and surveyed by these writers, the preservation of the record might partly reconcile us to the loss of the monument.[1] I should add that the nature and extent of the problem to be faced by an investigator of Offa's Dyke was clearly envisaged by one writer, the late Professor McKenny Hughes, who thirty years ago stressed the urgency and importance of the task in a suggestive paper published in volume 53 of *Archaeologia*.

The evidence, historical and traditional, which associates the great work with the King of Mercia is, as we have seen, very weighty, and (allowing for the possibility that it may incorporate earlier elements) a late eighth-century date is highly probable.

A field survey and excavation at selected points cannot fail to provide facts which will bear directly on the problem of date and origin of Offa's Dyke. If the historical evidence be considered adequate without further investigation, it may be remarked that it is a serious reflection on our scholarship that no scientific record of the structure, form or character of a monument of such political and historical importance exists.

With these considerations in mind I begin the archaeological survey of the Dyke; the method which it is proposed to follow is:

(1) To record, and illustrate on sections of the 6-in. O.S. map, the appearance and exact trace of the Dyke wherever it is recognizable. Reference will also be made to early editions of the 1-in. O.S. map where these record sectors of the Dyke now lost.

(2) At successive points throughout its course to determine its existing profile, and to prepare sectional diagrams illustrating this.

(3) To examine its relation firstly to the terrain through which it passes, and secondly to earthworks on or near its alignment.

(4) To note all facts that are likely to bear on the problems as to whether or no it is wholly a work of one period, and as to whether it was designed to define a frontier, or (in parts) to defend it.

(5) To note the extent to which the Dyke forms parish, county, or national boundaries.

(6) To excavate in order to determine the original profile of the ditch or ditches and the structure of the bank at successive points throughout its course.

(7) To excavate at points which seem likely to yield evidence bearing on the age of the Dyke.[2]

(8) Where recognizable traces are lacking for short distances, to indicate its probable course, or a reason for its absence, basing one's conclusions either on its character at either end of the lost portion, or on the behaviour of the Dyke on similar terrain elsewhere.

(9) To draw the attention of historical students in Wales to those sectors wherein traces of the Dyke for long stretches are not to be found; in the hope that docu-

---

[1] (1954) Guest, however, was unreliable: see p. 20, note 2.

[2] e.g. At the crossing-points of Roman roads, and adjacent to Roman settlements. Cf. *Montgomeryshire Collections*, 1896, vol. xxix, p. 105.

mentary evidence or local tradition may be brought to light which will enable the line of the Dyke, destroyed by road-maker or by farmer, to be identified.[1]

This programme is ambitious, and the writer's preoccupations may not permit him to carry out all of it; but it is a practical one which can be undertaken by more than one investigator.

Since, then, more than one person may be concerned in the work, it is necessary that uniform scales should be adopted for the large- and small-scale maps respectively and for the Profiles, so that the whole series may be available for comparative study.

The work which is urgently necessary is comprised in the first two desiderata. Long stretches of the Dyke can be properly examined in a season in the manner here indicated, and at the same time information bearing on the headings 3, 4, 5, 8, and 9 obtained. It is, of course, excavation which takes time and costs money; this can be postponed, but cannot be neglected if the survey is to be complete and adequate.

The considerations outlined above apply equally to Wat's Dyke, which for a considerable distance in the counties of Flint, Denbigh, and 'Salop' runs parallel to and eastwards of Offa's Dyke; and the investigation of the Offa's Dyke system cannot be considered complete until Wat's Dyke has in like manner been examined, and the relation of the one Dyke to the other considered in all its aspects.[2]

[1] It hardly needs saying that information of the latter character requires very careful and critical analysis. In villages where archaeological investigation of the Dyke has been carried out, and local interest aroused, local 'knowledge' may be second-hand and of quite recent acquisition.

[2] Note (1953). The programme was, in the event, carried out, excavation apart. It took nine years of my available time: 1925 to 1933. Very little excavation was done considering the extent of the earthwork. Trenches were cut through Offa's Dyke at the first Roman site met with on its course, and near the Forden Gaer where the Dyke was thought to be on a Roman Road; also at two other places, but it was soon realized that the only useful information one could be sure of obtaining from a section of any running earthwork, at any point other than a known early settlement site, was the original profile of the ditch! Neither time nor money was available for this minor gain in knowledge while the work was in progress, the overriding necessity of completing the survey within a reasonable time being always in mind.

As for the maps, the exact course of the Dyke was throughout recorded on strips of the 6-in. O.S. reduced to two-thirds for publication; the Profiles were prepared on the scale of $\frac{1}{10}$ in. to the foot reduced to three-quarters.

PART I

II. OFFA'S DYKE IN NORTH FLINTSHIRE (1926 AND 1953)

THE field work was begun at the northernmost sector, from the estuary of the Dee to Treuddyn, it being my intention to follow the course of the Dyke southward.

The most northerly point to which Offa's Dyke, as a *continuous* earthwork universally recognized by that name extends, is in Treuddyn parish in S. Flintshire. Its apparent termination is immediately to the W. of the mining area of Coed Talwrn (6-in. O.S. Flints., XVII NW.), where it is present as a high ridge on which the road from Llanfynydd to Treuddyn runs. Thomas Pennant notes that the Dyke ended near Treuddyn Chapel, a few hundred yards farther N.;[1] doubtless mining and related activities have combined to destroy this short stretch. (My first key-map, Plate VI,[2] shows the line of the Dyke from Treuddyn to Montgomery.) There is, in addition, an isolated stretch of earthwork unknown to Pennant, but recorded in 1703 in a letter written by Wm. Aubrey, published in Lhwyd's *Parochialia* (see Bibliography).[3] This mentions 'Clawdd Offa' on or about 'Tegangle' Mountain. This entry had been forgotten when Pennant's work of 1810 revived interest in the Dyke; the earliest record of rediscovery which I have come across is in a letter attached to a copy of the *Tours* in the National Museum of Wales. The relevant passage is as follows:

Dear Friend . . . Now I have no great doubt but that ye *Balk*, or *Offa's Dyke* as it is described in the old Deeds of the Talacre Family forming for a considerable length the boundary of our parish [Whitford, Flints. C.F.], traceable from the Race-course to Marian Newmarket, is the continuation of the one lost by Evans near Truddin Chapel. It is known everywhere under that denomination in the parishes where it is discoverable; and the deeds alluded to above are of the Reign of Edward the Sixth, so without doubt it bore that name for a considerable period. . . .

Yours most faithfully, HENRY PARRY.

(Dated in another but contemporary hand, 8 September 1832.)

My friend the Revd. Ellis Davies tells me that Henry Parry was vicar of Llanasa from 1798 to the year of his death, 1854. The deeds to which reference is made have not been traced.[4]

Lewis's *Topographical Dictionary*, published in 1833, described Offa's Dyke as present in Whitford parish (passing 'through the plantation of Pen-y-Gelli where it is quite perfect and ten feet high') and as forming the boundary for a certain distance between Newmarket and Llanasa parishes. H. L. Jones in 1856[5] mentions this sector, and Guest

---

[1] *Tours*, 1810, i, p. 351. See also A. N. Palmer in *Y Cymmrodor*, xii, p. 78.

[2] Redrawn in 1953, and printed by the Ordnance Survey.

[3] The late Professor Sir John E. Lloyd drew my attention to this.

[4] The Revd. Ellis Davies, M.A., F.S.A. endeavoured to trace these deeds with the kind assistance of Miss Clementina Mostyn, but without success.

[5] *Arch. Camb.*, 1856, p. 8.

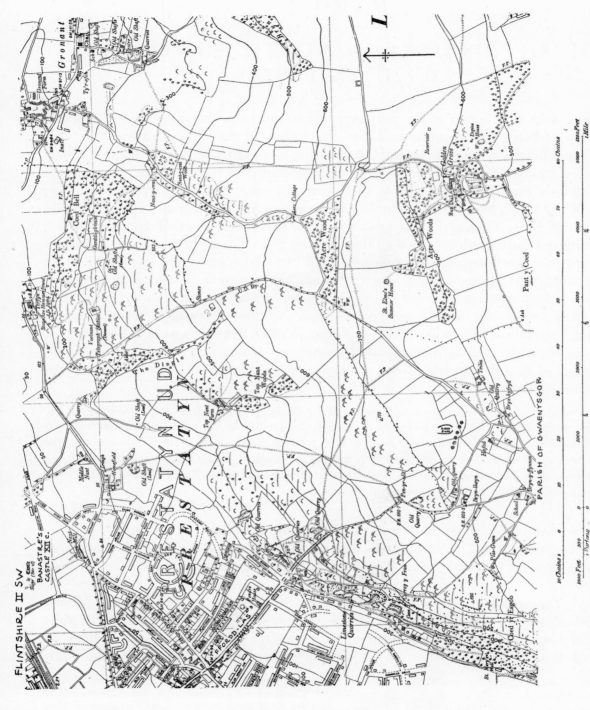

FIG. I. A portion of the 6-in. O.S. map, Flintshire, reduced to 4 in. to 1 mile. In this and (or) the following map ▬▬ represents portions of the Dyke clearly visible today; ∙∙∙∙ shows that faint traces of the Dyke are present or that the course is reasonably certain. ▬▪▬ represents banks of uncertain significance. ●∙∙∙● is drawn to Ffordd-las and Prestatyn Castle, in the NW. corner of the map.

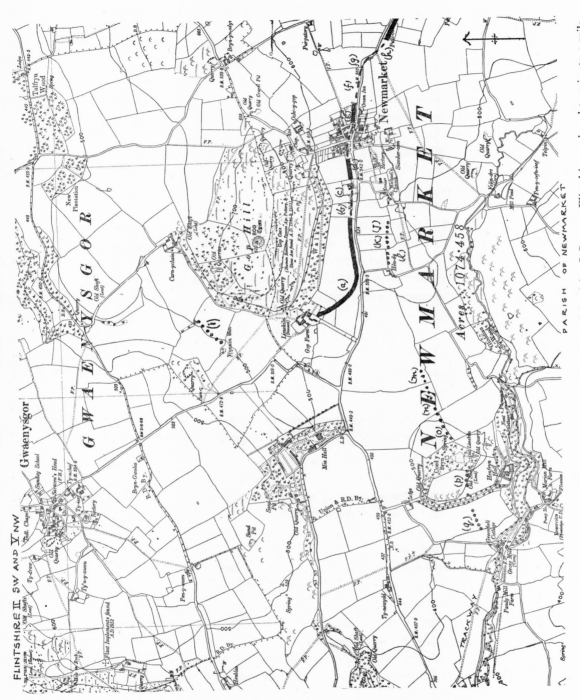

FIG. 2. Offa's Dyke from Gop farm to Marian, Newmarket. A portion of the 6-in. O.S. map, Flintshire, reduced to 4 in. to 1 mile.

(Reproduced by permission of the Controller of H.M. Stationery Office.)

describes its course more fully in 1858.[1] Part of it is marked on the quarter-inch O.S. maps.

This travelling earthwork, extending, as Parry remarks, from Marian, Newmarket, to the Holywell race-course, has a total length of about 5 miles. It is sited just where it might on *a priori* grounds be expected. If the map (Plate VI) be examined it will be seen that it is geographically-speaking a convincing fragment, and the traditional identification with Offa's Dyke may be unhesitatingly accepted.

The exact alignment and the character of this sector of the Dyke in the parishes of Newmarket, Llanasa, Whitford, and Ysceifiog will be first described, and then we shall consider whether any trace of it exists between Newmarket (Marian) and the sea, a distance of 3 miles, and between Ysceifiog and Treuddyn, 12½ miles. The descriptive parts of the record date from 1926 unless otherwise noted.

Here and throughout this work the large-scale maps are placed on the page in such a manner that the reader is looking at the line of the Dyke from the Welsh side, irrespective of the cardinal points. The official reference number or numbers are reproduced at the top of each map, and are therefore omitted from the cross-headings in the text. The fields through which the Dyke passes are numbered.

THE COURSE OF THE DYKE

The course of the Dyke between Marian and the Gorsedd–Babell road is set out on three sections of the 6-in. O.S. map, reduced to 4-in. to 1 mile (Figs. 3 to 5). Plate VI indicates the position in the sector of these large-scale maps.

FIGURE 3. *From Marian (outskirts of Newmarket) to spot-level 582, on the Newmarket–Holywell road. In the parishes of Newmarket, Llanasa, and Whitford*

1. The Dyke appears near Pwll-budr as a ridge in the pasture field (no. 1) parallel with the road; it is ploughed-down but unmistakable, and the rise in the western boundary hedge of this field, where the bank joins it, is confirmatory evidence. It is faintly traceable in meadow 3, in arable field 4, and in pasture field 6. It is present as a low ridge in field 7. In field 8 it first appears on the 6-in. O.S. map; it is represented by a low ridge here, as in parts of fields 9 and 10.

In 1840 this portion of the Dyke was more perfect than it is today. It is marked on the 1-in. O.S. map of that year (sheet 79 NW.) as extending without a break from the by-road to Pentre-bach across my field 5, to the steading of Min-y-ffordd, field 9.

At the hedge between fields 10 and 11, close to the steading of Min-y-ffordd, one may look along the line of the Dyke as it dips into the valley, rising and passing out of sight behind a crest line half a mile away, NW. of the farmstead of Tre Abbot-fawr. Though under plough, and much denuded, it reveals itself as a considerable work; traces of a ditch on either side are present but indeterminate. The ridge of the bank, 'spread' by ploughing, in the NW. corner of field 11, measured 23 yards in breadth and was over 1 ft. above the general level of the ground at this point. These measurements and this contour—a low

---

[1] *Arch. Camb.*, 1858, pp. 338–9.

wave-like ridge between two slight hollows—fairly represent the appearance of the Dyke in this sector, where it has been under the plough for a considerable period.

The alignment of the Dyke between the Min-y-ffordd and Tre Abbot-fawr crest lines, a distance of over half a mile, is not direct, the maximum deviation being 55 yards. Under present-day conditions a direct trace could be easily drawn; it is possible that the country-side was forested when the Dyke was built, preventing long views.

In pasture fields 12 and 13 the low ridge of the Dyke is clearly traceable along the line indicated on the O.S. map. The SW. hedge boundary of field 14 is on the line of the SW.

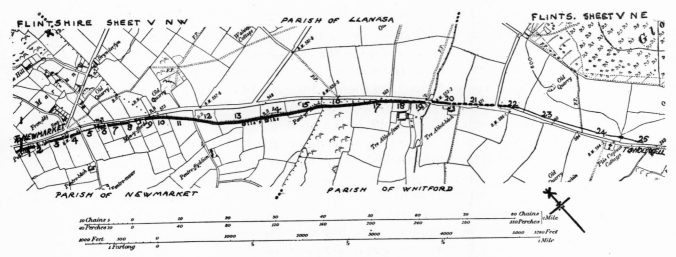

FIG. 3. Offa's Dyke from Marian, Newmarket, to spot-level 582 on Newmarket–Holywell road. A portion of the 6-in. O.S. map, Flintshire, reduced to 4 in. to 1 mile. In this and the following two maps ▬▬ represents portions of the Dyke clearly visible today; ▪▪▪▪ shows that faint traces of the Dyke are present; ——— represents the approximate alignment of the Dyke in 1840, transferred from the 1-in. O.S. map of that year.

(Reproduced by permission of the Controller of H.M. Stationery Office.)

ditch. The trace is apparent through field 15, and the right-angled bend in the boundary between this field and the next marks the line of the ditch on the NE. side of the Dyke. The pasture field 16 presents a steep slope on which the broad low ridge of the Dyke is clearly visible. Half-way across field 17 (the crest-line as seen from Min-y-ffordd half a mile away) the Dyke approaches the Newmarket–Holywell road; the roadside hedge marks its top from spot-level 583 to the south-eastward for a distance of 230 yards. The NE. side is here destroyed, but, viewed from fields 17, 18, and 19, the bank is well marked. It terminates abruptly as a prominent spur above the alluvium of a little brook, in the home-field of Tre Abbot-fawr.

Here the Newmarket–Holywell road crosses the Dyke, a bend in the road marking the point of passage. The high hedge-bank and hillocks on the waste land bordering the road adjacent to fields 20 and 21 are all that survive of the earthwork. In the W. corner of field 22 a slight rise in the ground and the high hedge-bank represent the Dyke; the trace dies away in the E. half of this field.

No definite trace survives in the rest of the sector included in Fig. 3, but there is evidence in the literature that the Newmarket–Holywell road represents its approximate course,[1] and reference to the 1840 O.S. map (sheet 79 NE.) shows that it was then visible on the N. side of the road (in fields 22, 23, and 24). Close to the road in field 25 there was, in 1840, a homestead, and the Dyke is not marked; the alignment of adjacent sectors of the earthwork on the old map suggests that it may here have coincided with the road. I have little doubt that the rise in the hedge between fields 24 and 25, 30 yards from the road on the NE. side and opposite Plas Captain cottages, represents the bank.

FIGURE 4. *From Llyn Marl to Coed Pen-y-Gelli, in the parish of Whitford*

The 1840 O.S. map mentioned above shows a stretch of the Dyke from a point half-way across the field marked 25 on my map up to the cross-roads by field 30. It is close to, and on the N. side of, the main road. In field 26, parallel to and 30–40 yards away from the road, a slight ridge is visible today, and there is little doubt but that the well-marked rise in an old pasture between Tyddyn-y-person and the road—shown on my map as enclosure 29—is the ploughed-down bank of the Dyke.[2]

East of the cross-roads the 1840 O.S. map marks the Dyke close to the S. boundary hedge of the main road (in fields marked on my map as 31 and 32). It would appear from this map (which is, it must be remembered, on a very small scale) to have continued on the same side of the road as far as field 35; but visible indications reveal a different alignment. In the enclosure, now a larch wood, marked 33 on my map, the Dyke is well marked, and here, on the shoulder of the hill above spot-level 604 at a point 35 yards from the road, it seems to have changed direction through an angle of about 47 degrees. The Dyke has been levelled in the western half of the wood; but the high level of the ground surrounding old decayed tree stumps, presumably cut down when the wood was planted, suggests that the Dyke approached the hill from a SSW. direction, that is from the N. corner of field 32.

These certainties and probabilities are shown on the map.

The next section, from the hill to an artificial mound at Brynbella, is of great interest. The Dyke is exactly aligned between these two mutually visible points, a distance of 500 yards; it has suffered from agricultural operations, and presents the wave-like character now familiar—a broad ridge between two depressions.

The Dyke crosses the by-road (to Cornel-cae-celyn) and the main road diagonally, being definitely present as a rise in the hedges at the SW. corner of field 34, by BM 596·1. It enters meadow 35 at a wooden enclosure marked on the O.S. map, and is exceptionally well marked in field 36; the top of the bank here is 4½ ft. above the ditch levels, and the over-all breadth is about 30 yards.[3] The ridge of the Dyke forms the hedge

[1] Lewis (*Top. Dict.* 1833, under Whitford) affirms that the Dyke was wholly on the NE. side of the main road in this sector. Guest (*Arch. Camb.*, 1858, p. 339) states that it crossed and recrossed the road several times.

[2] My friend Mr. W. J. Hemp, F.S.A. writes: 'I am certain that I saw faint but definite traces of the Bank in field 27. I remember, however, that I only saw this in a certain evening light after looking in vain on other days.'

[3] It is impossible to determine exactly the original over-all breadth of the Dyke here or at any point where it has been under the plough, without excavation.

boundary of the next three fields (37, 38, 39); this has to some extent prevented destruction and the Dyke is well-marked, the over-all breadth being 30 yards 1 ft. (For excavations at this point see p. 26 and Fig. 7, i.)

In the home-field (40) of Brynbella steading the ridge of the Dyke runs up to, and joins, the great Brynbella tumulus, 12 ft. high; the S. ditch of the Dyke passes to the S. of the barrow (Fig. 7, iii). The Dyke changes direction at the barrow through 32 degrees, being aligned on the spot now occupied by Rhydwen farm. This stretch is approximately straight, 370 yards in length.[1] The junction with the barrow is destroyed, a road having

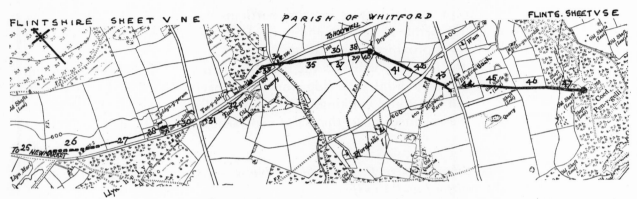

FIG. 4. Offa's Dyke from Llyn Marl to Coed Pen-y-gelli in the parish of Whitford. A portion of the 6-in. O.S. map, Flintshire, reduced to 4 in. to 1 mile.
(Reproduced by permission of the Controller of H.M. Stationery Office.)

been cut through the Dyke at this point; a patch of scrub (marked on the O.S. map), however, bordering the adjacent arable field 41, has preserved unusually well the original contours of the bank and N. ditch. (See Fig. 7, iv, and p. 22.) Farther to the S. of this field the bank has been ploughed down, but a rise in the hedge marks its passage to field 42. At the N. end of this field (which is scarred with old mine workings) a portion of the bank and the NE. ditch remains. The mining was probably undertaken prior to enclosure and has prevented cultivation; this part of the field by a mere chance has escaped being dug over. It is the only place in this sector, except possibly in a corner of field 41, where the ditch of the Dyke, apparently unaltered save by natural silting, can be seen. It is about 6 ft. broad and 3 ft. below the top of the bank, which has been partly levelled. Clearly the Dyke was not a formidable work here; it varies greatly in dimensions from point to point in its course, while preserving its character unchanged.

This field and the next form the opposing slopes of a small valley along the floor of which runs a brook, accompanied by a green lane. Rises in the hedges bordering this lane, especially that on the N. side, mark the crossing of the Dyke. Field 43 is pasture; on it the Dyke is visible as a low bank 12 yards broad (on which old trees stand) which goes straight to the buildings of Rhydwen farm.

At this homestead the Dyke changed direction, swinging eastwards through about

[1] The contours of the ground must have made exact alignment difficult.

24 degrees. Lost in the homefield (44) of Rhydwen-bach, it reappears as a well-marked rise in the hedge in the S. corner of this field, and can be seen crossing field 45. In the SE. corner the Dyke, though ploughed, is well defined, being a broad, rounded ridge 2½ ft. above the general level of the ground. Here, as elsewhere, it was ditched on either side, but the depressions are hardly apparent. Crossing field 46, where it is almost ploughed out, the Dyke is well marked on the steep slope of enclosure 47, Pen-y-Gelli wood. Breasting the hill, one notices a mound on the skyline; at this mound the Dyke ends. Whether it is a barrow or a mining dump is uncertain; the whole hill-side and hill-top are scarred with mine workings.[1]

The 1840 O.S. map confirms this trace in every particular, and fills in the gaps. It was, it is evident, then clearly visible in field 42 and in field 44; the S. boundary of this latter field must have been its approximate alignment.

No further trace of the Dyke is visible on the high hill, Pen-y-Gelli, and the 1840 map does not mark it beyond the mound. The ridge must have been crossed at the very crest, 760 ft. above O.D.; but the mine workings have destroyed all traces. From the crest apparently the Dyke was aligned on to the Rhydwen farm site 160 ft. below and over 600 yards distant.[2]

FIGURE 5. *From the eastern slope of Pen-y-Gelli to Llyn-du on the Gorsedd–Babell road. In the parishes of Whitford and Ysceifiog*

In this sector no trace of the Dyke is present until field 57 in Ysceifiog parish is reached. The figures on the map indicate a straight trace between Pen-y-Gelli tumulus and the ridge in this field; the numbered fields 47–56, and those adjacent, have been carefully searched without success. The point of passage of the Holywell road must have been near Pen-y-Parc, but no rise in the hedges (which are all probably post-enclosure) gives a hint as to its course.

Near the SE. boundary of field 57 already referred to, and in 58, a slight ridge is inter-mittently visible as indicated on the map. Crossing this field, one is on the old Holywell race-course, which has not been under plough for over a century; here the Dyke is definitely present as a low bank between two ditches, making for the Gorsedd–Babell road. So slight is the profile in this portion (see Fig. 9, v) that the complete destruction of the Dyke between Pen-y-Gelli and field 57 by the farmers can be readily understood. Guest, in 1858, met an old inhabitant of Caerwys who had crossed the Dyke in this lost sector 'hundreds of times when a boy before the common was enclosed'.[3]

On the Holywell race-course (marked as enclosure 59) is the Ysceifiog Circle with its Early Bronze Age barrow excavated by me in 1925.[4] The Dyke S. of the Circle is of

[1] It was described as a tumulus in Ormerod's account of the Dyke (*Arch. Camb.*, 1856, p. 8), and is marked as such on the 1840 O.S. map.

[2] A Roman road from the crossing of the Clwyd at St. Asaph to Basingwerk is shown on the O.S. map of Roman Britain crossing this ridge (but it is not on the 1-in. O.S. map). The alignment is that suggested by Mr. W. J. Hemp, F.S.A., but 'at no point have un-mistakable traces been discovered'. See Ellis Davies, *Prehistoric and Roman Remains of Flintshire*, 1949, p. 24 (C.F. 1953).

[3] *Arch. Camb.*, 1858, p. 339. This sector of the Dyke is not marked on the 1840 map.

[4] Ibid., 1926, pp. 48–85.

greater dimensions than N. of it, presenting an example of the variability in size coupled with uniformity of character which is a mark of the earthwork in this area. Here, as else-where, it is a bank ditched on both sides; the over-all breadth from ditch to ditch is 20 yards compared with 17 yards N. of the Circle. (See Fig. 9, vi.) It has apparently never been ploughed here; N. of the Circle traces of furrows are very apparent on the heath. A short section S. of the Circle is aligned on the barrow; hence the Dyke was in this area built from S. to N.[1]

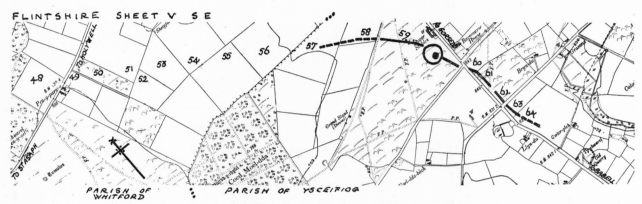

FIG. 5. Offa's Dyke from the E. slope of Pen-y-gelli to Llyn-du on the Gorsedd–Babell road: in the parishes of Whitford and Ysceifiog. A portion of the 6-in. O.S. map, Flintshire, reduced to 4 in. to 1 mile.
(Reproduced by permission of the Controller of H.M. Stationery Office.)

The Dyke crosses the Gorsedd–Babell road diagonally at the SE. corner of the race-course; in fields 60 and 61 it is apparent as a low ridge. Enclosure 62 is waste land, much disturbed; the Dyke is clearly marked at the southern end close to where it crosses a by-road; rises in the hedges bordering this road mark its passage. The next field, 63, shows a low ridge (almost effaced by the plough) continued as a rise in the hedge which divides it from field 64. On the steep slope of this arable field the Dyke is finally lost, the most exhaustive search having failed to reveal any trace of it, or hint as to its probable alignment.

In this last section the trace of the Dyke is curiously irregular; only short stretches, the longest not more than 200 yards, being in one alignment, as the map shows.

THE 'LOST' (OR UNCOMPLETED) PORTIONS

I. FROM PWLL-BUDR, MARIAN, IN NEWMARKET PARISH, TO THE SEA, A DISTANCE OF 3–3½ MILES[2]

It is not in doubt that the portion of the Dyke we have examined is part of the Offan frontier, or that this frontier reached, or was designed to reach, 'the sea'. I searched for

[1] A reference to Pant Asa in the preceding paragraph of Aubrey's letter quoted on p. 5 above, suggests that the sector on Holywell race-course may possibly be referred to, since this is only two-thirds of a mile from Pant Asaph. If so, the 'camp' mentioned in the letter as being near to the Dyke is doubtless the ring-work in Coed Moeldda, half a mile to the S. There is no apparent connexion between the two structures.

[2] This section is entirely rewritten (1953).

its continuation beyond Newmarket in 1925, on the ground and in the literature, but I could not satisfy myself that the evidence I had found, though suggestive, was adequate; it was, moreover, conflicting. My report (*Arch. Camb.* 1926, p. 177) contained the following sentence: 'I conclude, therefore, that while it is probable that Offa's Dyke passed through Newmarket to the west of the Gop Hill, and thence between Gwaenysgor and Golden Grove to the sea, its trace cannot be fixed at any single point.' I learnt in 1952 that my friend Mr. Arnold Taylor, M.A., F.S.A., Inspecting Officer for Wales of the Ancient Monuments Department, Ministry of Works, was interested in the problem of the Dyke's termination, and that he had made a discovery which materially extended the Dyke's alignment beyond Pwll-budr. I looked at this new portion with him and discussed other possibilities which he suggested; thereafter I invited him to re-examine the problem for publication in this book, withdrawing that part of my 1926 report which deals with it. His report follows:

(a) The Record Evidence

The documentary material bearing on the problem of Offa's Dyke from the point W. of Newmarket where my friend left it in 1926 (Fig. 2, right) consists of a single Norman-French record of late thirteenth-century date, which is printed in full below. In the phrase *Prestatun od le Deke* it contains what, so far as is known at present, is the only extant historical reference pointing to the Dyke's former existence in the Prestatyn area (Figs. 1 and 6). The meaning to be assigned to these words is, however, obscure. While there can be no doubt that *le Deke* refers to the Dyke, the exact connotation to be accorded to the name *Prestatun* is less certain. Earlier in the document it is used in its manorial sense, i.e. with reference to the commote or hundred of Prestatyn, which included, territorially speaking, the townships of Llanasa, Newmarket (Rhylofnoyd), Gwaenysgor, Meliden, and most of Dyserth, in addition to that of Prestatyn itself (Fig. 6). It may be so used here. The word *od* literally means 'with', and is twice so used in this same record. But, whichever interpretation is adopted for Prestatyn, this meaning hardly makes sense in the present context. One can only suppose, therefore, that *od* must here be used in a local sense of 'within'; the expanded meaning would then be 'Prestatyn (whether it be hundred or township) which is "within" the territory delimited by the Dyke'. If it is the township that is referred to, it will follow that the line of the Dyke passed it (or at any rate was considered in the thirteenth century to pass it) on the W. and not, as Edwin Guest claimed on the strength of local oral tradition in 1858, on the E. If, on the other hand, it is the hundred that is referred to, the passage would imply that the whole of its territory lay 'within' (i.e. on the English side of) the Dyke; this would mean that the frontier was regarded in the thirteenth century as coterminous with the S. boundary of the hundred, which demarcates Dyserth, Newmarket, and Llanasa from Cwm and Whitford (Fig. 6). For a short distance between Tre Abbot and Pant yr Abbot the hundred boundary does in fact follow the known line of the Dyke. The only certain conclusion that can be drawn from all this is that no unassailable theories as to the course of the frontier can be based solely on this one incidental mention of *Prestatun od le Deke*. If, however, it could be established that the reference to Prestatyn is indeed to the township, then these words would afford strong prima facie grounds for believing that the course of the Dyke, still a known and recognizable feature in the thirteenth century, must have passed close to it.

The right of Robert Banastre to the manor of Prestatyn with the appurtenances thereof in Englefield, 1278.[1]

Ce est le droit Robert Banastre al maner de Prestatun od les appurtennaunces en Englefeld. Ce est asaver ke Robert Banastre, le ancestre cestie Robert, vyent en Engleterre od le Cunquerur, e ont le vant maner, e plusours terres, ke ceste Robert tent uncore du Cunqueustre par le Cunquerur, e cely Robert ceosq' lung tens, e murrut en de cele terre vestu e seisi, e lessa son fiz Robert Banastre, ke ont vivi, ke en tens le Roy Richard ferma une tur a Prestatun, ke uncore este. E en son tens Oweyn ab Gweynor fu Seigneur de Wales, e mist gwere en la terre, tant cum le Roy Richard fu en la tere de outre mere, e prist le Chastel le Roy de Rothelan, e enchasa fors de la tere tutte la gent le Roy. E Robert le fiz Robert Banastre pardi sa tere en Wales a cel heure, e amena tut sa gent de Prestatun od le Deke en Contee de Lancastre, e uncore sunt apele le Westroys, et murrut cele Robert Banastre, e lessa troys fiz, Richard, Warin, e Thorstan Banastre, e en tut sun tens fu gwerre e tens Lewelyn le veyl. Thorstan se lessa murrir, e ont un fiz, ke ont a nun Robert Banastre, e ne fu fors ke de un an quant son pere murrut, si fu vint ans en garde, e quant il veyne a age, il ne vesqui for ke troys anz e murrut, si lessa un fiz, Robert, ke ore est demandant, ke fu en garde disenef anz, e pus ke il fu Seigneur de tere, la tere ad este en gwere, ke unk' ne fu establi la pes devant ore. . . .

Rotuli Parliamentorum, vol. i (1783), p. 2.

(b) The Bank near Hen-dy

Mention is made in the 1926 report (p. 177) of the remains of a bank in a direct line between St. Michael's Church, Newmarket, and the little steading of Hen-dy (shown on Fig. 2, field l), two sources of local tradition being quoted for the belief that this bank represents part of Offa's Dyke. The tradition is still current (1953). In a paper read to the Dyserth and District Field Club in 1949[2] Mr. W. S. Richardson, of Prestatyn, stated a case for the view that this bank near Hen-dy (Fig. 2, fields j, k, l) was indeed a section of the Dyke and that it pointed, when taken in conjunction with the apparent direction of the main earthwork where it is last visible by Pwll-budr, to the original line having continued through the Dyserth gap to Rhuddlan, rather than north-westwards past Gwaenysgor to Prestatyn.

At first sight this proposition has features to commend it. The seeming continuation by the Hen-dy bank of the slight curve which the Dyke begins to follow after it leaves the Llanasa–Newmarket boundary at Min-y-ffordd, and a hypothetical termination on the Clwyd at Rhuddlan (Fig. 6) give it much plausibility. Such a termination would not be seriously at variance with the sense of Asser's statement that the Dyke ran *de mari usque ad mare*, for Rhuddlan marsh, now reclaimed, was essentially a part of the coastline. The

---

[1] This is one of the lost parliamentary petitions of 6 Edward I, the originals of which were recorded by Prynne as still existing in the Tower of London in 1657. The printed text is that of a seventeenth-century copy made for Sir Matthew Hale and included in a volume (Hale MS. 5) of the large collection of manuscripts left by him in 1676 to the library of Lincolns Inn. Comparison of the 1783 edition with the Hale transcript reveals only negligible variations, and there is no reason to suspect that the crucial passage, difficult as it is, is not a correct version of the original petition.

[2] *Proceedings*, 1949, pp. 25–26.

crossing of the river at the head of the tidal estuary, immediately below the Norman *motte* (Twt Hill, Fig. 6), must have been a point of strategic importance from the earliest times. We know that the English were warring near Rhuddlan in 796, the year of Offa's death, and Offa himself, according to one text of the Welsh annals, had laid waste the territory of Rhuvoniog, beyond the river, in the previous year.[1] Moreover there can still be traced, at Rhuddlan,[2] a short length of bank and ditch, based on the river cliff and having very much the required alignment (Fig. 6), which might, if there were other grounds for believing the line lost at Newmarket to have been originally carried towards the Clwyd, have conceivably been related to the frontier system.[3]

These considerations led me to examine, both on the ground and on air-photographs, the fields separating the last recorded section of the Dyke near Pwll-budr from the Hen-dy bank, and also the whole country over which the Dyke might pass if it had followed a course from Hen-dy to Rhuddlan. There are, I am sure, no remains of earthwork likely to have been the Dyke on or S. of a line drawn between the W. boundary of Fox's 'Field 1' (Fig. 3) and Newmarket church. W. of the church the Hen-dy bank first clearly emerges in the field S. of spot-level 524 (Fig. 2, *j*). It is seen near to the southern hedge-bank and continues as a flattened ridge in field *k*. In field '*l*' again there is a well-marked bank which the map shows as a field boundary; it is this which—Sir Cyril tells me—constitutes the 'undoubted remains of a bank' mentioned in his 1926 Report (p. 177.)

The ground at Hen-dy has been much interfered with, but a deflection in the lane here may be related to the line traced so far. This is next visibly resumed as a ploughed-out bank in the SW. corner of field '*m*'. When this bank was seen under plough in 1953 the soil discolouration to be expected on the exposure of material thrown up from an excavated ditch was entirely absent. In the next field '*n*' the line is continued by a field balk, now only showing as a slight ridge, and is then carried along the S. boundary of field '*o*'. The level of this field is higher than that of the field to the S. of it, which points to the balk being an old-established one. The ground here ascends to the slight eminence of Coed y Bryn (*c.* 530 ft.), the central part of which is scarred by former stone and lead workings. On its W. side in field '*p*' the remains of a bank are visible for some 50 yards. The line is lost again before the Henfryn avenue is reached, but the avenue changes direction at this point, and, where its ledge cuts into the side of the field, the contour of a bank can again be seen in section. Field '*q*' beyond the avenue, plateau-like for a short distance, slopes steeply towards the Marian brook. On this slope there are again traces of a ploughed-down bank, which disappears before the lane leading to the crossing of the brook below Greenfield Cottage is reached.

Such traces, then, as there are of earthwork between Newmarket church and Greenfield Cottage are tenuous and intermittent. Nevertheless they seem to mark the course of a formerly continuous line. Can the suggestion that this line embodies the remains of

[1] Sir John E. Lloyd, *A History of Wales* (London, 1911), i, p. 201 and note; *Annales Cambriae* (Rolls edn.), p. 11.

[2] It is best seen on air-photographs, e.g. R.A.F. Sortie, 3G/TUD/UK/33, Part III (16 Jan. 46), print no. 5340, but the scale is too small for clear reproduction.

[3] It is more likely to have been part of the bank and ditch defence of the pre-Edwardian borough.

Offa's Dyke be sustained? On the whole it would seem that it cannot. In the first place, until the rise to Coed y Bryn is reached, it is not well sited; a better command of the country to the S. is obtainable from the lower slope of Gop Hill a hundred yards or so farther N. Secondly, such banks as survive do not resemble as closely as one would expect the spreading, gently rounded contour characteristic of the ploughed-out Dyke E. of Newmarket. Thirdly there is no satisfactory alignment connecting the known Dyke at Pwll-budr with the bank that first appears near Hen-dy. Finally, if in spite of these objections this could still be established as having been the course of the Dyke, how was the frontier continued beyond Greenfield Cottage? It would be in keeping with the Dyke builders' known readiness to incorporate river lines as integral parts of the frontier system if from here on the Marian brook had been so utilized.[1] Below Grove Mill the sides of the stream draw together more steeply, and, as Dyserth is approached, it carves out for itself a miniature limestone gorge, from which with dramatic suddenness it cascades to the valley below. If Offa carried settled English rule to the Clwyd, this would certainly have been the point at which to have effected the frontier's transition from the hills to the plain. The difficulty, however, is that, supposing for a moment this is what was done, no trace can be found of the earthwork between Dyserth and Rhuddlan.

What, then, is the explanation of our intermittent line from Hen-dy to Greenfield Cottage? Changes which have taken place in the line of the Newmarket–Dyserth–Rhuddlan road may provide it (Fig. 6). At Rhuddlan itself the course was altered as early as the thirteenth century, when the river bridge was established in its present position. Prior to that the route from Dyserth continued straight on at Spital (Fig. 6) towards the Norman borough and the old crossing below the *motte*, instead of making a turn N. towards the Edwardian borough; though no longer distinguishable on the ground, part of the old line shows clearly on air-photographs.[2] In the neighbourhood of Dyserth the change, which must be much later, has been radical. From a point near Tre-castell farm, about 200 yards E. of Dyserth station, to a point just short of spot-level 143 on the W. side of the town, the present main road diverges completely from the old route, which ran farther to the N. along a line still traversed almost continuously by lanes and footpaths, sketched on Fig. 6. It is fairly clear that on the Newmarket side it had continued what is still a well-marked track from the Greenfield Cottage–Grove Mill area (Fig. 2, *F.P.*) to the existing road immediately north of Tre-castell. It is suggested that the Hen-dy–Greenfield Cottage line represents preceding sections of the same early route, evidence of which also appears to have survived in the alignment of buildings on the N. side of Newmarket village and in a footpath to Llanasa which continues that alignment still farther towards the NE. The whole route is indicated on Fig. 6.

(c) *The Gop Farm Bank*

There is another bank which, in the words of the 1926 Report, 'extends for 200 yards from the Newmarket–Rhuddlan road at BM 506·5 (Fig. 2) towards Gop farm; this is in the right direction, SE.–NW., but is entirely isolated. It may be a roadway dating from

---

[1] For the Dee, see p. 47 and Plate XI, for the Severn, p. 85 and Plate XVIII.
[2] Loc. cit., Part II, print no. 5225.

B 3122   D

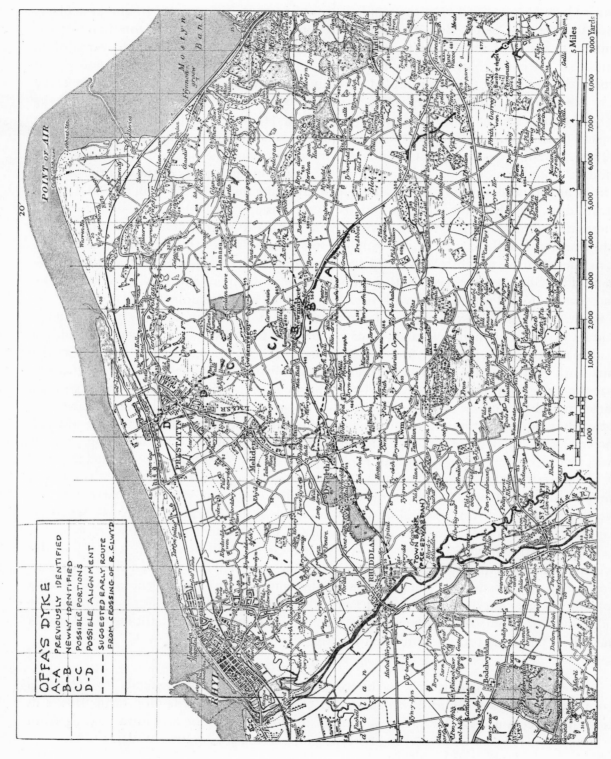

FIG. 6. The Offan Frontier in north Flintshire.

(Reproduced by permission of the Controller of H.M. Stationery Office.)

the time when the farmhouse was an important mansion.' This bank is much ploughed-down and is best seen in an evening light; its shallow, spreading outline is markedly similar to that of known sections of Offa's Dyke on the other side of Newmarket. If the isolation referred to could be shown to be more apparent than real, and a link established with the Dyke E. of Pwll-budr, the bank would at once become of great importance as indicating the probable course of the Dyke to its termination; its north-westward curve, following the contour of Gop Hill, rules out a continuation towards Rhuddlan.[1]

Although it has hitherto escaped notice, the required link exists. It is to be found in a length of ploughed-down bank in field 'e' on the N. side of the main road, opposite the Crown Inn, on the eastern outskirts of Newmarket (Plate IIIa). Any trace there might have been of the portion of the Dyke between here and the Pwll-budr section will have been destroyed in the straightening of the road bounding fields 'f' and 'g', but its former existence may be fairly presumed once the presence of the Crown Inn section is recognized and accepted. In Newmarket itself the exact line is lost, but immediately beyond the village, in the long field 'd' E. of the school and N. of the road, the slightly rounded outline of the bank can be seen though now almost obliterated; it lies some yards back from the road, as shown on the map and in Plate IIIb. The school and its playground now intervene, and W. of these a small housing estate (formerly field 'b') has destroyed any evidence that may have existed. Immediately W. of this again is field 'a' containing the Gop farm bank, which can be plainly seen curving up to the outer enclosing wall of the farm from a point nearly opposite the lane leading down to Hen-dy. It is, however, clear from an air-photograph[2] that the bank is not isolated, but is in fact the prolongation of a bank which runs parallel and close to the road all the way from beside the housing estate, although until the swing north-westwards begins it has been so much levelled as to be scarcely noticeable on the ground without the photograph's guidance. Thus there is evidence of a continuous line of earthwork, excepting where it is broken by the presence of buildings, from E. of the Crown Inn right up to the area of Gop farm, with a fair presumption of former continuity with the Dyke at Pwll-budr. There can be little doubt that this line is itself the continuation of the frontier, which is hereby claimed to be established as far as the point named.

The ground immediately NW. of Gop farm is much disturbed; none of the banks and ridges visible in this area could be adopted even tentatively as likely portions of the earthwork, and indeed at no point within a widening arc between here and the Dee can any section of the Dyke be certainly identified on the evidence at present available.

There are, however, two further lines of bank, both of which it is *possible* may have formed part of it. The first runs NE. from near Fynnon Wen (400 yards NNW. of Gop farm, Fig. 2) to a point above a second spring about 100 yards farther on, the line followed practically coinciding with the 500-ft. contour line marked on the map. The need to cling to the slope of Gop Hill to maintain adequate command over rising ground

---

[1] At one point this bank is less than 150 yards distant from the Hen-dy bank, and in these circumstances the transference of a tradition from the one bank to the other perfectly possible (cf. p. 15, above).

[2] R.A.F. Sortie 541/119 (30 July 48), print no. 4226.

to the W. could account for a SSW.–NNE. course at this point. The second line of bank (Fig. 1 and Plate V*b*) occurs on the top of the rise on the N. side of the valley, parallel to and just above the 700-ft. contour. It is only faintly traceable, running in a SE.–NW. direction for a little over 100 yards, but is very like the ploughed-down sections of the Dyke E. of Newmarket. If it be the Dyke, the contours suggest a course due W. to 'Old Quarry' lane, and along this to Pen-yr-allt, whence an ancient route, the so-called Fforddlas, descends in an almost straight course to Prestatyn (Fig. 1). Such a course to the shores of the Dee would place the older part of Prestatyn town, including the site of the Banastres' twelfth-century castle (Figs. 1 and 6), 'within' the Dyke, on the English side. Prestatyn is a name of English origin, and, though it is not recorded before the eleventh century, it is recognized that the majority of English place-names in Flintshire originated during the early period of Mercian colonization.[1] We may then regard as suspect any line for the Mercian frontier that would exclude Prestatyn from Mercia, such as Guest's view that Offa's Dyke reached the coast at Uffern.[2] The name Terfyn (Fig. 1), which he took as supporting evidence for the Offan boundary having passed nearby, may in fact be related only to the adjacent parish boundary.

(d) Summary

Important as the crossing of the Clwyd at Rhuddlan is likely to have been in the border warfare of the eighth century, the suggestion that Offa's frontier line was so constructed as to control it is not supported by archaeological evidence. There is, on the other hand, almost certain evidence that Offa's Dyke was built as a continuous work at least as far N. and W. as Gop farm, and the direction of its alignment when it is lost is strongly in favour of the Offan frontier having gone on to reach the coast near Prestatyn. This is so whether or no the two 'possible' lengths of bank referred to in section (c) above were parts of it. The likelihood of a final course to Prestatyn is reinforced to the point of probability by the association of Prestatyn with the Dyke in the 1278 petition, even though the literal interpretation of the text of that document remains uncertain. Finally place-name evidence, in particular the fact of English Prestatyn bordered on the W. by Welsh Meliden, suggests a frontier line passing to the W. rather than to the E. of the former place. There is, then, much to be said for supposing that Offa's boundary, in the final lap of its long march *de mari usque ad mare*, is marked today by the lane that sweeps down from the hills to the sea directly above Prestatyn itself (Fig. 6) where, as the main street of the modern town, it passes half a mile to the W. of the site of Prestatyn castle.

Note by the Author.

I accept Mr. Arnold Taylor's conclusions as set out in this summary, and express my appreciation of a piece of research by which the Survey as a whole is enriched.[3]

[1] B. G. Charles, *Non-Celtic Place-Names in Wales* (London, 1938), pp. xxii and 230–1.

[2] *Arch. Camb.*, 1858, p. 340. Edwin Guest is in any case a doubtful authority, whose standards of scholarship have not escaped severe criticism. Cf. W. H. Stevenson, 'Dr. Guest and the English Conquest of South Britain' (*Eng. Hist. Rev.*, 1902, pp. 625–42); for Maitland's opinion of Guest, see *Camb. Hist. Journ.*, 1952, p. 342. Uffern was NNW. of Terfyn.

[3] If a straight-edge be placed on the known, and assumed, alignments *A*, *B*, *C*, and *D* on Fig. 6, from Llyndu, that is, to Ffordd-las, a distance of 8 miles,

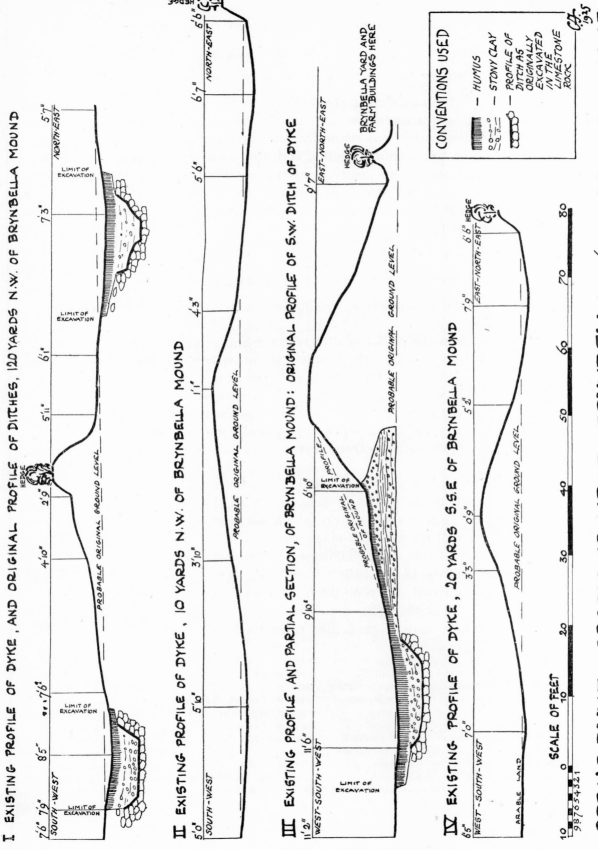

Fig. 7. Existing profiles, I to IV, and record of excavations.

II. FROM LLYN-DU, NEAR BABELL, IN YSCEIFIOG PARISH, TO COED TALWRN, IN TREUDDYN PARISH

We may now turn to the 12-mile gap (Plate VI) between the point S. of the Ysceifiog Circle, where the Dyke appears as a low ridge in the arable fields, and the spoil heaps of Coed Talwrn. Special attention was naturally first directed to the countryside in the neighbourhood of these two terminal points, and afterwards the intervening area was scoured. I could find no indications justifying even a tentative alignment, and unless and until documentary evidence or a chance discovery of its ditch in sewer- or water-pipe-laying, fixes its position at one or more points, I do not think it can be recovered.[1] It may never have been constructed.

THE EXISTING PROFILE OF THE DYKE

The Dyke was surveyed at two points—(*a*) in the neighbourhood of Brynbella, (*b*) near the Ysceifiog Circle.

(*a*) Fig. 7, i and ii, show the profile of the Dyke 120 and 10 yards respectively NW. of the Brynbella mound, and Fig. 7, iv, the profile SSE. of the mound. The table on p. 23 gives the essential measurements. The elevation of the bank is fairly constant, as is the depth of the ditches; but the over-all breadth varies considerably, from 81 to 131 ft. The exceptional breadth of the work 10 yards to the NW. of the mound is referred to below (p. 27). Plate II*b* illustrates the Dyke hereabouts; its ridge and the silted-up ditch on the SW. side of the work are visible. The three survey poles are set up in the ditches, and on the ridge.

In Fig. 7, i, a hedge-bank is seen on the ridge. This bank may be part of the original vallum. On the NE. side of the hedge the ridge has been almost entirely ploughed out.

The hedge on the SE. side of the trackway which has been cut through the Dyke close to the mound shows a well-marked rise which represents the bank; on the other side of this hedge the bank and NE. ditch are well preserved. Here the existing profile (Fig. 7, iv) was plotted. The ridge of the bank, about 5 ft. 6 in. above the original ground level, has probably never been ploughed; the SW. ditch has been levelled up.

(*b*) Fig. 9, v and vi, show the existing profiles of the Dyke on the same scale as the foregoing, 130 yards NW. and 43 yards SE. respectively of the Ysceifiog Circle. The

the directness of the whole layout, allowing for the tactically necessary bulge westward at Gop Hill (820 ft.) will be apparent. This is a feature characteristic of Offa's Dyke (p. 44 and p. 80 below) and greatly strengthens the likelihood of the accuracy of Mr. Taylor's discoveries and inductions.

[1] The Dyke is not at any point in this sector recorded on the 1840 O.S. map. Guest records (*Arch. Camb.*, 1858, p. 339) a local tradition that the Dyke passed 'over the Halkin Mountain to Mold parish'. The parishes through which it may have passed between Ysceifiog and Treuddyn are Halkyn, Northop, Cilcain, Mold Rural, and Nerquis. *Not* Caerwys. A stretch of hummocky ground in this parish accepted as Offa's Dyke by the R.C.A.M. (*Flints. Inventory*, no. 27) is, I am convinced, the result of quarrying along a natural outcrop. Lewis (*Top. Dict.*, 1833) is certainly in error in stating that the Dyke 'enters the parish of Caerwys and passes on the west of Llyn Helyg'. A reference in Lhwyd's *Parochialia* may *possibly* relate to a lost portion of the Dyke on Halkyn Mountain. The topography of the record is, however, very obscure.

character of the work is the same as at Brynbella, but it is only half the size. The Table of Measurements indicates that the average over-all breadth here is 55·5 ft., and at Brynbella 100·7 ft.

Table of Measurements

No. of Profile	Position	Height of bank	Present dimensions		Over-all breadth	Result of excavation
			Depth of SW. ditch	Depth of NE. ditch		
		ft. in.	in.	in.	ft.	
I	120 yds. NW. of Brynbella mound	4 0	11	13	90	Ditches originally 4 ft. 7 in. and 5 ft. 11 in. deep, and about 12 ft. broad at the top
II	10 yds. NW. of do.	4 0	10	17	c. 131	
IV	20 yds. SSE. of do.	5 6	5	14	c. 81	
V	130 yds. NW. of Ysceifiog Circle	0 11	7	6	c. 51	Ditches probably originally 3 ft. 3 in. and 3 ft. deep respectively
VI	43 yds. SE. of do.	2 0	11	21	c. 60	SW. ditch probably originally 4 ft. 2 in. deep
III	Brynbella mound	. .	4	. .	. .	SW. ditch 3 ft. 7 in. deep and c. 15 ft. broad at top

EXCAVATION

Like travelling earthworks in general, well-defined changes in direction of the Dyke often coincide with hill-crests. The use of barrows for the same purpose is, as we have seen, a feature of this section. The relationship of the Ysceifiog barrow and its Circle to the Dyke seemed so remarkable as to justify the devotion of the greater part of the time at my disposal for excavation to the examination of this monument. The structure consists of a circular enclosure, defined by a bank and a ditch, some 350 ft. in diameter. Within the Circle (but not at its centre) is a barrow; and on this barrow Offa's Dyke, approaching from the SE., is aligned. The peculiar feature which imparts special interest to the relationship between Dyke and barrow is that the Dyke stops short at the ditch of the Circle (see Fig. 8[1]), commencing again at the ditch on the opposite side. The Ysceifiog barrow proved, however, to be much older than the earliest date to which the Dyke might be assigned and no late (Saxon) secondary interments were found. We must, then, suppose that a tradition of sacredness still attached to the site in the eighth century A.D., or that one-half of the bank of the Circle was regarded as the boundary.

Other excavation work carried out in 1925 consisted of attempts to determine the original depth and profile of the ditches at three separate points. Time was also found for a partial examination of the Brynbella mound.

Determination of the original dimensions of the Dyke was first attempted in the neighbourhood of the Ysceifiog Circle. Sections were cut 130 yards to the NW. and 43 yards to the SE. of the junctions of the Dyke with the ditch of the Circle. These sections are

[1] Figure 8 was published as Fig. 1 of the Ysceifiog Barrow report, *Arch. Camb.*, 1926, pp. 48 ff.

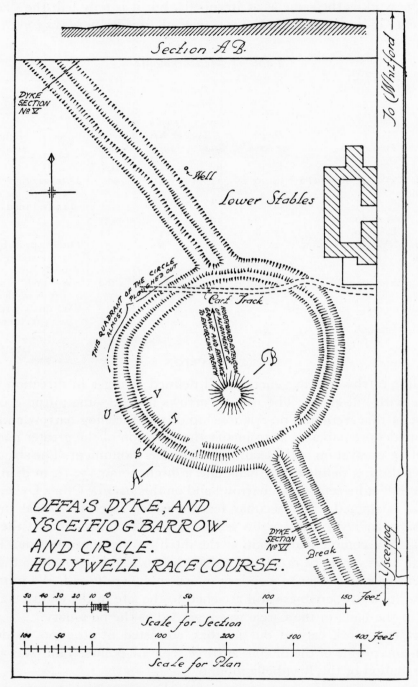

Section A.B.

To (Whitford →

DYKE
SECTION
Nº V

Well

Lower Stables

THIS QUADRANT OF THE CIRCLE
ALMOST PLOUGHED OUT

Cart Track

NORTHWARD EXTENSION
OF ALIGNMENT OF
GRAVE AND ENTRANCE
TO ENCIRCLING TRENCH

B

V

U

F

S

A

OFFA'S DYKE, AND
YSCEIFIOG BARROW
AND CIRCLE.
HOLYWELL RACE COURSE.

DYKE
SECTION
Nº VI

Break

Ysceifiog

50 40 30 20 10 0   50   100   150 Feet
Scale for Section

100   50   0   100   200   300   400 Feet
Scale for Plan

FIG. 8. Plan of Ysceifiog Circle, Flintshire, showing junction with Offa's
Dyke, and sites of excavated sections, V and VI, of the Dyke.
(From *Arch. Camb.* 1926, p. 50.)

planned on Fig. 9. The visible dimensions, as we have seen, indicate a work of very slight importance; the heights of the bank are 11 in. and 2 ft. respectively above the original ground level.

In the section NW. of the Circle the subsoil is a very stiff glacial clay full of stones and with contorted streaks of sand here and there. The original ground level below the bank could not be determined. This was not surprising, for the bank was almost entirely denuded; but failure to find the original floors of the ditches was unexpected. In order that the character of the subsoil might be studied, the trench was widened and deepened,

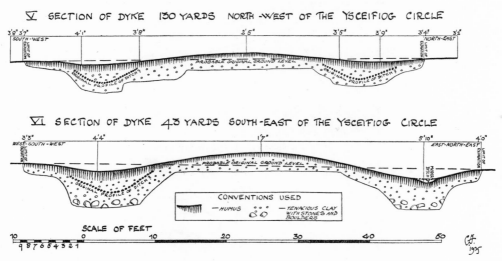

V SECTION OF DYKE 130 YARDS NORTH-WEST OF THE YSCEIFIOG CIRCLE

VI SECTION OF DYKE 43 YARDS SOUTH-EAST OF THE YSCEIFIOG CIRCLE

CONVENTIONS USED
— HUMUS
— TENACIOUS CLAY WITH STONES AND BOULDERS

SCALE OF FEET

OFFA'S DYKE : SECTIONS NEAR YSCEIFIOG CIRCLE 6 INCH O.S. MAP FLINTS V SE

FIG. 9.

being carried well into the undisturbed ground underlying the bank, as is shown in Fig. 9, v. The probable original form of the ditches, as indicated in the sectional plan, is the result of very careful scrutiny. I do not think certainty is possible, and can only claim high probability for the profiles here recorded, which represent depths of 3 ft. 3 in. and 3 ft. respectively. The photograph (Plate IV*a*) shows the existing profile of the Dyke in perspective; the white sticks in the deep trench indicate the probable original profile of the SW. ditch.

A bank built up of such tenacious clay as this grows practically no vegetation for many years. From the moment it is completed the silting of the ditches commences; the muddy stony clay thus replaced in the hole whence it came being free from decayed vegetation, is of the same colour and character as the undisturbed subsoil, and is therefore undistinguishable from it.

Precisely the same difficulties were experienced in the case of the section SE. of the Circle. Here the closest scrutiny failed to reveal any indication in the eastern ditch by which silting might be distinguished from the undisturbed clay, nor could the original ground level under the bank be detected. In the SW. ditch a slight change of colour in the deposit suggested that the original profile was as indicated in Fig. 9, vi. Both the trenches were taken down to a depth of over 6 ft. to an undisturbed layer of large limestone blocks. Plate IV*b* shows the Dyke at this point in perspective, the pegs as before marking the probable profile of the SW. ditch.

It was clear to me that further investigation of the Dyke in this area was useless; a fresh site with a rock subsoil was therefore sought. This was found at Brynbella (Fig. 10). The work done here was only such as could be carried out in the few days left for the investigation.

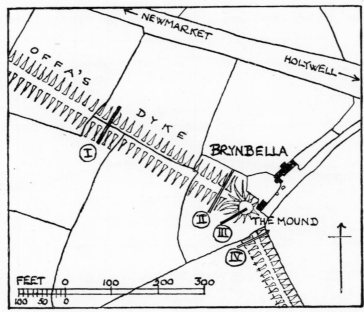

FIG. 10. Offa's Dyke and Mound at Brynbella, Whitford, showing places surveyed or excavated.

Trenches were dug across the ditches on either side of the bank, 120 yards NW. of the Mound. These were found to have been cut in the limestone rock, which is disjointed with pockets of clay between the blocks, and was probably quarried without difficulty. The black lines in the section (Fig. 7, 1) mark the profile of the ditches as far as they can be determined; above the rock level, where stony clay grades up into humus, the profile is necessarily uncertain. The profiles differ on the two sides, one being flat-floored, the other V-shaped; evidently two gangs were at work on the Dyke, one on each side. The dimensions of the ditches (4 ft. 7 in. and 5 ft. 11 in. in depth by about 12 ft. in width at the top) show that the vallum when perfect cannot have been of greater height than 7 ft.; the Dyke was clearly a boundary earthwork only. The filling of the ditches is stony clay grading up into humus; the stones are much more numerous in the SW. than in the NE. ditch. No artefact was found in these cuttings.

The last two days available for excavation were devoted to an examination of the relation between the Dyke and the Brynbella mound which was utilized for its alignment.

A section was cut across the line of the SW. ditch of the Dyke fronting the mound; its position is indicated in the plan (see Fig. 10, iii and Plate IIa). The ditch was shallow, flat-floored, and of similar profile to the SW. ditch at a point 120 yards away (Fig. 7, iii). It was cut (like those at section 7, i) into the disjointed limestone rock. The filling consisted of a thick layer of humus grading down into clayey earth-with-stones. It was proved to be the ditch of the Dyke, and not the (hypothetical) ditch of the mound; its long axis was exactly aligned with the long axis of the Dyke NW. of the mound, and the depression marking the silted-up ditch of the Dyke was continuously present for several hundred yards from the point of excavation north-westward.

Mr. Thomas Price, to whose kindness I have elsewhere alluded, did not wish the Brynbella mound to be mutilated, as it adjoined his house and its green bulk made a pleasant prospect. He, however, very kindly permitted me to dig into its face; I gladly took the opportunity thus afforded of extending my trench in order to study its stratification (Plate IIa). This was fairly regular and approximately level; a layer of reddish-sandy clay with stones was overlaid by yellowish sandy clay, above which was stony clay. There was very little humus. The contour of the mound here (Fig. 7, iii) suggested that it had been dug away in modern times.

Though little evidence is available, I hold it to be probable that the mound is sepulchral, older than the Dyke; utilized as a sighting mark, and incorporated—without mutilation—in the earthwork.[1] On this view the exceptional breadth at Profile ii was due to the engineer in charge of the work expanding the Dyke to include the barrow. The NE. ditch of the Dyke probably crossed the Brynbella farmyard (compare Profiles ii and iii, Fig. 7).

The last point that emerges from a careful study of this interesting site is that the change in direction which pivoted on the mound commenced, as far as the SW. ditch is concerned, at a point S. of the mound, under the trackway leading to the Brynbella steading.

SUMMARY[2]

A stretch of country from the sea coast near Prestatyn, to Treuddyn, Flintshire, a distance of 19 miles, is covered in this chapter. From Gop farm, ½ mile W. of Newmarket, to Llyn-du farm in Ysceifiog parish, Flintshire, about 5¾ miles in all, the Dyke can be traced almost continuously, ¾ mile at the northern end having been added to its extent as known

---

[1] If the mound were a structure contemporary with the Dyke we should expect the SW. ditch to become broader and deeper as it passes the mound, in order to provide the extra quantity of material required. On the contrary, the ditch is shallower than in the adjacent field (Fig. 7, i and iii). The inference is that the mound was already in existence. It is probably a barrow of the Bronze Age; the material for such was often brought from a distance. It might be thought an easy matter to determine the relative age of the two structures by a cross trench driven along the axis of the ridge of the Dyke at its junction with the mound. If the mound is older the material of the Dyke will lie unconformably, as the geologists say, on the slope of the mound; if contemporary the stratification should be continuous; if later the mound should over-lie the bank. The Dyke, however, at its junction with the mound is only 3 ft. 3 in. above the original ground level, and the mound has been quarried. Allowing 1 ft. for humus, we have only 2 ft. 3 in. vertical to work with; inadequate, when the material (a stony clay with limestone blocks) is considered, for a delicate stratigraphical determination. This, at all events, was my experience.

[2] Recast in 1953.

in 1926, by Mr. A. J. Taylor, F.S.A. I am much indebted to him for this addition, and for his survey of the problem of the Dyke's termination in the light of this new knowledge (pp. 17 ff).

Gop farm is 2½ miles from the seaboard, to which the Dyke is pointing when it fades out; two short stretches of earthwork, and the straight road from the cliffy scarp of the upland near Pen-yr-allt (770 ft.) to the sea at Prestatyn, possibly indicate the line taken by the frontier. From Llyn-du farm to Treuddyn on the other hand (Plate VI), nearly 11 miles, no trace of the Dyke could be found.

It may then be that King Offa—who died, as we know from a Welsh source, at Rhuddlan 3 miles beyond his frontier in 796, presumably in border warfare—never completed his work.

Character.—The Dyke in the Gop farm–Llyn-du sector traverses a limestone plateau country, its alignment varying in elevation from 520 to 700 ft. It is uniform in type, consisting of a bank between two ditches, but varies in dimensions, the over-all breadth being at one point only about 50 ft. Clearly it is a boundary, and not a defensive work. This conclusion is to some extent confirmed by its trace; an alignment in the same general direction, but giving a much wider view to the SW. could have been chosen. On the other hand, the inclusion of Gop Hill (820 ft.) within the Dyke, which bends N. at the foot of this striking natural feature, the knobby western terminal of a dominant ridge, suggests that visual control over Welsh territory, at the point where the coastal track from the Rhuddlan ford of the river Clwyd leads eastwards into Mercian territory, was an important factor in the layout. Since the Dyke is structurally of boundary bank type, this is the only indication in the area that military considerations influenced its construction. The general direction of the Dyke, NW.–SE., is well maintained, the maximum deviation from a straight line, on either side, being 220 yards.[1] Within these limits, however, the alignment is curiously variable. Changes of direction are frequent and often coincide with mounds—barrows—which were used as sighting marks. One of these barrows, in Ysceifiog parish, was examined in 1925 and found to be of the early Bronze Age.

The alignment chosen by the builder of the Dyke, in so far as it is known, cut off from Wales the southern shore of the estuary of the Dee and the rich mineral deposits of Halkyn Mountain. The Dyke is a political boundary, a frontier; its course here suggests, since this is militarily and economically advantageous to the Power on the E. side, that Mercia was the dominant partner in the arrangement that resulted in its (partial) construction.

[1] The Dyke hereabouts may have been more directly planned than this figure indicates: see p. 20, note 3.

PLATE II

a. Brynbella Mound, Whitford, taken from point III on Fig. 10

b. Offa's Dyke NW. of the Brynbella Mound, taken from the SW. side

PLATE III

a. Offa's Dyke N. of Crown Inn, E. side of Newmarket: Figure 2(*e*)

b. Offa's Dyke on W. outskirts of Newmarket, looking E. Figure 2(*a*)

PLATE IV

b. Section of Offa's Dyke 43 yards SE. of Ysceifiog Circle

a. Section of Offa's Dyke 130 yards NW. of Ysceifiog Circle

PLATE V

a. Bird's-eye-view of Offa's Dyke from Coed Talwrn, Treuddyn, Flintshire, to Brymbo Hill, Denbighshire, a distance of over 2½ miles. Taken from the N. side of Brymbo Hill at point marked E on map, Fig. 12

b. Bank in Gwaenysgor parish, Flintshire (see Figure 1). In the middle distance is Gop Hill, near Newmarket (Figure 2).

PLATE VI

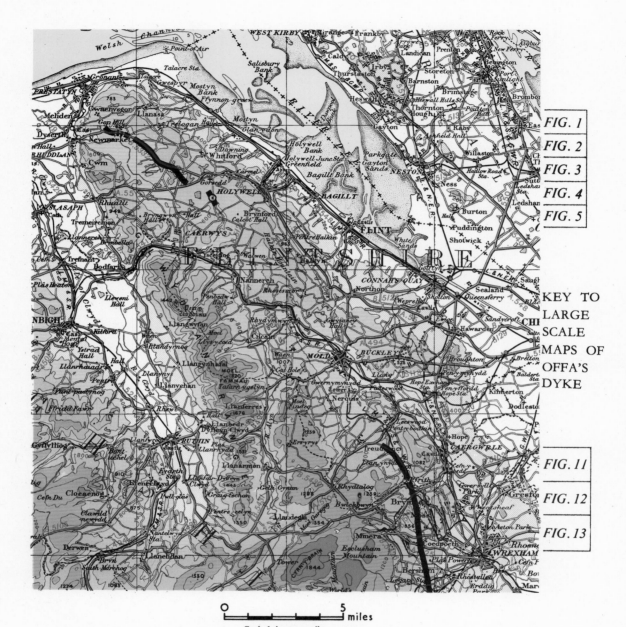

FIG. 1
FIG. 2
FIG. 3
FIG. 4
FIG. 5

KEY TO
LARGE
SCALE
MAPS OF
OFFA'S
DYKE

FIG. 11
FIG. 12
FIG. 13

Scale ¼ in. to 1 mile

Offa's Dyke in Flintshire and East Denbighshire
(Chapters II and III)
See pages 5, 8, 22, 29, 30, 39, 44, 278, 287

III. OFFA'S DYKE IN SOUTH FLINTSHIRE AND EAST DENBIGHSHIRE (1927)

TREUDDYN, where the survey of 1925 ended, is 'the most northerly point to which the Dyke, as a continuous earthwork universally recognized by that name, extends'. In this chapter the investigation (in 1926) of a sector 5 miles in length, extending from Coed Talwrn, in Treuddyn parish, to the N. end of Plas Power park, Bersham is described. If the key map, Plate VI, be referred to, the position and direction of this sector will be readily understood, Plas Power park being due W. of the town of Wrexham.

The Dyke is, on the whole, well preserved. Gaps occur, but the general direction is never in doubt. The earthwork is, moreover, not of that slight and indeterminate character which it presents in N. Flintshire, but is for the most part a striking feature of the landscape it traverses—a countryside 400 to 800 ft. above sea-level, foot-hills of the mountain mass lying between the Vale of Clwyd and the plain of Cheshire—a northern outlier of the Berwyn Mountains, cut off from the main range by the gorge of the Dee. Along the E. slopes of this upland, deeply intersected by small tributaries of this river, flowing eastward, the Dyke is aligned; and, having regard to the difficulties of the terrain, its course is singularly direct.

The first identifiable traces of the Dyke are on the flat crest of a low ridge 600 ft. above O.D. between the river Cegidog and a tributary (Plate VII*a*). It follows this rapidly narrowing ridge in a SE. direction for 900 yards; descending to valley level, it crosses the tributary and clings to the E. flank of the narrow Cegidog valley for a distance of over a mile, at between 500 ft. and 400 ft. (Figs. 11 and 12). Descending to the valley floor at Ffrith, it crosses, first the Cegidog, and then another tributary of the Cegidog, at 394 ft. above O.D. Five hundred yards farther on it crosses a third tributary streamlet, and breasts the steep slopes of Brymbo Hill, rising to over 800 ft. above Cae-llo brickworks. Its course from this point to the end of the sector surveyed is nearly due S. and very direct, its maximum lateral deviation from a straight line for $2\frac{1}{3}$ miles being only 100 yards. It is here sited on fairly level upland, bisected by one ravine. There is a gradual descent from Brymbo Hill (850 ft.) to Vron (700 ft.); then, after a sharp dip into the ravine of the river Gwenfro the upland is regained, and the Dyke runs at about 600 ft. above O.D. across terrain offering no topographical features to Plas Power park, where this year's survey ends.

Down the valley of the river Cegidog (1 mile); on Brymbo Hill (300 yards); and from Brymbo reservoir to Vron ($\frac{1}{2}$ mile), the Dyke is definitely aligned in such a manner as to give a field of view to the W. On the Treuddyn ridge ($\frac{1}{2}$ mile) the crest line which was chosen gives an excellent view to the W., and incidentally an equally good view to the E. At no point is there evidence that an eastward-facing alignment was selected in preference to one facing W.

The detailed record follows.

THE COURSE OF THE DYKE

Three sections of the 6-in. O.S. map, reduced to 4 in. to 1 mile (Figs. 11 to 13), represent the entire stretch of country traversed by the earthwork between Coed Talwrn and
Plas Power park. Plate VI indicates the position in the sector of each of these large-scale
maps.

FIGURE 11. *Spot-level 621 (Coed Talwrn) to by-road to Glandwr on Treuddyn–Llanfynydd–
    Ffrith road*

Throughout this portion the above-mentioned road is either on, or immediately adjacent
to, the Dyke. The Dyke first appears at a point 100 yards SE. of the Tan-llan colliery
tramway, on the margin of the ground disturbed by mine workings; here the Treuddyn–
Llanfynydd road, which has hitherto been on the natural ground level, rises on to a bank
which is seen to be the flattened crest of the Dyke. This bank is of considerable breadth
and height (Fig. 14, vii and viii), and its absence farther northward, already recorded, is
all the more remarkable.

For a distance of 700 yards the road, which throughout this distance descends at an
even gradient towards the valley floor, remains on the crest of the Dyke (Plates V*a* and
VII*a*). The drainage of the plateau has been partly deflected into the ditch—here on the
SW. side—which has thus been maintained probably at its original depth; the brook
leaves the ditch at the E. boundary of field 4. Throughout this distance, the fields immediately adjacent to the Dyke on the NE. side show a rounded hollow close to its line, as
though some of the material required for its construction had been gathered from this
side. Its bulk indeed is here greater than can be accounted for by the size of the western
ditch.

The line of the Dyke from this point (field 4) is by no means easy to trace, but I am
convinced that the sharp termination of the ridge in field 5 is partly artificial, and is the
rampart of the Dyke. Here then the road has left the crest and runs below the rampart,
its position being probably in part determined by the platform which on this steep slope
may have represented the (western) ditch.

As is commonly the case with travelling earthworks, no clear trace survives on the
valley floor, but it was noticed that the prolongation of the alignment of the Dyke would
carry it across the NE. angle of a field in the valley (no. 6). The ground hereabouts was
seen to be unusually stony when the field was under plough in April 1926, and this stony
soil was probably the remains of the bank.

The Dyke is certainly present close to the farm buildings in field 8 as a ridge sloping
steeply up from the E. towards the road. With this clue, it is easy to recognize the bank
extending along the roadside boundary of this field, and its well-nigh shapeless remains
in the southern angle of field 7. Thus, the line of the Dyke across the valley suggested by
its alignment on the farther side is seen to be approximately, and perhaps actually, the
line of the modern road.

In the enclosure, now a garden, in the N. angle of the cross-roads by Penuel chapel, an isolated fragment of the bank of Offa's Dyke, some 6 ft. in height, survives to mark its course. In field 9, the ploughed-down bank, an imposing whale-backed ridge 22 yards in breadth, runs close to the road; it was cut away to build the chapel. The S. boundary of this field is a marshy flat, probably in former times a small mill pool. The road crosses the tiny watercourse (now piped) at this point, and so has destroyed the beginning of the bank at the farther side of the stream. The gap, however, is a short one (32 yards

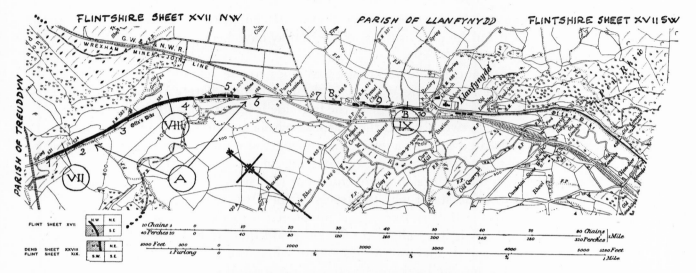

FIG. 11. The Dyke from Coed Talwrn to by-road to Glan-dwr on Treuddyn–Llanfynydd road. A portion of the 6-in. O.S. map, Flintshire, reduced to 4 in. to 1 mile. In this and the following two maps ▬▬ represents portions of the Dyke clearly visible today; ▬ ▬ ▬ shows that faint traces of the Dyke are present; ——— represents the approximate alignment of the Dyke where it is now lost, as recorded in 1838 on the first 1-in. O.S. map, or as indicated by a respectable tradition.

Roman numerals in circles point to the exact position where the sectional plan with the corresponding number was made; letters in circles and arrows indicate the approximate position and direction of the camera when the illustration with the corresponding letter was taken. For the significance of the arabic numerals on the maps, see the text.

The key plan at the left-hand corner of this map shows the position of the Dyke on the 6-in. sheets here reproduced in part.

(Reproduced from the Ordnance Survey map with the sanction of the Controller of H.M. Stationery Office.)

or so) and the Dyke reappears on the W. side of the road (field 10) as a magnificent rampart with traces of a ploughed-in ditch at the lower (W.) slope (Pl. VIII*b* and Fig. 14, ix). It is here 8 ft. high, but its original breadth has been lessened by road widening.[1]

The Dyke is not now visible in the gardens and closes of Llanfynydd, but it must have passed to the W. of the post office. The main road, which takes a devious course through the village, recovers its previous alignment opposite the school.

From here to the bridge across the Cegidog at Ffrith, a distance of nearly 1 mile, the road runs at a fairly constant level on the E. hill-side (which is at times very steep) some 20 ft. above the valley floor. There is thus continuously present a steep scarp below the

[1] No indication of the course of the Dyke between BM 503·2 (Flints. XVII NW.) and Llanfynydd, a distance of 850 yards, is given on the O.S. maps.

road, and this has been by all observers identified as Offa's Dyke. The identification is supported by a respectable tradition, and the Dyke is marked on this alignment on the 6-in. O.S. maps. It is highly probable on general grounds; definite traces of any artificial construction other than the modern road in this section are, however, very scanty.

(1) Between the station and the school at Llanfynydd there is a narrow ditch half-way up the steep slope which separates the station road from the main road. This may be the ditch of Offa's Dyke, for it is in the correct alignment; but it owes its existence to the bank which defines it on the lower side, and which may have been thrown up during the construction of the station.

(2) Greater certainty and much importance attaches to the remains of a bank some 550 yards farther to the SE. on the W. side of the road, immediately W. of the cottage known as Cerrig-llwydion. Here the slope of the hill-side is less steep, and the road swings inwards leaving a space between it and the scarp which flanks the valley. On the edge of the platform thus presented there is a low rounded ridge, at its best 9 ft. across and some 2 ft. high. This must have been built up on the edge of the steep scarp created by the scour of the river with material taken from the inner (E.) side.

We are thus able to understand why the traces of the Dyke are so slight. A very little levelling would turn the earthwork into a convenient platform which would form a trackway, and later a road, down this valley; the Dyke would quickly be obliterated, and the only chance of recognizable survival would occur when the road happened to swing inwards (eastwards) leaving the bank on the edge of the natural scarp. Road widening has been carried out in this section during the last few years, and many traces similar to that referred to above may have been destroyed.

FIGURE 12. *From a point 450 yards NNW. of the bridge over the river Cegidog at Ffrith to the mine-tip of the Brymbo colliery*

At a point 230 yards NNW. of the bridge over the river Cegidog, at the entrance to Ffrith village, a low rounded bank is seen with an inner ditch, on the upper (E.) margin of the valley pasture, at the foot of the scarp; and though the connexion of this bank with the reputed alignment of the Dyke *on* the scarp, recorded in the preceding paragraphs, is lost, the bank is, I believe, Offa's Dyke, which is here carried to valley level, below the scarp, preparatory to the negotiation of the river crossing. The bank follows the foot of the scarp, making for the river close to the bridge; at the edge of the alluvium it is lost.[1]

The correct determination of the course of the Dyke from this point—the bridge over the Cegidog—onwards through Ffrith village to Pont Newydd-y-ffrith, the bridge over the tributary stream descending from Nant-y-ffrith, is important. It is indeed one of the crucial points on its alignment, because the area was occupied by a Roman settlement of

---

[1] The occurrence of the E. ditch here is interesting. From Coed Talwrn to Llanfynydd the ditch was on the W., but on the scarp from L. to Ffrith the material for the bank seems for practical reasons to have been taken entirely from the inner (E.) side. It is easy to under-stand why the practice was continued in the short stretch of some 200 yards under consideration; it differentiated the earthwork from the scarp which backed it.

some sort; if the Dyke here has not been destroyed, excavation should enable us to determine whether it antedates or postdates the Roman occupation. On the large-scale map, Fig. 16, the position of Roman foundations, of pottery and other finds, which constitute the evidence for Roman occupation at Ffrith is indicated.[1] The site has been called a small 'Roman Station' and is marked as such on the O.S. map, but the lines of its defences have not been traced, and the character of the settlement is not known.[2]

The course of the Dyke at Ffrith is not recorded on the O.S. map, but the road through the village is in alignment with the fragment just described, and in view of the close association between Dyke and road already manifested in this section it seemed probable

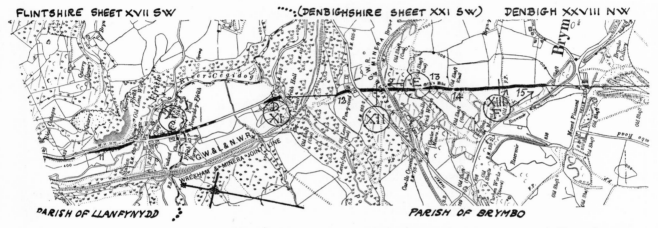

FIG. 12. The Dyke from 450 yards NNW. of bridge over river Cegidog at Ffrith, to the Brymbo Colliery. A portion of the 6-in. O.S. map, Flintshire and Denbighshire, reduced to 4 in. to 1 mile. For the significance of the symbols and letters employed see Fig. 11.

(Reproduced from the Ordnance Survey map with the sanction of the Controller of H.M. Stationery Office.)

that traces might be found on or close to it. This proved to be the case. A well-marked bank[3] is visible practically the whole distance between the two bridges, the E. row of cottages fronting the street being built on it. The bank is especially well marked N. of spot-level 397 (Fig. 16)—where it is 3 ft. above the street level—and between the post-office and Pont Newydd-y-ffrith, where it is 4 ft. high; at the latter point its forward slope has been cut away, and the ridge revetted by a stone wall. The contours of the bank render it highly improbable that the ditch was to the E., and it may safely be assumed that the road marks the line of the ditch.

Further evidence in favour of the view that this bank is Offa's Dyke is afforded by the fact that on the other side of Pont Newydd-y-ffrith the road is for over 200 yards raised above the ground level on either side; the ramp on which it runs can hardly be other than the flattened crest of the Dyke.[4] Proof that these inductions were correct was discovered

[1] Details of these and references will be found in a paper by Miss M. V. Taylor on 'Roman Flintshire' in the *Flints. Hist. Soc. Journ.*, vol. ix (1922), and in *Roy. Com. Anc. Mon.*, Flints. Inventory, p. 166.

[2] See Taylor, loc. cit., for a reference to tiles stamped

LEGIO XX, found near Ffrith.

[3] Noted by Taylor, loc. cit.

[4] The course of the Dyke is shown on the W. side of the road in Fig. 43, *Roy. Com. Anc. Mon.*, Flints. Inventory. No visible indications justifying this align-

at Ffrith Hall, 400 yards beyond the bridge. Here the road swings eastward; but in the grounds of the Hall, in the correct alignment, a well-preserved fragment of the Dyke survives. Traces of the ditch are apparent on the W. side; this is in agreement with the probable position of the ditch in Ffrith village. The position of the constructions identified as Offa's Dyke in this important sector are shown on Fig. 16.

S. of Ffrith Hall there is a ravine, the ground then rising steeply to field 12 by Pen-y-coed farm, 250 ft. above the Hall. This wooded scarp is pitted with mines and scarred with landslips, and all traces of the Dyke have vanished; but it was in existence here as late as 1838, being shown on the 1-in. O.S. map of that date (no. 74 Llangollen NE.). The alignment is here indicated (Fig. 12).

At the point where the steep scarp gives place to an easy slope, 100 yards N. of Pen-y-coed, the Dyke reappears as the E. boundary of the field mentioned in the previous paragraph. It is a low bank, about 5 ft. high, steep on the W. face; there is no visible ditch, but the contours of the bank point to its having been on the W. At this point, as we shall in due course note, a major alignment begins.

Crossing the Minera road by the farm-house, the Dyke appears as a broad low ridge with a W. ditch, 54 ft. over-all, making for the Brymbo Hill sky line. From the road to the hill-top it is continuously present, save at the point where the Minera–Wrexham railway cuts through it.[1] The ditch is consistently on the W. The scarp of the Dyke is very steep on the slope S. of the railway, which it ascends diagonally.

On reaching the plateau-like slope of Brymbo Hill (from which the photograph shown in Plate V*a* was obtained), the Dyke forms the W. boundary of field 13, and is quite definite. After crossing a marshy hollow at the N. end of field 14, where it can hardly be said to exist, it rises on to the crest of Brymbo Hill, well over 800 ft. above sea-level, and then descends a gentle slope towards Brake road and the Brymbo colliery mining area. On the hill the Dyke, as the photograph (Plate VII*b*) shows, forms a striking feature. The ditch was certainly on the W. side, but has been ploughed in; agricultural operations, moreover, have steepened the slope of the bank on both sides (see Fig. 15, xiii).

Near the S. margin of field 15 the Dyke disappears in disturbed ground; a damaged fragment is visible 180 yards farther on in the back-yard of the cottages bordering Brake Road on the S.,[2] and the Dyke then disappears for a further 300 yards under the mountainous spoil-heaps of Brymbo colliery.

Looking back from this mine-tip an excellent view of the layout across Brymbo Hill is obtained. The neglect of eastward-facing alignments already noticed as characteristic of the Dyke is here strikingly exemplified. The Dyke is sited on the crest of the hill where the W. slope begins; there is, therefore, a good view of the hill country to the W., and a very limited view in the opposite direction. An alignment a few yards to the E. would have

---

ment exist. It is based, I suppose, on what are topographically speaking the very confused statements regarding the relation between the Dyke and Roman remains contained in *Arch. Camb.*, 1875, p. 277, and *Archaeologia*, 53, p. 481. In neither account are the presumed remains of the Dyke described or their position recorded.

[1] Sixty yards of the Dyke N. of the railway are not marked on the 6-in. O.S. map, 1914 edition.

[2] The bank forms the W. boundary of the yard, and is revetted by a low stone wall.

given the builders, had they desired it, control of a long slope, and beyond, one of the finest views of the marches, embracing portions of half a dozen counties.

On the farther side of the mine-tip the Dyke is easily identified, in the same alignment. It is marked as continuously present in this area on the 1838 1-in. O.S. map (no. 74, Llangollen NE.)—the result of a survey made prior to the industrial development.

FIGURE 13. *From Reservoir near Brymbo Hall to the northern end of Plas Power park*

The Dyke forms the E. boundary of field 16, being here 6–7 ft. in height, 18–20 ft. in breadth, with a steep W. slope; there are indications of a ditch on the W. side. South of

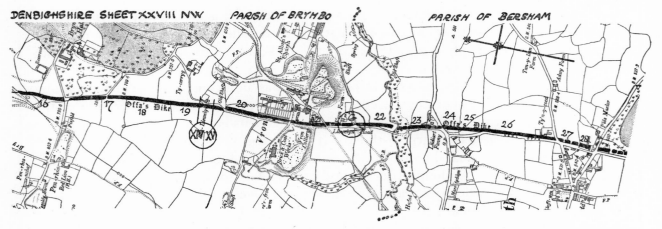

FIG. 13. The Dyke from Brymbo Hall to N. end of Plas Power park. A portion of the 6-in. O.S. map, Denbighshire, reduced to 4 in. to 1 mile. For the significance of the symbols and letters employed see Fig. 11.
(Reproduced from the Ordnance Survey map with the sanction of the Controller of H.M. Stationery Office.)

the Brymbo Hall cross-roads the ploughed-in ditch and the scarp of the Dyke can be seen on the W. of the road skirting Brymbo Hall grounds; near the cross-road the road is *on* the bank. At the road angle by field 17 definite traces of the Dyke cease for a few yards, but the steep scarp which forms the E. boundary of this field, as also of field 18 is undoubtedly the Dyke, and is so marked on the O.S. map. The ditch (on the W. side) is very well marked in field 19, as the diagram (Fig. 15, xiv) shows; the bank is ploughed down at the point where the section was measured, but in the SE. corner of this field it is undamaged save by time (Fig. 15, xv). The Dyke now crosses the road, and shows a well-preserved stretch of bank in the pasture field no. 20; its probable height above natural ground level, as shown by a modern cutting, is 5 ft.; the breadth is 20 ft. The road-side hedge is on the scarp, and the ditch is filled in with rubbish.

From field 16 (close to the mine-tip) to field 20, the Dyke is aligned on a gentle W. slope, parallel to a small brook tributary to the Gwenfro. The view to the W. is thus ample; the view to the E. is restricted.

The houses of Vron colliery are on the site of the bank (as the 1-in. map of 1838 shows), and a much-ravaged fragment survives on the S. side of the light railway which divides the row of cottages from a colliery building. In a garden (enclosure 21) immediately S. of the latter the bank of the Dyke is very impressive, being 27 ft. across and 7 ft. in height, as shown by a transverse cutting. It maintains this amplitude, and is well wooded, as far as the entrance to Vron farm; the Llewelyn road, falling steeply to the river Gwenfro, occupies the ditch. S. of Vron farm both bank and ditch are in field 22, the former being represented by a whale-backed grass ridge (Plate VIII*a*), sloping steeply to the river; the silted-up ditch is on the W. side. The rampart continues to within 28 yards of the existing course of the stream, that is to say it ends abruptly on the valley floor, which is only some 40 yards wide. It may originally have continued as far as the bank of the stream; but since floods would quickly plane the valley floor clean of obstructions its present termination must be very ancient. This portion, from Vron to the river, is an interesting example of the structure of the Dyke when crossing a steep-sided valley. It may here be noted that the 1838 1-in. map already referred to shows the Dyke as continuous and complete from Ffrith Hall to the Gwenfro.

On the S. side of the Gwenfro the Dyke is present as an inconspicuous bank ascending the steep scarp; it does not align accurately with the portion on the other side of the stream. Directly the plateau is reached, the Dyke regains its normal proportions and usual profile, presenting a steep scarp to the W. It forms the W. boundary of field 23; it is partly destroyed at Llidiart Fanny, but for a very short distance only, as the map shows.

In field 24 the Dyke is ploughed down and forms a low rounded ridge; the line of the ditch on the W. side is clearly apparent. In field 25 the Dyke is almost completely levelled; in field 26—the homefield of Tyn-y-coed, dotted with lime and oak trees—it is seen close to the hedge, the road being on the line of the ditch. On the W. side of the Tyn-y-coed farm buildings the bank is now revetted by a stone wall.

In the ploughed field 27, beyond the cross-roads, the almost obliterated bank is visible in evening sunlight on the alignment shown, and in continuation with this line the ploughed-down but quite clearly marked ridge of the Dyke is visible in enclosure 28, close to a chapel. It may be noted that a hamlet adjacent to the Dyke is known as Adwy'r clawdd, indicative of the existence of an ancient (but not necessarily original) gap in the earthwork.

The Dyke now enters Plas Power park. It is well marked in a ruined enclosure, overgrown with brushwood, in the N. corner of the Park, and the line of the levelled rampart can, without difficulty, be traced as far as the right margin of the Figure.[1]

THE EXISTING PROFILE OF THE DYKE

The Dyke in N. Flintshire was an inconsiderable work—a boundary bank with ditches on both sides. The earthwork in the sector under review presents the character generally associated with Offa's Dyke—that of a considerable work ditched on the W. side, inviting comparison with the better-preserved portions of Wansdyke in Somerset. The profiles in Fig. 14 are from surveys taken N. of Ffrith; those in Fig. 15 from surveys taken S. of that

---

[1] The line of the earthwork for the last 400 yards here recorded is not noted on the printed O.S. map.

OFFA'S DYKE: PROFILES IN TREUDDYN AND LLANFYNYDD, FLINTSHIRE

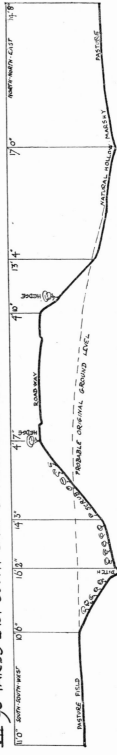

VII 90 YARDS EAST·SOUTH·EAST OF SPOT·LEVEL 621 ON TREUDDYN—LLANFYNYDD ROAD [6"O.S. FLINTS. XVII N.W.]

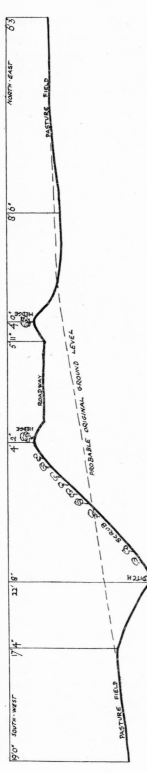

VIII 50 YARDS SOUTH·EAST OF SPOT·LEVEL 585 ON TREUDDYN—LLANFYNYDD ROAD [6" O.S. FLINTS. XVII N.W.]

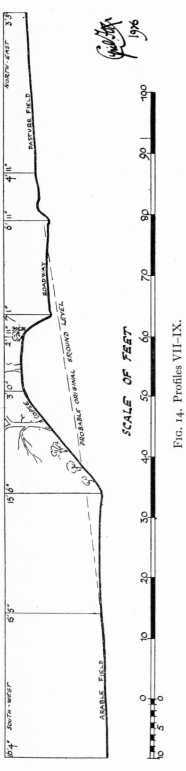

IX 50 YARDS N.E. OF ROAD JUNCTION AT ENTRANCE TO LLANFYNYDD VILLAGE [6" O.S. FLINTS. XVII S.W.]

SCALE OF FEET

Fig. 14. Profiles VII–IX.

village; the exact positions are indicated on the maps (Figs. 11 to 13). Some of these profiles show Offa's Dyke much reduced and damaged; the bank ploughed down, the ditch ploughed in or filled up. Where circumstances have been favourable to the preserva-

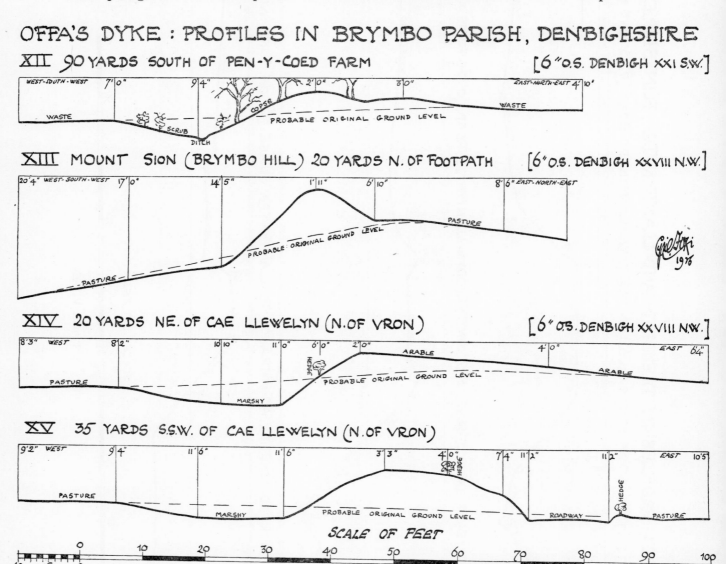

FIG. 15. Profiles XII–XV.

tion of the earthwork, however, it is revealed as a construction of striking and massive character, a work of man which would be impressive in any landscape, and which is particularly so in the broken country of S. Flintshire and N. Denbighshire. From certain view-points, the great Dyke can be seen extending for miles, pursuing a course singularly direct across hill and valley.

Surveys such as these are of value for comparative purposes, and graphic presentation to a constant scale renders comparison easy. In order that a long series of such profiles may ultimately be studied with ease and convenience, it is desirable also to present the essential dimensions in the form of a table, and this offers difficulties, for without excavation the dimensions can only be approximately stated. On the plans, the probable original ground level under the Dyke (from which the height and breadth of rampart is computed) is in each case recorded; this has been worked out with care from a study of the terrain.

The Profiles (Figs. 14 and 15) are numbered consecutively with those in Chapter II, and are plotted to the same scale.[2] The tabular summary shows that the over-all breadth of the work as originally planned must have been in this sector fairly constant round about 60 ft., and that the height of the bank approximated to 7 ft. The ditch is usually filled in or silted-up; an original depth of 7 ft. seems probable from the available evidence. It will be observed that the dimensions as shown in the table are more constant than the variety of outline (due to partial destruction as well as to differences in the lie of the ground traversed by the earthwork) shown in the diagrams would lead one to expect.

The impression gained by the survey work in this sector is that of unity, and of visual control to the W. consistently attained (Plate VI). Though differences of scale and method of construction exist, these are to a large extent determined by the terrain. The whole of the Dyke in this sector is the work of one period.

TABLE OF MEASUREMENTS*

In Treuddyn and Llanfynydd, Flintshire; and Brymbo, Denbighshire

No. of Profile†	Position	Estimated dimensions of bank		Estimated dimensions of ditch		Estimated over-all Breadth
		Height	Breadth	Depth	Breadth	
		ft. in.	ft.	ft. in.	ft. in.	ft.
VII	90 yds. ESE. of spot-level 621 on Treuddyn–Llanfynydd road	7 0	38	6 0	24 0	62
VIII	50 yds. SE. of spot-level 585 on Treuddyn–Llanfynydd road	7 9	38	7 4	24 0	62
IX	50 yds. NE. of road junction at entrance to Llanfynydd village	7 2	32	2 6	24 0	56
X	In Ffrith village	5 0‡	?	?	?	?
XI	At Ffrith Hall	6 8‡	46§	?	?	?
XII	90 yds. S. of Pen-y-coed farm . . .	3 0	32	3 0	22 0	54
XIII	Mount Sion (Brymbo Hill)	7 6	24	1 4	?	55
XIV	20 yds. NE. of Cae Llewelyn, Vron . .	4 0	46‖	4 0	30 6	64
XV	35 yds. SSW. of Cae Llewelyn, Vron . .	6 6	34	2 0	30 0	64

* These measurements are necessarily approximate.
† The numeration is carried on from Chapter II.
‡ Exact dimensions determined by excavation.
§ Bank 'spread', probably by denudation; it is composed of gravel.
‖ Bank 'spread', probably by ploughing.

[1] The profiles and sections on Fig. 17 (nos. x and xi), referred to later, are plotted to scales not hitherto adopted.

EXCAVATION

The excavation work carried out in 1926 consisted of: (1) determination of the structure and lower limit of date of the bank in Ffrith village, and (2) examination of the structure of the bank and determination of the position of its ditch in the grounds of Ffrith Hall.

A. *In Ffrith Village*

It has already been noted that the cottages on the E. side of the street in Ffrith village are built on a bank identified as Offa's Dyke. A short stretch of this bank close to the

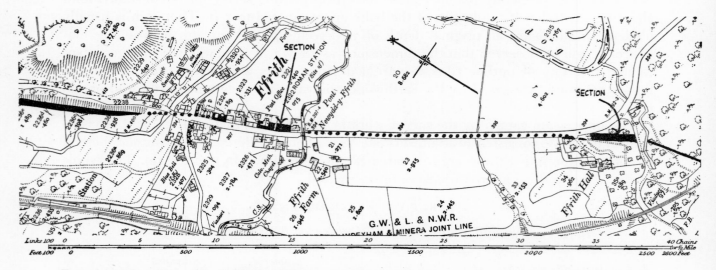

FIG. 16. Portion of the 25-in. O.S. map of Ffrith, reduced by one-half (to 12·5 in. to 1 mile) showing an existing bank, identified as Offa's Dyke ▬▬▬; the probable alignment of Offa's Dyke • • • • •; and the alignment shown on the 1-in. O.S. map of 1838 ▬▬▬▬. The positions of the excavations are shown by arrows, and of Roman remains E. and SE. of the Blue Bell Inn by two crosses.

(Reproduced from the Ordnance Survey map with the sanction of the Controller of H.M. Stationery Office.)

post office is not built on, and in view of the known presence of Roman buildings in the immediate neighbourhood, it was a good place to find out whether it is pre- or post-Roman. If pre-Roman, potsherds and other dateable articles would be present *on* the bank, but not *under* it; if post-Roman, such would be found in the ancient surface soil under the bank. By the courtesy of Mr. E. W. Smallwood, owner of the field, and of Miss E. Hughes, tenant, I was permitted to dig a trench in order to test the matter. Fig 16, the 25-in. map of the area (reduced to 12·5 in. to the mile) shows the position of the excavation, and Plate IX*b* the appearance of the bank from the E.

Description.—The trench was cut as close to the road as was desirable in view of the ruinous condition of the revetment wall and the presence of disturbed ground in its neighbourhood. The trench thus limited, extended up to the crest of the bank. Below the crest the ancient surface soil was struck at a depth of 5 ft. The core of the mound was composed of water-worn boulders. Black (charcoal-stained) soil interpenetrated these and extended beyond them; over this black soil was stony clay with dark patches here and there. A thick layer of humus covered the whole.

Numerous fragments of Roman tile and pottery, all small and the majority abraded, were found in the material composing the bank. The black-soil layer and patches were richest in these artefacts. Fragments of iron and glass, the head of an ox femur sawn across, and a bronze rivet were also recovered. In all fifty-two fragments of pottery and tile, one piece of glass, the bronze rivet, and one fragment of iron were found in the upper layers of the deposit; in the black-soil layer thirty-six fragments of pottery and tile, two broken animal bones and an iron nail were found. There was no oyster shell and no coin. Recognizable pottery fragments included one of Samian form 37, one of 18/31, one of 27, and one of 67 (Plate X). Coarse red and grey wares and chips of tile formed nine-tenths of the finds. All were definitely of the Roman period save one piece of modern porcelain found immediately under the turf.

Plate IX*a* shows the appearance of the section, looking W.; the black-soil layers and the boulders are clearly visible. The floor of the trench is the original surface of the ground. The boy in the upper left-hand corner of the photograph is standing in the roadway—on the presumed site of the ditch.

The subsoil under the bank was then carefully examined. Charcoal was commonly present in the upper layers; the artefacts included ten fragments of pottery (one of Samian 18/31—Plate X,5) four of coarse red, three of grey, and one of buff ware), one iron nail and one piece of glass (Plate X, 4). There were also at the ancient surface level two shallow basin-shaped holes full of charcoal, one of which contained three worn fragments of pottery, the other a fragment of tile; and one post hole which is of some interest. The top of this hole, which was 1 ft. 8 in. deep, was blocked by three waterworn boulders; there was *no filling*, and no trace of decayed wood. A post must have been placed in it shortly before the bank was thrown up[1] and wedged in position with stones. *When the bank was under construction the post was withdrawn*; the boulders remained in, blocking the hole and preventing its being filled with soil.

The potsherds found in and under the bank were for the most part small and abraded, but it is safe to say that no fragment to which an approximate date can be assigned is later than the second century A.D.

If the reader will turn to Fig. 17 the main results of the excavation will easily be grasped. The small-scale diagram shows the relation of the bank to the road and the probable position of the ditch; the large-scale diagram shows the stratification of the artificial deposits, the position of the post-hole, and the distribution of the finds.

The deductions to be drawn from the facts revealed by excavation may be stated as follows:

(i) The bank is not pre-Roman.

(ii) Apart from one fragment of porcelain found immediately under the turf (which is of no moment), the bank contains only objects definitely Roman (potsherds and tile,

---

[1] Had it been in for any length of time worms and rain would have caused the interstices between the stones to be filled with soil.

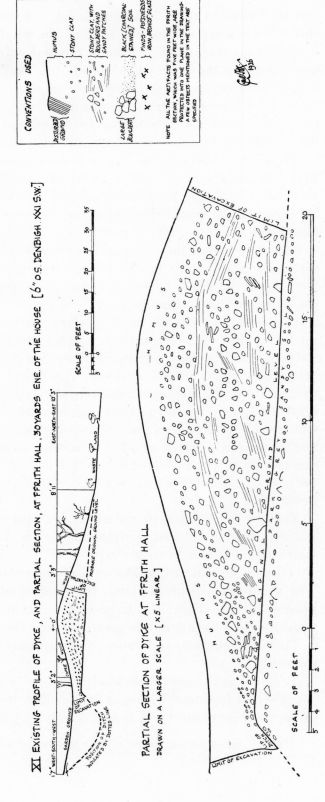

FIG. 17. Profiles X–XI and transverse sections.

bronze, iron and glass—ninety in all) or not incompatible with Roman date (animal bones). Hence the bank was erected anterior to the development of the modern settlement. There is, moreover, no trace of disturbance in the stratification (save in the area near the road and revetment wall which was not excavated).

(iii) The ancient surface soil under the bank contains numerous Roman artefacts and nothing which can be dated later than the Roman period. These artefacts (potsherds, pieces of tile, glass) are small and for the most part abraded, as though they had been in the ground for some time before they were covered up.

(iv) The datable sherds, whether in or under the bank, seem all to be early, i.e. not later than the second century. The fragmentary condition of the sherds, their frequent abrasion, and the absence of groups of fragments of individual vessels, suggests that the bank was not constructed until after the accumulation of rubbish—that is, until after settlement—had ceased. We do not know when this occurred at Ffrith. Intensity of occupation in the early Roman period evidenced by the finds here recorded is in accordance with recent evidence bearing on the occupation of inland Wales. Coins and other finds, as Miss M. V. Taylor has shown, extend the settlement at Ffrith into the third century,[1] but the later occupation may have been slight and intermittent. We may conclude that the bank is later, and probably considerably later, than A.D. 200.

(v) The contours of the ground render it certain that there was no ditch on the E. side of the bank. Throughout the sector of the Dyke under investigation the ditch is on the W. side wherever the ground is level, and there is no reasonable doubt that the village street here marks its site. The character of the material composing the bank at Ffrith shows that it was largely obtained from an area containing Roman rubbish pits. The ground in the neighbourhood of the Roman building uncovered in 1910—only 90 yards away—is recorded to have been 'dark coloured' and as containing 'numerous fragments of charcoal and bones' as well as pottery[2]—evidently it was of similar character to the earth composing the greater part of our bank. I was informed that 'numerous animal bones' were found under the post office, when this was built before the war, and I have no doubt that evidence similar to that which I have obtained underlies every house built on the bank in the village of Ffrith.

(vi) The bank, which I hold to be, without any reasonable doubt, our Dyke, then, is, on the one hand, certainly later than A.D. 200, and probably later than A.D. 400; on the other hand, it is not modern. The evidence, then, in no way contradicts the traditional ascription of the Dyke to Offa, c. A.D. 785, and is indeed entirely consonant with this ascription. It may be noted that this evidence is closely similar to that which I obtained at the Devil's Dyke, Cambridgeshire, long considered to be pre-Roman, but certainly a work of the Dark Ages.[3]

(vii) The post-hole almost certainly illustrates the method employed to guide the gangs engaged in building the Dyke. Posts were doubtless set up at convenient intervals along the line which the bank was to occupy, and removed one by one as a gang reached them.

[1] Roman Flintshire, loc. cit., p. 14.
[2] Roy. Com. Anc. Mon., Flints. Inventory, no. 166, p. 55.
[3] Camb. Antiq. Soc. xxvi, p. 122.

The charcoal-filled holes in the ground may also be contemporary with the erection—sites of the camp fires of the workmen; the few fragments of Roman pottery found therein were abraded, and there is no reason to suppose them to be contemporary.

(viii) Nothing bearing on the supposed existence of a Roman fortified station at Ffrith was found.

B. *At Ffrith Hall*

The only point reasonably close to Ffrith village where the Dyke was undamaged save by time and of characteristic profile, was at Ffrith Hall, 470 yards to the SE. (see Fig. 16 and Plate V*a*), and it was thought worth while to test the Dyke here for the presence of Roman remains. With the kind permission of Mr. Davies, owner of the Hall, a trench was dug through the rampart; its maximum height above ancient ground level was shown to be 6 ft. 8 in., and the existence of the ditch on the west side thereof proven. No artefacts of any sort were found; the site is evidently well outside the settlement area. Profile and section are shown on Fig. 17, plotted on the same scales as the Ffrith village excavation.

SUMMARY

Five miles of Offa's Dyke extending from Coed Talwrn, in Treuddyn parish, Flintshire, to Plas Power park in Bersham parish, Denbighshire (Plate VI), is described in this chapter. The Dyke is a considerable work, and of fairly uniform character; where undamaged (save by time) the over-all breadth is about 60 ft., the bank about 7 ft. high, the ditch correspondingly deep. No hill-forts, barrows, or other earthworks presumably pre-Norman lie on or near its alignment. Gaps occur, but its entire course in this sector can be recovered with reasonable certainty. On level ground the main ditch is always on the W.; but in the Treuddyn–Llanfynydd area some of the material composing the bank seems to have been obtained from the E. side, and on the slope falling steeply to the W. between Llanfynydd and Ffrith, the ditch may have been—for convenience of construction—on the upper (E.) side.

The purposeful directness of the alignment of the Dyke shows that its course was not determined by local advantages of terrain, but it is remarkable how consistently within the manifestly narrow limits permitted by this essential directness, an alignment giving a field of view to the W. is chosen. The Dyke follows a ridge giving a wide view to the W. from Coed Talwrn to the point where this ridge dips to the valley of the little river Cegidog. Thence onwards to Ffrith the alignment of the Dyke follows the steep E. scarp of this narrow valley. From Ffrith to Brymbo Hill no opportunity for selection arises; but on the hill (850 ft.) the deliberate choice of a line giving a field of view to the W. is notable. From Brymbo colliery to Vron again, control of the foreground to the W. is desired and obtained (see p. 79 below).

It may be supposed that these facts point to the Dyke being constructed in this sector as a military barrier, a defence. With such a conclusion I cannot agree. I would, however, go as far as to say that on the evidence yielded by this year's survey it was built under the direction of men trained in a military tradition, and that to the builders, Wales was

PLATE VII

a. Panoramic view in two parts showing Offa's Dyke aligned along the crest line of a spur in Treuddyn parish. The upper portion lies to the north of the lower. The position of the Dyke is shown by arrows; the photographs were taken from the point to the westward marked A on the map, Fig. 11

b. Offa's Dyke on Brymbo Hill, looking E. Taken from point marked F on map, Fig. 12

PLATE VIII

a. Offa's Dyke, descending the slope from Vron farm to the ravine of the river Gwenfro. Taken from the entrance to Vron farm—G on Fig. 13

b. Offa's Dyke, NW. of Llanfynydd village, looking NE. Taken at point marked B on map, Fig. 11

PLATE IX

a. Offa's Dyke in Ffrith village; transverse section, looking west. The survey poles are on original ground level

b. Offa's Dyke in Ffrith village, looking west

PLATE X

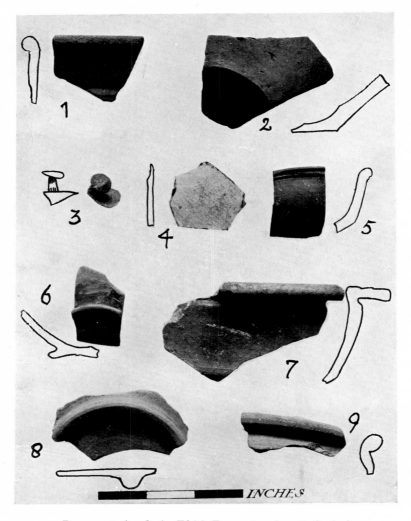

Representative finds, Ffrith Excavation (1926). Scale ½

1. Fragment of rim. Coarse pinkish-grey ware. Black soil layer.
2. Fragment of base. Coarse red ware. Stony layer.
3. Bronze rivet. Stony layer—1 ft. 11 in.
4. Roman glass. Old surface soil under bank.
5. Samian, Form 18/31. Old surface soil under bank.
6. Samian, Form 67. Black-soil layer—3 ft. 8 in.
7. Fragment of flat-rimmed bowl, grey ware. Black-soil layer—3 ft. 2 in.
8. Base of red-ware jug. Black-soil layer.
9. Fragment of rim, coarse red ware. Stony layer—2 ft. 6 in.

an enemy country. I would also point out that the alignment of the Dyke in this sector is high up on the foothills of the Welsh mountains, bordering the Midland Plain; the significance of this may await more extended survey.

Modern roads follow the line of the Dyke for nearly the whole length here surveyed. The earthwork was doubtless at a very early date utilized for *lateral communications* in this broken country where most of the natural lines of traffic are E. and W.

Excavation of a bank in Ffrith village, identified as the rampart of the Dyke, shows it to have been constructed later—probably considerably later—than the second century A.D., and prior to the development of the modern village in the nineteenth century. The ascription of the Dyke to Offa is consistent with these facts.

Certain portions of the Dyke here dealt with are specially worthy of preservation. These are detailed in an appendix (p. 298).

PLATE XI

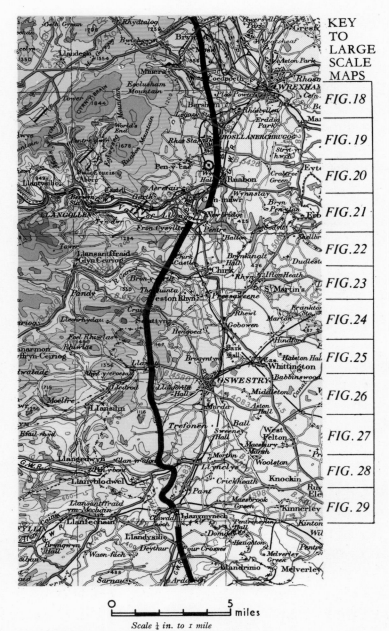

KEY
TO
LARGE
SCALE
MAPS

FIG.18

FIG.19

FIG.20

FIG.21

FIG.22

FIG.23

FIG.24

FIG.25

FIG.26

FIG.27

FIG.28

FIG.29

0 ——————— 5 miles

Scale ¼ in. to 1 mile

Offa's Dyke in East Denbighshire (*continued*) and North-
west Shropshire

(Chapter IV)

A small hillfort (Pen-y-gardden) is also shown

See pages 47, 75, 80, 81, 83 *n.*, 278, 286

IV. OFFA'S DYKE IN EAST DENBIGHSHIRE AND NORTH-WEST SHROPSHIRE (1928)

THIS chapter records the survey of a portion of Offa's Dyke some 22 miles in length; the distance in a straight line between the northern end of Plas Power park, Bersham, Denbighshire, where the investigation began, and the churchyard of Llanymynech, Shropshire, on the left bank of the river Vyrnwy where it ended, being exactly 19 miles.

The small-scale key map, Plate XI, shows the course of the Dyke in relation to the main topographical features. It will be seen that the portion examined is divided into two unequal parts by the valley of the Dee, and that these present distinct geographical characters. In the northern, the Dyke continues the course referred to in Chapter III, along the foothills of the mountain mass which lies to the west. Here the securing of visual control to the W., and directness of alignment, involve very skilful planning. The Dyke maintains a moderate elevation, the maximum being 600 ft. at Plas Power park, the minimum 190 ft. where it reaches the river Dee in Hopyard wood; 400 ft. is the average level. In this part the Dyke passes through a country-side extensively industrial but mainly agricultural, offering no marked physical features other than the ravine of the river Clywedog and the Pentrebychan brook, and the steep northern flank of the Dee valley. The underlying rocks are the Coal Measures.

In the southern part the Dyke crosses country largely mountainous, intersected by two river valleys. It ascends gradually from the right bank of the Dee to Chirk park (621 ft.), crosses the trough valley of the Ceiriog, and sweeping westward in a broad arc surmounts the easternmost hills of the Berwyn range. Mount wood (1,175 ft.), Selattyn Hill (1,200 ft.), Baker's Hill (1,124 ft.) are thus included. The highest point reached by the Dyke in this part of its course is about 1,120 ft. in the centre of the arc due west of Selattyn Hill. Descending from Craig Forda (1,000 ft.) to the Morda valley (500 ft.) it crosses a belt of country without marked physical features; it then follows the contours of Whitehaven and Llanymynech hills on their western sides at the 600–700-ft. level, descending from the latter to the river Vyrnwy (200 ft.). The country-side is mainly upland pasture and moorland, but between the river Dee and Mount wood and between the river Morda and Whitehaven Hill it is agricultural. The underlying rocks are 'millstone grit' alternating with limestone.

THE COURSE OF THE DYKE

The course of the Dyke is set out on twelve sections of the 6-in. O.S. map, reduced as before to 4 in. to 1 mile (Figs. 18 to 29). These represent the entire stretch of country traversed by the earthwork between Plas Power Park and the river Vyrnwy. Plate XI indicates the position in the sector of each of these large-scale maps.

FIGURE 18. *North end of Plas Power park to north end of Pentre-bychan park, passing through Bersham parish and between the parishes of Esclusham Above and Below, Denbighshire*

There is no trace of the Dyke in the copse close to spot level 609,[1] but immediately to the S. of this woodland a fragment (+2 ft.) of the bank is seen, close to the park wall. From this point to Park Cottage the traces are not very marked, but are quite definite; the park wall is on the line of the ditch, and the old oak-tree at the N. end of the cottage enclosure is on the reverse slope of the bank.

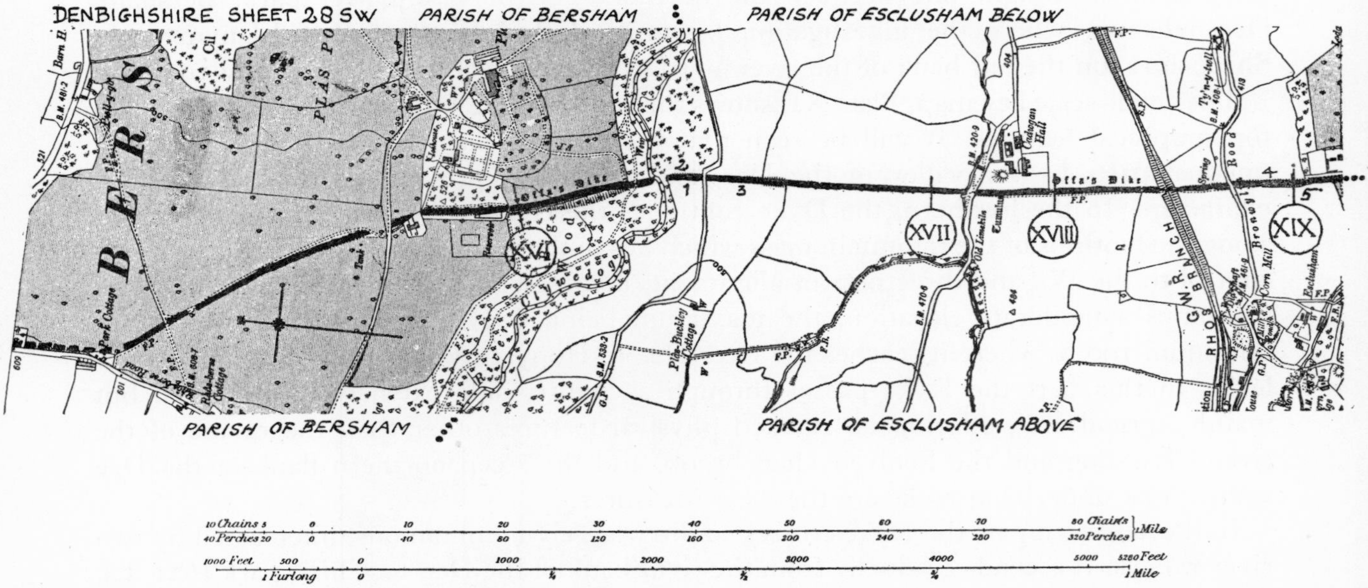

FIG. 18. The Dyke from N. end of Plas Power park to N. end of Pentre-bychan park. A portion of the 6-in. O.S. map reduced to 4 in. to 1 mile.

In this and the following eleven maps ▬▬ represents portions of the Dyke clearly visible today; ▪▪▪▪ shows that faint traces of the Dyke are present; ——— represents the approximate alignment of the Dyke where it is now lost, as recorded on the first 1-in. O.S. map, or as indicated by a respectable tradition.

Roman numerals in circles point to the exact position where the sectional plan with the corresponding number was made; letters in circles and arrows indicate the approximate position and direction of the camera when the illustration with the corresponding letter was taken. The Arabic numerals are inserted for convenience of textual reference.

(Reproduced from the Ordnance Survey map with the sanction of the Controller of H.M. Stationery Office.)

At Park Cottage the Dyke changes direction through 20 degrees. There is nothing in the topography to account for so sudden an alteration (but see p. 82, *Note*, below). The Dyke is destroyed where the change took place; the 1838 O.S. map shows three cottages here, and the levelling was probably carried out then. Thirteen yards from the Park Cottage enclosure the earthwork, much denuded, is again apparent, and it continues on a fairly straight alignment across the park. For a distance of 700 yards it has been much damaged (mainly by cultivation), and small portions of the bank have been completely levelled and the ditch filled in. Its position is, however, certain;[2] the ditch (now used as a field drain)

[1] It was present here in 1838. See the 1-in. O.S. map of that year, sheet 74.

[2] Visible traces, confirmed by the 1838 O.S. map.

was consistently on the W. side, and the best preserved portions[1] show that the Dyke was here of normal scale and proportions.

On the S. side of the E. and W. track across the park, and to the N. of the cottages marked on the map, the Dyke is present, undamaged save by time, with old trees on bank and counterscarp. There is a low bank on the counterscarp here (see p. 74).

The Dyke now crosses a patch of woodland, both bank and ditch being well marked and of characteristic scale; the scarp is notably steep. The construction of the 'Reservoir' which occupies the ditch has not seriously damaged the bank; immediately S. of it there is a gap (cart track). Emerging again on to parkland, the Dyke descends a rapidly steepening slope to the river Clywedog, its continuity broken only by one modern cross-track. The overdeepened ditch (p. 78) here is well shown on the map, and is illustrated in Profile xvi, Fig. 30; on the bank are well-grown oaks. The earthwork ends abruptly on the edge of the rapidly flowing stream and begins afresh, equally abruptly, on the opposite scarp only 35 yards away. The intervening area is certainly swept by winter floods, and we have here an excellent illustration of what is evidently a characteristic feature of the Dyke (previously exemplified at Vron),[2] namely, the reduction of openings and gaps necessitated by the topography to a minimum.

From the right bank of the stream straight stretches extend across meadow and pasture land to Pentre-bychan Hall, the earthwork throughout being an imposing work and but little damaged. It is especially fine passing between field no. 1 and the plantation marked 2; the gap permitting the passage of the adjacent roadway is obviously not original. From this road to the brook NW. of Cadwgan Hall the Dyke is continuous and presents a striking appearance. At the SE. corner of field 3 the ditch has been widened to form a pond; S. of this point the contours of the ditch have been to some extent flattened and the crest of the bank lowered by the plough.[3] Profile xvii, Fig. 30, is characteristic. S. of the gap near Cadwgan Hall, where the brook and a trackway cross it, the Dyke presents a similar appearance. The bank is dug away at the point where the base of the Cadwgan mound[4] most closely approaches it, and there are narrow gaps (not original) by the O and e of Offa's Dike. No. xviii is a characteristic profile; the low bank on the W. of the ditch is part of a later enclosure. It is certain that the Dyke is present under the railway embankment;[5] from this embankment to 'Bronwylfa Road' it is much damaged. The bank by S of Spring is, however, very fine, with a steep scarp; the ditch, as is usual in this area, is to some extent ploughed in. A nearby gap, probably original, permits the passage of the water-flow.

The Bronwylfa roadway has been cut through the earthwork, which is very imposing from this point onwards to Pentre-bychan Hall. The reverse slope of the bank has been ploughed up to the crest, but in the greater part of this sector the ditch is well marked, especially in the SE. corner of field 5. It may have been widened in one place to form a cattle-pond; the floor here is flat and marshy (see Profile xix). There is a narrow field gap by the SW. corner of field 4.

---

[1] At one point the bank is 8½ ft. (vertical) above the ditch floor, the overall breadth of the work being 72 ft.
[2] Chapter III, p. 36.

[3] As much as 3 ft., by the SE. corner of field 3.
[4] See p. 75.
[5] See the 1838 ordnance map.

FIGURE 19. *Pentre-bychan Hall to spot-level* 393 *on Wrexham–Ruabon road, passing between the parishes of Esclusham Above and Below, through the parish of Rhosllanner-chrugog and on the boundary between Rhosllanerchrugog and Ruabon parishes, Denbighshire*

Except in the immediate neighbourhood of the Hall, the Dyke at Pentre-bychan has been but little damaged by man; ancient oaks are on scarp and crest. S. of the Hall, on

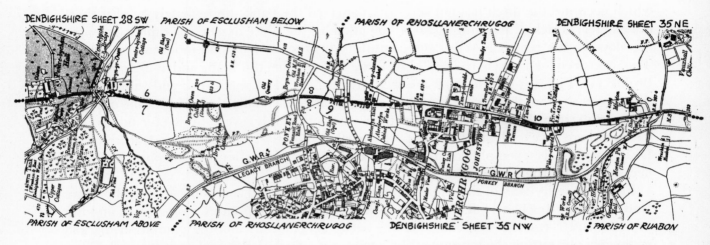

FIG. 19. The Dyke from Pentre-bychan Hall to spot-level 393 on Wrexham–Ruabon road. A portion of the 6-in. O.S. map reduced to 4 in. to 1 mile. For the significance of the symbols and letters employed see Fig. 18.
(Reproduced from the Ordnance Survey map with the sanction of the Controller of H.M. Stationery Office.)

the slope of the Pentre-bychan brook, the bank is much 'spread' and the ditch is a mere hollow; but this is probably due to a change in the character of the subsoil of and in which it is constructed.

The Dyke ends abruptly on a steep scarp 15 ft. above the stream, and there is little doubt that it was present in a similar position on the opposite side of the narrow ravine, but it has been destroyed to make room for the farm buildings of Bryn-yr-Owen. It reappears—damaged, as is usual near old farmsteads—immediately to the S. of the steading. The Dyke now resumes an alignment of familiar type, passing along the W. side of a hill with fine views to the W., the outlook to the E. being limited by the crest line. A trackway marks the levelled crest as far as Bryn-yr-Owen colliery; here a minetip fills the ditch. The Dyke is now in agricultural country partly industrialized, and has suffered accordingly. The ditch is for the most part indistinct (but quite definitely on the W. side); the scarp of the bank, being a hedgerow and parish boundary, is steep; the Dyke was probably here originally of dimensions normal to the area. There are gaps between fields 6 and 7 and immediately S. of Bryn-yr-Owen colliery; the 'Old Quarry', moreover, cuts through the Dyke which is present, much ravaged, between it and Bryn-yr-Owen farmstead. An ancient oak immediately N. of the latter house is on the remains of the bank.

The Dyke reappears as a broad ploughed-down ridge in the pasture field marked 8; in the N. part of the field 9 it is almost entirely destroyed, but it reappears (as the W. boundary of Aber-derfyn croft) in the S. portion of the field. Between Aber-derfyn road and the main Wrexham–Ruabon road cultivation has obscured and modified its profile and in places the Dyke has been destroyed by recent building; it is, however, quite certainly present in the places marked on the map, and is indeed at one spot, W. of Tan-y-clawdd-uchaf, an imposing bank crowned by old pine-trees. The W. ditch, in this portion, is filled in.

The Dyke joined the Wrexham–Ruabon main road at an acute angle at BM 437·0. The adjacent New Inn, here set askew to the road, was probably built on the line of the earthwork.[1] N. of the Inn and immediately S. of Charles Street the ground is 4 ft. above the road level, and this represents the bank of the Dyke. From BM 437·0 to Moreton Inn, a distance of half a mile, the main road is on the line of the Dyke. Old farmsteads here have suggestive names: Tan-y-clawdd-canol, Tan-y-clawdd, and Plas-y-clawdd,[2] and the road is a raised causeway. This feature is well marked as one looks S. along it from Tan-y-clawdd; the large pasture-field no. 10 slopes steeply up to the road and undoubtedly represents the reverse slope of the bank of the Dyke. Its vertical height opposite the last house (on the S.) of Belgrave Terrace is 5·5 ft. The Dyke has in this urban area been aligned on the axis of a low N. and S. ridge; in the more open stretch extending from Fir Tree Cottage to within a few yards of Moreton Inn, this topographical character is clearly visible, as is the fact that the road is a causeway. It would appear that this road, originally a narrow track on the flattened crest of the Dyke, has been widened by the addition of fresh ballast on the W. side, the site of the ditch.

Between Moreton Inn and spot-level 393 the road dips slightly, and visible evidence that it is on the levelled bank of the Dyke is lacking.[3]

FIGURE 20. *The hamlet of Afon-goch to the Home farm, Wynnstay park, Ruabon; on the boundary between Rhosllanerchrugog and Ruabon parishes, and through Ruabon parish, Denbighshire*

From spot-level 393 on the main road (see Fig. 19) to the *F* of *F.P.* the road is raised, and is evidently on the Dyke; the stream, Afon Goch—which runs parallel and close to it on the W.—is in the ditch. We have here another example of the use of the ditch as a drainage channel (see p. 49). When the stream diverges from the road the bank of the Dyke reappears adjacent to it, *and the road immediately falls to a lower level.* The topography here requires careful description; it is where the new alignment (on to Selattyn Hill, Plate XI) begins, which will be discussed later. The existing remains of the Dyke are (*a*) a fragment of the bank on the E. of the single-line railway, and (*b*) a well-marked ridge, pointing towards a known section farther on, on the W. of the railway. This latter portion, though only 35 yards in length, is important, for it enables us to fix the alignment

---

[1] The Dyke is shown as continuously present from Bryn-yr-Owen to the New Inn on the 1838 O.S. map, sheet 74.

[2] See a note on these in *R.C.A.M.*, Denbighshire,

no. 611.

[3] The lower level of the ground to the E. here seems to be artificial.

of the Dyke through the deeply scarred ground of the brickfields.[1] NW. of Tatham brickworks the Dyke reappears on the full scale, climbing the eastern slope of the spur on which Pen-y-gardden fort is sited. The Dyke is wooded, and the bank has never been under the plough (see Profile xx, Fig. 31). By the farmstead of Tatham the Dyke is almost completely destroyed, but the core of its bank is present at the point marked on the map. Beyond, the houses named 'Offa's Cottages' are on its line, but it is not now visible on the steep slope descending to Afon Eitha. On the S. side of this stream the Dyke is present as a high bank bordering the road (which is on the site of the filled-in

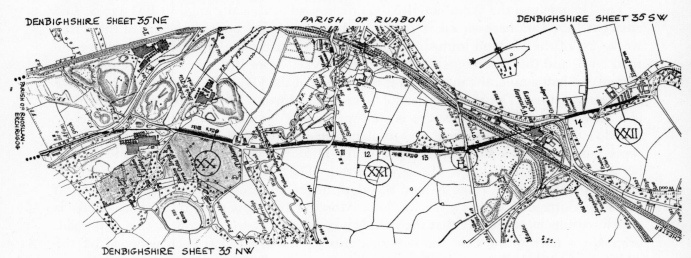

FIG. 20. The Dyke from the hamlet of Afon goch to the Home Farm, Wynnstay Park, Ruabon. A portion of the 6-in. O.S. map reduced to 4 in. to 1 mile. For the significance of the symbols and letters employed see Fig. 18.
(Reproduced from the Ordnance Survey map with the sanction of the Controller of H.M. Stationery Office.)

ditch) as far as the cross-road by the Grammar School. Road widening has steepened the scarp and gaps have been cut through the vallum, notably near the Grammar School (p. 77), but it is still an imposing monument, at best over 10 ft. above original ground level.

From BM 423·3 to Tîr-y-fron farm the Dyke, aligned across level country-side, is a magnificent work. The bank is wooded and has never been ploughed; the ditch is old pasture; in fields 11 and 12 the latter is but little damaged, in field 13 it is filled in. No. xxi, Fig. 31, gives a characteristic profile. Near Tîr-y-fron farm the Dyke is gapped and damaged, but the bank is well marked between the farm-house and the Ruabon–Llangollen road, where it changes direction. Tile Green is unenclosed; the bank is a whale-backed ridge extending to the railway, with a passageway cut through it close to the road; the ditch is traceable and occupied by a footpath. This portion—illustrated in Plate XIIa—is a favourable example of the present appearance of the Dyke in industrial areas; beyond the Green it is completely destroyed, first by the railway and then by the Wynnstay colliery workings. The deflection of the Ruabon–Newbridge road bordering the colliery on the E. marks its alignment; it was immediately to the W. of the road here,

[1] A native of the district, Mr. Pritchard, aged eighty-four, remembers the 'big bank' before it was destroyed for brickmaking.

as the 1838 O.S. map shows. From this point to Tan-y-cut on the right bank of the Dee, a distance of 1½ miles, the course of the Dyke is unrecorded on this or any map. It is quite certain that the direction of the preceding section is maintained, and that the Dyke enters Wynnstay Park at the Green Lodge.[1] The track to the Home farm is undoubtedly on the levelled vallum, the scarp and ploughed-in ditch being clearly visible in the field (no. 14) on the W. side of the track.

At spot-level 360 a second track crosses the first diagonally and the Dyke fades out. Beyond, in the correct alignment, is a ravine which opens out into the valley of the Dee as a deep and narrow gorge, today thickly wooded. Such country did not appear very hopeful, but on following the line indicated a ledge or berm was discovered cut on the face of the scarp of the ravine, at the point indicated on the map (see Profile xxii, Fig. 34).[2] I was at once reminded of the Llanfynydd–Ffrith section of the Dyke on a similar west-ward-facing scarp,[3] and had little doubt that the determination of its course to the Dee was within reach. The ledge extends for a short distance only, the construction of the Home farm buildings, the filling up of the ravine, and the piping of the stream having altered the original topography for a distance of 250 yards.

At this stage in the investigations I made inquiries locally without mentioning my own opinions. Sir Watkin Williams-Wynn's bailiff, whom I first approached, informed me without hesitation that the older workers on the estate knew the course of Offa's Dyke between the Home farm and the Dee; that it was on the E. side of the ravine in Hopyard wood, and was in use as a footpath.[4]

When the line of the Dyke, thus pointed out to me, was examined it was found to be a westward-facing shelf on the steep scarp of the ravine, exactly like that at the head of the gully which had already been identified, and which, not being in use as a footpath, had been apparently forgotten. The lower shelf commences at the point where the piped stream reappears. Retracing one's steps, the Dyke is seen to be aligned, for half a mile, on to Pen-y-gardden spur (p. 79 below).

FIGURE 21. *Hopyard wood, Ruabon, to the neighbourhood of Plas Offa farm, Chirk, in the parishes of Ruabon and Chirk, Denbighshire*

The shelf on the scarp, identified as Offa's Dyke, clings to the 300-ft. contour as far as the spur (324 spot-level on map) where the ravine opens out into the main valley and the footpath on to an arête. At a point 120 yards to the N. of this spot-level there is a low bank on the edge of the shelf, elsewhere this is merely a narrow platform.

From spot-level 324 to the river traces of the Dyke are slight and indeterminate, one or two isolated hummocks, apparently artificial, on the steeply sloping ridge being all that is discoverable. The ground is, however, rough and broken and landslips (which have certainly occurred) may account for the slightness of the traces met with. It should be

---

[1] Lewis's *Topographical Dictionary* (1833) confirms this (see under 'Ruabon').

[2] It is most unfortunate that the construction of the roadways referred to obscures the very interesting transition from a raised bank on the plateau to a shelf on the scarp of the ravine.

[3] Chapter III, pp. 31–2.

[4] Mr. Pritchard, whose name has been mentioned before, when asked where the Dyke reached the Dee, said 'in Hopyard wood'.

noted that the shelf on the scarp identified as the Dyke is a very slight work (such as might easily have been cut as a track or path in later times) and that something more imposing and definite might have been expected. Thus the *visible* traces of the Dyke between the head of the ravine and the Dee are in themselves by no means convincing. Moreover, Lewis in his *Topographical Dictionary* (1833)[1] states that the Dyke leaves Wynnstay Park 'near the Waterloo Tower', which is on the spur above Cefn Station. I am, however, convinced that the alignment of the Dyke is as indicated, because I could find no trace of the Dyke on the plateau between the Green Lodge—where it certainly

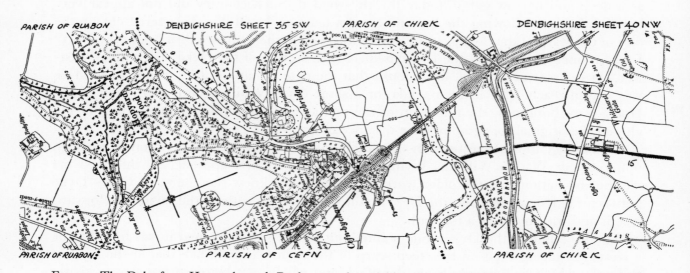

Fig. 21. The Dyke from Hopyard wood, Ruabon, to the neighbourhood of Plas Offa farm. A portion of the 6-in. O.S. map reduced to 4 in. to 1 mile. For the significance of the symbols and letters employed see Fig. 18.
(Reproduced from the Ordnance Survey map with the sanction of the Controller of H.M. Stationery Office.)

exists—and Waterloo Tower,[2] nor between that Tower and the river; and because it is certain that the Dyke *enters* the ravine, and its character and trace lower down, as preserved by local tradition, are consistent with its character and position at the point of disappearance north of the Home farm.[3]

No such difficulties as those with which we have been faced on the left bank of the Dee present themselves on the right bank. Here the Dyke is well marked close to the river, and its course is thenceforward, for many miles, well known.

The starting-point is on a level pasture-field near to the dwelling known as Tan-y-cut, W. of the viaduct; the Dyke is here an imposing grassy bank. The river foams at the foot of the precipitous scarp bordering this field, and has by erosion caused in recent years heavy falls of rock (sandstone), including part of the Dyke. The river is here widening its alluvial plain and many yards of the earthwork may have been destroyed.

---

[1] See under 'Ruabon'.

[2] The ridge on which Cefn wood is situated is the crucial area. There is no trace of the Dyke here.

[3] Pennant (*Tours*, 1810, ed. i, p. 351) gives no help in the determination of the alignment in this area.

The reader will naturally ask whether it is certain that the builder of Offa's Dyke utilized the Dee between Hopyard wood and Tan-y-cut (a distance of 1 mile as the crow flies, and nearly 1½ miles along the river bank) as the boundary, equivalent to and in place of the earthwork. From this conclusion there is, I think, no escape. I am satisfied that no visible trace of the Dyke is present on either bank of the river between these two points, and that there is no dependable tradition of its former existence.

Little trace of the ditch of the Dyke is apparent on the flat by the river,[1] but it is quite clearly on the W. side when, at Tan-y-cut, the Dyke ascends the slope which forms the S. flank of the Dee valley. The ground from here to Chirk park is wholly agricultural, now mainly meadow and pasture.

Tan-y-cut lies on the Dyke, which in its immediate neighbourhood is much denuded, and to the S. of this dwelling the garden and outbuilding of a modern bungalow occupy the levelled bank. The construction of the Shropshire Union Canal and the light railway adjoining, moreover, have obliterated the earthwork, but on the hill-slope S. of the water-way it reappears on the full scale, and continues in good condition as far as Offa's Cottages.[2] There is one modern gap near the canal. The ditch is especially well marked close to the cottages, being in use as a pathway. The modern highway to Llangollen cuts through the Dyke; an older (but probably not original) opening is present on the N. side of this road.

From the road to the S. boundary of field no. 15 (just off the map, Fig. 21) the Dyke is well marked, the ditch forming a water channel; it is damaged in the neighbourhood of Plas Offa, a modern farmstead, and there is a modern gap on the S. side of the steading; but beyond this it is very fine, with old oaks on its bank.

FIGURE 22. *The neighbourhood of Wern Cottage to Chirk Castle, through the parish of Chirk, Denbighshire*

At the S. end of field 15 the hedge which hitherto has been on the crest of the bank swings westward on to the counterscarp. For a few yards the earthwork is well-marked on a patch of uncultivated ground, but it then passes on to ploughed land (field 16) and from this point to the Wern Cottage cross-track is with difficulty discernible as a low ridge. It is of the same character in the pasture field (17) S. of the track, Wern wood boundary being on the counterscarp. It crosses the next field (18) as a low rounded ridge and in the NE. corner of field 19 again becomes a field boundary, the hedge being, as usual, on the bank. From this point to the cross-track by the first *f* of *Offa*, the Dyke is gapped and damaged, but where it crosses the eastern-facing rise SE. of Caeau-gwynion it is an imposing work, crowned by old trees, with well-marked W. ditch (see Plate XII*b* and Profile xxiii). This character is maintained as far as the Little Gate cross-track; the Dyke then crosses the arable field (20) as a ploughed-down ridge and hollow.

In this undulating agricultural country the course of the Dyke is direct though sinuous; actually it was, I think, aligned in short straight stretches a few hundred yards in length.

[1] N. of Tan-y-cut there is a hollow on the E. side of the bank; this is, I think, modern.

[2] Hereabouts it was aligned on the point where the Dyke leaves the Hopyard wood ravine (E. of Bodylltyn on Figure 20) and crosses Wynnstay park, that is, where it is first visibly present on the left bank of the Dee; the northerly trend past Tan-y-cut brings it by a shorter route to the right bank (1954).

Such straight portions are clearly seen at Plas Offa and in Chirk park. If the country was then forest, as is likely, such a method—the general line having been previously determined—may have been the most convenient.

The Dyke now crosses a by-road and enters Chirk park; from the by-road to the lake it is remarkably fine, the bank steep and crowned by old trees, the W. ditch well defined. There are several cross-tracks in the parkland (enclosure 21), but the earthwork is undamaged in Pool wood. Though obliterated on both margins of the artificial lake, it is present on its floor and can be seen in dry seasons. Between the lake and Chirk Castle

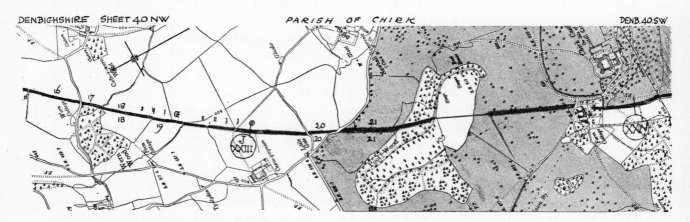

FIG. 22. The Dyke from the neighbourhood of Wern Cottage to Chirk Castle. A portion of the 6-in. O.S. map reduced to 4 in. to 1 mile. For the significance of the symbols and letters employed see Fig. 18.
(Reproduced from the Ordnance Survey map with the sanction of the Controller of H.M. Stationery Office.)

stables the Dyke is present as a low ridge with definite traces of a W. ditch. Its breadth (over 60 ft.) is indicative of its original dimensions, which must have been those normal to the district. The earthwork now passes to the W. of the knoll on which the Castle is situated; it is destroyed from the Park boundary to the S. boundary of the estate office enclosure; it is present, though in a damaged condition, in the Castle gardens immediately to the S., and reappears on the full scale (see Profile xxiv, Fig. 31) on a slope trending S. towards the Ceiriog valley. Its crest is here marked by stag-headed oak trees. The Dyke now follows the eastern flank of a small N. and S. re-entrant, the ditch at one point coinciding with the streamlet which created the re-entrant.

FIGURE 23. *The southern end of Chirk park to the Crogen wood–Mount wood area; through the parish of Chirk, Denbighshire, and on the boundary between Denbighshire (Glyn Traian parish) and Shropshire (Weston Rhyn parish)*

At a gap in the Dyke, by *F* of *F*.P., the re-entrant referred to above becomes a deep ravine,[1] and the Dyke fades out on a steep scarp which fronts the Ceiriog valley. From this point to the Glyn valley road no definite traces are present, and such are entirely absent

[1] Originally the bank here may have been more imposing. The ravine has probably grown wider during the past thousand years, partly at the expense of the Dyke.

between road and river. One cannot expect that any indication of its presence would have survived on this flood-swept valley floor, but its absence on the slopes is noteworthy.[1] Immediately S. of the river, however, quite definite traces, hitherto unrecorded, are present on the steep scarp and in the gardens and closes of Pen-y-bryn hamlet; these traces coincide with the line of the boundary between Denbighshire and Shropshire.

From Pen-y-bryn farm—where the denuded bank is present in the yard—to the Nant Eris ravine, the Dyke is continuously present (save for infrequent gaps permitting farm traffic), and in places is of striking profile. It climbs diagonally up the steep hillside, having

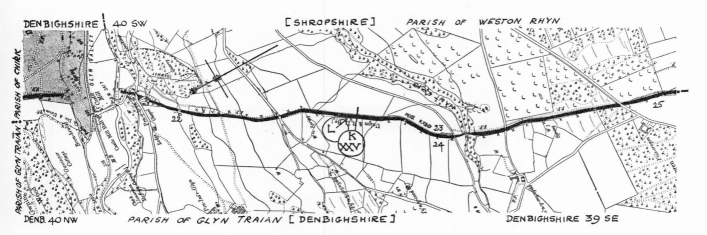

FIG. 23. The Dyke from the S. end of Chirk Park to the Crogen wood–Mount wood area. A portion of the 6-in. O.S. map reduced to 4 in. to 1 mile. For the significance of the symbols and letters employed see Fig. 18.
(Reproduced from the Ordnance Survey map with the sanction of the Controller of H.M. Stationery Office.)

a broad embayment to the W.; hence the views up the Ceiriog valley are magnificent, those to the E. limited. Throughout this stretch the Dyke is well wooded; on the slope, the adjacent fields now mostly pasture have formerly been under cultivation and the ditch is in places ploughed in;[2] when the upland is reached (close to 'Spring' on map) the area W. of the Dyke is moorland pasture and both ditch and bank are practically undamaged save by time. The highest point is over 1,000 ft. above O.D. The Dyke here is cut through the limestone; hence the bank has a steep slope and the ditch maintains its angular contours. (See Profile xxv, Fig. 32, and Plates XVIIb and XVa.) Between fields 23 and 24 the Dyke is much damaged by rabbits and foxes, and between the adjacent road and the ravine it is lowered by cultivation. On the other side of the brook which flows at the bottom of the gully, the Dyke presents a remarkable appearance, commencing as it does on the edge of the stream and rising at a steep angle up the wooded scarp with an immense V-shaped ditch on the W. side silhouetted against the southern skyline. This ditch is another example of overdeepening due to water action.

[1] This is *Adwy'r beddau*, the gap of the graves. There is no adequate authority for associating the gap with the defeat of Henry II by the Welsh in the Battle of Crogen in 1165. *R.C.A.M.*, Denbigh, p. 192.

[2] In the field marked 22 there are ill-defined banks and holes adjacent to the Dyke, and a trackway leading through it thereto. These I judge to be of recent origin.

From the Nant Eris ravine to the Plas-crogen trackway the Dyke crosses level moorland well above the 1,000-ft. contour.[1] It is not inferior in scale to the previous portion, but owing to the soil of which it is composed the bank is in places much spread, and being overgrown with bracken and gorse, is less impressive. The ditch is marshy or forms a watercourse.

FIGURE 24. *The N. flank of the Morlas brook valley to the plateau S. of Orseddwen farm; on the boundary between Denbighshire (parish of Glyn Traian), Shropshire (Weston Rhyn and Selattyn parishes) and through Selattyn parish*

From the Plas-crogen trackway (Fig. 23) to the Morlas brook the Dyke descends a slope gradual at first, but becoming steep as the stream is approached; the northern part is open moorland, the southern part is pasture and the Dyke is tree-clad. Adjacent to field 25 the ditch is perfect, marshy; the bank has been damaged, a berm having been cut on its scarp to form a pathway. From the S. boundary of this field to BM 967 the earthwork is perfect and of normal dimensions, its line unbroken save by one cross-track. The ditch has become the bed of a streamlet, and is thus over-deepened on the rapidly steepening slope. At this bench-mark a few yards of the bank have been levelled and the streamlet passes across it to the eastward.

The Dyke is very imposing in the short stretch between the streamlet and the Morlas brook, and it ends abruptly on the steep slope which borders the narrow ribbon of flat land, subject to floods, which here forms the floor of the ravine. It is seen between the stream and the road on the other side of the gully; it is quite definite, though smaller than on the near side. Its position on the S. side of the valley road is marked by a stone tower of nineteenth-century date, inscribed 'Offa's Dyke', and the earthwork can be seen in the woodlands breasting the steep slopes diagonally, its ditch to the W., the wall bounding Craignant Wood being on the bank. It climbs the hill on the eastern side of a small re-entrant, and emerges on the open upland at the S. border of Craignant wood. A certain amount of the material of the bank has apparently been taken from irregular holes dug on the E. side in this section, especially in the field 26 N. of 'Woodside' cottage, but the regular depression in this field (parallel to the bank) is a natural drainage line. The Dyke now crosses open ground, pasture and moorland, as a grassy bank with steep scarp and well-defined ditch; its highest point is on the easy westward-facing slopes of Selattyn Hill (1,200 ft.), its exact course being determined by the contours of this hill.

An uncommon feature is well represented on the Hill; a low bank on the edge of the counterscarp. Closely examined, this in places shows a core of dry walling, and is, I suspect, the remains of a later field boundary. The ditch of the Dyke, moreover, is here unusually narrow; this is due to the fact that much of the material needed to raise the bank to the required height was taken from the E. side. There is no ditch, properly speaking, on this side; the irregular depressions show where the limestone was quarried, close to the bank. These characters are shown in Profile xxvi.

[1] Traces of dry stone walling on the bank here and also in the upland country to the S. are not to be regarded as original. The bank throughout the sector included in this report is wholly earthen or of stones mingled with earth.

The Dyke having changed direction through 40 degrees descends a gentle slope to Orseddwen farm; the special features noted above continue no farther than the S. end of field 27. Half-way along the E. boundary of this field is a gap, possibly original (see Fig. 24, Plate XVIIa and p. 75). SE. of the farmstead of Orseddwen there is another gap (field road) and from here to the stream the Dyke shows a deviation from alignment, for which the existing topography offers no explanation (Plate XVIa). The site is a fairly level one, the stream a mere ditch in a wide landscape presenting no marked features. The problem is discussed on p. 76.

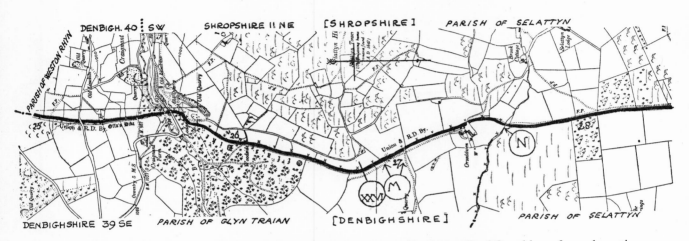

FIG. 24. The Dyke from the N. flank of the Morlas brook valley to the plateau S. of Orseddwen farm. A portion of the 6-in. O.S. map reduced to 4 in. to 1 mile. For the significance of the symbols and letters employed see Fig. 18.

(Reproduced from the Ordnance Survey map with the sanction of the Controller of H.M. Stationery Office.)

The Dyke is present on both margins of the little stream referred to, and the gap is very narrow. S. of the stream the earthwork, bare of trees, crosses moorland country in places afforested. It is of normal contour on the rising slope, but on the broad plateau-like crest beyond it has spread, owing to the sandy soil of which it is composed. The ditch, passing through enclosure 28, forms a marsh or pools: it is wet from this point onwards for some distance.

FIGURE 25. *The moorland N. of Careg-y-big farm, Selattyn, to the N. end of Craig Forda; through the parishes of Selattyn and Oswestry Rural, Shropshire*

The ground now falls towards Careg-y-big, and the ditch of the Dyke as far as the footpath by field 29 is overdeepened by serving as a drainage channel.[1] At the SE. corner of this field the water passes through a gap in the Dyke which may be original, since a spring rises here. From the spring to the cross-road N. of Careg-y-big[2] the Dyke is very fine, steep-scarped, with well-grown pines on its crest. The ditch and bank are

---

[1] There is a bank on the edge of the counterscarp here, probably a hedge bank.   [2] See p. 76, footnote 2.

perfect and thickly wooded NE. of Careg-y-big; E. of the farm-house the Dyke is much damaged. Crossing the road, it is present as a low rounded ridge with a hollow on either side in the N. half of the arable field 30; in the S. half of the field the bank is undamaged, and its mass has clearly been derived from the E. side as well as from the W. ditch. Breasting the slope the Dyke passes an old quarry (enclosure 31) where it has been considerably damaged; but beyond the gap marking the SW. corner of this enclosure the Dyke emerges on the moorland of Baker's Hill (1,100 ft.) as a magnificent monument, undamaged save by rabbits. Plates XIII *a* and *b* indicate its appearance, and Profile

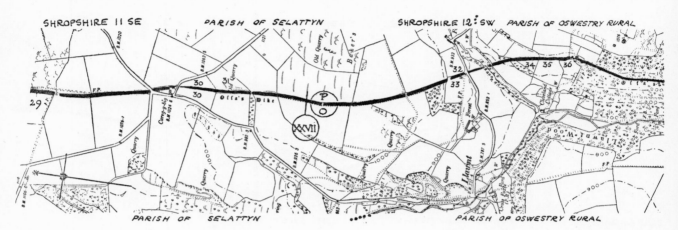

FIG. 25. The Dyke from the moorland N. of Careg-y-big farm, Selattyn, to the N. end of Craig Forda. A portion of the 6-in. O.S. map reduced to 4 in. to 1 mile. For the significance of the symbols and letters employed see Fig. 18.

(Reproduced from the Ordnance Survey map with the sanction of the Controller of H.M. Stationery Office.)

xxvii its character, on this dominating hill-top. The main ditch is on the W., but a shallow depression on the E. shows that material for the bank has continuously been taken from this side also. From the crest of the hill to the Oswestry–Llawnt road and beyond the Dyke descends to a ravine opening westwards on to the Morda valley. From the slope of Baker's Hill the view of this valley, with Craig Forda in the foreground, is magnificent: the Dyke can be seen rising up the opposite flank of the lateral ravine, and its course is visible through the pinewoods which hang on the steep scarp of the Craig.

In its descent the Dyke maintains its fine character as far as fields 32–33; the material for the bank is apparently wholly derived from the W. ditch. Between these fields the Dyke is present though somewhat damaged; in the pasture field beyond the road it has been ploughed down, but its ridge is clearly apparent. No trace of it is to be expected on the precipitous flanks of the ravine, but it is present in a patch of meadow on the S. side thereof, close to an ancient trackway.

The diagonal course of the Dyke up the steep slope S. of the trackway, across pastures and woods, can easily be followed; in field 34 it has been ploughed down, presenting an appearance similar to that in field 30 S. of Careg-y-big (above). In fields 35 and 36 the Dyke forms a grassy bank of normal character ditched on the lower (W.) side, and somewhat damaged by man and rabbits; it has now reached the westward-facing flank of the Morda valley and the views to the W. are very extensive. Utilizing the outcrop of rock (on which a cottage stands),[1] the Dyke proceeds, at the level of the rock crest, through a plantation as a berm or platform on the steep hill-side usually with a low bank on the W. Profile xxviii in Fig. 34 explains the mode of construction.

FIGURE 26. *Craig Forda to the neighbourhood of Pentreshannel farm, through the parish of Oswestry Rural, Shropshire*

The platform above referred to is present on the hill scarp for a distance of 600 yards at a constant level below the 1,000-ft. contour. Three hundred feet below the Morda

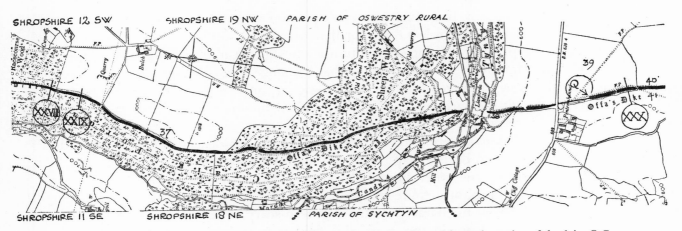

FIG. 26. The Dyke from Craig Forda to the neighbourhood of Pentreshannel farm. A portion of the 6-in. O.S. map reduced to 4 in. to 1 mile. For the significance of the symbols and letters employed see Fig. 18.
(Reproduced from the Ordnance Survey map with the sanction of the Controller of H.M. Stationery Office.)

brook, swollen by summer rains, races along its stony bed; at this height a low murmur indicates its presence. The choice of so dominating an alignment for the great earthwork is notable, influencing conclusions as to its purpose and significance.

After passing through the plantation the Dyke forms the boundary between hill pasture and beechwoods; the hill-side is doubly scarped—above to form the bank, and below to form the ditch—as Profile xxix, Fig. 34, shows. The reason for this change is interesting; the hill-side has become less steep and the construction of the normal W. ditch once more possible. For half a mile the course is level between 1,000 and 900 ft. above O.D., save at a point E. of the *d* of For*d*a, where a dip in the level of the plateau affects the scarp. Here a trackway (and the Vyrnwy aqueduct) passes through the Dyke.

Opposite to field 37 the bank is almost entirely constructed with material taken from the upper (E.) side, the W. ditch being represented by a narrow berm. The woodland here is plantation of young conifers. East of the *r* of C*r*aig a fairly sharp descent to the valley floor is begun, the course of the Dyke being diagonally down the hill-side through natural

[1] This outcrop was a definite point in the layout of the Dyke; it changes direction from E. of S. to W. of S. here.

woodland scarred with disused limestone quarries. It is at first a bank of no great size scooped from above out of the hill-side, with a narrow berm below; its course (by no means easy in places to follow) is accurately set out on the O.S. maps. Destroyed for a short distance E. of the *C* of *C*raig, it reappears as a broad bank with upper and lower ditch, having a modern boundary wall on its crest. It is composed mainly of quarried limestone, and such material from the adjacent pits may have been cast on to it in recent times.

S. of the gap admitting passage of a bridle road (*BR* on the map) the slope on which the Dyke is aligned becomes steeper, and directly it approximates to the steepness of the N. end of Craig Forda the lower berm dies away, and the character already described—upper ditch or berm only—reappears.

Thus we may generalize from the remarkable portion of the Dyke which extends along the Craig that whenever possible a ditch (or the equivalent) on the W. was planned; and only when the steepness of the slope made it impracticable to throw earth or stone upwards was it omitted. Moreover, we have learned that a change in character of the Dyke does not necessarily mean a change in design, or of designer, but that the builders constructed various types to suit the variations of contour on their mountainous alignment.[1]

The last few yards of the steep descent to the valley through the wood are not marked on the O.S. map. There is here a rocky bank with indications of a trench on either side. The alignment is shown on the map; it is pointing directly at the ford of the Morda. A rounded hummock on the other side of the stream, E. of Llanforda Mill, may be the remains of the Dyke, but for definite traces one must proceed to the southern hillside, an easy slope very different in character to the northern scarp, where it is present as the E. boundary of field 38. Immediately S. of this field it is seen as a magnificent work of character normal to such terrain with a deep ditch to the W. and none to the E. Between this point and the road by Pentreshannel farm it is gapped and somewhat damaged by agricultural operations; a trackway follows the line of the ditch. From the road southwards for a distance of 150 yards slight traces only of the levelled bank are seen in field 39;[2] the ditch has here been widened and deepened to form a duck-pond. Thence onwards for 230 yards the Dyke is exceptionally fine with deep W. ditch and undamaged bank (see Profile xxx, and Plate XIV*b*). It is crossed by a footpath, and forms the boundary between fields 40 and 41 as far as the angle in the hedge.

FIGURE 27. *The hamlet of Trefonnen to the hamlet of Treflach wood, in the parish of Oswestry Rural, Shropshire*

From fields 40 and 41 onwards for a distance of a mile the Dyke crosses an undulating agricultural countryside and has been much damaged. It occupies—as a ploughed-down ridge—the western border of field 40. Gapped by the adjacent trackway, it forms the boundary between fields 42 and 43, the bank and (W.) ditch being well marked as far as

---

[1] The E. ditch, however, or rather the abstraction of material from the E. side for the bank, does occur in places other than those where it is a necessary feature of the construction, and this presents a special problem which will be considered later (p. 80).

[2] The levelling was carried out after 1837; the Dyke is shown as present here on the 1-in. O.S. map of that year.

the footpath crossing these fields; beyond, the earthwork is less distinct.[1] In the N. half of field 44 the Dyke is present as a rounded grassy bank with traces of ditch to W.; in the S. half of this field the remains, though unmistakable, are shapeless.

The Dyke bank now follows the line of the houses bordering the road. In places the high level of the gardens reveals its former existence,[2] and N. of the *B* of *LB* by Trefonnen cross-roads, in a small close, a fragment survives 19 yards in breadth and 4 ft. high. The deep (W.) ditch corresponding to this fragment was being filled up when I saw it in July 1927.

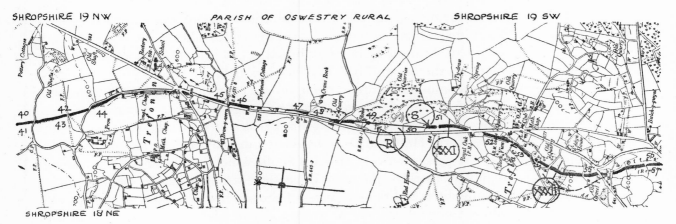

FIG. 27. The Dyke from the hamlet of Trefonnen to the hamlet of Treflach Wood. A portion of the 6-in. O.S. map reduced to 4 in. to 1 mile. For the significance of the symbols and letters employed see Fig. 18.
(Reproduced from the Ordnance Survey map with the sanction of the Controller of H.M. Stationery Office.)

The garden of the cottage N. of *I* of *I*nn is above normal ground level and represents the bank. The Dyke then crosses the main road diagonally and is present close to the road as a grassy bank in field 45. Near the brook it disappears, having been dug away, but is again visible as a hump-backed ridge in field 46 close to the highway. The Dyke has here been aligned along the western-facing slope of a N. and S. re-entrant; the road is in places on the line of the W. ditch. The ploughed-down bank of the earthwork is visible as a ridge in field 47; the hedge bordering this field on the S. shows a marked rise 12 yards from the road. Enclosure 48 is an ancient limestone quarry, and the Dyke has here been extensively destroyed; but it is present as a high grassy bank at the S. end of this enclosure.

At the N. end of the large quarry, enclosure 49, the Dyke has a well-marked ditch on the W. and a less noticeable hollow on the E. The structure is obscured by undergrowth in the neighbourhood of the *S* of *S*tone, but is clearly visible on the freshly worked quarry face close to this point as a ridge rising 7 ft. above the ancient ground level (see p. 77, and Plate XIV*a*). Its course in field 50 is as shown on the map, but the ground has been much disturbed and the present contours of the bank here do not accurately record its original form. In field 51 the Dyke is undamaged, and its alignment and profile are of great interest.

[1] Hills and holes in field 42 have no connexion with the Dyke.

[2] The line of the ditch is marked on the 1837 1-in. O.S. map, sheet 74.

This field is in part a westerly facing slope, in part flat and boggy. Entering the field from the N., the Dyke runs in a straight line to the edge of the marsh. There is then a narrow gap, 4 yards in width, and the Dyke begins again with a sudden deviation from the alignment. This deviation enabled the constructors to follow the edge of the high ground to the E. Thus the Dyke, though mainly on the marsh, is partly composed of material taken from the E. side, where the ground begins to rise. This E. hollow or ditch is confined to the marshy portion of the field; it is wet and the gap now drains it. I do not think that this gap is an original opening (see Profile xxxi, Fig. 34, and Plate XV*b*). For a distance of over 500 yards the Dyke is *similarly sited on a marshy floor and on the margin of the higher ground lying to the E.*; its course is not easy to follow through the fields, closes, and trackways of the hamlet of Treflach Wood. Crossing the main road by the Royal Oak Inn it is very well marked in field 52 on the line indicated,[1] having a broad *wet* W. ditch; Rock View cottages are on the reverse slope of the bank. The Dyke borders field 53 as a steep scarp, wet-ditched on the W., the accommodation road being on the crest of the bank. Crossing the track, its trace can be distinguished in the garden of a cottage (letter P. on map), and it is clearly marked in the adjacent grassy close (enclosure 54) as a broad bank, ditched on both sides,[2] at the foot of the scarp. Here the Dyke leaves the marshy floor, and rising steeply up the adjacent hill-side it passes between the two knolls which mark the crest, the angle here present in its alignment marking the point of passage, which is just below the 700-ft. contour. The depth of the ditch and the steepness of the scarp adjacent to the cottage are remarkable;[3] it is difficult not to associate this grandeur of scale with the fact that the Dyke is commanded at short range by the western knoll. The convex curve of the Dyke here seems to have been forced on the designer by the topography, and having pushed so far to the W., it is, at first sight, difficult to understand why he excluded the western knoll (700 ft.). Possibly the alignment necessary to secure the high ground created an acuter angle (the line is indicated on Fig. 27) than he cared about. On the other hand, a W.-facing alignment sufficiently dominant could have been secured by carrying the Dyke higher up the shoulder of Whitehaven Hill (near Wddyn House). Usually the reasons governing the choice of alignment are clear to the modern observer, but in this case it seems probable that factors unknown to us, not directly connected with the topography, may have influenced the engineer responsible for the layout of the Dyke.[4]

The Dyke is well marked as it descends the gentle S. slope of the knoll with a deep ditch on the W.; there is a slight E. ditch in field 55. Crossing a by-road (position marked by rise in hedge) the bank descends steeply to a small farmstead, and is aligned across a re-entrant on the western hill-side of Whitehaven. It is here broad and flattened with a ditch on the W.; material has also been taken from the E. side. At the S. end of fields 56 and 57 the Dyke is much damaged.

[1] Not marked on the 6-in. O.S. map, but recorded on the 1837 survey map, sheet 74, SE.

[2] The E. ditch is cut, I think, to differentiate the bank from the hill-slope immediately adjacent. See Chapter III, p. 32, footnote 1.

[3] The Dyke could not be surveyed here owing to hedges and trees, but Profile xxxii, Fig. 33, shows the well-defined though less imposing scarp of the Dyke on the N. slope of the hill.

[4] The course taken enabled 600 yards of the Dyke to be dug in soft and tractable subsoil, instead of being quarried out of the limestone. I have, however, more respect for the designer than to suppose him influenced by such considerations.

FIGURE 28. *Whitehaven Hill to Llanymynech Hill in and between the parishes of Oswestry Rural and Llanyblodwel, Shropshire, and on the boundary between Shropshire (Llanyblodwel parish) and Montgomeryshire (Careghofa parish)*

The Dyke crosses the main road (which has been cut through it diagonally), and can be seen to follow the curve of Whitehaven Hill, gradually ascending from the 600- to the 700-ft. contour; its bank usually forms a field boundary, in fields 58 to 64. Though not as a whole very impressive on this hill-side—which is meadow, rough pasture, or woodland—

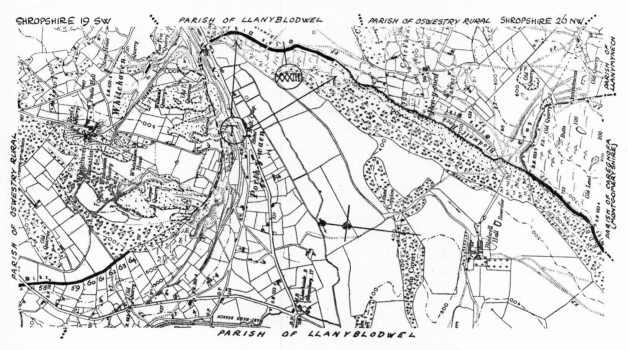

FIG. 28. The Dyke from Whitehaven Hill to Llanymynech Hill. A portion of the 6-in. O.S. map reduced to 4 in. to 1 mile. For the significance of the symbols and letters employed see Fig. 18.
(Reproduced from the Ordnance Survey map with the sanction of the Controller of H.M. Stationery Office.)

the well-defined broad W. ditch surviving in field 64, with the bank above, shows that in its original condition the Dyke here was of normal character. The usual evidence on such slopes of material being taken from the E. side as well as from the W. ditch is here present in places. At the SE. corner of field 64 all traces of the Dyke are lost; but in view of its known alignment on the slopes of Llynclys Hill there can be little doubt that the parish boundary (between Llanyblodwel and Oswestry Rural), which has followed the Dyke for 230 yards, preserves its course along the hillside for at least another 250 yards. This ancient boundary is here buried under spoil heaps, and beyond the hill-side has been extensively quarried. It may be suggested that the parish boundary marks the line of the Dyke as far as the 'Old Quarries'; this is, however, unlikely, because the upland S. of Whitehaven House is not quarried, and there is no trace of the earthwork on the parish boundary here. The boundary, moreover, is set well back from the edge of the scarp of

B 3122   K

the hill, which was, I think, the alignment selected. I conclude that the Dyke may have followed the line indicated on the map; quarries are continuously present along this line as far as the head of the valley, and the absence of all visible traces of the earthwork is thus readily accounted for.

The Dyke crosses the Porth-y-waen re-entrant at BM 329·8, being definitely present in the schoolhouse garden at this point as a rounded ridge lying at right angles to the axis of the valley. Crossing the light railway SE. of the school (not shown on map) the Dyke can be seen as a well-marked bank ditched on the W. in the adjacent cottage garden; it then climbs steeply to the open moorland of Llynclys Hill. It accommodates itself to the contours of this hill, rising gradually to the 600-ft. level and making for the point where the steep western slope becomes precipitous (Plate XVI*b*). The Dyke on this hillside is quarried out of the limestone; the W. ditch or berm is present throughout, but the material for the bank is mainly taken from the upper (E.) side (see Profile xxxiii). The depression on this side, very irregular, a series of holes, is clearly a quarry and not a true ditch. The earthwork is here of moderate size.

The cliff referred to above, practically unscalable, now takes the place of the artificial barrier. The cliff is again replaced by a steep slope at the point where the western defences of the hill fortress of Llanymynech begin.[1] The equation of these defences with the Dyke is based on a respectable tradition,[2] but I doubt whether the Ordnance Survey authorities were justified in including the western vallum and ditch of the Blodwel Rock outwork as part of the line of the Dyke. The whole problem has been discussed in the 1926 volume of *Archaeologia Cambrensis*[3] and the conclusions there arrived at in respect to the Dyke are embodied in the maps (Figs. 28 and 29).

FIGURE 29. *Llanymynech Hill to the Church, Llanymynech; partly on the boundary between Shropshire (Llanyblodwel and Llanymynech parishes) and Montgomeryshire (Careghofa parish) and partly in Careghofa parish*

This map includes the greater part of Llanymynech hill-fort and of that portion of the defences which is equated with Offa's Dyke. These defences terminate at spot-level 740; the cliff face and the steep scree which extends its line eastward are held to represent the S. boundary of the fortress and the line of the Dyke. Quarrying has destroyed all traces of the original escarpment beyond the scree; but it is fairly certain that Offa's boundary clung to the hill up to the point where the modern county boundary leaves it, because this boundary, from the foot of the scarp onwards, is coincident with the Dyke.

The evidence may now be detailed. Immediately below the quarry, adjacent to Pen-y-foel cottages, we see a bank with a steep scarp to the west—a typical 'Dyke' profile. This bank extends as a rounded hummock into pasture field 65. The bank which forms the W. boundary of the northern part of field 66, moreover, is artificial, as a partial cutting shows, and this is without doubt the vallum of the Dyke. It fades out on the E. scarp of the knoll

---

[1] i.e. on the boundary between Shropshire and Montgomeryshire.

[2] It is noted by Pennant, *Tours*, 1810 ed. iii, p. 219.

[3] C. Fox and W. J. Hemp, *Arch. Camb.*, 1926, pp. 395–400; also *Montgomeryshire Collections*, xi, pp. 202 ff.

through which the Pen-y-foel–Llanymynech road is deeply cut, and no trace of the Dyke can definitely be seen today from this point onwards to the end of the sector dealt with in this chapter. There is, however, ample traditional and documentary evidence available to show that the modern boundary between England and Wales marks the line of the bank through Llanymynech village. Fewtrell describes it as in part existing or remembered on this alignment in 1878,[1] and states that the western wall of the churchyard is supposed to be built on the vallum. This is very probable, the wall being on a grassy bank fronting the street (which is on the line of the filled-in ditch). Pennant, moreover,[2] noted

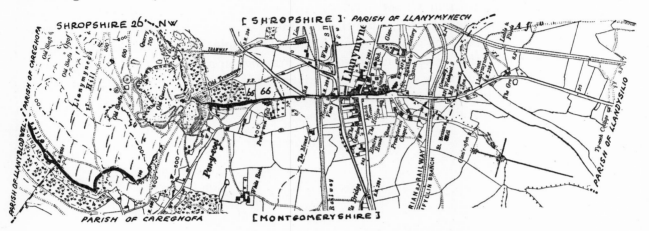

FIG. 29. Llanymynech Hill to the Church, Llanymynech. A portion of the 6-in. O.S. map reduced to 4 in. to 1 mile. For the significance of the symbols and letters employed see Fig. 18.
(Reproduced from the Ordnance Survey map with the sanction of the Controller of H.M. Stationery Office.)

its presence in St. Agatha's churchyard. I have little doubt that the river Vyrnwy at the time the Dyke was built flowed at the foot of the knoll on which the church stands, and that the Dyke ended at this point. The modern causeway to the bridge obscures the ancient topography, but no trace of the Dyke is in any case to be expected on the alluvial flat beyond the church, seamed as it is by old river channels.

THE PROFILE OF THE DYKE

Apart from human destruction, the extent to which the original profile of the Dyke is preserved depends on the nature of the subsoil of and in which it is constructed. In limestone country it is seen at its best—the ditch well defined, the scarp steep, the reverse slope fairly steep, the crest a narrow ridge. In soil with a large admixture of sand the bank tends to spread, losing shape and character, while the ditch tends to become a rounded hollow. In such soils rabbits flourish and complete the ruin. In the sector at present under

[1] 'Parochial History of Llanymynech', *Mont. Coll.* xi, p. 212.

[2] *Tours in Wales*, 1810, ed. iii, p. 219. 'The Wall' (presumably the W. wall) 'of the churchyard is placed on the former' (i.e. Offa's Dyke). It will be observed that the older houses of Llanymynech village are on the E. side, that is, on the bank. The village of Fen Ditton, Cambs., is similarly placed in relation to the Fleam Dyke.

consideration the subsoils (limestones and shales) are on the whole favourable to the preservation of the work, but sandy patches occur in the mountain zone.

Eighteen profiles are reproduced in the five figures, nos. 30, 31, 32, 33, 34, and these are fully representative of the character of the Dyke in this sector. They show that the scale of the work is similar to that seen in the Ffrith district (Chapter III, Figs. 14, 15); the range of variation in size is, however, wider. This fact may most readily be demonstrated by a comparison of 'overall breadths', i.e. the width of ground covered by western ditch and bank. The accompanying table of measurements gives this and other details. In the sector dealt with in Chapter III (p. 39) the minimum recorded was 54 ft., the maximum 64 ft.; in the present sector the minimum is 49 ft., the maximum 77 ft. It is evident that the short stretch examined in Chapter III (5 miles) was insufficient to indicate the extent to which the Dyke varies in scale; it may be supposed that the 20 miles now under consideration gives in this respect a much truer picture of the character of the earthwork. It is to be observed that only portions of the work sited on fairly level ground (and therefore comparable) are included in these tables.

Table of Measurements

No. of Profile*	Position	Estimated dimensions of bank		Estimated dimensions of western ditch		Estimated overall breadth of bank and western ditch
		Height	Breadth	Depth	Breadth	
		ft. in.	ft.	ft. in.	ft.	ft.
XVI	Plas Power park, Denb. (Fig. 30) . .	6 0	39	11 1‡	28	67
XVII	N. of Cadwgan Hall, Denb. (Fig. 30) .	5 3	—§	3 2	—§	—
XVIII	Cadwgan Hall, Denb. (Fig. 30) . .	5 9	35	4 3	22	57
XIX	N. of Pentre-bychan park, Denb. (Fig. 30)	4 8	35	5 0	25‖	60
XX	Tatham farm, Denb. (Fig. 31) . .	7 0	40	3 5	—**	—
XXI	Ruabon, Denb. (Fig. 31) . . .	10 0	48	4 7	29	77
XXIII	Near Chirk park, Denb. (Fig. 31) . .	7 1	28	3 8†	24†	52
XXIV	Chirk park, Denb. (Fig. 31) . . .	6 0	40	6 3	29	69
XXV	Near Tyn-y-Mynydd, Denb. and Salop border (Fig. 32)	8 4	38	6 4	27	65
XXVI	Selattyn Hill, Denb. and Salop border (Fig. 33)	5 10	33	4 0	16	49
XXVII	Baker's Hill, Salop (Fig. 32) . .	9 8	36	6 0	21	57
XXX	Pentreshannel farm, Salop (Fig. 32) .	7 4	45	7 7	26	71
XXXI	Treflach Wood, Salop (Fig. 34) . .	6 4	39	—††	—††	—

* The numeration is carried on from Chapter III. Only the profiles on fairly level ground are included in this list.

† The original dimensions of the ditch determined by excavation were: depth 7 ft. 7 in., breadth, 18 ft.

‡ The ditch is 'overdeepened'; its original depth was probably about 8 ft.

§ Bank 'spread' by ploughing, ditch ploughed in. No estimates can possibly be reliable.

‖ Ditch probably widened for use as cattle pond.

** Roadside hedge-bank probably occupies part of ditch. Breadth of ditch cannot be estimated.

†† Marshy. Cannot be determined or estimated.

Not only does the Dyke vary in scale at comparable points in its course, but it also varies in character. In the portion N. of the Dee surveyed in this chapter the material composing the bank seems to have been derived wholly from the western ditch; S. of the

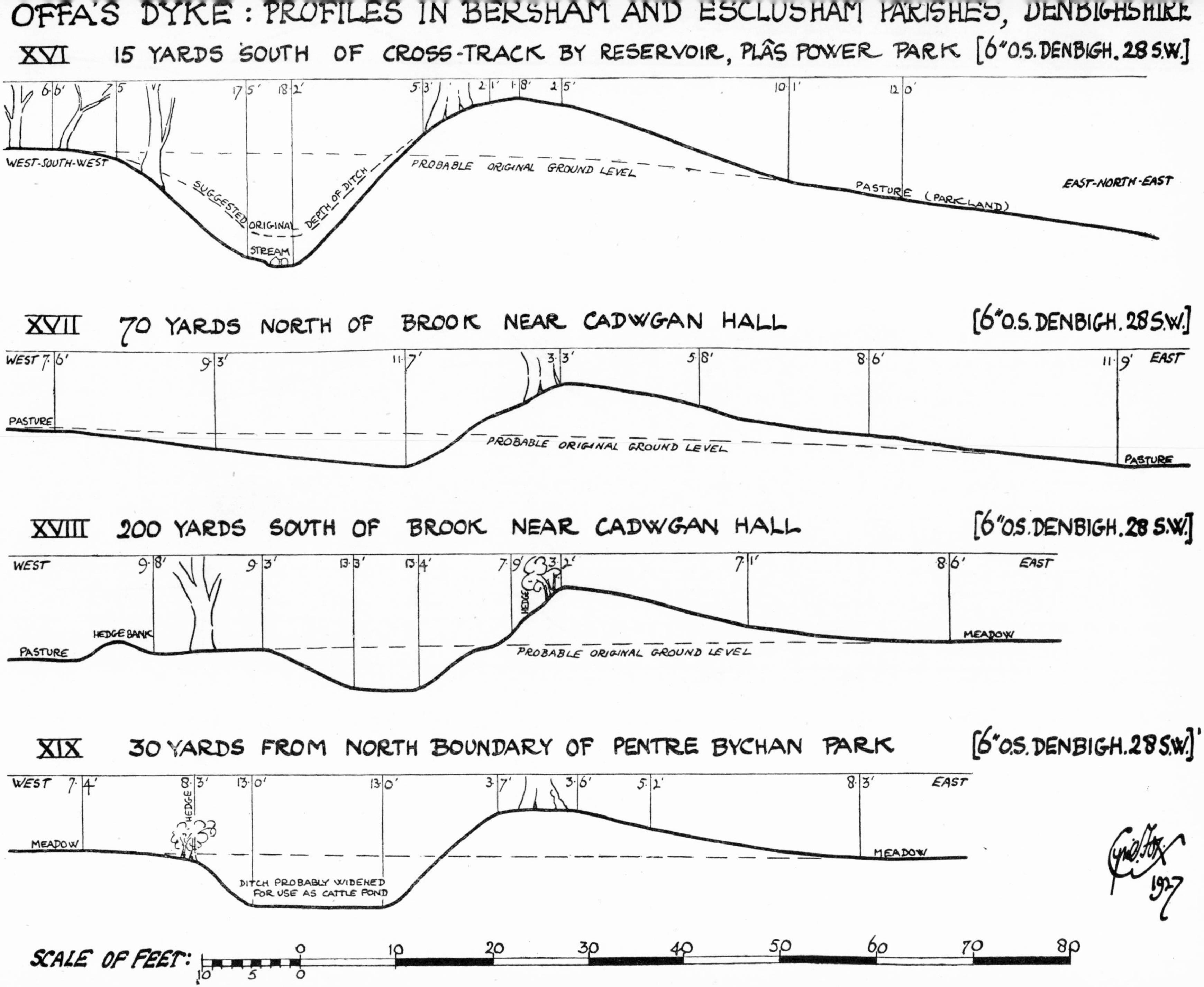

OFFA'S DYKE: PROFILES IN BERSHAM AND ESCLUSHAM PARISHES, DENBIGHSHIRE

XVI   15 YARDS SOUTH OF CROSS-TRACK BY RESERVOIR, PLÂS POWER PARK [6" O.S. DENBIGH. 28 S.W.]

EAST-NORTH-EAST

PASTURE (PARK-LAND)

12.0'   10.1'   1.5'   1.8'   2.1'   5.3'

PROBABLE ORIGINAL GROUND LEVEL

DEPTH OF DITCH

SUGGESTED ORIGINAL

17.5'   18.1'

STREAM

WEST-SOUTH-WEST

6.6'   7.5'

XVII   70 YARDS NORTH OF BROOK NEAR CADWGAN HALL   [6" O.S. DENBIGH. 28 S.W.]

EAST

11.9'   8.6'   5.8'   3.3'

PROBABLE ORIGINAL GROUND LEVEL

11.7'

9.3'

WEST 7.6'   6.6'

PASTURE

PASTURE

XVIII   200 YARDS SOUTH OF BROOK NEAR CADWGAN HALL   [6" O.S. DENBIGH. 28 S.W.]

EAST

8.6'   7.1'   3.3'   7.9'

HEDGE

PROBABLE ORIGINAL GROUND LEVEL

13.4'

13.3'

9.3'   9.8'

WEST

HEDGE BANK

MEADOW

PASTURE

XIX   30 YARDS FROM NORTH BOUNDARY OF PENTRE BYCHAN PARK   [6" O.S. DENBIGH. 28 S.W.]

EAST

8.3'   5.1'   3.6'   3.7'

HEDGE

PROBABLE ORIGINAL GROUND LEVEL

13.0'

13.0'

DITCH PROBABLY WIDENED FOR USE AS CATTLE POND

WEST 7.4'   8.5'

MEADOW

MEADOW

SCALE OF FEET: 0   10   20   30   40   50   60   70   80
                 0   5   10

Fig. 30. Profiles XVI–XIX.

OFFA'S DYKE : PROFILES IN RUABON AND CHIRK PARISHES, DENBIGHSHIRE

XX 100 YARDS NORTH-EAST OF TATHAM FARM, NEAR RUABON [6" O.S. DENBIGH. 35 NW.]

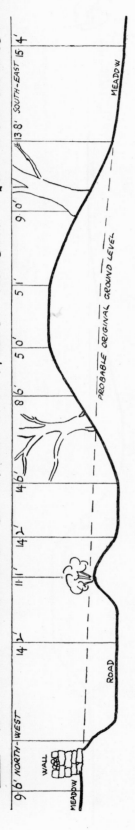

XXI 210 YARDS SOUTH-WEST OF PONT ADAM ROAD, RUABON [6" O.S. DENBIGH. 35 SW.]

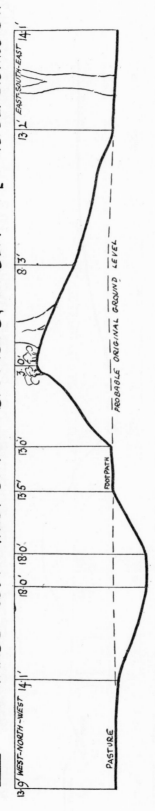

XXIII 400 YARDS NORTH-EAST OF N. BOUNDARY OF CHIRK PARK [6" O.S. DENBIGH. 40 NW.]

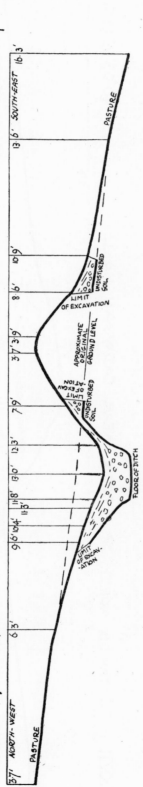

XXIV 150 YARDS SOUTH-SOUTH-WEST OF GARDENS, CHIRK PARK [6" O.S. DENBIGH. 40 NW.]

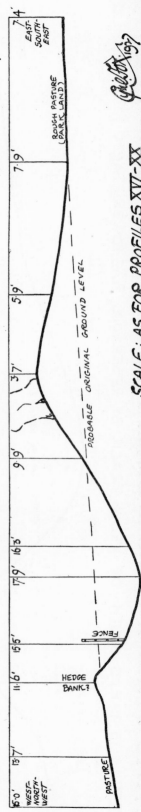

SCALE: AS FOR PROFILES XII–XX

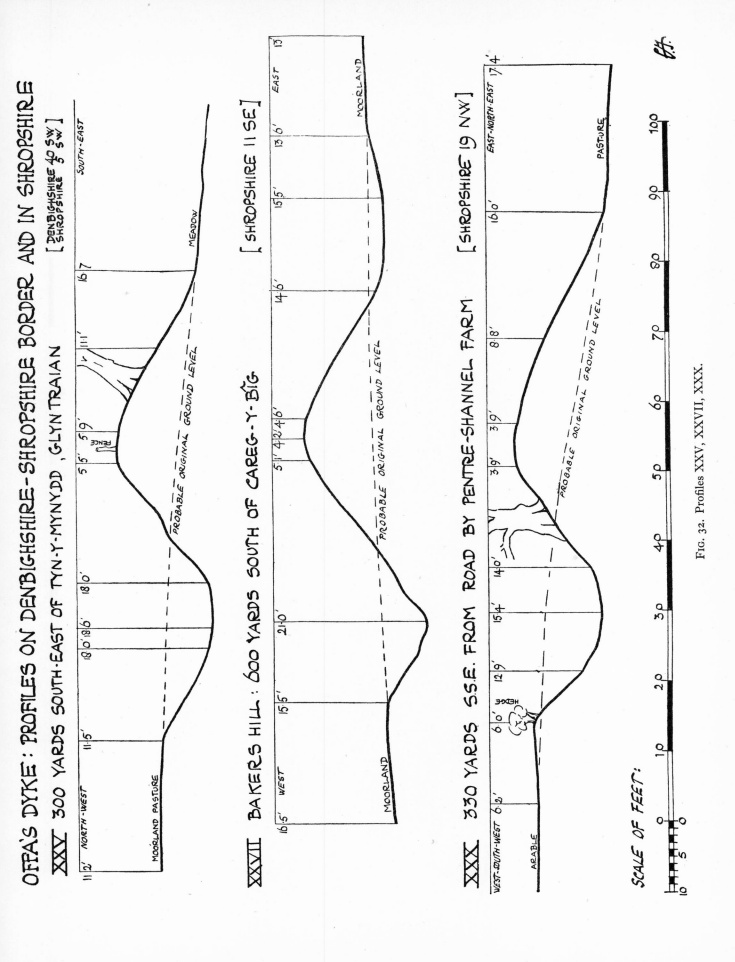

OFFA'S DYKE: PROFILES ON DENBIGHSHIRE–SHROPSHIRE BORDER AND IN SHROPSHIRE

XXV 300 YARDS SOUTH·EAST OF TYN·Y·MYNYDD, GLYN TRAIAN [DENBIGHSHIRE 40 SW / SHROPSHIRE 5 SW]

NORTH-WEST ... SOUTH-EAST

11·2' 11·5' 18·0' 18·6' 18·0' 5·5' 5·9' 11·1' 16·7

FENCE

MOORLAND PASTURE

MEADOW

PROBABLE ORIGINAL GROUND LEVEL

XXVII BAKERS HILL: 600 YARDS SOUTH OF CAREG·Y·BIG [SHROPSHIRE 11 SE]

WEST ... EAST

16·5' 15·5' 21·0' 5·11' 4·2' 4·6' 14·6' 15·5' 13·6' 13

MOORLAND

MOORLAND

PROBABLE ORIGINAL GROUND LEVEL

XXX 330 YARDS S.S.E. FROM ROAD BY PENTRE·SHANNEL FARM [SHROPSHIRE 19 NW]

WEST·SOUTH·WEST ... EAST·NORTH·EAST

6·2' 6·0' 12·9' 15·4' 14·0' 3·9' 3·9' 8·8' 16·0' 17·4

ARABLE

HEDGE

PASTURE

PROBABLE ORIGINAL GROUND LEVEL

SCALE OF FEET:

0 ... 5 ... 10

0 ... 10 ... 20 ... 30 ... 40 ... 50 ... 60 ... 70 ... 80 ... 90 ... 100

ft.

Fig. 32. Profiles XXV, XXVII, XXX.

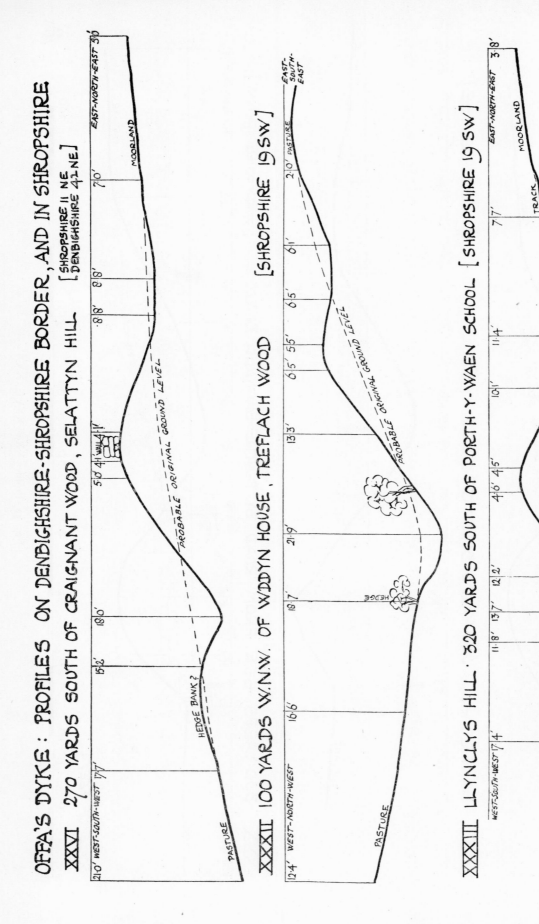

OFFA'S DYKE : PROFILES ON DENBIGHSHIRE-SHROPSHIRE BORDER, AND IN SHROPSHIRE

XXVI 270 YARDS SOUTH OF CRAIGNANT WOOD, SELATTYN HILL [SHROPSHIRE 11 NE DENBIGHSHIRE 42 NE]

XXXII 100 YARDS W.N.W. OF WIDDYN HOUSE, TREFLACH WOOD [SHROPSHIRE 19 SW]

XXXIII LLYNCLYS HILL · 320 YARDS SOUTH OF PORTH-Y-WAEN SCHOOL [SHROPSHIRE 19 SW]

SCALE OF FEET:

Fig. 33. Profiles XXVI, XXXII, XXXIII.

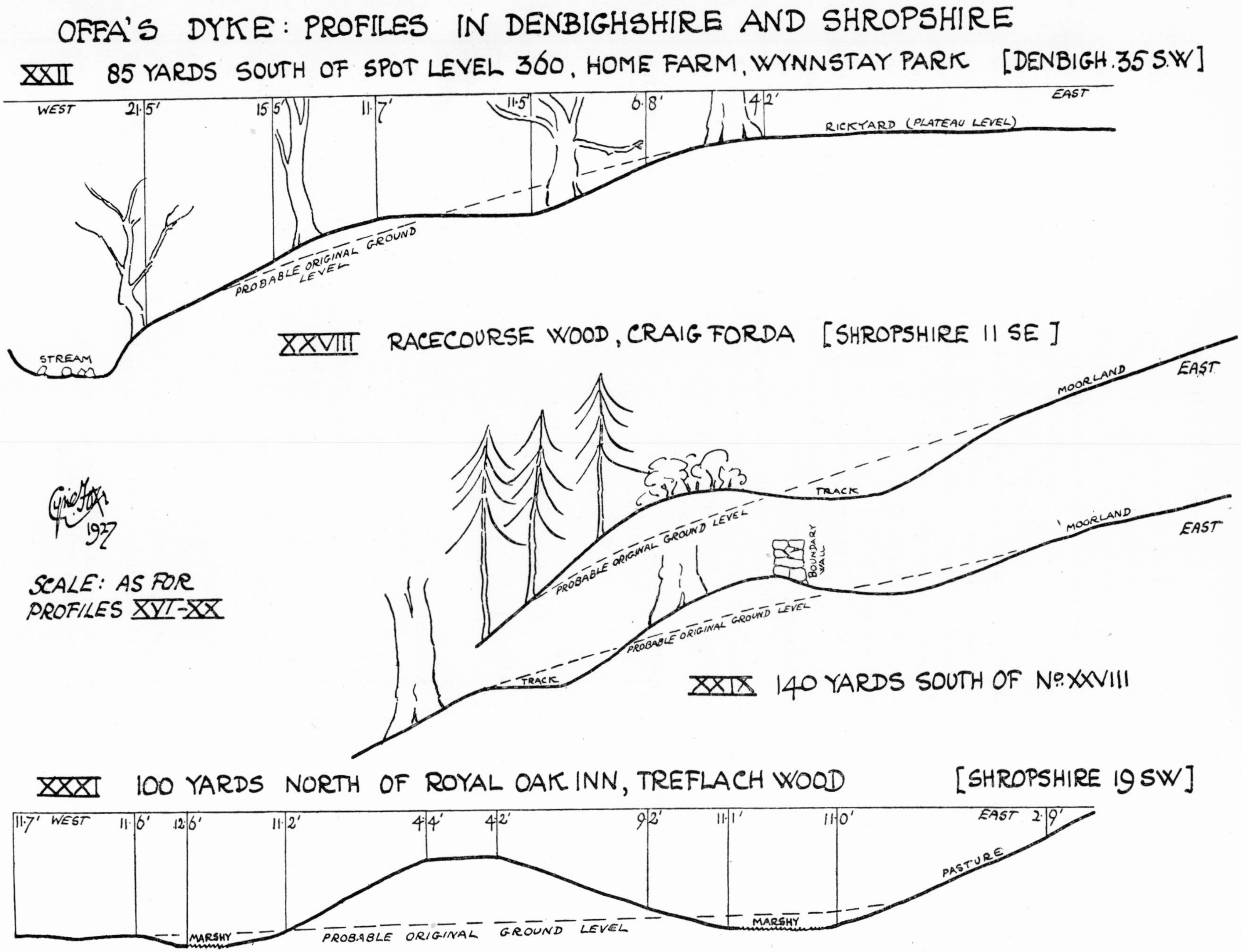

OFFA'S DYKE : PROFILES IN DENBIGHSHIRE AND SHROPSHIRE

XXII 85 YARDS SOUTH OF SPOT LEVEL 360, HOME FARM, WYNNSTAY PARK   [DENBIGH. 35 S.W.]

EAST

RICKYARD (PLATEAU LEVEL)

4.2' 6.8' 11.5' 2' 15.5' 21.5'

PROBABLE ORIGINAL GROUND

PROBABLE ORIGINAL LEVEL

WEST

STREAM

XXVIII RACECOURSE WOOD, CRAIG FORDA   [SHROPSHIRE 11 S.E.]

EAST

MOORLAND

TRACK

PROBABLE ORIGINAL GROUND LEVEL

EAST

MOORLAND

BOUNDARY WALL

PROBABLE ORIGINAL GROUND LEVEL

TRACK

XXIX 140 YARDS SOUTH OF No. XXVIII

Gindar
1927

SCALE: AS FOR
PROFILES XVI-XX

L

XXXI 100 YARDS NORTH OF ROYAL OAK INN, TREFLACH WOOD   [SHROPSHIRE 19 S.W.]

EAST 2.9'

PASTURE

1.10' 11.11' 9.2' 4.2' 4.4' 11.2' 12.6' 11.6'

MARSHY

PROBABLE ORIGINAL GROUND LEVEL

PROBABLE ORIGINAL GROUND LEVEL

MARSHY

11.7' WEST

FIG. 34. Profiles XXII, XXVIII, XXIX, XXXI.

B 3122

Dee the material may be gathered in part from spoil holes on the E. side of the bank (e.g. at Selattyn and Baker's hills, Profiles xxvi and xxvii, Figs. 33 and 32).[1] A definite E. *ditch* occurs, however, in short lengths of the Dyke at Treflach Wood (e.g. Profile xxxi, Fig. 34). For these the local topography provides explanations (pp. 63 and 64).

The effect of the plough on the contour of Offa's Dyke is well shown in our series of profiles. Fig. 32 as a whole may be compared with Fig. 30; the profiles in the former reveal the earthwork undamaged save by time, those in the latter show that the reverse (eastern) slope of the bank has been to a greater or less extent ploughed down. The effect is to make the bank broader and flatter. Sometimes the ditch receives similar treatment, and is ploughed in; an example is no. xvii of Fig. 30. In extreme cases such as this measurement of the present overall breadth of the Dyke is valueless, because it is so much greater than its original breadth.

An exceptionally high bank is recorded in three places; 10 ft. near Ruabon, north of the Dee (Profile xxi, Fig. 31), and $8\frac{1}{3}$ and $9\frac{2}{3}$ ft. on the mountain S. of the Dee (Profiles xxv and xxvii, Fig. 32). These indicate ramparts originally 10 ft. to 12 ft. high and ditches correspondingly deep; remarkable dimensions for a boundary bank.

Other features of the Dyke as revealed by the profiles have already been referred to; of these 'overdeepening' (pp. 49, 57 f., 59 f.) and the mode of construction on steep western-facing slopes (pp. 61 ff.) are of special interest.

Slight banks which occasionally occur on or near the edge of the counterscarp (as no. xviii, Fig. 30, no. xxiv, Fig. 31, and no. xxvi, Fig. 33) are not, I think, part of the Dyke as originally designed.

THE GAPS IN THE DYKE

The numerous gaps in Offa's Dyke hitherto met with fall into two classes. Firstly, those which must be original, present where the Dyke crosses rivers, streams, and brooks; and secondly those which mark the crossing points of roads and tracks, or give access to fields. Of the latter some may be original, but the great majority is certainly later than the construction of the earthwork.

It has been shown that the gaps in the Dyke necessitated by the existence of streams and brooks were made as narrow as possible. Such gaps as those at Plas Power (p. 49), at Morlas brook (p. 59), and at Nant Eris (p. 57) are only a few yards across; moreover, the winter torrents have certainly made them wider than they were originally. There is, it is true, a broad stretch across the Ceiriog valley whereon no trace of the Dyke can be seen. But the greater part of this is an alluvial flat subject to floods, and any construction offering a barrier to the waters would certainly be swept away.

Gaps of the second class which show no obvious indication of modern origin are alike in this: that none shows any trace of incurving or thickening of the banks at the point of passage, as do the entrances to defensive constructions such as hill-forts. The only test

---

[1] No attempt has been made (in the Table of Measurements) to include these irregular and ill-defined spoil trenches in calculating the overall dimensions of the Dyke.

of original design thus lies in the contour of, and vegetation on, the banks flanking the openings. These usually present a flattish plane, with recognizable angles where the cut surface meets the scarp or reverse slope of the embankment, and with turf noticeably thinner and poorer on the face than on the lateral surfaces of the bank (see Plate XV*b*). Such characters reveal the adjacent opening as a recent alteration. If the bank contours and vegetation pass the test, one looks for a causeway across the Ditch on the natural ground level with vegetation similar to that on the adjacent undisturbed ground. It is not very hopeful to look for original passage-ways (save perhaps in place nomenclature— e.g. Adwy'r clawdd[1]) in inhabited country, for even original openings will almost certainly have been widened and the flanking banks will thus present the marks of late work; but on such hills as the Selattyn range the inquiry is worth while.

On this moorland gaps of any sort are few; this is a striking feature, for the early roads and tracks in Wales are mostly hill-ways. I consider that like the Devil's, Fleam, and Bran Ditches in East Anglia[2] the Dyke was intended to present a barrier almost complete, legitimate traffic between the two peoples concerned being limited to defined routes few in number.

The only gap which struck me as presenting definitely original characters was that on Selattyn Hill, Plate XVII*a* and p. 59 above. There is a slight hollow on the line of the ditch, but the rounded slopes of the bank facing the gap are in character and vegetation indistinguishable from the adjacent scarp and reverse slopes. The opening is not now in use, and there is no indication on the rough moorland pasture which adjoins it on the E. of any trackway having formerly existed. The opening is therefore ancient. It is situated at the highest and the most westerly point reached in this area on the plateau W. of Selattyn Hill, 1,200 ft. (see pp. 58 and 80 f.), where the Dyke changes direction.

EARTHWORKS ON OR NEAR THE DYKE

North of the Dee the only ancient earthworks now visible on or near the alignment of the Dyke are the mound at Cadwgan Hall in Esclusham Below parish (Fig. 18), and the hill-fort of Pen-y-gardden in Ruabon parish (Plate XI and Fig. 20).

The mound at Cadwgan Hall is situated close to and on the E. side of the Dyke, its base on the W. being some 12 yards from the vallum, which is here dug away. It is only partly artificial, being situated on the northern edge of the knoll on which Cadwgan stands; it is therefore impossible to determine its dimensions without excavation. It does not resemble a motte, nor is its position that usual for a prehistoric barrow. It may be a mill mound; but the possibility that it is a sepulchral mound of the Saxon period, contemporary with or later than Offa's Dyke, cannot be excluded. 'Armour', probably medieval, is said to have been found in it in 1804.[3] The slight change of direction of the Dyke at the mound does not necessarily imply the priority of the latter; the existence of the bluff on which the mound is situated is, in itself, sufficient to account for it.

[1] Chapter III, p. 36.
[2] C. Fox, *Archaeology of the Cambridge Region*, p. 130; *Communications, Camb. Antiq. Soc.* xxvi, p. 90.

[3] *R.C.A.M.*, Denbighshire, no. 178. The height (20 ft.) stated in this record is manifestly erroneous. (See also A. N. Palmer in *Y Cymmrodor*, xii, p. 83.)

The contour fort of Pen-y-gardden[1] lies to the W. of and 450 yards from Offa's Dyke. It is situated at the end of a spur facing E. nearly 600 ft. above O.D. and encloses an area of 4 acres. It was defended by double banks and ditches, now in places levelled, an additional bank being present on the S. and E. sides. Though it occupies a commanding position, it is a work apparently of no great strength; the soil of which it is built up is, however, light, and the defences may have been much denuded. The problem of its relation to the Dyke is discussed on pp. 79 f.

South of the river Dee the contour hill-fort of Llanymynech and its northern outlier Blodwel Rock are the only earthworks connected with the Dyke. The relationship is referred to on pp. 66–67 of the present chapter. The inclusion of these earlier works within the boundary represented by the Dyke may be regarded as due to the tactical value of the dominating rock mass on which they are situated rather than to any military importance then possessed by the works themselves.

My friend Mr. W. J. Hemp is inclined to regard the road running SW. from Selattyn and crossing the Dyke immediately to the N. of Careg-y-big[2] farm-house (Fig. 25) as Roman. In case this should at some future date be established, it is worth noting that the terminations of the Dyke on either side of this road are abrupt and create the impression that the gap is not original.

The deflection of Offa's Dyke by the farm of Orseddwen, Glyn Traian (Fig. 24 and Plate XVIa), is curious, and inexplicable on topographical grounds. It is possible that the slightly rising ground on the chord of the arc here described by the earthwork was the site of a prehistoric monument, now destroyed; and that on reaching its neighbourhood the diggers changed direction in order to avoid injury to the structure. The result of my investigation of the Ysceifiog Circle (*Arch. Camb.*, 1926, p. 167, and p. 23 of this work) provides a parallel sufficiently close, I venture to think, to justify this suggestion. It is known that the Orseddwen district was occupied by early man; there are at least two Bronze Age cairns in the immediate neighbourhood.[3] The only further fact which may have a bearing on the problem is that a small limestone monolith, which has been exposed for a very long period (as is shown by the weather-worn hollows on its upper face), is set up as a gate-post at the adjacent steading.

THE CONSTRUCTION OF THE DYKE

The portion of the Dyke described in this chapter provided no known sites likely to yield evidence bearing on its date. Excavation was therefore confined to a determination of the original depth and form of the ditch at one point. The site selected was at Caeau-gwynion in Chirk parish (Fig. 22 and Plate XIIb); I have to thank the owner, Colonel Myddelton, and the tenant, Mr. Evan Evans, for permission to carry out the work. The ditch was found to be flat-floored, 6·5 ft. in breadth on the floor and about 18 ft. in breadth

---

[1] Op. cit., no. 615.

[2] The megalith from which the farmstead Careg-y-big takes its name is not on the Dyke, but lies to the NW. and 500 yards from it.

[3] *R.C.A.M.*, Denbighshire, nos. 186, 187. These can be seen from the Dyke, but had no influence in determining its alignment. (See also A. N. Palmer in *Y Cymmrodor*, xii, pp. 81, 82.)

at ground level; *the depth of the silting varied from 3 ft. 9 in. to 4 ft. 10 in.* We thus have a useful check on the figures in columns 5 and 6 of the Table of Measurements in this sector. The line of the original ground level was determined by excavation in the scarp and reverse slope of the bank; this enabled the original maximum depth of the ditch to be fixed, within narrow limits of error, at 7·7 ft. The bank was composed of gravelly and sandy clay, the ditch silt of similar material overlaid by a considerable depth of fine soil. (See p. 68, and Profile xxiii, Fig. 31.)

At three other points information bearing on the construction of the Dyke was obtained.[1]

1. *By the Grammar School, Ruabon.*—A roadway was cut through the bank in 1922 to give access to the new buildings of the Grammar School. The bank is here very impressive, and its height above the original ground level is 10 ft. 6 in. The cross-section showed that there were numerous large waterworn boulders placed at the base of the bank on either side[2] (but chiefly on the E.) evidently with the object of preventing the sandy stony soil of which the bulk of the vallum was composed from 'spreading', I have not observed this constructional feature elsewhere.

2. *On the right bank of the Dee.*—The cross-section of the earthwork on the cliff scarp referred to on p. 54 is not sufficiently well defined for measurement, but the bank is seen to be composed of river pebbles in a sandy matrix.

3. *In the Old Quarry, Treflach Wood.*—The quarry face gives, as Plate XIV*a* shows, an excellent cross-section of the bank. This bank is composed of gravel and clayey sand in diagonal layers (which have been outlined). The nucleus of the bank was, it is evident, cast on to the edge of the (W.) ditch, and it was brought to full size by adding material to the reverse slope and the crest.[3] The vertical quarry-face prevented accurate planning of the cross-section, but the height of the bank was determined; it is 7 ft.

On levelling the Dyke for the purpose of rebuilding Pentre-bychan Hall (Fig. 19), in 1824, 'several Saxon coins' were found.[4] Had this discovery been recorded in detail, it might have been important to us.

COMMENTARY

(i) *Course*

The course of the Dyke between Plas Power park and the river Vyrnwy is for the most part certain. In the portion N. of the Dee, wherein an industrial and agricultural area is traversed, it has been in some places destroyed and in others much damaged. It is, however, seldom unrecognizable, and where destroyed in recent years the 1837–41 1-in. O.S. map, local knowledge, and place-names, enable its course to be fixed. In the portion S. of the Dee, wherein it traverses country for the most part upland or moun-

[1] A tentative excavation in the ditch of Offa's Dyke near Oswestry, made in 1922, is referred to in the *Bulletin of the Board of Celtic Studies*, i, p. 286. No detailed record was published.

[2] Information kindly supplied by Rev. D. J. Bowen, M.Sc., the Headmaster: confirmed, as far as the vegetation permitted, by my own observation.

[3] This is the usual method of making such earthworks; the only bank known to me which was constructed on the opposite plan, that of placing the primary deposits at a point farthest away from the ditch and building the vallum *inwards*, is the Devil's Dyke, Cambridgeshire. (*Camb. Antiq. Soc.* xxvi, p. 90.)

[4] Lewis's *Top. Dict.* (1833) under 'Esclusham Below'.

tainous, it is remarkably perfect, extending undamaged save by time, by rabbits, and by occasional gaps cut for trackways or farm roads, for mile after mile. The only areas whereon there is any real difficulty in plotting its exact course are from Wynnstay collieries, Ruabon, to the river Dee, and from Whitehaven Hill to Llanymynech. In the former section the Dyke is held to have taken a direct course to the river bank, the river then forming the boundary for a distance of $1\frac{1}{2}$ miles; in the latter, part of the prehistoric defences of Llanymynech Hill seem to have been utilized.

(ii) *Character*

Direct alignments are short, straight stretches longer than 400 yards being uncommon; the 700-yard stretch from the river Clywedog to the knoll N. of Cadwgan Hall is, perhaps, the longest. The course in general, though sinuous, is remarkably direct for long distances. In the hill country it swings from side to side of the straight course to take advantage of dominant features within reasonable distance or to accommodate itself to changes of level. The most remarkable detour made by the Dyke is that between Whitehaven and Llanymynech hills, which is due to the determination of the engineer (exemplified so frequently in this—the Selattyn Hill—sector) to take advantage of all commanding westerly facing hill-slopes. Instead of crossing the Porth-y-Waen valley floor to Llanymynech and the Vyrnwy, the Dyke clings to the slopes of Whitehaven Hill, crosses the Porth-y-Waen re-entrant higher up, and, breasting the slopes of Llynclys Hill, reaches the plateau of this great limestone outlier, from which it ultimately descends to Llanymynech village.

The scale of the Dyke in the zone examined this year is on the whole as fine as that dealt with in Chapter III. Equally striking profiles can be found in upland and in lowland country, but the dimensions vary considerably from point to point.

The Dyke consistently shows a ditch on the W. side in level or fairly level country. On *gentle* westward-facing slopes, and even on level ground S. of the Dee, material for the bank is frequently obtained from spoil holes on the east side as well as from the western ditch. This has not been noted in the part N. of the Dee included in this year's survey, but has been seen near Coed Talwrn in Flintshire (Chapter III, p. 30). Occasionally a definite E. ditch is present in addition to the W. ditch. On *steep* westward-facing slopes the Dyke may be represented by a shelf or berm only, as at Hopyard wood and Craig Forda, by a shelf with western ditch (Craig Forda), or by a bank with eastern hollow and slight western ditch (Craig Forda). The mode of construction of the Dyke in the Cegidog valley (Flintshire) was probably very similar (Chapter III, pp. 32, 44). A feature of the Dyke in the present area is the occasional over-deepening of the ditch. This is strikingly exemplified where it descends the steep slope of Plas Power park to the Clywedog river. Its construction has here provided an artificial drainage line for much of the rainfall on the adjacent plateau, and erosion has converted the ditch into a gully.

(iii) *Relation of farmsteads to Dyke*

A number of homesteads lie on or close beside the Dyke in the agricultural area north of the Dee, the number noted being undoubtedly higher than a line drawn by chance across country would bisect. I do not at this stage in the inquiry,[1] however, see any reason for concluding that these or any one of them originated as police posts or sentinel stations at important points on the boundary, as has been suggested. A much simpler explanation suffices; it is that the Dyke formed a convenient N. and S. pathway in many parts of its course, and where this pathway was crossed by E. and W. traffic lines human habitations were very likely to spring up.[2]

The well-wooded character of the country-side through which the Dyke runs and the nature of the woodland before it was destroyed as a result of agricultural and other activities, are shown by the frequency with which well-grown or ancient oaks occur on the bank of the Dyke. Exceptionally fine examples survive in Plas Power, Pentre-bychan, and Chirk parks.

(iv) *The Layout*

The unity of design of the Dyke in the area is shown by the use made of lateral re-entrants in approaching E. and W. valleys. Such re-entrants are chosen in the descent from the Ruabon plateau to the river Dee, from Chirk park to the river Ceiriog, and from Selattyn Hill to the Morlas brook, the side of the re-entrant which faces W. being in each case made use of for the alignment. The tendency, moreover, of the engineer of the Dyke to select an alignment on the westward edge of a plateau, ridge, or knoll, exemplified in the sector dealt with in Chapter III, is continued. The earthwork, for example, crosses the hill (503 ft.) above Bryn-yr-Owen colliery (Fig. 19) near the crest on the W. side, and through Johnstown its course conforms to the axis of a low N. and S. ridge divided from the Rhosllannerchrugog upland by a valley and a streamlet. In this portion of the Dyke N. of the Dee there are, however, remarkable examples of indifference to tactical position. The Dyke is on the reverse slope of the spur occupied by Big Wood, in Plas Power park: only a short stretch, 100 yards in length, is, however, involved. Failure on a larger scale to secure commanding ground is seen near Tatham, in Ruabon parish, where the Dyke runs just above the 400-ft. contour on the slope of the spur on which Pen-y-gardden fort is situated.[3] This fort is 160 ft. above the Dyke and 450 yards to the W. of it. In the approach to the Dee, moreover, the dominant western-facing spur on which the Waterloo Tower is sited is neglected for a more easterly alignment down the Hopyard ravine. S. of the Dee, on the other hand, practically all the advantages offered by the terrain are seized;[4] not only does the Dyke swing westward to include the spurs of the Berwyn mountains, but every effort is made to site it on dominant westward-facing slopes. Its alignment on the scarp of Craig Forda, on Whitehaven and Llynclys hills is

---

[1] Nor at any later stage (C.F., 1933).

[2] Villages and hamlets apart, the list for this portion of the Dyke is as follows:

   1. One at road crossing NW. of Plas Power park (destroyed).
   2. Cadwgan Hall.
   3. Pentre-bychan Hall.
   4. Bryn-yr-Owen, S. of Pentre-bychan.

   5. Bryn-yr-Owen by the road to Ponkey.
   6. Tatham, near Pen-y-gardden camp.
   7. Tîr-y-fron, near Ruabon.

[3] The implications of this alignment are considered below (p. 81).

[4] The only feature of tactical importance in this sector not occupied is in the hamlet of Treflach Wood. It is of minor character. (See p. 64.)

evidence of this. The whole alignment between the Dee and Vyrnwy is laid out with remarkable skill; though it includes so many vital tactical points, its maximal deviations from the direct line between Selattyn Hill and the Dee, and Selattyn Hill and the Vyrnwy, are only 250 and 750 yards respectively. In respect of this part it is legitimate to infer not that the Dyke is a military defence, but that the Power occupying the lowlands desired to include within its territory key positions giving visual control of this part of the mountainous borderland.

(v) *Unity of Design*

It may be urged that two different engineers were responsible for the portions respectively N. and S. of the river Dee (assuming that they are of the same date), or, alternatively, that the Dee–Selattyn Hill–Vyrnwy section was an earlier and local work of defensive character included in the larger scheme by Offa. Neither of these views is, I think, probable. A convincing argument for unity of design and date can be briefly stated: it is that a major change in direction rendered necessary by the decision to include Selattyn Hill within the line of the Dyke begins (or ends), not on the right bank of the Dee—a natural starting-point for a local work, giving a protected flank—but, as the map reproduced in Plate XI shows, at a point without any tactical features near Pen-y-gardden fort, $2\frac{1}{2}$ miles to the N. of the river, in the sector above referred to. Thus the creator of the Dee–Selattyn Hill–Vyrnwy alignment also controlled the layout of the northern portion of the Dyke.

This conclusion is, I submit, not vitiated by the fact that in a minor detail of construction—namely, the tendency shown by those who built the southern portion to gather material for the bank from the eastern side as well as from the western ditch—a difference between the portions N. and S. of the Dee is present. This feature shows that different gangs and different foremen were employed in the two areas; it does not necessarily imply different designers.[1]

(vi) *Technique of Construction*

I am, on the archaeological evidence at present available, led to the view that the Dyke was constructed in the following manner. One master-mind was responsible for the planning of the work.[1] The course having been by him laid out and the dimensions and character of the work in general terms defined, the localized social and economic organization of the Mercian state was utilized. It is possible that each landowner on the Border was made responsible for a certain length of the Dyke, this length being proportionate to the resources at his command or to the extent of his estates. I doubt whether the King who built the Dyke expended a single penny on labourers, though the planning and the organization of the work and the taxation which had to be remitted because of it, imposed, we may hold, a severe economic strain on the leading men of Mercia, and on the royal treasury.

---

[1] 1953. This view set out in 1928 was confirmed by subsequent study of the Dyke. The suggestion that King Offa himself provided the master-mind would now be acceptable.

PLATE XII

a. The Dyke in an industrial area: Ruabon, Denbighshire. Taken at point H, Fig. 20

b. The Dyke at Caeau-gwynion farm, Chirk. Taken from point J, Fig. 22

PLATE XIII

a. The Dyke on Baker's Hill, from the E. Taken at point P, Fig. 25

b. The Dyke on Baker's Hill, from the W. Taken at point O, Fig. 25

PLATE XIV

a. Cross-section of the Dyke at Old Quarry, Treflach wood. Taken from point R on Fig. 27

b. The Dyke at Pentreshannel farm. Taken at point Q on Fig. 26

PLATE XV

MARSHY FLAT: SITE →
OF WESTERN DITCH

RISING GROUND →
TO EAST

b. The Dyke near the Royal Oak Inn, Treflach Wood. Taken from point S on Fig. 27

a. The Dyke on a limestone upland. Taken from point L on Fig. 23

PLATE XVI

a. The Dyke at Orseddwen farm. Taken from point N on Fig. 24

b. The Dyke on Llynclys Hill. Taken from point T on Fig. 28

PLATE XVII

a. The Dyke near Selattyn Hill, showing a gap, probably original. Taken from point M on Fig. 24

b. The Dyke on a limestone upland: on the boundary between Shropshire and Denbighshire. Taken from point K on Fig. 23

c. Offa's Dyke on Rushock Hill: the right-angled corner. The figure is standing in the ditch. Taken from point K2, Fig. 64

This view serves to explain not only differences in method of construction, but also the differences in scale which were constantly met with in comparable portions of the Dyke as one proceeded along the sector under review. I infer that the scale of the work was (within the limits laid down by higher authority) dependent on the resources of the locality and the energy of, and command of technique possessed by, the gangers in charge of the actual work of digging.

(vii) *Political (?) Influences on Alignment*

Acceptance of the theory of unity in design leaves us with a serious problem: why was the spur on which Pen-y-gardden fort is situated excluded? The alignment of the Dyke here is the first indication met with which suggests that the designer had not an entirely free hand in its selection. The exclusion of the Waterloo Tower spur might be explained on the ground that the Hopyard wood alignment, which utilizes a loop of the Dee, saved the labour of constructing three-quarters of a mile of the Dyke; but this explanation is hardly adequate, and I think that if we shall discover a sound reason for the omission of the fort, we shall at the same time find the explanation of the neglect of the Waterloo Tower spur. The simplest explanation is that the Welsh held Pen-y-gardden,[1] and that the plans of the Dyke builder were conditioned by this fact, whereas he had a much freer hand S. of the Dee. It follows that the alignment of the Dyke in general may not represent, as I have been disposed to hold, the free choice of a conquering race, but a boundary defined by treaty or by agreement between the men of the hills and the men of the lowlands. The latter, one would say, although clearly the dominant partners in the arrangement, did not have matters all their own way.

This view is in accordance with the remarkable fact that the trace of the Dyke for 3 miles to the N. of Pen-y-gardden was based on the exclusion of this commanding Dee-side site. The passage of the Dyke to the E. of it is thus definitely not a local deflection of an otherwise direct alignment (Plate XI).

Such tactical inferiority cannot but reflect a contemporary political and military situation of great interest. Excavation having provided evidence which tends to assign the Dyke to the Dark Ages, and its unity of design having been, so far as the inquiry has proceeded, established, we are, I think, justified in discussing its problems on the assumption that, as tradition and historical record both Welsh and English assert, it was wholly constructed by King Offa towards the close of the eighth century. Accepting this basis, then, there are certain data available to us which may throw light on the situation referred to.

North of the river Dee, about 6 miles to the W. of Pen-y-gardden, is the pillar[2] set up by

---

[1] Reoccupation of hill-forts in the Dark Ages in Wales is referred to in the *Arch. Camb.* centenary volume, 1946, pp. 109–10; no positive evidence of this is at present available.

[2] Close to Valle Crucis Abbey, marked on map, Plate XI. This pillar is not *in situ*, but the available evidence indicates that it was set up not far from its present position. The inscription on it is well known;

its significance has been discussed by, among others, Rhys in *Y Cymmrodor*, xxi, pp. 39 ff., Sayce in *Arch. Camb.* 1909, pp. 43 ff. Since this was written a translation and analysis has been published by Dr. V. E. Nash-Williams in *The Early Christian Monuments of Wales*, 1950, pp. 123–4. He dates the pillar in the first half of the ninth century.

I am much indebted to my friend, Dr. (now Professor)

Concenn (Cyngen), King of Powys, probably in the middle third of the ninth century, to the memory of his great-grandfather Eliseg; nearby, we may suppose, there was a favourite residence of the Powysian dynasty in this part of their dominions. That the late-eighth-century representative of that House should have concentrated his efforts in the field and at the council table to secure a serviceable frontier adjacent to a country-side in which he was specially interested, is to have been expected.[1]

(viii) *The Will, and the Task*

It has been noted that the alignment of the Dyke in each of the three great stretches included in this season's work, though sinuous, is singularly direct. This fact deserves to be stressed. The intellectual quality, the eye for country, the intimate knowledge of the district manifested by the creation of these alignments carried out in very broken and mountainous country intersected by deep river valleys, involving stretches of 6, $7\frac{1}{2}$, and (if the line be carried to the Severn) 12 miles, without the aid of accurate maps, is

William Rees, for the following genealogical table of Kings of Powys mentioned in the record, with their actual or approximate dates:

to the theory of the 'agreed frontier' involving some withdrawal on the part of the English. He regards the Pillar as being *in situ*, though reset.

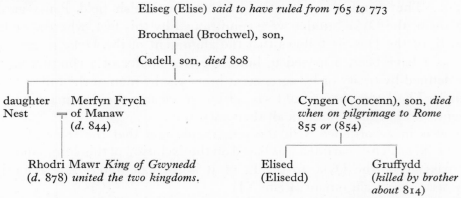

Eliseg (Elise) *said to have ruled from 765 to 773*
|
Brochmael (Brochwel), son,
|
Cadell, son, *died* 808

daughter Nest — Merfyn Frych of Manaw (*d.* 844)
Rhodri Mawr *King of Gwynedd* (*d.* 878) *united the two kingdoms.*

Cyngen (Concenn), son, *died when on pilgrimage to Rome* 855 *or* (854)
Elised (Elisedd)
Gruffydd (*killed by brother about* 814)

The inscription is obscure, but we gather that Concenn and his great-grandfather Eliseg both waged successful war against the English; the achievements of Cattell (Cadell) and Brochmael are not mentioned.

It will be noticed that while Eliseg is in part a contemporary of Offa, the period 784–96 within which the construction of the Dyke may with most probability be assigned, is that of Brochmael or of Cadell. There appear to have been two great Mercian attacks on Wales in 778 and 784; and it is to the latter date that tradition assigns the Dyke. The political and military recovery of Powys, with which the achievements referred to by Concenn (Cyngen) may be equated, are in all probability to be placed, Dr. Rees informs me, after A.D. 825.

I should add that a recent reassessment of the evidence by Mr. C. A. Ralegh Radford, sometime Inspector of Ancient Monuments for Wales, in a Ministry of Works pamphlet *The Pillar of Eliseg* (1953) regards the reference to King Eliseg: 'It was Elise who united the inheritance of Powys (laid waste for nine years) from the hand of the English with fire and sword' as a reference

[1] Note (1954). These views have been criticized, and I have re-examined their foundations, the topography of the country N. and S. of Pen-y-gardden in relation to the Dyke. The facts justifying the N. alignment are set out in lines 5 to 10 of the section dealing with the layout (p. 79); here other points can be added. The remarkable change of direction of the Dyke—off the Gardden spur—at the N. end of Plas Power park (Fig. 18) enabled the alluvial flat of the Clywedog stream to be crossed at right angles, and the two Cadwgan brooks and the two Pentre-bychan brooks to be crossed E. of their respective mergings into one stream; thereafter it can be said that the alignment along the Bryn-yr-Owen ridge (503 ft.) and the slightly lower ridge through Johnstown (with a stream to the W.) has better local command of ground than a layout on to the spur could provide hereabouts. Thus it is in general a sound one.

On the S. flank of Pen-y-gardden two points should be stressed. First, that the starting-point of the Dyke from the Dee at the Hopyard wood ravine on its northward

remarkable.[1] The selection of an alignment which, while including essential tactical points on the adjacent hills, provides on both sides of the Ceiriog valley westward-facing slopes for the earthwork through the skilful use of re-entrant and embayment is especially note-worthy. It is difficult to imagine anything more indicative of strenuous purpose and successful achievement than the straight course of the whale-backed ridge of Offa's Dyke in broken country. This was first borne in upon me when I was following its course with difficulty across the ravines N. of the Dee; further experience, in mountainous country, confirmed and amplified this impression of a firm and undeviating will, applied to what must have been, having regard to the resources of a primitive state, an almost impossible task.

course had been arranged for when the alignment S. of the Dee was planned (Plate XI and p. 80). Second, that the Dyke was aligned from this point direct on to the Gardden spur, for half a mile, thereafter breaking away to conform with the northern alignment below the spur (Fig. 20).

Thus the alignments on both flanks of Pen-y-gardden show features suggesting alteration of plans.

It cannot be denied that these alterations, involving the passage of the Dyke 160 ft. below such a vantage-point, overlooking the Dee valley, as Gardden, having regard to the efforts made in the Selattyn sector to control the upland, provide a contrast in aim or out-look which has to be taken into account in any study of its genesis and planning.

[1] The sector of the Dyke described in Chapter III forms part of the first of these three alignments. The maximal deviations from the direct course on these stretches are:

Pen-y-Coed to Pen-y-gardden (6 miles), 170 yards.
Pen-y-gardden to Selattyn Hill (7½ miles), 300 yards.
Selattyn Hill to R. Severn (12 miles), 750 yards.

The zigzag course necessitated by the topography at Whitehaven and Llanymynech hills accounts for the deviation being greater in this latter sector than in the others.

Key map XI includes all save a small portion of the northern alignment (from Coed Talwrn to Ffrith). For this see key map VI.

PLATE XVIII

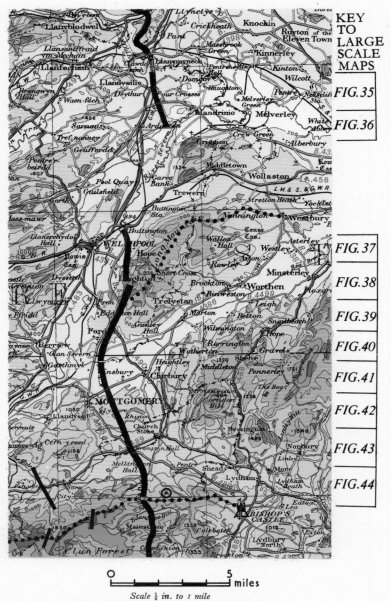

KEY
TO
LARGE
SCALE
MAPS

FIG. 35

FIG. 36

FIG. 37

FIG. 38

FIG. 39

FIG. 40

FIG. 41

FIG. 42

FIG. 43

FIG. 44

Scale ¼ in. to 1 mile

Offa's Dyke in East Montgomeryshire

(Chapter V)

The dotted lines show ridgeways and the narrow black lines 'short dykes'. A castle and a motte-and-bailey are also indicated

See pages 85, 88, 113, 115, 117, 278, 286

V. OFFA'S DYKE IN EAST MONTGOMERYSHIRE (1929)

THIS chapter records the course and character of Offa's Dyke in the county of Montgomery; its trace is approximately N. and S. across the eastern borders of the shire.

The survey commences at the river Vyrnwy in Llandysilio parish and ends at a point 400 yards south of the county boundary, near Ringfield on the Kerry Hill, in Mainstone parish, Shropshire. The distance in a straight line between these points is 20 miles; the total length visible today of the Dyke, which follows a fairly direct course, is about $15\frac{1}{4}$ miles. There is reason to suppose that for 5 miles the Severn formed the boundary. Other breaks in the continuity of the Dyke are few and relatively unimportant.

The Dyke traverses very varied country, ranging in elevation through over 1,000 ft., from under 200 ft. on the flats bordering the Severn to 1,251 ft. on Kerry Hill.

The map, Plate XVIII, shows the trace of the Dyke in relation to the main topographical features. It first crosses the belt of alluvium, clay, and river gravels between the Vyrnwy and the Severn. Ending on the left bank of the Severn, it begins afresh on the right bank at Buttington, 5 miles away, and ascends diagonally the western slopes of the Long Mountain which are deeply serrated by ravines, reaching an elevation of nearly 1,000 ft. E. of Leighton Hall. The Dyke then descends by easy gradients (varied by one slight ascent), to the valley of the Camlad (270 ft. above O.D.). The underlying rocks hereabouts are Silurian and Ordovician, the shaly characters of which are well seen where the Dyke is aligned on forested slopes bare of undergrowth. Stony clay presumably of glacial origin forms the superficial deposits at many points, chiefly on the lower levels. From the alluvial flat of the Camlad the Dyke crosses fertile farmlands overlooked by the Castle of Montgomery; the Lymore Park–Brompton Mill area, a plateau 400–500 ft. in elevation, follows; then the Dyke, crossing a diversified countryside, rises to 600 ft. before ascending the steep northern slopes of the Kerry Hill ridge which is passed near Ring Hill at 1,251 ft. above O.D.

The country traversed varies in character with the elevation. It is agricultural—now almost entirely grassland—varied by water-meadows on the alluvial flats, and by stretches of park and woodland, between 200 and 500–600 ft.; above this level, on the ravines of the Long Mountain it is forest (of recent origin), on Kerry Hill upland sheep pasture.

THE COURSE OF THE DYKE

The course of the Dyke is set out on ten sections of the 6-in. O.S. map, reduced as before to 4 in. to 1 mile (Figs. 35–44). Two represent the stretch of country between St. Tysilio's church, Llandysilio, and the Severn NE. of Rhyd-esgyn, and eight that between Buttington and the Kerry ridgeway. Plate XVIII indicates the position in the sector of each of these large-scale maps.

FIGURE 35. *The Street, Llandysilio to the School Brook bridge; passing through Llandysilio parish, and on the boundary between Llandysilio and Llandrinio parishes, Mont.*

The first definite traces of Offa's Dyke to the S. of the river Vyrnwy are in Llandysilio rectory garden (close to the entrance gate) on the N. side of the Llanymynech–Llandysilio road. Here begins the partially levelled reverse slope of the bank, the road being on the site of the ditch. From this point to Hafod Offa traces are frequent, on the same alignment. An irregular ridge in field 1 (pasture) may represent the levelled bank, which is certainly present at the school a few yards farther on. This building is erected on the ridge of the

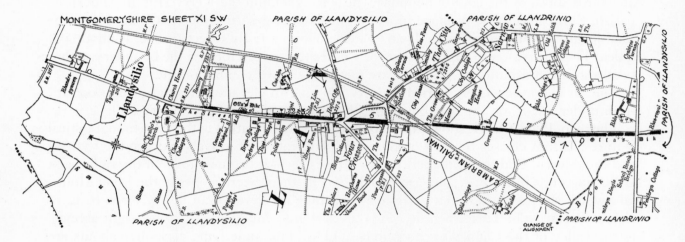

FIG. 35. The Street, Llandysilio, to the School Brook Bridge; passing through Llandysilio parish, and on the boundary between Llandysilio and Llandrinio parishes, Montgomeryshire.

A portion of the 6-in. O.S. map reduced to 4 in. to 1 mile. In this and the following nine maps a thick black line ▰▰▰ represents portions of the Dyke clearly visible today; the *degree* of thickness illustrating the relative size of the work at different points in its course. An additional line close to and parallel with the principal one indicates the presence of a bank on the counterscarp. A thick broken line ▬ ▬ ▬ shows that faint traces of the Dyke are present; while a hair line —— represents the approximate alignment of the Dyke where it is now lost, as recorded on the first 1-in. O.S. map, or as indicated by a respectable tradition.
Roman numerals in circles point to the exact position where the sectional plan with the corresponding number was made; letters in circles and arrows indicate the approximate position and direction of the camera when the illustration with the corresponding letter was taken. Certain fields and enclosures on the line of the Dyke are identified by arabic numerals.
Sketch contours — · — · — · indicate important natural features on the line of the Dyke not clearly brought out on the Ordnance map.
(Reproduced from the Ordnance Survey map with the sanction of the Controller of H.M. Stationery Office.)

Dyke which (spread by former cultivation) occupies the whole breadth of the playground. Farther on the Dyke becomes more clearly marked; in field 2 it presents a rounded hump, in the adjacent garden (enclosure 3) a higher bank, while in field 4 it is 5 ft. in height and apparently but little denuded save that the scarp has been dug away here and there, probably to mend the adjacent road. Slight traces exist in the garden of Hafod Offa.

Having established the line of the Dyke at Llandysilio, we must return to deal with the problem of the gap, nearly 1 mile (1,700 yards) in breadth, which separates Llandysilio rectory from Llanymynech Church (Fig. 29) the point on the left bank of the Vyrnwy river, where it was clearly seen that the Dyke must have ended.

A northward extension of the known alignment near the right bank would carry the Dyke diagonally across the road to the farm-yard of Church House beside St. Tysilio's church, and there is little doubt that it began again here on the edge of the alluvial flat.

This flatland is certainly subject to floods and the parish boundaries show that the river hereabouts has changed its course since these were defined. We have no means of determining the alignment of the Offan boundary between the two churches; it is possible that in the eighth century the river Vyrnwy formed a loop extending across the alluvium from church to church; it nearly does so today.[1]

We may now turn to Hafod Offa. Here the road divides;[2] the Dyke, known as the 'Clawdd', maintains its alignment and is present in pasture-field 5 as a broad low grassy ridge with definite traces of a ditch, on the W. as heretofore. The alignment of the Dyke along the Cambrian Railway sidings is preserved by a footpath, but no traces survive.[3] On the farther side of the railway it reappears as a broad grassy bank with a hedge boundary on its W. margin; passing Y Gornel, it presents similar characters in fields 6 and 7. The Dyke in field 8 is instructive, as it clearly reveals the ditch as unilateral and on the W.; we have little doubt that this was the case in the Y Gornel area, where modern drainage channels obscure the original profile. The Dyke crosses field 9 as a broad flattened-out ridge at the N. end, higher and narrower at the S. end, where it is over 6 ft. in height; here, however, it is damaged by cross-drains and other excavations. The W. ditch is a modern field drain, and can bear but little relation to the original ditch.

On the S. side of the high road the Dyke has been dug away for some 40 yards; thence for over 100 yards it forms a narrow steep-sided ridge about 4 ft. in height.[4]

FIGURE 36. *Rhos Royal farm to the Severn opposite Severn House, on the boundary between Llandysilio and Llandrinio parishes and in Llandrinio and Guilsfield parishes, Mont.*

For over 250 yards the crest of the Dyke forms a hedge boundary; the bank is 'spread', but must have been of considerable size; there is a field drain on the E. and no definite trace of a W. ditch. From the cross-track—where it is levelled and extensively quarried—the Dyke is seen to extend across open level pasture (field 10) for about a third of a mile. It is a broad (18–21 yards) flattened bank, without definite trace of a ditch on either side. At the S. end of this pasture-field a flood-bank has been constructed to bridge a narrow gap in the Dyke; a small portion of the Dyke (on which are two oak-trees) then follows: from this a similar bank extends in a SW. direction, 40 yards of the Dyke in the corner of the field having been levelled to make it. The Dyke reappears, much denuded, as the boundary between fields 11 and 12.

For a distance of 275 yards beyond the adjacent road the Dyke bank, much eroded by man (and rabbits), forms the E. hedge boundary of the trackway leading to the marshes past Neath farm. Then the lane opens out into a grassy ribbon of meadow (field 13) of which the Dyke, heightened to form a flood-bank, forms the chief feature.

In the next field (14) the bank is reinforced by a stone revetment: it is still on the line of the Dyke, and is presumably on its foundation. When the Bele brook is reached, the

---

[1] Written in 1953.
[2] This point was called the Bwlch. See *Mont. Coll.* xxxi, 1900, p. 277.
[3] The 1836 O.S. map, sheet 60, shows that it was present here before the railway was built.
[4] This originally carried a hedge on the crest, which accounts for the profile.

flood-bank swings eastward; but in the correct alignment, in a loop of the brook, on the left bank, is a shapeless mound (+3 ft.) which may well be the remains of the Dyke.

Tradition and the O.S. map record the Dyke as extending to the river Severn. The structure lying between the Bele brook and the Severn which is marked as the Dyke consists of a broad and low (+2 ft.) but quite definite ridge. This may well be a characteristic dyke construction planed off by floods, and since it is in the correct alignment there is no reason to doubt its antiquity. From the Bele brook to the New Cut a narrow field bank is superposed on, or in places dug out of, the ancient bank; between the New Cut and the

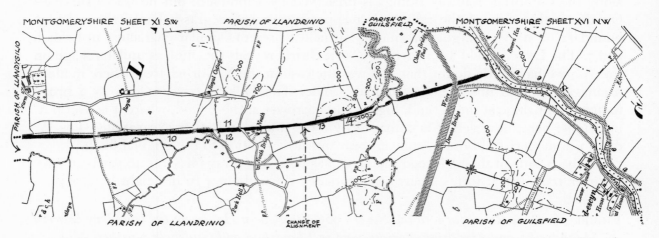

FIG. 36. Rhos Royal farm to the Severn opposite Severn House, on the boundary between Llandysilio and Llandrinio parishes, and in Llandrinio and Guilsfield parishes, Montgomeryshire.
A portion of the 6-in. O.S. map reduced to 4 in. to 1 mile. For the significance of the symbols and employed letters, see Fig. 35.
(Reproduced from the Ordnance Survey map with the sanction of the Controller of H.M. Stationery Office.)

Severn no later construction is associated with it, and it crosses the open pasture, fading out on the bank of the river, high above the summer level of the water. In places between Bele brook and the New Cut the bank is as much as 20 yards broad; the ditch seems to have been on the W.

The course of Offa's Dyke between the Vyrnwy and the Severn is singularly direct. The greater part seems to have been laid out on two alignments (Plate XVIII), the first extending from the bluff by St. Tysilio's Church to a point S. of Y Gornel, a distance of 1,830 yards, the second from this point to the end of the Neath farm trackway (the edge of the flood plain, Fig. 36), a distance of just under 1 mile. The change in direction at the junction of these two alignments amounts to only 7 degrees. The remaining stretch, half a mile in length, is in its centre (field 14) deflected slightly from a straight alignment, but this portion—that faced with stone—may have been rebuilt. The section was probably aligned from the edge of the dry land to the Severn.

The Dyke between the rivers is nowhere of striking proportions; this is probably due mainly to the soil (clay, alluvial silt, or gravel) of which it is composed. The ditch is usually filled in, silted up, or ploughed in, but the Dyke reveals no definite evidence of being double ditched, and we are of opinion that as originally constructed the ditch was consistently on the W.

FIGURE 37. *Buttington to Goppas wood; in the parishes of Cletterwood and Hope, Mont.*

The direct alignment of the Dyke on to the Severn and its presence on the very bank of the river shows that we must look for its continuation on the opposite bank. This is easily found, since there is an authentic and well-recognized stretch, beginning at the school house, Buttington. This stretch is, however, 5 miles away, and 450 yards from the

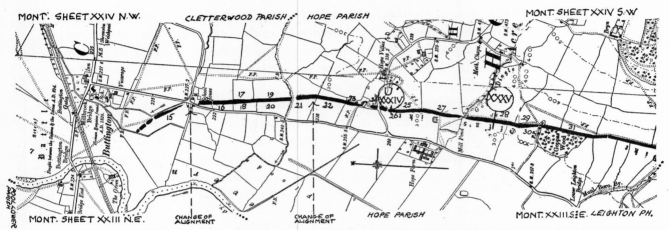

FIG. 37. Buttington to Goppas wood: in the parishes of Cletterwood and Hope, Montgomeryshire.
A portion of the 6-in. O.S. map reduced to 4 in. to 1 mile. For the significance of the symbols and employed letters, see Fig. 35.
(Reproduced from the Ordnance Survey map with the sanction of the Controller of H.M. Stationery Office.)

river on any alignment which it could, having regard to its trend S. of the school house, be expected to follow.

The difficulty has, by some writers, been met by the assumption that the Dyke was originally present on the right bank of the river N. of Buttington; the O.S. map, indeed, marks a stretch over a mile long, near Trewern Hall (Mont. XVI SW.) as the 'site of' Offa's Dyke.

These and other possible alignments were examined; they are flood—or hedge—banks. The absence of the Dyke suggests that the Severn was utilized as the boundary,[1] an assumption which would become a certainty if an extension of the Dyke from Buttington school house in the direction of the river could be demonstrated.

Such an extension can be shown to exist. A raised ridge is seen close to and parallel with the NE. boundary of field 15; its continuity with the known portion of the Dyke is, of course, broken by the road junction, but anyone who studies the area cannot doubt that the ridge is part of the Dyke. This impression is confirmed as one proceeds along the field, the Dyke bank becoming more distinctly marked, though crossed by drains and

[1] This obvious explanation is given in Lewis's *Top. Dict.* 1831 (see under Buttington), and by others since: e.g. Thomas Price in *Mont. Coll.* xxxi, 1900, p. 276.

channels. At its best, it is about 2 ft. high and 15 yards broad. Beyond the NW. boundary of this field no indication of the Dyke is to be found, but since it can be traced right on to the alluvial flat of the Severn within 150 yards of the present course of the river,[1] and since it is pointing directly at the river, we are justified in assuming that the construction of the Dyke, intermitted for 5 miles, was recommenced in the immediate neighbourhood of Buttington church and bridge.[2]

The selection of this point is interesting and deserves the attention of topographer and historian. Ancient roads and tracks lead towards Buttington bridge (or the ford which preceded it) from either side of the river, and there are traces of a rectangular earthwork (p. 115) on the rising ground on which the church and school are set. The Dyke then was so placed as to give access from Mercian territory to an important crossing of the Severn. It was at Buttington that the English levies overtook the Danes in A.D. 894, as the Anglo-Saxon Chronicle records.[3] This circumstance strengthens the probability that it was a nodal point on the traffic lines of the border.

The topographical narrative may now be resumed. Passing from the school house garden, the shed of which is placed on the bank, the Dyke is seen to cross pasture-field 16 as a ploughed-down ridge crossed by one drainage channel, the ditch being on the W. It forms the boundary between fields 17–18 and 19–20, the bank having been lowered—probably by ploughing—before the field divisions were made. It then crosses the open field 21 (arable) as a very low rounded ridge, the southern hedge of the field showing its position by a well-marked rise.

From the school house to this point (560 yards) the Dyke is directly aligned; it is at the foot of the slope of the Long Mountain, and is making a very gradual diagonal ascent of that slope. At the S. end of the field the direction changes, through 13 degrees. The new alignment is maintained for nearly $1\frac{1}{4}$ miles, ending close to the (N.) Lodge of Leighton park (Fig. 38). The course is remarkably direct, the maximum deviation from the straight line being not more than 25 yards.

An examination of the contours on Figs. 37 and 38 will reveal the engineer's achievement. For reasons which will later be discussed he had to carry the Dyke from the 225-ft. level at Buttington to the 1,000-ft. contour on the Long Mountain slopes in Leighton parish. This he determined to achieve by a gradual ascent, the intermediate goal being the Old Quarry spur (500 ft.) close to the North Lodge. The reason for the change in direction at field 21 is readily grasped; it is high enough up the hill-side to bring the objective into full view.

---

[1] The Severn may, in the eighth century, have followed a course nearer to the high ground.

[2] C. W. Dymond, in *Mont. Coll.* xxxi, 1900, p. 346, roundly states that the Dyke extended to the earthwork at Buttington church and was 'levelled to form the Leighton road'. There is no evidence on the ground to support this assertion.

[3] 'þa hie þa ealle gegaderode wæron, þa offoron hie þone here hindan æt Buttingtune. on Sæferne staþe, ond hine þær utan besæton on ælce healfe, on anum

fæstenne. þa hie ða fela wucena sæton on twa healfe þæer(e) é,'... Earle and Plummer, *Two Saxon Chronicles Parallel*, i, p. 87. The identification of Buttington Tump, Tidenham, as the site of the battle is topographically improbable having regard to the phrases used by the contemporary chronicle, quoted above, and those in the same annal describing the route taken by the Danes—'Foron þa up be Temese,' &c.

See also C. W. Dymond, *Mont. Coll.* xxxi, 1900, pp. 337 ff.

In field 22 the Dyke is nearly ploughed out; the W. boundary of field 23 is on the scarp, here very steep and measuring 20 ft. on the slope. The adjacent farm-house stands on the Dyke; in its home-field (no. 24) is a massive fragment adjacent to a deep holloway. When this obstacle is crossed, the Dyke is found to be a formidable barrier on the slope of the hill, overlooking the vale of Powys.[1] The scarp is steep, and old oaks crown the crest, which forms a hedge boundary between fields 25 and 26 (Profile xxxiv, Fig. 48); here there is an ancient and probably original opening (p. 112 and Plate XIX*b*). Passing on towards the Goppas dingle the crest of the bank is seen to have been ploughed down and its scale much reduced thereby, but the steepness of the scarp is maintained. After crossing the Goppas streamlet a very perfect section of the Dyke is seen. The hedge boundary here being on the W. edge of the ditch instead of on the crest of the bank, the ditch has not been ploughed—or filled—in, and a clear impression of the original character of the earthwork on these hill-slopes can be obtained. As Profile xxxv shows it is in scale and form identical with characteristic portions N. of the Severn; the scarp is steep, the crest a narrow ridge. At the S. end of field 28 the hedge swings on to the crest of the bank, and the ditch, being unprotected, has been ploughed in; the contrast in character between two adjacent portions of the Dyke in this field shows that accidental and apparently insignificant factors largely determine the present-day condition of travelling earthworks.

In field 29 the crest of the bank has been ploughed down and the W. ditch (in field 30) ploughed in, but the steep scarp remains. It ends abruptly on the edge of a deep hollow in which a spring rises;[2] on the farther side of this hollow the Dyke passes along the E. margin of Goppas wood. At the N. end of the wood the ditch is a drainage channel, being over-deepened where it descends to the above-mentioned spring. At the S. end of the wood the ridge of the bank emerges on to the pasture-field 31 and the (W.) ditch is largely silted or filled up.

The Dyke continues to form field boundaries for the next 350 yards; it is, for the most part, very poorly preserved, but the scale of the work is such that destruction is difficult, and its course is easily traced.

FIGURE 38. *Pentre Mill to Pole Plantation, in the parishes of Hope and Leighton, Mont.*

From the SW. angle of field 32 the course of the Dyke across the ravine (here opening out into a narrow flat-floored valley) of the Pentre Mill brook is by no means easy to trace. A fragment of the bank remains E. of the *s.* of 'Offa'*s*', and in this alignment there are quite definite traces of a ditch and bank on the valley floor N. of the farm buildings, in continuation of the portion already traversed. The O.S. map, however, seems to regard the steep scarp to the E.—the natural flank of the valley—as the continuation of the Dyke. This is erroneous. From the farm the Dyke rises steeply on to a spur which forms the W. flank of the little valley; visual control over the vale of Powys is thus cleverly maintained without any alteration of alignment. Unquestionably this was taken into consideration

---

[1] It is of a size last seen at Treflach Wood hamlet, 12 miles away: Chapter IV, p. 64.

[2] The inclusion of the spring head within the Mercian frontier may have been intentional; a slight deflection to the E. would have avoided the obstacle which it creates.

when the line was staked out. An ancient trackway follows the (W.) ditch and thus has preserved it; the bank has been extensively ploughed down; it is not here marked on the O.S. map. The track opens on to a farmyard across which the Dyke has been obliterated, but it is clearly seen as a ploughed-down ridge crossing the next field (no. 33). A cottage here intervenes, immediately beyond which the Dyke is seen as a massive ridge. Crossing the estate road, it is easily found in a belt of trees on the E. of the Lodge, rising steeply up the slope. We have reached the (lower) Quarry spur, and the end of the straight alignment which has continued for over a mile.

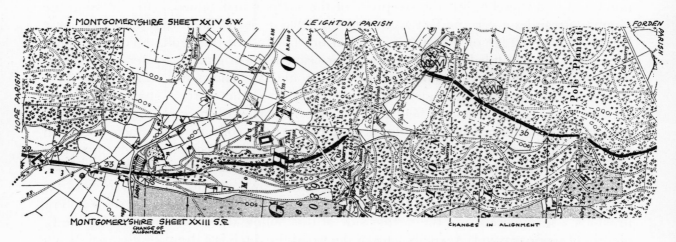

FIG. 38. Pentre Mill to Pole plantation, in the parishes of Hope and Leighton, Montgomeryshire.
A portion of the 6-in. O.S. map reduced to 4 in. to 1 mile. For the significance of the symbols and employed letters, see Fig. 35.
(Reproduced from the Ordnance Survey map with the sanction of the Controller of H.M. Stationery Office.)

From this point, about 500 ft. above O.D., the Dyke follows for nearly 2 miles a devious course closely related to the relief of the country (which is very hilly and deeply dissected by lateral valleys), through the plantations overlooking Leighton park (see Figs. 38 and 39). Rising to nearly 800 ft. by Tank Cottages it drops to about 590 ft. in the Viaduct ravine; leaving this ravine higher up just below the 800-ft. contour, it ascends to the 'Pole Plantation' plateau, nearly 1,000 ft. up, by two short direct alignments, and follows a straight course on it. Descending a steep slope diagonally, it follows for $\frac{3}{4}$ mile the indentations of the hill-side, reaching the S. boundary of the park and open cultivated country at 650 ft., to the E. of the Old Quarry. From here an extended direct alignment is once more possible and is chosen.

The course in this area may now be described in detail. On the slope by the Lodge the earthwork can be traced through thick underwood, gardens, and closes, emerging on to a forested hill-side, which it ascends diagonally. Material for the bank on this hill-side is seen to have been taken from either side; the work is of full scale, measuring 27 ft. on the scarp close to the Q of the lower Quarry. As the slope steepens the Dyke takes on the familiar character of a scarped berm or platform (cf. Craig Forda, Chapter IV, p. 61), which is maintained as far as a deep holloway which crosses it (this holloway is 200 yards

S. of the *Q* of the lower *Quarry*). On the farther side of the holloway, the Dyke emerges, at 650 ft., on to a patch of more open country (marked 34 on map), a rounded knoll indicating its position. Beyond this point a maze of tracks and banks on the hill-side obscures its trace. A survey in advance of this complex reveals a berm, of familiar character, in the correct alignment. It is composed of loose shaly material and has been degraded by the activities of rabbits; it rises on an easy gradient diagonally up the hill-side, here exceptionally steep. A lower (W.) ditch or shelf, formed by steepening the scarp, is clearly apparent in places. No difficulty was experienced in tracing the berm, once found, until the W. end of the bar of the *H* of LEIGHTON was reached. Here it dies away for 20 yards, completely lost in dense woodland. Crossing the E.–W. fence shown on the map the Dyke is found again in the same alignment; berm, steepened scarp, and lower shelf are clearly apparent. It reaches its highest point in this area (790 ft.) just below the modern roadway round the western face of the knoll which forms the crest-line of the massif as seen from Leighton Park farm. No path marks, through bracken and woodland, the course of the Dyke here; but its character once grasped, no doubt as to its identification can arise. Emerging from the dense growth into the comparatively open area below the 'Tank' (black spot on map) one sees cross-sections of the bank on either side of the cutting made for a pipe line down the hill-side, and, immediately beyond this, the well-defined portion marked on the O.S. map. The bank here identified as Offa's Dyke was, it may be remarked, tracked through dense woodland without the use of map or compass, and the exact point where a known portion exists was reached at the first attempt. Field archaeologists will agree that no better proof of the correctness of the line followed could be produced.

Offa's Dyke now descends the shoulder of the hill as a broad, flattened bank, making for a point beside the 'Old Quarry'; here on the very steep slope overlooking the Viaduct ravine it fades out, reappearing on the full scale some 450 yards farther on.

The line of the Mercian boundary between these two points is unknown.[1] The problem of its course is interesting, because the relief of the country-side is so complex. Fig. 47 represents the bare elements of the topography. It will be observed that the Dyke fades out on the flank of a deep re-entrant which forks a short distance above, and that it reappears on the other side of the re-entrant higher up, on the edge of the brook which flows W. towards the Severn. The brook, it should be added, runs in the deep and narrow gully which it has eroded, and this is difficult to cross.

A sufficient length of the Dyke has now been studied to enable generalizations to be formulated as to the chief engineer's probable choice of route in any type of country met with. When proceeding along a hill-side in broken country (such as this) *small* lateral re-entrants are crossed in a direct manner, the Dyke dipping to the floor of the little valley and up again the other side. In the case of larger re-entrants the Dyke swings inwards for a moderate distance, dips slightly to cross the valley at the higher level thus attained, and then swings outwards to regain the correct alignment.

It was anticipated that the latter course would have been adopted at the Viaduct ravine, but no trace of the earthwork was found on the northern flank of the little valley. Further

---

[1] No evidence is presented on the 1836 1-in. O.S. map, sheet 60, or on the modern 6-in. map.

consideration suggested that the reason lay in the existence of the branch valley and streamlet (see Fig. 47) which would have to be negotiated before the main re-entrant (trending NW.) was approached.

Much afforestation was carried out in the area in the 70's of last century when the Viaduct was built, the road up the ravine made or remade, the quarry (near which the Dyke fades out) dug, and the brook which flows down the ravine dammed to form a series of ponds; but since the course of the Dyke here is not shown on the first edition of the O.S. map (1836) it cannot be affirmed that the earthwork was destroyed by these activities. The course which may have been adopted by the Dyke builder is a simple one. The stream itself is in line with the adjacent portion of the Dyke on the N. side; indeed, the trace of the Dyke seems here to have been set out with the object of striking (or leading away from) the ravine at the elbow above the Viaduct—the most convenient point. From the elbow[1] the gully, it is suggested, formed the Mercian boundary until a point was reached when a direct course could be struck for the edge of the plateau, the highest point aimed at in the Long Mountain sector.[2] The Dyke builder has in effect used the Viaduct brook as he utilized the Dee and the Severn; the abrupt way in which the Dyke is recommenced at the point where the brook is no longer of service is, moreover, exactly paralleled at Tan-y-cut on the former river (Chapter IV, p. 55, Fig. 21).

Offa's Dyke, then, begins afresh on the left bank of the Viaduct brook, at about 760 ft. above O.D., as a blunt-nosed mass on the precipitous slope of the gully; it is difficult to locate here owing to the dense undergrowth. By the hedge which separates the copse from an open pasture there is a broad trackway beyond which the Dyke is present as a magnificent bank measuring 25 ft. on the (W.) slope, and with a silted-up W. ditch. The photograph (Plate XXa) shows its appearance from the E. side. From this point onwards for one-third of a mile the Dyke is constructed on the grand scale, and has been but little denuded; Figs. 48 and 49 show characteristic profiles. It climbs up the steep N. face of the re-entrant to the shoulder of the plateau, having been set out in two straight alignments of 140 and 170 yards. The plateau being reached, a second slight change of direction is manifest, and a straight course is set ending 320 yards away at the Keeper's cottage; this lies directly above a deep embayment of the hill in Pole Plantation.

There is a Roman quality about engineering work of this class which compels admiration. The directness of the approach to the plateau up a slope which, for 70 yards, has a gradient of 1 in 2 is especially striking; the Dyke is aligned exactly on to the margin of the plateau (by the *O* of *Offa's*, see map).

The surface conditions are varied. After crossing the open field (no. 35) by the brook, the Dyke passes into thick forest (plantations); but at the angle of the plateau and in a clearing farther on (no. 36) the original plant association—downland turf—is present, and there are magnificent views embracing the vale of Powys and the mountains beyond.

---

[1] The steepness of the slope by the Quarry and the shaly rock of which it is composed, together with the presence of a modern road on the valley floor close to the elbow of the gully, are sufficient to account for the loss of a small part of the Dyke—about 70 linear yards.

[2] The possibility that there was no break in continuity and that the Dyke closely followed the right flank of the gully was considered. But no trace could be found on this alignment.

The Keeper's cottage already referred to is set partly on the bank of the Dyke, which is here cut away, exposing the shaly material of which it is composed. Crossing the adjacent trackway the Dyke is seen to descend the very steep slope of the Pole Plantation embayment, keeping a very straight alignment (having regard to the relief) as far as the stream bed at the foot of the slope. It is of no great size here, but is readily recognizable, though not recorded on the 6-in. O.S. map.[1] The ditch is on the W. Landslips and modern trackways have rendered the trace obscure for the next 40 yards, and then a long and almost complete stretch begins, which extends as far as the S. end of the park. This stretch is sinuous in its trace and fairly level, following on a steep slope the contours of the hill; it is a comparatively slight work, of the character usual on slopes and fully exemplified at Craig Forda (Chapter IV, p. 61); a small portion falls within Fig. 38. This portion has been formed by heaping up a ridge with soil from above, and steepening the scarp to form a ditch below. The Dyke swings round the hill on the 800-ft. contour, affording, since the plantations have been recently felled, an extensive view; it then dips into another embayment.

FIGURE 39. *Green Wood to Kingswood hamlet, in the parishes of Leighton and Forden, Mont.*

The Dyke continues for a short distance to follow the 800-ft. contour, and then sinks nearly 100 ft., still following the curves of the hill. It is more clearly marked here, and is formed in the manner indicated above. It should be placed on record that in Green Wood there is ample evidence that periodical deforestation is most destructive to the earthwork; its shaly soil unprotected by grass is exposed to denudation by heavy rainfall, and it has also been damaged by the removal of felled trees.

From the letter W ('well') on the map to the point where the Dyke emerges on to parkland from the forested area it has been destroyed,[2] a trackway used for log-hauling occupying its site. In the parkland (enclosure no. 37) it leaves the 700-ft. contour line, making a steep descent; its character changes, and though quarried and gapped the remains of a high and broad bank with W. ditch are manifest. A holloway burrows deep behind the reverse slope of the Dyke (Profile xxxviii, Fig. 49), following its line; it is the Long Mountain ridgeway making for the lowlands (p. 116).

The change in scale, it will be noted, occurs directly the relation of the Dyke to the relief of the country changes; the Dyke is normally *small when the contour of a steep hill is being followed*, or when such a hill is descended diagonally, *large when it is descended directly*. It also tends to be large on the flat crest of a hill or ridge.

At the end of the park a magnificent sweep of pastoral and agricultural country lies before one; the straight alignment of the Dyke is resumed, the gentle fall and slightly undulating character of the country favouring this. For the mile and a half (2,980 yards) which separates this point from Nant Cribau park (Fig. 40), its course is nearly direct; so straight that it has been widely assumed that it follows the line of a Roman road. A handsome compliment to the man who wrought it in the Dark Ages, nearly 400 years after the

[1] The 1836 1-in. O.S. map, sheet 60, records its trace here.

[2] The 1836 1-in. O.S. map, sheet 60, records its trace here.

end of the Roman power in the West. The changes of direction, though slight (7° and 2° 30′) are sufficient to reveal the engineer's design; he set the course in three straight lengths, the first of 1,430 yards to a point near the Cock Inn, the second of 800 yards to the Nant Cribau Gaer, the third of 750 yards to the end of Nant Cribau park. The course into the hollow beyond, and over the Hem ridge, is not directly aligned.

To resume the narrative: in field 38 the Dyke is of full scale. At an opening the bank is seen to be about 8 ft. above ground level, its breadth about 40 ft. At another point near-by the scarp is 29 ft. on the slope (Profile xxxviii). The holloway continues to flank the

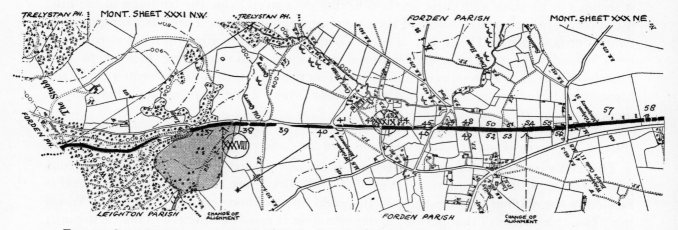

FIG. 39. Green Wood to Kingswood hamlet, in the parishes of Leighton and Forden, Montgomeryshire.
A portion of the 6-in. O.S. map reduced to 4 in. to 1 mile. For the significance of the symbols and employed letters, see Fig. 35.
(Reproduced from the Ordnance Survey map with the sanction of the Controller of H.M. Stationery Office.)

Dyke on the E., becoming shallower as the hill-side becomes less steep (see p. 115). In field 39 a large portion of the Dyke has been dug away (as shown on the O.S. map). In field 40 the W. ditch remains and has probably been widened; the bank is present, tree-clad, but of smaller size than hitherto. We are now at the foot of the Long Mountain slope (500 ft. above O.D.). The old road now swings across on to the line of the ditch, but an opening in the Dyke near the N. end of field 41 seems to mark an earlier crossing point. The bank is hereabouts of moderate size, +4 to 5 ft.

At the S. end of field 42 the old road leaves the lines of the Dyke, but a footpath follows it through a rich country-side broken up into small pasture-fields, for half a mile—as far as the Welshpool–Bishops Castle road junction. The Dyke has suffered at the hands of the farmers, having been much ploughed-down, but is still a considerable work easily traceable: its ditch is consistently on the W. The Dyke crosses fields 43 (see p. 115) and 44 as a broad ploughed-down ridge, the hedges being on the line of the ditch. The W. hedge of field 45 is on the bank and the footpath is mainly on the site of the ditch; the bank is denuded in the SW. corner of the field. A well-preserved portion of the (W.) ditch is present in the SE. corner of the adjacent field 46. Crossing a by-road, the Dyke is seen to breast the slope of the opposite field (47); its profile is characteristic of the lowlands where the plough has been at work—steepish scarp and gentle reverse slope. Between fields 48 and 49 a hedge-bordered footpath follows the crown of the ridge; hereabouts the view to the W. is limited, the ground falling gently towards the E. The hedge dividing fields 50 and 51 from 52 and 53 is on the lowered crest; the Dyke is wholly within fields 54 and 55, the W. hedges of these fields being on the counterscarp of the ditch—the latter is quite well marked. The farm-house adjacent to the Bishops Castle road is on the bank, the ditch being in the home-field, no. 56. Crossing the road, the ridge of the Dyke, undamaged, is seen in a small close, the ditch forming a pool; it is present also in the garden beyond. In field 57 the Dyke is ploughed down, but is still clearly visible; in field 58 it is almost completely levelled.

FIGURE 40. *Nant Cribau Gaer to the Pound House, in the parish of Forden*

A 5-ft. rise in the hedge bordering field 58 on the S. marks the line of the Dyke, and shows that the levelling to which it has here been subjected is of comparatively recent

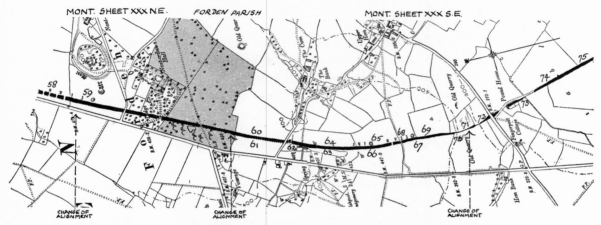

FIG. 40. Nant Cribau Gaer to the Pound House, in the parish of Forden, Montgomeryshire.
A portion of the 6-in. O.S. map reduced to 4 in. to 1 mile. For the significance of the symbols and employed letters, see Fig. 35.
(Reproduced from the Ordnance Survey map with the sanction of the Controller of H.M. Stationery Office.)

date. In field 59 the ploughed-down dyke is clearly traceable. Crossing the by-road which leads to Nant Cribau the Dyke enters a small enclosure, the W. hedge of which is in the ditch; it then passes through two fields, formerly park land and now rough pasture. The bank is gapped and damaged in places, but the (W.) ditch has not been filled in and the earthwork is still a striking monument. Descending a gentle slope the Dyke (much ploughed down) forms the boundary between arable fields; the W. hedge of field 60, irregularly aligned, is mainly on the scarp, the ditch being in field 61. Crossing a by-road, a cottage is seen on the bank; in the croft beyond a high and broad ridge is present, the ditch being in field 62.

From here onwards, up the slope of Hem Hill, the ground falls gently to the W. giving an ample field of view. For over 700 yards the bank of the Dyke forms the hedge boundaries of large fields; it traces a wide curve over the flattened crest of the hill.

Turning to detail, the scarp of the Dyke forms a steep slope in field 63, the reverse slope in fields 64 and 65 having been to some extent spread by cultivation. In field 66 the ditch is almost entirely ploughed in, but the scarp still measures over 20 ft. on the slope at favourable points. The Dyke now passes on to the flat hill-top, the course chosen between fields 68–69 and 67 giving a very limited field of view to the W. It is reduced to a mere hedge bank, and the ditch is filled in. Crossing the S. boundaries of these fields we are on a very steep scarp overlooking the Camlad valley; the line of the Dyke can be seen far beyond the stream, and, when the course is known, in the valley itself. The trace here requires careful description, as the remains of the Dyke for 1,300 yards though sufficiently evident are unrecorded on the 6-in. map.[1]

Down the upper part of the steep slope previously referred to the ditch of Offa's Dyke is on the E. margin of field 70; it then swings into the rough (enclosure 71) and becomes a modern drain bordering field 72. The bank can be seen in the rough; though levelled in field 72 its traces can be seen when the sun is near the horizon, and there is a rise in the S. hedge bordering this field. An unmistakable fragment of the Dyke survives in the angle between Pound House trackway and the by-road.

The Dyke is next seen in field 73 as a bank, 3 ft. in height, which ends on marshy land 20 yards from an ancient watercourse. Looking back, one sees definite traces of the bank in the garden of Pound House, in the correct alignment. Crossing the marshy patch, here 70 yards in breadth, the Dyke is again seen as a low ridge, +1 to 3 ft., following the W. margins of fields 74 and 75: occasionally the ditch, on the W., is traceable.

FIGURE 41. *The Camlad stream to the Montgomery–Shrewsbury road (and beyond) in the parish of Chirbury, Shropshire*

The Dyke fades out within a few yards of the present course of the Camlad; it can be readily picked up on the other side of the stream, immediately to the S. of the floodbank (field 76). Within 60 yards it attains remarkable dimensions having regard to its position on an alluvial flat, presenting a whale-backed ridge 33 ft. across and $3\frac{1}{2}$ ft. above natural ground level, which carries two ancient oaks.

The course of the Dyke for a short distance is obscured by trenching, by a pond (the Devil's Hole?),[2] and by watercourses, but the trackway which borders field 77 is on the flattened bank. This bank fades out at a second watercourse, but beyond the rivulet it reappears, on the W. side of the trackway. We are now leaving the floor of the valley, which is here over half a mile broad, and the change is marked by the increasing size of the Dyke as it rises up the slope, and by its reappearance on the O.S. map.

The recovery of this valley sector is of interest. It provides another example of the determination of the builders to leave no portion of the boundary in doubt. Under the most favourable physical conditions one can postulate, the construction of the Dyke across a valley the drainage system of which can hardly have been, in the eighth century, under control, must have offered considerable difficulties. If, moreover, a straight-edge be passed along the line thus recovered it will be seen that it is direct from the foot of

---

[1] The 1836 ordnance map, sheet 60, carries the line of the Dyke as far as the foot of the slope, immediately N. of Pound House.   [2] See the same map.

Hem Hill to the Camlad (a distance of 800 yards), and that the surviving fragments of the Dyke on the valley floor S. of the stream prolong, to the river, an exact alignment from (or to) Rownal Covert, a prominent knoll ¾ mile (1,350 yards) away. The two stretches are indeed almost in the same straight line, the change in direction at the Camlad amounting to 5 degrees only. The only noticeable deviation developed during construction was in the hollow at Rownal (enclosure no. 79), invisible from the sighting points.

To return to the detailed survey; rising from the alluvial floor (in field 77a), the Dyke is a notable feature of the landscape. A cottage in field 78 is on the Dyke, which then

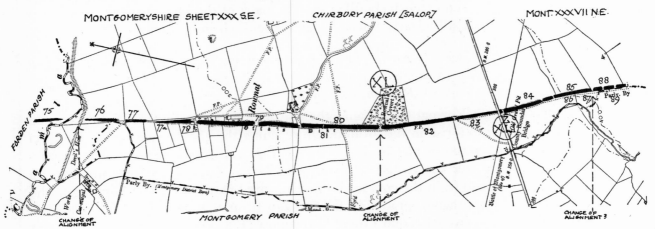

FIG. 41. The Camlad stream to the Montgomery–Shrewsbury road (and beyond) in the parish of Chirbury, Shropshire.

A portion of the 6-in. O.S. map reduced to 4 in. to 1 mile. For the significance of the symbols and employed letters, see Fig. 35. (Reproduced from the Ordnance Survey map with the sanction of the Controller of H.M. Stationery Office.)

passes behind a row of deserted cots with their gardens, as a broad ridge with traces of W. ditch. The gap in the dip at Rownal (field 79) is occupied by a water channel; it may be an original opening for drainage, widened in modern times. The W. hedge of this field is on the counterscarp, thus permitting the preservation of the W. ditch, which is, at its best, 6 ft. deep. The scarp is here 26 ft. on the slope, the whole work being very imposing. The Dyke then crosses a garden, and a partial section of the bank is seen in the adjacent farm roadway; it appears to be mainly composed of stony clay, but no stratification can be detected. Beyond the roadway the Dyke forms a narrow belt of woodland with well-grown oaks, on the W. of field 80; it is undamaged; the reverse slope measures 20 ft., the scarp 26 ft., and the W. ditch is present. The general appearance and scale is strongly reminiscent of Pentre-bychan (Chapter IV, p. 50). In the centre of field 80 the boundary passes for a short distance on to the scarp of the Dyke, and the unprotected W. ditch—in field 81—is under the plough.

The earthwork is equally fine in Rownal Covert (Profile xl, Fig. 49); the (W.) ditch is marshy;[1] there is a traffic gap on the crest of the knoll (see p. 113) from which the view to the W.—Montgomery and the hills beyond—is very extensive.

[1] The W. ditch hereabouts does not seem broad enough to supply all the material for so massive a bank, but there is no trace of spoil holes on the E. side.

The Dyke now changes direction through 10 degrees; it is much reduced in field 82, being in places a mere hedge bank; the ditch is completely filled in. In field 83 most of the bank has been carted away, the E. hedge marking its line; a hollow parallel and close thereto indicates the original breadth of scarp and ditch.

Crossing the main road, the Dyke is seen as a high ridge with deep W. ditch. A narrow gap marks the original crossing point of the highway, which has been straightened in modern times (Plate XIX*a*, and Profile xli). At the S. end of field 84 the bank has been lowered; in field 85 it is well marked but eroded by rabbits; the ditch in this area (in fields 86 and 87) has been extensively filled in. The bank of the Dyke has been ploughed down in field 88 but is still clearly traceable, as is the ditch in field 89.

FIGURE 42. *Dudston Covert to north flank of Lack brook valley, on the boundary between Wales and England: In Montgomery and Church Stoke parishes, Montgomeryshire, and Chirbury, Brompton-with-Rhiston, Shropshire*

The Dyke between Rownal Covert and the end of Fig. 41 presents a slightly curved trace correspondent to a rise in the ground. On reaching the 400-ft. contour (in field 85) it enters on a long stretch of plateau-like country (Fig. 42) which rises on a hardly perceptible gradient to over 500 ft. (a ring contour at Lower Gwarthlow) in a little over a mile, reaches about 520 ft. in the course of a few hundred yards, and then, dipping to the Lack brook, and rising again, gradually falls to 446 ft. at the crossing of the Caebitra (Caebutrach?) brook, a mile beyond Lower Gwarthlow (Fig. 43). The course is direct but sinuous, and the method of alignment is not readily grasped. The straight-edge reveals a change of general direction through 4 degrees in the neighbourhood of the 500-ft. contours referred to, the highest points reached (as can be seen in Fig. 42), and we have no doubt that the course in this area was laid out in two extended stretches of $1\frac{1}{4}$ miles from the 400-ft. contour to the first 500-ft. ring contour at Lower Gwarthlow, and $1\frac{1}{4}$ miles from the second 500-ft. crest line near Gwarthlow to the Caebitra.

A closer study of the line of the Dyke in the first sector between the 400-ft. contour and Gwarthlow yields interesting results. Though the line chosen at no point corresponds for more than a hundred yards or so with a straight line joining the two ends, the maximum lateral deviation from absolute directness in this long distance is only 30 yards (at Dudston Covert). It seems probable therefore that one is analysing a technical process of alignment identical with that observed in several of the preceding sectors; the engineering skill of the designer is even more manifest here (since there are no *dominant* sighting points), but the constructional work is less accurately carried out.

Turning to the second sector, the straight-edge shows that the Dyke approximates even closer than in the first to exact alignment; for 1,100 yards indeed the correspondence is absolute. This part is the S. half of the sector, a flat region extending from field 101 near the Ditches farm to the Caebitra (Fig. 43); the sinuous part is topographically more diversified and includes the Lack valley. Thus, on the same alignment the Dyke is partly sinuous, partly straight. The sinuosity must be in some measure due to the fact that the line of the Dyke on the N. flank of the Lack valley was invisible from the sighting point near Gwarthlow; discussion as to whether any other factors operated may conveniently be deferred (see pp. 118 ff.).

To return to the detailed survey: the bank of the Dyke in field 90 (and the ditch in 89) is clearly traceable; there is then a gap some 17 yards wide representing an old traffic line, and the Dyke reappears as a high bank forming the boundary of Dudston Covert. The W. ditch is marshy and, to some extent, silted up with peaty deposit; the earthwork as a whole is well preserved, but is not on its greatest scale. At the end of the Covert the Dyke passes on to parkland; in a well-preserved (and, for the area, unusually massive)

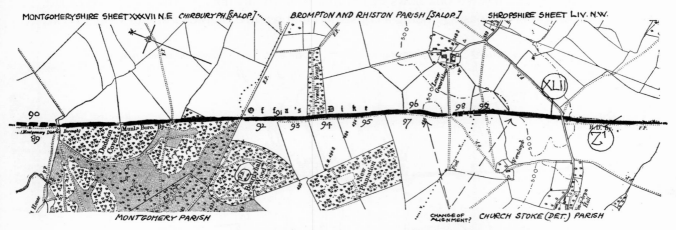

FIG. 42. Dudston Covert to north flank of Lack brook valley, on the boundary between Wales and England; in Montgomery and Church Stoke parishes, Montgomeryshire; and Chirbury and Brompton-with-Rhiston parishes, Shropshire.

A portion of the 6-in. O.S. map reduced to 4 in. to 1 mile. For the significance of the symbols and employed letters, see Fig. 35. (Reproduced from the Ordnance Survey map with the sanction of the Controller of H.M. Stationery Office.)

portion here[1] the scarp is 24 ft. on the slope, the ditch 4–5 ft. in depth. Ancient oaks and thorns are on the bank, which in places is much spread; the reverse slope all along this woodland stretch has been under the plough.

Leaving Lymore park the Dyke forms the boundary between pasture-fields 91 and 92–93, being much lowered by cultivation; the ditch is filled in. In fields 94 and 95 the scarp and ditch are fairly well preserved, being densely overgrown with scrub, and are full of rabbits. The scale of the work in this area is definitely smaller than at Rownal. After a gap the field boundary, usually on the crest of the bank, swings to the W. edge of the ditch; a short sector of the work (in field 96) is thus almost undamaged, the scarp measuring 21 ft. on the slope. In field 98 and the N. half of 99, the bank is levelled but still traceable; from here onward to the Pen-y-bryn Hall by-road the whole work is well preserved, apart from rabbit burrows and an occasional gap; it forms a belt of scrub between fields (Profile xlii, Fig. 50).

Crossing the road the Dyke dips to the Lack valley, in open pastoral country. On the slope both bank and (W.) ditch are very well defined, but when the level flat is reached the

[1] Opposite the triangular extension of the park (see Fig. 42).

former is much spread and gapped, the ruin forming a narrow belt of rough woodland (pp. 107-8 and Plate XX*b*).

FIGURE 43. *Lack brook to Mellington wood; on the boundary between Wales and England; in Brompton-with-Rhiston parish, Shropshire, and Church Stoke, Montgomeryshire*

The Lack brook, where it crosses the Dyke, is deflected to the SE., following the line of the ditch for a distance of 22 yards before essaying the passage; the remains of the bank can be identified here, despite the intermittent flooding of the vale. The actual gap in the Dyke through which the brook flows was probably originally not more than 12 yards broad, the narrowness of the passage being a constructional feature characteristic of Offa's Dyke.

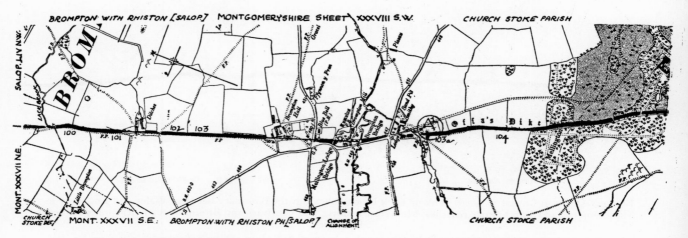

FIG. 43. Lack brook to Mellington wood; on the boundary between Wales and England; in Brompton-with-Rhiston parish, Shropshire, and Church Stoke, Montgomeryshire.

A portion of the 6-in. O.S. map reduced to 4 in. to 1 mile. For the significance of the symbols and employed letters, see Fig. 35.
(Reproduced from the Ordnance Survey map with the sanction of the Controller of H.M. Stationery Office.)

An adjacent tributary stream now utilizes a second gap nearby; both were doubtless canalized by the Dyke builder to pass at one point.

From the stream to the end of field 100 the Dyke is a low, flat, broad bank, well wooded; an excavated area adjacent may have supplied material for this bank, which is too bulky to have been entirely derived from its W. ditch, traces of which are apparent. In field 101 the Dyke is a high ridge gapped at the S. end, and there are traces of the W. ditch. The work is levelled where it passes by the Ditches farmstead; the yard shows a slight hump on its line, and the ridge of the bank reappears alongside the accommodation road. In the fields which follow, 102 and 103, the bank is present, the W. boundary hedges being on the scarp. The Dyke then enters a narrow strip of woodland, in which it is well marked; the W. ditch is to some extent ploughed in. All traces have been eliminated in the neighbourhood of Brompton Hall; crossing the main road the ridge is seen in the garden and orchard of the Bluebell Inn. A watercourse intervenes, immediately beyond which a mutilated fragment of the bank is present. From here to the Caebitra it has been entirely destroyed, doubtless when the adjacent motte-and-bailey castle was constructed (p. 115). A deflection of the stream by the bridge preserves the alignment of the ditch, as was the case at the Lack brook; immediately beyond the stream traces of the ditch are clearly seen; the bank then reappears, reaching its full height at spot-level 447.

There is a change of direction at the Caebitra through 8 degrees; the Dyke follows a sinuous but direct course by Mellington park and up the steep slope of Mellington wood. From the S. end of the park (Fig. 44) to Cwm, a distance of over half a mile, the course is practically a straight line, and was, it may be supposed, controlled by an observer on the slope of the hill which rises steeply south of Cwm hamlet. From the hamlet it ascends the lofty Kerry Hill; here the Dyke builder abandons the method of straight alignment and follows a course sensitive to the bold relief of the country, swinging to the W. to keep clear of the eastern-facing re-entrant (S. of Drewin) on the alignment hitherto followed (Fig. 44). The policy governing the layout of the Dyke is here strikingly manifested.

To return to the detailed survey: between Mellington Hall lodge and a nearby rivulet the Dyke is present, gapped and otherwise damaged; crossing the brook the W. ditch is seen, and, within a few yards, a well-marked bank which for over 500 yards forms the W. boundary of Mellington park. The ditch forms a drainage channel and is overdeepened, especially near the brook.

Extending due W. from the counterscarp of the ditch close to the above-mentioned brook is an outwork with S. ditch, ending near the margin of the gully in which the rivulet flows and covering its junction with the Dyke (see plan, Fig. 45, ii, and photograph, Plate XXI). It is less than 20 yards in length but is an imposing mound with a scarp measuring 24 ft. on the slope, and a crest higher than that of the Dyke opposite. It commands a wide view over flat country (field 103a). There is no satisfactory explanation for this unusual structure. The possibility that Offa's Dyke originally swung through a right angle at this point and that the direct course of the Dyke to the rivulet is a later cut, cannot be excluded. The bank in the direct alignment between the outwork and rivulet is of very slight relief. The overdeepening referred to above has left the ditch of the outwork high above the floor of the main ditch (Plate XXI); if the outwork be the original Dyke, the new cut must have been made before erosion developed; in short, it may be a contemporary alteration of the original design.

For some 75 yards beyond this point the bank is poorly preserved, having in part slid into the broad and overdeepened ditch. The Dyke then recovers its full scale, presenting a high rounded bank, gapped in places. The overdeepening of the ditch, which shows progressive diminution, ends in the N. corner of field 104. From the s to the i of Offa's Dike the bank, crossing a flat and ill-drained patch, is much spread and relatively small. As the Dyke rises off the flat its condition improves, and on entering Mellington wood it is a high undamaged ridge with a deep (W.) ditch.[1] This character and condition is maintained on the slope and on the upland as far as the 'Fish pond' by Mellington Hall, and this sector is a finely preserved stretch. At a typical point the overall breadth of the work is 54 ft., and the scarp measures 20 ft. on the slope.

[1] The sudden change has a physical basis; it is related to the passage from an ill-drained flat to a well-drained slope.

FIGURE 44. *Mellington Hall to the Kerry Hill ridgeway: in Church Stoke and Castlewright parishes, Montgomeryshire, and Mainstone parish, Shropshire*

From the 'Fish pond' to the SW. corner of field 105 the bank of the Dyke is in good condition, but the ditch is not well marked. For 50 yards, across a drainage line, the Dyke is much reduced; it quickly recovers its normal scale, and presents an undamaged bank with a slightly overdeepened ditch, in a belt of scrub, as far as the S. hedge of field 106. The Dyke is gapped at the N. end of field 107, up the slope of which it climbs. The W. ditch, extensively filled in, is in the arable field 108. The Dyke and the little Cwm valley

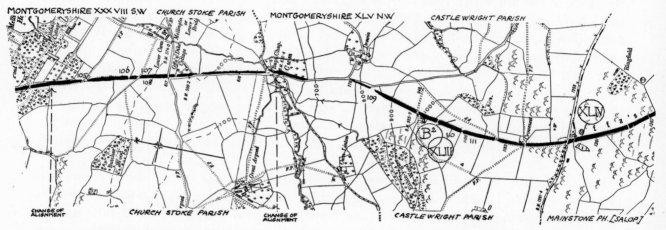

FIG. 44. Mellington Hall to the Kerry Hill ridgeway: in Church Stoke and Castlewright parishes, Montgomery-shire, and Mainstone parish, Shropshire.

A portion of the 6-in. O.S. map reduced to 4 in. to 1 mile. For the significance of the symbols and employed letters, see Fig. 35. (Reproduced from the Ordnance Survey map with the sanction of the Controller of H.M. Stationery Office.)

to the E. are now converging, and the field of view to the W. is very limited. A by-way is crossed, deeply eroded, but later than the Dyke, as its deflection at the crossing-point shows, and the earthwork is then accompanied by a lane on a switch-back course to Cwm hamlet. This lane is on the line of the ditch, and traffic has in places (e.g. at spot-level 616) cut into the scarp of the Dyke. In the hollow near spot-level 599·2 the bank is almost entirely eliminated by the curve in the road, but from this point onwards to Cwm it is very prominent. It fades out by the brookside, but presents a massive fragment fronting the road by the Chapel. A nearby cottage is on the ridge of the Dyke, beyond which both bank and ditch are seen in a wooded belt bordering the road. From this belt onwards for 300 yards—a steep ascent—the road is on the flattened crest of the Dyke; scarp and W. ditch are clearly visible beside it at the lower (NE.) end of field 109. The road now swings to the SE. and the Dyke, gapped at the point of divergence, is seen ascending the steep slope as a grassy ridge from which there are magnificent views up the Cwm-y-Lladron— 'robbers' ravine'—and across the lowlands to the N.

The photograph (Plate XXII*a*) and Profile xliii (Fig. 50) illustrate its general character on this hill-side; the shaly rock in which its (W.) ditch is cut yields a clean and sharp outline. The scale is moderate; a scarp 15 ft. on the slope is usual.

As the Robbers' ravine recedes the field of view to the W. becomes restricted and between fields 110 and 111 the Dyke is on a well-marked reverse slope. The field of view becomes less limited as the flattened crest of the Kerry ridge is approached. The Dyke has been damaged by cultivation near spot-level 1106 and in the neighbourhood of Crows-

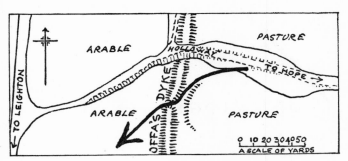

FIG. 45. i. The opening near Hope farm, Hope (p. 112).

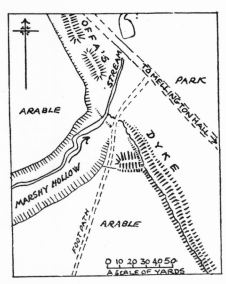

FIG. 45. ii. The out-work at Mellington Park (p. 103).

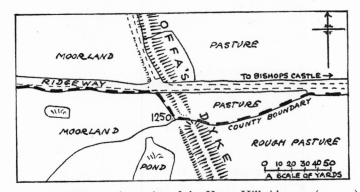

FIG. 45. iii. The crossing point of the Kerry Hill ridgeway (p. 113).

nest farm; here its remains are present W. of the house. From Crowsnest to the ridgeway we are on upland pasture; the Dyke is a high bank, the ditch being in use as a farm road. An opening, manifestly modern, permits the passage of the ridgeway;[1] in an arable field to the S. (enclosure 112) the ploughed-down bank of the Dyke is visible. Crossing the S. hedge of this field, where there is a gap, we are on open moorland. From this point to the end of the sector surveyed in this chapter—spot-level 1267—the Dyke is wrought on the grand scale so often seen on moorland plateaux, and apart from a modern cross-track or

[1] Yr Hên Ffordd, the old road (see *Mont. Coll.* xxiii, 1889, p. 95).

two is undamaged. At a favourable point the unusual figure of 27 ft. for the length of the scarp was recorded (Profile xliv). The views to the W. are extensive across a lateral valley of the river Unk; the main valley is visible to the S.

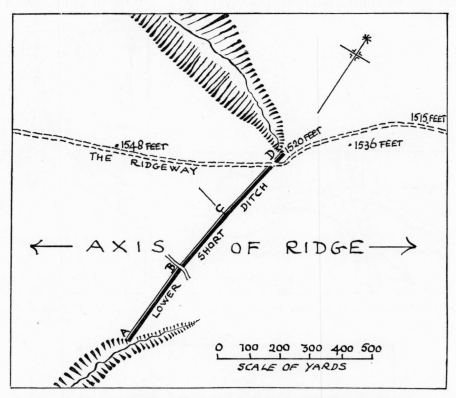

FIG. 46. The Lower Short Ditch across the Kerry Hill ridgeway, showing construction in three straight stretches AB, BC, CD (see p. 113).

THE PROFILE OF THE DYKE

Eleven profiles are reproduced in three figures, nos. 48–50; several have already been mentioned. One, Profile xxxix, represents the Dyke reduced to a low, broad ridge by cultivation. The section cut through this ridge (see p. 115) shows incidentally how impossible it is to determine, by observation and survey alone, the original form of an earthwork partially levelled by the secular processes of agriculture. The remaining profiles illustrate well-preserved portions of the Dyke in the county. Surveys were made where the Dyke is sited on hill-sides as well as on the level, but no example showing its construction on *steep* slopes was considered necessary, the profiles met with this year on such slopes above Leighton park being similar to those on Craig Forda illustrated in Chapter IV, Fig. 34. The Table of Measurements shows that the size of the Dyke in Montgomeryshire is normal, the estimated overall breadths ranging from 50 ft. 6 in. to about 70 ft., and the greatest estimated height of the bank 7 ft. At the points where nos. xxxvi, xxxvii, xl, xliv were recorded the Dyke was unmodified save by some denudation of the bank and silting of the ditch, and the overall breadths recorded, 54·6, 61, 55, and 52 ft. are probably a close approximation to the true figures. These dimensions, recorded many miles apart, do not vary very widely, and it may be concluded that the Dyke in Montgomeryshire was, on the whole, fairly uniform in size.

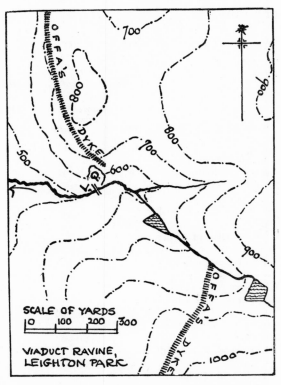

FIG. 47. The break in the Dyke at Viaduct ravine,
Leighton (see p. 93).

The Montgomeryshire survey confirms the conclusion arrived at in Chapter IV (p. 67) as to the importance of the soil or rock of and in which the Dyke is built in determining its present-day condition. Agriculture is a leveller of banks, a filler-up of ditches; in Montgomeryshire the Dyke crosses extensive tracts of farm-land and has suffered accordingly. The assaults of the plough, however, are capricious and selective, not universal; and since the whole course of the Dyke between Vyrnwy and Severn has been traversed without any portion showing original contours having been met with, the farmer cannot be regarded as the prime destroyer. The bank of the Dyke indeed, constructed as it is here of alluvial silts, gravels, and clays, could not be expected to preserve sharpness of outline. The hills to the E. and S. of the Severn valley—the Long Mountain and the Kerry Hill— on the other hand, composed of Ordovician shales, provide several stretches of the Dyke but little altered by the passage of time. A notable example of this contrast occurs near the

Lack brook. On the northern flank of the small valley formed by this streamlet, Ordovician shales form the subsoil, but on the floor these are overlaid by stony clays probably of glacial origin. The result is that an exceptionally fine and clear-cut stretch of the Dyke gives place within a few yards to a series of sprawling, shapeless hummocks, only a foot or two above ground-level. The point of junction of the strata is illustrated in Plate XX, *b*, it is on the right side of the photograph. The extent of degradation of an earthwork, therefore, is not a measure of its antiquity.

Table of Measurements

No. of Profile*	Position	Present dimensions of bank (estimated)		Present dimensions of western ditch (estimated)		Present overall breadth of bank and western ditch (estimated)
		Height	Breadth	Depth	Breadth	
		ft. in.	ft. in.	ft. in.	ft. in.	ft. in.
XXXIV	110 yds. due E. of spot-level 260 on Buttington–Leighton road (Fig. 37) .	6 4	40 0	†	†	
XXXV	200 yds. N. of N. end of Goppas wood (Fig. 37)	5 0	28 0	4 10	22 6	50 6
XXXVI	140 yds. W. of N. end of Offa's Pool, Leighton (Fig. 38) . . .	6 5	30 0	4 0	24 6	54 6
XXXVII	270 yds. SW. of SW. corner of Offa's Pool (Fig. 38)	7 0	37 0	4 2	24 0	61 0
XXXVIII	50 yds. S. of S. end of Leighton Park (Fig. 39)	6 4	32 0	†	†	
XL	Rownal Covert, Chirbury (Fig. 41) .	6 1	33 0	5 0	22 0	55 0
XLI	30 yds. S. of Montgomery–Shrewsbury road (Fig. 41)	6 0	43 0‡	4 8	28 0	71 0‡
XLII	40 yds. N. of crossing-point of road from Pen-y-bryn Hall (Fig. 42) .	6 2	32 0	3 4	25 0	57 0
XLIII	80 yds. N. of spot-level 1106, Kerry Hill (Fig. 44)	5 0	36 0	3 6	25 0	61 0
XLIV	60 yds. S. of Kerry Hill Ridgeway (Fig. 44)	6 10	30 0	5 4	22 0	52 0

* The numeration is carried on from Chapter IV. Only sections on fairly level ground are included.
† Ploughed in: therefore measurements unreliable.
‡ These figures are probably too large. The reverse slope of the bank has been ploughed down.

Throughout the sector the ditch of the Dyke is normally on the W. side.[1] The special constructional features met with on hill-sides in Denbighshire and Shropshire occur also in Montgomeryshire (p. 95).

PASSAGE-WAYS AND GAPS IN THE DYKE

The point made in Chapter IV (p. 74) that gaps necessitated by streams and brooks were, by the Dyke builder, made as narrow as possible receives confirmation in the Montgomeryshire sector in the valleys of the Camlad and Lack brook. There is, however, no visible trace of the Dyke on the alluvial flat of the Vyrnwy, 1 mile wide; this cannot be

[1] See p. 89 for notes on the ditch in the Vyrnwy–Severn area.

OFFA'S DYKE: PROFILES IN HOPE, LEIGHTON AND FORDEN PARISHES, MONTGOMERYSHIRE

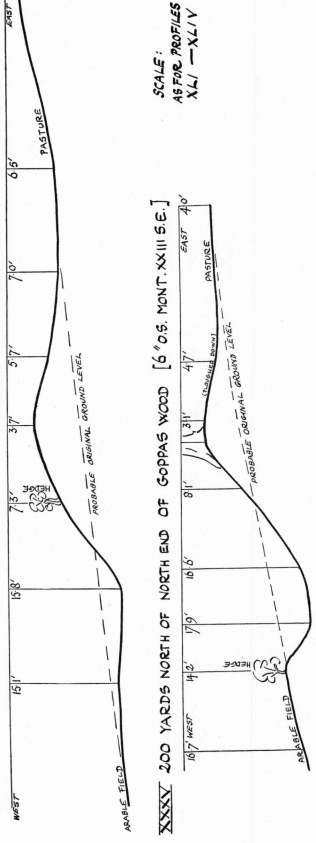

XXXIV 110 YARDS DUE EAST OF SPOT-LEVEL 260 ON BUTTINGTON - LEIGHTON ROAD [6" O.S. MONT. XXIII N.E.]

XXXV 200 YARDS NORTH OF NORTH END OF GOPPAS WOOD [6" O.S. MONT. XXIII S.E.]

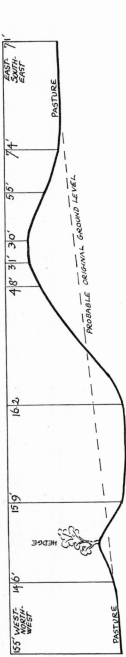

XXXVI 140 YARDS DUE WEST OF NORTH END OF OFFA'S POOL, LEIGHTON [6" O.S. MONT. XXIV SW.]

SCALE:
AS FOR PROFILES
XLI — XLIV

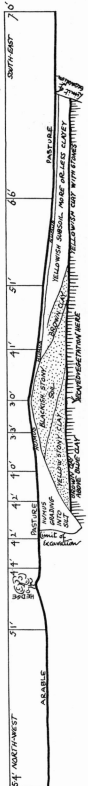

XXXIX 350 YARDS WEST-SOUTH-WEST OF COURT HOUSE, FORDEN [6" O.S. MONT. XXX N.E.]

Fig. 48. Profiles XXXIV–XXXVI, XXXIX.

OFFA'S DYKE: PROFILES IN LEIGHTON AND FORDEN PARISHES [MONT.] AND CHIRBURY [SALOP.]

XXXVII 270 YARDS SOUTH-WEST OF SOUTH-WEST CORNER OF OFFA'S POOL [6" O.S. MONT. XXIV S.W.]

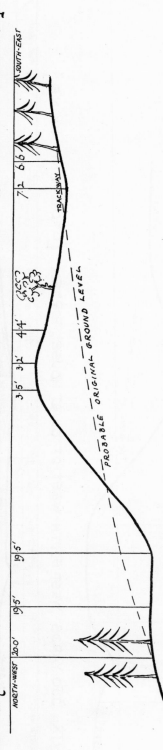

XXXVIII 50 YARDS SOUTH OF SOUTH END OF LEIGHTON PARK [6" O.S. MONT. XXX N.E.]

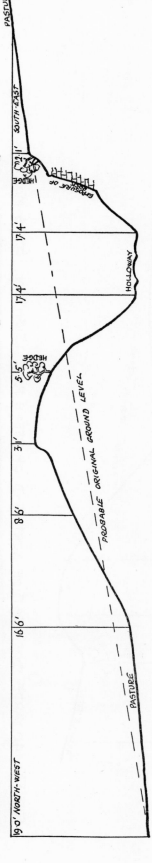

XL THE MIDDLE OF ROWNAL COVERT, CHIRBURY [6" O.S. SALOP. XLVI N.E.]

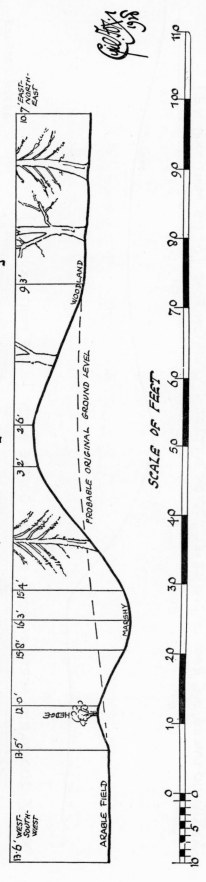

SCALE OF FEET

FIG. 49. Profiles XXXVII, XXXVIII, XL.

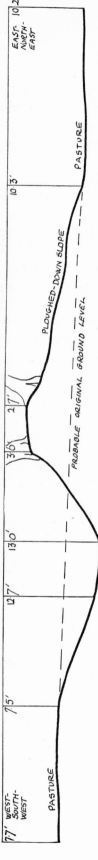

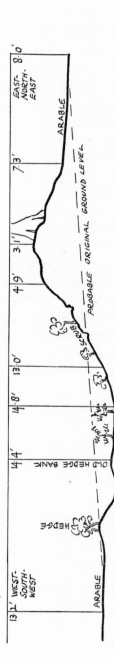

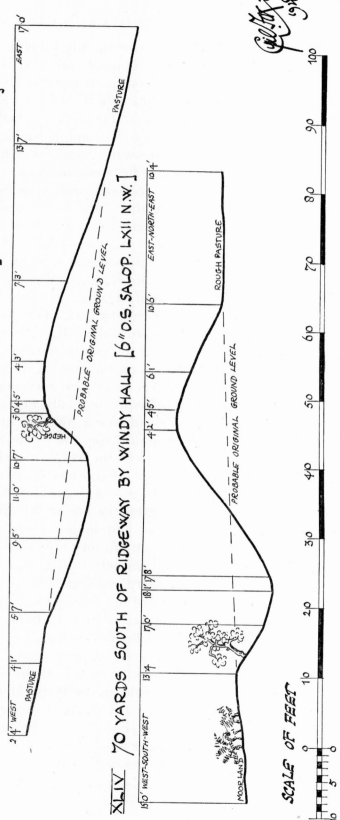

OFFA'S DYKE. ... AND ON THE BOUNDARY BETWEEN THESE COUNTIES

XLI 30 YARDS SOUTH OF MONTGOMERY-SHREWSBURY ROAD [6" O.S. SALOP. LIII N.E.]

XLII 40 YARDS NORTH OF CROSSING-POINT OF ROAD FROM PEN-Y-BRYN HALL [6" O.S. MONT. XXXVII N.E.]

XLIII NORTH OF WINDY HALL – 80 YARDS NORTH OF SPOT-LEVEL 1106 [6" O.S. MONT. XLV N.W.]

XLIV 70 YARDS SOUTH OF RIDGEWAY BY WINDY HALL [6" O.S. SALOP. LXII N.W.]

SCALE OF FEET

Fig. 50. Profiles XLI–XLIV.

regarded as surprising, for the whole belt is subject to floods, and may have been, in the eighth century, a marshy jungle full of pools and seamed by half-silted watercourses. It seems at first sight inconsistent that the Dyke thus intermitted near the Vyrnwy should be carried to the very bank of the adjacent Severn; but the difference in treatment seems to have a geological basis. The Severn is here deeply entrenched, cutting its way through glacial deposits of stony clay, and its banks, though at times flooded, are normally dry— very different from the water meadows of the Vyrnwy.

Openings for traffic are numerous. The majority are obviously of later date than the Dyke; of only two indeed can contemporaneity be confidently asserted, while the claims of a third deserve mention. The first is near Hope farm in the parish of Hope (Fig. 37 and Plate XIX*b*). A secondary road which leads from the Severn valley to the hamlet of Hope, 500 ft. above O.D., is crossed by the Dyke, being hereabouts a deep holloway: 30 yards to the S. of this holloway is an original opening in the Dyke. The two terminals are neither thickened nor recurved; they are not in the same straight line but have a slight set outwards (westward). Commanding the opening on the E. side is a bluff which may have been artificially emphasized, and a well-marked depression in the (pasture) field leads to the opening from the NE. This depression (which can be followed down the slope) is without doubt an ancient trackway; it can be traced far enough up the hill-side to show that it was the continuation of the route from Hope hamlet to the Severn valley, which was, from the point of junction onwards, subsequently deflected into its present-day course. The difficulty normally experienced of identifying original passage-ways through the Dyke is, of course, that the evidences of contemporaneity are entirely destroyed by long-continued use; the flanking terminals are cut back to widen the gap, or dug into for material to fill the wheel ruts. Here, fortunately, a new cut was made deflecting all the traffic, before the constructional features of the original opening were damaged. Figure 45, i, shows the gap, with the bluff which commands it, and also the present roadway; the arrow indicates the line of the original track. It was at first assumed that the depth of the holloway now in use would provide a useful indication of the extent of erosion resulting from traffic on a hill-slope in a thousand years, more or less; but inquiry made locally elicited the information that the road floor had been lowered some sixty years ago to ease a sharp gradient.[1]

If the view expressed in Chapter IV (p. 75), that 'the Dyke was intended to present a barrier almost complete, legitimate traffic between the two peoples concerned being limited to defined routes few in number', be correct, the opening at Hope must have linked important lines of communication.

On the English side the road leads by a winding route which conforms to the bold relief of the country-side, to the Welsh Harp, a meeting place of trackways on the Long Mountain, at a point 1,100 ft. above sea level, where cols approach the ridge on either flank and notch the skyline. This is the geographical centre of the great massif, which covers about 100 square miles of country, and must always have been the key-point on it. One of the trackways passing the Welsh Harp inn, moreover, was a highway into Mercia,

---

[1] There was evidence on the ground to support this statement.

linking up with the Roman road to Wroxeter.[1] On the Welsh side the gap in the Dyke lies opposite Welshpool, the geographical situation of which suggests early development as a trading centre.

The second passage-way (Fig. 44) is adjacent to *Yr Hên Ffordd*, the Kerry Hill ridgeway. This must always have been one of the most important routes from Wales to England, leading as it does from the heart of the Cambrian Mountains into Shropshire without leaving the high plateau country, and without negotiating a single stream (see Plate XVIII). It passes through the Dyke by a gap obviously modern; but a few yards to the S. of the point of passage, close to an ancient hedgerow, the high ridge of the Dyke abruptly terminates, presenting what is manifestly one flank of an original (and very narrow) opening (see Fig. 45, iii). The terminal is neither recurved nor in any way strengthened. The other flank on the opposite (N.) side of the hedge is in an old patch of cultivation and has been ploughed down. Here, we felt certain, was the original opening left for the passage of the ancient highway. Confirmatory evidence of the correctness of this view, almost amounting to proof, is provided by the 6-in. map, which shows that the boundary between Wales and England, coincident, for miles on either side of the Dyke, with the existing trackway, is sharply deflected from it near the earthwork, passing through the opening under consideration.

The third gap referred to is at Rownal Covert (Fig. 41). This is in woodland, and is narrow; that it may be original is suggested by its position on the crest of a knoll where the Dyke changes alignment. The terminals are neither thickened nor recurved.

EARTHWORKS ON OR NEAR THE DYKE

(i) *Defensive Works (Short Ditches) in the Kerry Hill area*

There is a group of works in the Kerry Hill area which, though situated at a considerable distance from the Dyke—the nearest is over 2 miles away—merit attention. The chief of these are the cross-ridge dykes which span the Kerry ridgeway.[2] Two of these—the Upper and Lower Short Ditches—are shown on the map (Plate XVIII) together with the line of the ridgeway, discussed hereafter. The Lower Ditch, the nearest to Offa's Dyke, may be described in detail. It presents (see Fig. 46) the usual characters of a cross-ridge barrier, bestriding the ridge where this is constricted by lateral ravines; it commences at the head of a ravine on one side, and ends at a ravine on the other. It is thus sited at a point where the traffic along the ridge can be controlled with the least expenditure of effort in construction and maintenance. Its total length is half a mile. It consists throughout of a single bank and ditch, the ditch being on the W. It is damaged at the crossing point of the ridgeway, but the opening was almost certainly simple, like those through Offa's Dyke. Thus we appear to have an earthwork skilfully sited by lowland folk as an outlying barrier against dwellers in the mountain zone, who used the ridgeway

---

[1] On Plate XVIII, the *h* of Wels*h*pool is the position of the Hope gap, the *M* of *M*ountain the junction of the trackway with the ridgeway; this ridgeway is shown as a dotted line.

[2] These have never been scientifically studied. See *R.C.A.M.*, Mont., Index 'Dykes'. This was written in 1929. For later work, including that by Mr. Noel Jerman, see pp. 160–8 below.

as a line of approach to their territory. When was the Lower Short Ditch constructed? Before answering the question a further fact about it should be noted. It is formed in three direct alignments, corresponding respectively to the N. slope, the flat crest, and the S. slope of the ridge, the whole work being as nearly as possible in one straight line. Thus the mode of construction is identical with that of considerable portions of Offa's Dyke.[1]

Cross-ridge dykes were not the only means employed by the lowlanders for dealing with the menace of attack from the Kerry Hill area. In the early Middle Ages the Bishops of Hereford had a castle at the lowland terminal of the ridgeway (Bishop's Castle) and they had previously constructed a 'motte-and-bailey' (Bishops Motte) on the ridge 2 miles E. of Offa's Dyke.[2] A similar mode of protection seems to have been used at an earlier date; 1 mile E. of Offa's Dyke is the small plateau ring-fort, known as Caerdin. It lies (as the map shows) to the N. of the present ridgeway; but the deep trackway which passes across the enclosure, utilizing the original openings, suggests that when it was occupied a good deal of the ridgeway traffic was deflected in order to pass through it. Attention is drawn to this fort because it possesses a feature by no means commonly met with;[3] namely that in plan it tends to be polygonal with rounded angles; in other words, its defences seem in part to have been designed in straight stretches. The possibility that we see here the technique of the Dyke builders applied to a hill-fort cannot be excluded; to state the case in another way, it may be suggested that straight alignment, being a well-recognized technique in Dark Ages earthwork, may well have been applied, in so far as structural requirements permitted, to hill-forts of the traditional form. The entrances to this fort are simple, like the original passage-ways through the Dyke.

There is thus some reason to believe that the Short Ditches of the Kerry Hill region belong to the Dark Ages, and it is possible that the Caerdin hill-fort is of the same period. Are we to regard these works as contemporary with or in any definite relation to Offa's Dyke?

It is a notable fact that Offa's Dyke is at no pains to cross the ridgeway at a favourable *tactical* point, where the ridge is narrow, such as that chosen for the Lower Short Ditch. Its line is selected on broader principles, those indeed to which we have been accustomed in dealing with the earthwork. Though the ridge is wide at the point of passage the alignment of Offa's Dyke thereover is such as to make use of westward-facing slopes; on the N. side that provided by the Cwm valley (p. 104), on the S. that afforded by the basin of the Unk. I am disposed to suggest, as a working hypothesis, that the Short Ditches—and possibly the Caerdin fort—represent the military activities of Mercians (in their defensive aspect) in the pre-Offan period when the tide of English conquest ebbed and flowed on the frontier; and that when the lowlanders had realized the limits of their power to advance and consolidate, Offa's Dyke formed an agreed boundary (not a defensive barrier) across the debatable land.

---

[1] Across the adjacent valley there is another similar work, the Wantyn Dyke, ditched on the W., and directly aligned for at least 1 mile of its course.

[2] Eyton, *Antiq. Salop.* xi. 194 ff. and 203.

[3] Not at all events in S. England; but here the practice of building hill-forts probably ceased at an earlier date than in the W.

(ii) *Other Earthworks or Constructions*

The only earthwork which stands on the line of Offa's Dyke in Montgomeryshire is the motte-and-bailey[1] at Brompton on the Caebitra in Chirbury parish, Shropshire. The Dyke hereabouts has been extensively levelled, but its line appears to have been immediately to the W. of the motte. It changes direction at the crossing of the Caebitra, but as a similar change of alignment is present at the crossing of the Camlad (p. 98), where no castle exists, the suggestion that the mount was a sighting point used by the Dyke builders need not be entertained, and we may regard the whole structure as a typical earthwork of the twelfth century.

The following earthworks near Offa's Dyke ought perhaps to be mentioned: (*a*) Crosswood Camp, an ill-preserved ring-work about 130 yards in diameter, is situated 550 yards to the E. of the Dyke at Rhos (Fig. 36). (*b*) The earthwork at Buttington church (Fig. 37), which has already been referred to (p. 90), may have been used to control the adjacent crossing of the Severn. It lies about 150 yards away from the Dyke on the Mercian side; there is no apparent relation between the two structures.[2]

The main road in Llandysilio parish (Fig. 35) along which the Dyke runs is called the Street; but no recorded finds or constructions associate the area with Roman activities.

THE EXCAVATION OF THE DYKE

The portion of the Dyke examined in this chapter included one part in which there was a possibility of finding evidence bearing on its date. This is the straight stretch extending from the S. end of Leighton park to the neighbourhood of the Cock Inn, Forden (Fig. 39 and p. 96), which is accompanied for part of its length by the ancient ridgeway which, at a higher level, has followed the long axis of the Long Mountain (Plate XVIII). At the N. end of the Mountain this ridgeway joins the main Shrewsbury road, at the village of Westbury. Now the Roman road from Wroxeter to the W. can be traced, straightly aligned, as far as Westbury, and it may be supposed that one of its objectives was the Forden Gaer (Plate XVIII), long known to have been a Roman fort and recently shown to have been occupied in the first to third centuries A.D.[3] If so, it may well have crossed the Long Mountain and is indeed assumed to have taken this course by the editor of the Ordnance Survey map of Roman Britain (second ed.). The remarkable straightness of Offa's Dyke from the point where the ridgeway joins it at the S. end of Leighton park suggested, therefore, that the Dyke was thrown up on top of a straight stretch of Roman road which led from the Long Mountain towards the Forden Gaer and the Upper Severn.

Since it was an easy matter to test this hypothesis by excavation, this was undertaken; a trench being cut through the ridge of the Dyke close to Court House.[4] The structure of the bank (which was normal) was revealed; its breadth (36 ft.) was determined; the lip of

[1] Marked 'tumulus' on the O.S. map.
[2] For details see *R.C.A.M.*, Montgomery, 145, and *Mont. Coll.* xxxi, 1900, p. 346.
[3] *Bull. Celtic Studies*, 1928, pp. 277–8; see also *Arch.*

Camb., 1927, pp. 353–4. The fort is of Flavian date.
[4] By courtesy of Captain Murray Naylor, owner, and Mr. R. L. Davies, tenant.

the ditch was exposed and the position of the ancient land surface was fixed (Fig. 48, Profile xxxix, and Plate XXII*b*). The subsoil was tenacious stony clay. No artefact was found and there was no trace of a metalled road under or adjacent to the bank.

The result of this investigation suggests that the lower portion of the Long Mountain ridgeway—that portion which follows the line of the Dyke—is not older than the Dyke itself. The depth to which it has been eroded in its course beside the earthwork (see Profile xxxviii, Fig. 49,) is thus the result of about 1,100 years' use, and represents 1 foot for every 64 years. Of few holloways can the age be computed with such high probability.

COMMENTARY

(i) *Course and Character*

The plotting of the course of Offa's Dyke in Montgomeryshire offers few difficulties. There are three places in which it cannot be traced. The first is the crossing of the valley floor of the Vyrnwy from Llanymynech church to Llandysilio church, where it was probably never constructed. The second is down the Severn valley for a distance of 5 miles between Severn House and Buttington, and the third extends for 450 yards in the Viaduct ravine, Leighton. In these two places it was, I hold, definitely not constructed; the river and the ravine respectively seem to have formed the boundary, the principle adopted— the utilization of an existing obstacle or natural boundary—being that already demonstrated in the Dee valley and on Llanymynech Hill (Chapter IV, pp. 53 ff., 66 ff.). Thus there is evidence that the Montgomeryshire portion of the Dyke was created by the engineer who was responsible for the part already examined farther N.

The Dyke is on the whole well preserved, the degradation of certain low-lying portions being due as much to the nature of the soil—glacial clays and silts—as to the action of man. The mode of construction on the steep hill-slopes in Leighton park is the same as that on similar terrain farther N. The ditch of the Dyke, steep slopes apart, is on the W.

Of the numerous openings for cross-traffic which are seen in the Dyke at least two appear to be original. One of these is on the W. slope of the Long Mountain and from it a road, probably ancient, leads to the ridgeway on the crest of this massif. The other permitted the passage of the Kerry Hill ridgeway, a route into and from the core of the central mountain system of Wales, the importance of which is shown by the 'cross-ridge' dykes which traverse it, by the hill-fort 'Caer-din' which commands and the 'Bishop's Mote' which controls it. That no special constructional features mark these passage-ways through the Dyke is a notable fact.

The structure of the Dyke is simple, a single bank and corresponding ditch; and only one unusual detail has been noticed. This is a short spur, ditched on the SW., on the W. side of the earthwork, situated near the entrance to Mellington park (Plate XXI).

Each portion of the Dyke which has hitherto been examined has presented problems inviting analysis and speculation; this one is no exception, for its alignment is in many respects remarkable.

(ii) *Alignments analysed*

The term 'alignment' in connexion with a travelling earthwork has a dual significance; it is primarily concerned with the plan and general layout in relation to the main features of the country, and secondarily with the mode in which the course is set out and the earthwork constructed from point to point within the directional limits thus determined. The Lower Short Ditch (Fig. 46) provides a convenient illustration. It was *planned* as a barrier across the Kerry Hill, and its ends were to rest on natural obstacles—ravines—which flanked the ridge. The shortest possible course between these fixed points being desirable, the Ditch was *constructed* in three straight stretches, the changes in direction—which are very slight—coinciding with crest-lines.

The map of the course of Offa's Dyke in Montgomeryshire shows three well-marked divisions. The first, from the Vyrnwy to the Severn, $2\frac{1}{2}$ miles, is very direct, and is a prolongation of the alignment from Selattyn Hill to the Vyrnwy, which was considered in Chapter IV (pp. 78 ff). The second ($5\frac{2}{3}$ miles) extends from Buttington to Hem Hill; the third ($6\frac{3}{4}$ miles) crosses the basin of the Camlad and its tributaries, from Hem Hill to the Kerry Hill. The latter two alignments illustrate the method of laying out the course in long stretches, with well-defined changes in direction at the junctions, which was adopted by the Dyke builder in the Denbighshire area, and they, in consequence, carry the demonstration of the unity of the work a stage further.

Hem Hill, on which the chief alignments in Montgomeryshire hinge, is the most southerly outlier of the Long Mountain massif, and dominates the Camlad valley. From this hill southward a straight course to the Kerry ridge was projected, but northward to Buttington the chosen line was less direct. The map, Fig. 52, shows that the shoulder of the Long Mountain, in full view of Hem Hill, was selected as an intermediate point; from the shoulder to the Quarry Spur, Leighton, a winding trace was imposed by the difficult character of the country; from the Quarry Spur to Buttington a straight course was again practicable.[1]

The choice of Hem Hill as a key position, and the high level on the Long Mountain selected for the northern alignment, are the features in the layout most needing consideration.

Military necessities could hardly have been responsible for the decision to include Hem Hill in the line of the Dyke, for the earthwork is not carried far enough forward, on the crest of the hill, to secure complete visual control of the Severn valley. The choice of the hill may, then, have been due merely to its obvious convenience and suitability as an intermediate sighting point. The map suggests another possible explanation. It is that Mercian settlers had pushed up the Rea brook valley (see Plate XVIII) and had occupied the S. slopes of the Long Mountain and the Chirbury area; the convex line of the Dyke across the valley may then have been designed to render their tenure secure.

[1] Here the course is described as being laid out from S. to N.; on pp. 90 and 96 the alignments in the same area are treated as being set out from N. to S. The major and minor phases of alignment seem to differ in just this particular, and the treatment in the text has a reasoned basis. [As will be seen, it subsequently became likely that the digging of Offa's Dyke was begun in the Mountain Zone; this footnote (1929) is the first indirect hint of the probability, see pp. 168 ff. (1953).

No explanation based on convenience will serve for the Long Mountain alignment. A course involving a climb to nearly 1,000 ft. has here no topographical justification; a more direct alignment, as the map shows, would have followed the 400–300-ft. contours along the easy lower slopes of the mountain. This easy course, moreover, provides ample views to the W. over the vale of Powys (if this were an essential condition).

This is a new problem in the survey of Offa's Dyke. It will be remembered that in the Oswestry sector (Chapter IV, Plate XI), the Dyke swings *westward* on to the uplands to include within the Mercian boundary Selattyn and other hills overlooking the high plateaux of Wales; *here* the Dyke is swinging *eastward* high up the slopes of a range of hills which was in any case controlled by Mercia. The alignment which was adopted offered no military advantages to the Angles which might account for its selection; had the Dyke followed the lower slopes, the security of Mercian territory (in so far as this was attained by the inclusion within the frontier of tactical and strategic points) would not have been lessened one iota.

In the same chapter (p. 81), commenting on an unfavourable lay-out of the Dyke near Pen-y-Gardden, Denbighshire, I suggested that 'the alignment of the Dyke in general may not represent, as I have been disposed to hold, the free choice of a conquering race, but a boundary defined by treaty or by agreement between the men of the hills and the men of the lowlands. The latter, one would say, although clearly the dominant partners in the arrangement, did not have matters all their own way.' A likely explanation of the alignment at Leighton then is that the King of Powys demanded, as he certainly received, a large portion of the westward-facing slopes of the Long Mountain. To implement this (presumed) arrangement, the engineer of the Dyke had to make a considerable deflection from his ideal route.

(iii) *Methods of 'setting out'*

The mode of setting out the Dyke, by the engineer in charge of the work, within the limits thus defined by higher authority, now claims attention. In the first place the trace was as usual designed to give, wherever possible, a wide view to the W. The course of the Dyke over the Kerry ridge (Fig. 44) is especially interesting in this connexion; the deflection to the westward, manifestly made to avoid steep eastward-facing slopes, has several parallels farther N. and is another valuable piece of evidence in favour of the unity of the structure.

The reader will have noted in the survey (see maps) that the course of the Dyke varies from absolute straightness between two mutually visible points to a winding trace governed by the relief of the country-side. Three types now emerge from the analysis:

Type I. Parts of the earthwork which are either demonstrably straight between two mutually visible points, or which were almost certainly so laid out, though now gapped and damaged.[1] Sectors thus classed occasionally show localized deflections from the straight line. These bends (Type I A) are seen to be confined to hollows

---

[1] It is important to note that direct alignment cannot easily be detected on the ground without the aid of a 6-in. map, owing to the unequal size and spread of the Dyke, and to trees and hedges which block the view.

or small valleys invisible from the sighting point, the exact line being thus only temporarily lost. (This detail shows that the exact alignment of the Dyke depended on no elaborate calculation, but on the simple process of setting a row of posts in line from a given sighting point to the next crest line (see p. 99, Rownal).)

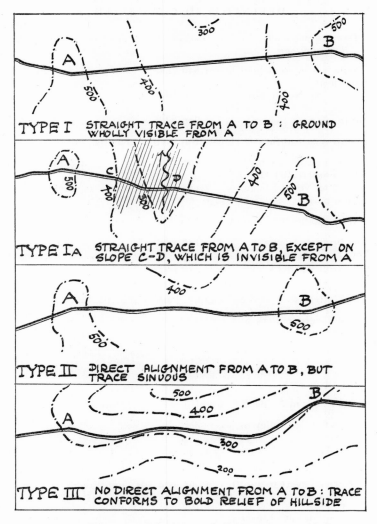

FIG. 51. Diagram of the types of alignment met with in Montgomeryshire.

Type II. Parts of the earthwork which between two mutually visible points are sinuous, but which at no point markedly diverge from the straight line.

Type III. Parts of the earthwork which, within the broad limits of general direction, are sensitive to the relief of the country-side.

The accompanying diagram (Fig. 51) illustrates all these types, and in the Table which follows practically the whole course of the Dyke in Montgomeryshire is analysed on the same basis; by reference to the maps the reader is in a position to check the generalizations.

OFFA'S DYKE: ALIGNMENTS IN MONTGOMERYSHIRE
DEFINED AND CLASSIFIED

Letters and reference	Terminal points of direct lay-out	Length	Change in direction	Character of work as carried out	Type
(a) Fig. 35	St. Tysilio's Ch. to School brook (near)	1,830 yds.		Straight	I
(b) Figs. 35–36	End of (a) to Neath farm trackway	1,700 yds.	7°	Straight	I
(c) Fig. 36	End of (b) to river Severn	870 yds.	13°	Probably straight	? I
River Severn (near) to School House, Buttington, 280 yds., not directly aligned?					
(d) Fig. 37	Schoolhouse, Buttington, to 300 ft. contour (near), Hope	560 yds.		Straight	I
(e) Figs. 37–38	End of (d) to North Lodge, Leighton park	2,120 yds.	13°	Sinuous. Maximum deflection, 25 yds.	? II
North Lodge to 'Viaduct' brook, 1,070 yds., not directly aligned.					III
(f) Fig. 38	Viaduct brook to trackway	140 yds.		Practically straight	I
(g) Fig. 38	End of (f) to plateau	170 yds.	24°	Practically straight	I
(h) Fig. 38	End of (g) to Keeper's Cottage	320 yds.	12°	Straight	I
Keeper's Cottage to S. end of Leighton Park, 1,400 yds., not directly aligned					III
(j) Fig. 39	S. end of Leighton Park to point SE. of Cock Inn	1,430 yds.		Straight	I
(k) Figs. 39–40	End of (j) to Nant Cribau Gaer	800 yds.	7°	Straight	I
(l) Fig. 40	End of (k) to BM 436·7, Nant Cribau park	750 yds.	2° 30′	Straight	I
Nant Cribau Park to N. flank of Camlad valley, 1,170 yds., not directly aligned					III
(m) Figs. 40–41	N. flank of Camlad valley to the Camlad	800 yds.		Straight	I
(n) Fig. 41	The Camlad to Rownal covert	1,350 yds.	5°	Straight, save for one localized deflection*	I
Rownal covert to 400-ft. contour, 970 yds., not directly aligned					III
(p) Figs. 41–42	400-ft. contour to 500-ft. ring contour at Lower Gwarthlow	c. 2,100 yds.	12°	Sinuous. Maximum deflection 30 yds.	II
500-ft. ring contour to plateau SW. of Lower Gwarthlow, c. 370 yds., not directly aligned					III
(q) Figs. 42–43	Plateau SW. of Lower Gwarthlow to the Caebitra	c. 2,000 yds.	4°	Sinuous 900 yds. Straight 1,100 yds.	II I
(r) Figs. 43–44	End of (q) to Mellington Hall and woods	c. 1,500 yds.	8°	Sinuous. Maximum deflection 25 yds.	II
(s) Fig. 44	End of (r) to Cwm	c. 1,000 yds.	15°	Straight	I
Cwm to end of Sector, 1,800 yds., not directly aligned					III

* This is in the hollow in field 79 (see p. 99).

PLATE XIX

a. A characteristic view of the Dyke, looking E., taken at point Z on Fig. 41. The opening on the left, probably not original, was the point of passage of the ancient Montgomery–Shrewsbury road

b. The opening in Offa's Dyke near Hope farm, Hope, from the E. Taken at point U, Fig. 37

PLATE XX

a. Offa's Dyke in Leighton parish, near the head of the Viaduct Ravine, from the E.
Point W, Fig. 38

b. Offa's Dyke on the N. flank of the Lack brook, looking SE. Taken from point Z,
Fig. 42

PLATE XXI

The Mellington park out-work, and its ditch, on the left: the ditch and bank of the Dyke on the right. Point A1, Fig. 43

PLATE XXII

a. Offa's Dyke on the N. slope of the Kerry Hill from the W., showing an opening made for farm traffic. Point B2, Fig. 44

b. Section through the bank of the Dyke near Court House, Forden: the extent of the cut as seen from the N. side. Point Y, Fig. 39

Results. The results detailed in the Table may be summarized as follows:

Type	Number of separate stretches	Range of length	Total length classified	Percentage of whole length of Dyke in county
I	14	140–1,830 yds.	7 miles, 500 yds.	48·5%
II	4	900–2,120 yds.	3 miles, 1,340 yds.	25·0%
III	6	370–1,800 yds.	3 miles, 1,500 yds.	25·6%

This summary presents points of interest. The high percentage of Type I, representing exact or approximately exact alignment, is remarkable. We see that in nearly one-half of the length of the Dyke in the county this technique was employed. Exact alignment has been noted in portions of the earthwork previously studied, but here it is exceptional in extent. What is the explanation? Exact alignment may well have depended upon three factors: country not of marked elevation, flat or with moderate variations in level, and free from dense woodland, that is country between 200–600 ft. above O.D. and over large uninterrupted areas either intensively pastoral or arable. The requisite natural conditions have not infrequently been present; but it may be that human activity was, in the regions hitherto examined, less widely prevalent. We may suppose that the patches of open pastoral country thereabouts lacked the reinforcement of a vigorous agriculture.

The portion of the Dyke under investigation crosses the upper valley of the Severn; this is just the countryside in which a wedge of agriculturists might at an early date have forced their way westward from the lowlands of Britain into the highland zone, the natural home of pastoralists and hunters, whose agriculture was comparatively limited and undeveloped. When the area is studied in detail from this point of view it is seen that straight stretches characterize the districts most favourably situated for early agriculture (see Fig. 52). We may here mention the fertile lands at Llanymynech and between the Vyrnwy and the Severn, and the lower slopes on the right bank of the Severn at Buttington; the warm SW. slopes of the Long Mountain; the Camlad valley; and the Caebitra valley. The distribution of Domesday vills gives a hint as to the probable centres of settlement in the Dark Ages in the area S. and W. of Buttington. Of special interest are *Heme* (Hem), and *Urbetune* (Wropton)—both in the Forden (*Fortune*, D.B.) area,[1] where the longest straight stretches occur. What was probably the original centre of another Domesday vill, *Muletune*, is the old site of Mellington Hall,[2] which lies close to the N. end of the last straight stretch in our sector, that from Mellington Hall to Cwm.

Alignments of Type II may now claim attention.

We have seen that the slight deviation from absolute straightness over long distances, in the alignments thus classified, makes it highly probable, if not certain, that the technique of setting out was the same as for Type I, that is, the shortest distance between two mutually visible points was chosen as the line of the Dyke. Why, then, was the constructional work less accurate? Some deflections on these alignments are due, doubtless, to irregularities in the ground; but the deviations are too extensive to be attributed wholly

---

[1] Extracted from *V.C.H.*, Salop. i, pp. 309 ff.

[2] Accepting the provisional identification in *V.C.H.*, op. cit., p. 343.

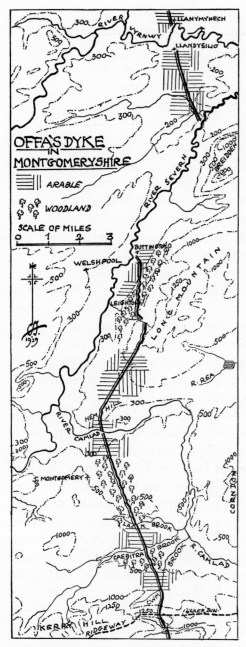

FIG. 52. Map of the course of Offa's Dyke through Montgomeryshire, showing suggested distribution of arable and low-level woodland in the eighth century. (The upper levels were probably moorland pasture varied with patches of scrub and woods.)

to this cause. There are two alternatives; either different and less skilful gangs were employed, or the superficial conditions in Type II areas differed from those in Type I areas. Is it possible that the former were in the eighth century densely wooded, untouched jungle, thus contrasting with the areas which it has been suggested were then cleared and settled? To drive a straight trench across arable fields is easy; in the woodland, a layout which avoids the thickest clumps of oak trees will commend itself to labouring men. Evidence in favour of this theory comes from an unexpected quarter. Of the three Type II stretches, two coincide today wholly or in part with large areas of park or woodland—Lymore Park with Rockley wood in one case, Mellington Park and woods in the other. The former certainly represents ancient forest, while the perfect condition of the Dyke in Mellington wood is good evidence that the area has never been under cultivation. The third sinuous stretch, on the NW. slopes of the Long Mountain, is even more interesting. It lies between the 300- and 500-ft. contours, levels which on the SW. slope are crossed by straight stretches of the Dyke. The line of reasoning which we are following provides a complete explanation of this contrast; it is due to the difference in aspect of the two slopes. In a country-side incompletely cleared by agriculturists, the S. slopes of the hills are, other things being equal, certain to be the first to be tilled, more extensively and to a higher level than the N. slopes.[1] The extent of forest on these NW. slopes in the eleventh century is indicated by the D.B. record. In *Lestune* (Leighton) 'wood(land) there 2 leagues long (which) is sufficient for fattening 200 swine'. The entry for *Edritune* (Edderton Hall, close to Leighton), yields similar testimony.[2] The forest was certainly not less extensive 300 years earlier. As for Type III, it is almost entirely confined to stretches where the relief of the country-side is bold, or which give limited visibility along the *projected* course of the

[1] There are geological factors reinforcing this selective process. The heavy forest-bearing clays of the glacial drift are thicker and have suffered less erosion on the N. slopes of the hills than on the S. slopes. (Information from Dr. F. J. North, F.G.S.)

[2] *V.C.H.*, Salop, i, pp. 325 and 318.

Dyke. It can be well studied in Fig. 44 from Drewin to spot level 1267 where the relief is bold, and in Figs. 38 and 39, from North Lodge to Viaduct Brook, and in Green Wood, respectively, where visibility is limited.

(iv) *Distribution of arable and woodland deduced*

I conclude, therefore, that the distribution in Montgomeryshire of alignments of Types I and II respectively represents roughly the distribution of arable and woodland in the eighth century on the line traversed by the Dyke. Furthermore, it is safe to hold that the boldly contoured country in which Type III alignments are found was, in the upland, rough pasture, with patches of scrub and wood; in the lower land, cultivated where the slopes are not too steep or inconvenient. The presumed condition of the countryside, then, in this century is as shown in Fig. 52; it may be briefly summarized as follows: the S. slope of Llanymynech Hill and the area between the Vyrnwy and Severn was arable and meadowland; a narrow belt bordering the Severn near Buttington up to the 300-ft. contour was arable, above that was woodland, above that again forest (waste); the short straight stretches at the 800–1,000-ft. level in Leighton parish represent, of course, not arable but open downland. On the SW. slope of the Long Mountain the rich lands were cultivated up to the 600-ft. contour, the whole area as far as Rownal being, except for Hem Hill, an agricultural countryside. From Rownal to within a thousand yards of the Caebitra there was thick woodland; thence to the Caebitra was arable. Passing upwards through another belt of woodland the crest of the Mellington Hall spur is reached, whence arable fields and meadows extended to the hamlet of Cwm; from here the Dyke sweeps in a broad arc up the steep slope (pasture and forest or waste) of the Kerry Hill.

If these views are well founded it follows that the survey of Offa's Dyke is providing information bearing on the early economic and cultural history of the Welsh border which could hardly on *a priori* grounds have been regarded as within the range of the research. It is, moreover, possible that the principles here enunciated may have a wider application. A study from this aspect of the travelling earthworks of England, which may be claimed as sub-Roman or post-Roman, might yield interesting evidence bearing on the economic condition of the country in the Dark Ages.

PLATE XXIII

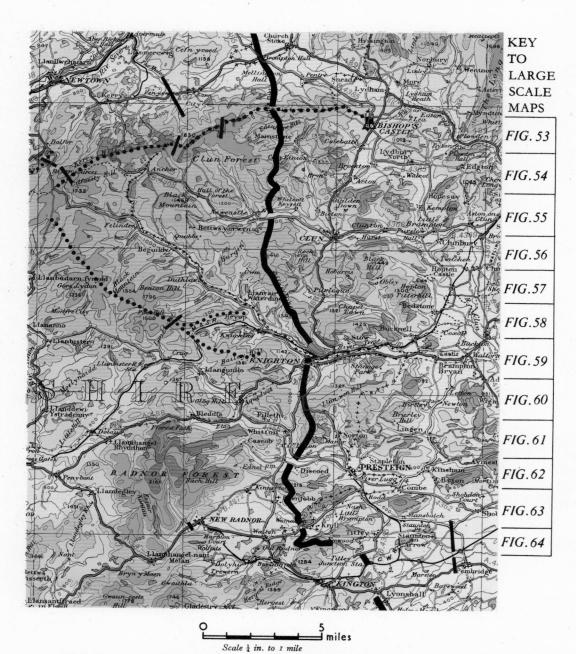

KEY
TO
LARGE
SCALE
MAPS

FIG. 53

FIG. 54

FIG. 55

FIG. 56

FIG. 57

FIG. 58

FIG. 59

FIG. 60

FIG. 61

FIG. 62

FIG. 63

FIG. 64

Scale ¼ in. to 1 mile

Offa's Dyke in the Mountain Zone—South Shropshire and East Radnorshire
(Chapter VI)
Dotted lines show ridgeways (controlled by 'short dykes'). Rowe Ditch is also plotted
See pages 125, 126, 127, 164, 278, 285, 286

VI. OFFA'S DYKE IN THE MOUNTAIN ZONE (SOUTH SHROPSHIRE AND EAST RADNORSHIRE) (1930)

IN this chapter the course and character of that portion of Offa's Dyke which traverses SW. Shropshire, E. Radnorshire, and the NW. corner of Herefordshire is surveyed.

The survey commences 400 yards S. of the Montgomery county boundary, in Mainstone parish, Shropshire, and ends at the 'Three Shepherds' on Rushock Hill on the boundary between Lower Harpton and Kington Rural parishes, Herefordshire, $1\frac{1}{2}$ miles S. of the Radnorshire border. The distance as the crow flies is $19\frac{2}{3}$ miles; there is a long stretch ($18\frac{2}{3}$ miles) to Herrock Hill, almost due N. and S., and a short one (1 mile) from Herrock to Rushock Hill, E. and W. The course taken by the Dyke involves a total distance of $21\frac{5}{6}$ miles ($20\frac{2}{3}+1\frac{1}{6}$); the actual length of Dyke visible today is nearly as great, being $20\frac{5}{6}$ miles ($19\frac{2}{3}+1\frac{1}{6}$).

The country crossed by the Dyke is part of a well-defined mountain mass isolated on the W. from the Cambrian mountains by the upper valleys of the Wye and Severn. The crests on the eastern fringe of this mass (with which we are alone concerned) range from 1,260 to 1,418 ft., the general level being about 1,100–1,200 ft.; but it is deeply dissected by drainage lines which run from W. to E. These form ravines with steep scarps (Plate XXIV) or narrow river valleys with well-defined flanks (Plate XXVIII), the floors of which are about 500–600 ft. above sea-level. The mass is structurally a high plateau (Plate XXVI), but denudation along the lines indicated has proceeded so far as largely to obscure this basic character. The line of the Dyke being across the grain of the country, it tends to present a switch-back course; but minor features, such as re-entrant valleys at right angles to the main drainage system, are seized upon to provide westward-facing slopes and more easy gradients. SW. of Presteigne the Dyke is aligned along the steep-scarped hills, natural bastions, which front the plain of New Radnor. Since the rivers are crossed at right angles, and the hills though steep show no rock-walls, there are no natural features which could conveniently replace the Dyke as a frontier line, and the earthwork as originally designed shows no material breaks in continuity. The extreme range of variation in elevation of the Dyke in the sector is 918 ft.: it crosses Llanvair Hill at 1,408, and the river Lugg at 490 ft. The rock structure of the country is such as to have assisted in the preservation of the Dyke, which is dug and built of Upper Silurian shales, save where it crosses narrow belts of alluvium in the valleys of the Teme and Lugg, and glacial gravels or clays N. of Burfa farm, in the Hindwell brook valley and on Rushock Hill. In the alluvium it has largely vanished, or was never built; in the gravel it is well marked, though much eroded by rabbits.

The maps, Plate XXIII and Fig. 69, show the traverse of Offa's Dyke in relation to the main topographical features. From Kerry Hill it descends and rises successively, to cross four streamlets which ultimately feed the river Clun and to surmount the uplands which separate their ravines. It then dips to cross the alluvial flat of the Clun valley (Plate XXVIII), and rises on to the high plateau country of Spoad Hill and Llanvair Hill. Dipping to a lateral ravine which carries a tributary of the Teme, the Dyke rises to the crest of Cwm-sanaham Hill and follows the continuation of this upland (Panpunton Hill) until it descends to cross the Teme valley at Knighton. Between the Teme and the next river valley, that of the Lugg, the highest point reached is *c.* 1,300 ft. at Hawthorn Hill; the Lugg is crossed W. of Presteigne and the Dyke follows the W. edge of the hill country between the Lugg and the Hindwell Brook at a less, but still considerable, elevation (Plate XXIX). The Hindwell brook group of streams, which, though tributary to the Lugg, have a watershed of similar area to that river, are crossed opposite the dominating mass of Herrock Hill. Up the ascending ridge of this hill the Dyke climbs, swings round to its S. face (Plate XXX), and passes on to Rushock Hill (Plate XXXI). The 1929 survey, and this chapter, end at the point where the Dyke commences the descent of Rushock Hill, making for the lowlands of Herefordshire.

The country traversed is agriculturally and pastorally of very varied character. The hill-tops, plateaux, and steep slopes are chiefly moorland or rough pasture-land (where the Dyke is frequently deep in bracken), occasionally woodland; but a good deal of corn-land (oats) is crossed at considerable elevations. The lower levels of the upland are mainly meadow and pasture; the alluvial flats in the river valleys are water meadows. Owing to the mountainous character of the country and the resultant scantiness of the population, the Dyke has been but little damaged throughout the greater part of its course.

THE LAYOUT OF THE DYKE

From a few salient points the layout of the Dyke in this country-side can be studied, and there is little doubt that from these—Edenhope, Spoad, and Llanvair hills, Hawthorn Hill, and Herrock Hill—the traverse was in its main outlines sketched by the chief engineer. Edenhope and Spoad are mutually visible; from Llanvair the gorge of Knighton and Hawthorn Hill can be seen; the latter and Herrock Hill are mutually visible.

The problem was not merely that of getting reasonably direct alignments, but of securing that these alignments should be such as to permit the utilization of westward-facing slopes, and the selection of the most convenient crossing points of rivers and ravines. The sequel will show how admirably this design was achieved. As Plate XXIII suggests, there were in all probability three major alignments.[1] The first extends from Edenhope Hill to Llanvair Hill; the second from Llanvair Hill to the gorge of the Teme at Knighton; the third from Knighton to Herrock Hill. Of the last, Plate XXIX gives a good impression. These alignments are *circa* 6¼ miles, 4¾ miles, and 8½ miles in length respectively.[2] It should be noted that the *highest* points of the hills which are held to have been utilized by the surveyors are not necessarily crossed by the Dyke, which usually traverses the west-

---

[1] The difficult character of the country, involving as it does considerable deflections from any ideal alignment, precludes certainty on this point.

[2] The major alignments previously studied are:
Coed Talwrn to Pen-y-gardden   .   8   miles

Pen-y-gardden to Selattyn	. .	7½ miles
Selattyn to R. Severn	. .	12 miles
Buttington to Hem Hill	. .	5⅔ miles
Hem Hill to Kerry Hill	. .	6¾ miles

ward-facing slopes[1] of such hills. The exact line taken by the Dyke here, as elsewhere, is secondary to the general layout. Consequently, a definite angle in the Dyke is not usually present at the point where the major alignments hinge.

The maximum deflections of the Dyke from the direct line on each of these three major alignments are as follows:

Edenhope Hill to Llanvair Hill, 283 yards.
Llanvair Hill to the scarp of the Teme valley N. of Knighton, *c.* 280 yards.
Knighton gorge to Herrock Hill, 1,000 yards.[2]

The secondary alignments of the Dyke are discussed in the narrative which follows, and on pp. 151–3.

THE COURSE OF THE DYKE

The course of the Dyke in this sector is set out on twelve sections of the 6-in. O.S. map, reduced as before to 4 in. to 1 mile (Figs. 53–64). Plate XXIII enables the position in the sector of each of these large-scale maps to be found by the reader. An attempt has here been made, by varying the thickness of the line which marks the Dyke, to indicate its varying dimensions.

FIGURE 53. *Nut wood to Knuck Bank; in Mainstone parish, Shropshire*

From the downland above Nut wood, where the 1928 survey ended, the Dyke follows a sinuous course, determined by the contours, along the W. face of the plateau. The W. ditch and bank are well defined and of moderate size; the latter is much eroded by rabbits. Near spot-level 1177 the Dyke enters Nut wood and descends, diagonally, a steep slope to the valley of the Unk. Here, as at Craig Forda (Chapter IV, pp. 61–62), it presents a small berm on the lower (W.) side of the bank and a well-marked ditch on the upper side. The Dyke is gapped by the shallow trackway to Upper Edenhope, and fades out at the lower margin of the wood. Crossing a hedge the Dyke can be traced (as an artificial heightening of a scrubby scarp) nearly to the stream, the eroding action of which has destroyed a few yards of it.

Traces of the Dyke are difficult to find on the valley floor immediately beyond the stream, which is probably swept by floods; but within 50 yards the bank is well marked. It is breached again near spot-level 997, the gap being 11 yards wide; changing direction, it soon rises, reaching spot-level 1105 within 200 yards.[3] There is no visible ditch on the valley floor but this reappears on the slope.

The layout of the Dyke here is interesting. At the point where the Unk is crossed, a lateral valley, dry in summer, meets the main valley, forming a Y-fork. A steep-ended

[1] e.g. on Ringhill (1,321 ft.), Llanvair (1,418 ft.), Hawthorn Hill (1,328 ft.) and, previously, Selattyn Hill (1,200 ft.).

[2] Westward-facing slopes for the Dyke-frontier are secured along practically the whole length of this stretch by the utilization of every available hill and lateral valley. This involves a very irregular trace, and illustrates the Mercian attitude.

[3] The Dyke is marked as unbroken, on this valley floor, on the 1836 O.S. map, sheet 60.

spur divides these; the Dyke is aligned from the edge of the Kerry Hill plateau on to the foot of this spur (near spot-level 997), and when this is passed a new alignment is taken.

Crossing a hedge at spot-level 1105, the Dyke, now on a steep slope, presents a striking appearance. The W. ditch is overdeepened, forming a ravine or dingle, but the scour being held up by the hedge there is a V-shaped flat of silt at the base of the dingle abutting on the hedge. We can now explain the absence of a ditch in the valley below; before the hedge was made the silt was carried down, filled the ditch, and spread over the plain.

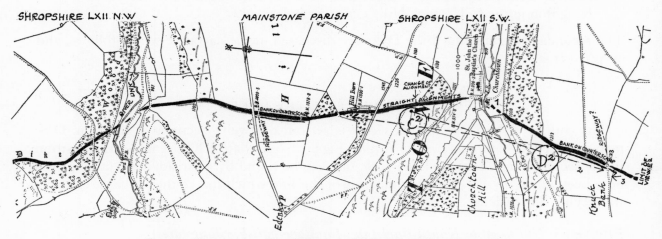

FIG. 53. Nut wood to Knuck Bank, in Mainstone parish, Shropshire.

A portion of the 6-in. O.S. map reduced to 4 in. to 1 mile. In this and the following eleven maps a thick black line ▬▬ represents portions of the Dyke clearly visible today; the *degree* of thickness illustrating the relative size of the work at different points in its course. An additional line close to and parallel with the principal one indicates the presence of a bank on the counterscarp. A thick broken line ▬▬▬ shows that faint traces of the Dyke are present; while a hair line —— represents the approximate alignment of the Dyke where it is now lost, as recorded on the first 1-in. O.S. map, or as indicated by a respectable tradition. A broken hair line — — — represents the probable frontier where the Dyke was not constructed.

Roman numerals in circles point to the exact position where the sectional plan with the corresponding number was made; letters in circles and arrows indicate the approximate position and direction of the camera when the illustration with the corresponding letter was taken. Certain fields and enclosures on the line of the Dyke are identified by arabic numerals.

Sketch contours — · — · — · indicate important natural features on the line of the Dyke not clearly brought out on the Ordnance map.

(Reproduced from the Ordnance Survey map with the sanction of the Controller of H.M. Stationery Office.)

As the crest of the ridge (Edenhope Hill) is approached, the view to the W. opens out; the overdeepening ends, and the Dyke becomes more sharply defined, presenting a high narrow bank and well-marked W. ditch.

Crossing a modern trackway at BM 1309·5 and an older, possibly original, gap (p. 157) immediately to the S. the Dyke follows a straight course up a gentle slope between arable fields for 250 yards. It is on the full scale hitherto characteristic of plateau country, reminding us of Baker's Hill (Chapter IV, Plate XIII), but is in places eroded by rabbits. There is here a small but definite bank on the counterscarp of the (W.) ditch. The view from the crest of Edenhope Hill (at BM 1378·8) over the Welsh hills is extensive, but there is dead ground in front. The Dyke now begins the descent to Mainstone and visual control becomes more complete; the bank is in a plantation and much dug over (fox-earths); the ditch, in a field, is ploughed in. Passing a cross-track, the Dyke bank, well preserved, forms a ride in a second plantation adjacent to Hill Barn; the W. ditch is well marked, the scale of the whole moderate.

Another track now intervenes, crossing which the Dyke is seen descending to the narrow valley of the Mainstone Brook, and, beyond, rising to Knuck Bank (spot-level 1313). Throughout this portion the Dyke is carried out on the grand scale, and is complete save on the valley floor; the factors governing its layout are manifest, as is the technique employed. There is no stretch in the Dyke hitherto surveyed in which this can be better studied, or in which the mental processes of the engineer are more clearly revealed.

The Mainstone valley is 300 ft. below the shoulders of the hills which flank it. The hamlet and church are sited where two ravines meet to form it; these ravines are separated by a high whale-backed ridge (Churchtown Hill), and the Dyke is aligned, as in the Unk valley, on the point where they meet, thus avoiding the switch-back which a straight alignment would involve, and giving the diagonal descent and ascent which are almost always chosen on steep hill-sides. Plate XXV shows the meeting point of the two ravines, and the Dyke rising to Knuck Bank; Plate XXIV, taken from the slope of the Bank, and looking N., shows the Dyke descending Edenhope Hill. The latter photograph shows a change of direction in the Dyke. The change coincides with a definite steepening of the slope: on reaching this point, the observer finds that the valley suddenly opens out, and that a straight line can be taken to the stream. The physical characters of the opposite slope are similar and have likewise determined the alignment of the Dyke; the change is at spot-level 1213 on the map and just above the wood in Plate XXV.

The reader will notice that there is one remarkable difference in the character of the Dyke as revealed by these photographs. Plate XXIV shows a straight (Type I), Plate XXV an irregular (Type II) alignment. This is a good example of the contrast between alignments of Type I and Type II stressed in Chapter V.[1] That the differences at Mainstone are due to surface conditions can hardly be doubted; the assumption that there was forest on one side and not on the other will, we think, be accepted when it is realized that the straight Dyke is on a steep slope facing due S., the irregular on a steep slope facing due N.

The analysis of this interesting portion may be supplemented by a few details. The ditch is on the W. throughout, but on the steepest slopes material is derived from spoil holes on the E. side. Below the 1,000-ft. contour the Dyke is much damaged, and the earthwork ends 12 yards from the NW. angle of the churchyard. Its definite reappearance is on the upper edge of the pasture below the wood on the opposite (S.) side of the valley; but there can be no reasonable doubt that the Dyke formed an obtuse angle at the 'Ford' where a rivulet draining the northern ravine meets the main stream. There are traces of the levelled Dyke in the lower part of the pasture field (no. 1) reinforcing this probability, and the inhabitants of the hamlet identify the 'Ford' as the point of passage.

Near spot-level 1213 (where the slope of the ascent eases), a rounded bank, some 15–18 ft. broad and 2 ft. high, appears on the counterscarp of the Dyke; it is present in arable field 2, and fades out in field 3, being thus present for some 270 yards. The (W.) ditch is unusually broad thereabouts, and the Dyke is well preserved, but gapped in two places, one of which may be original (p. 157).

---

[1] Type II alignments are of two kinds, irregular as illustrated here, or sinuous.

FIGURE 54. *Middle Knuck to Bridge farm. In Mainstone parish, on the boundary between Mainstone and Clun parishes, and in Clun parish, Shropshire*

The Dyke now descends an easy slope to cross a small dingle; here the ditch has been ploughed in. The necessity for crossing this drainage channel high up has determined the alignment of the Dyke, which here changes direction slightly, making for Hergan.

From Hergan to the river Clun, a stretch of over 2 miles, the engineer of the Dyke found, as we shall see, convenient western-facing slopes on which to align it; but the selection of this advantageous route involved him in difficulties. Between the crossing-point of the Mainstone brook, already fixed by geographical necessities, and Hergan, the upland has a definite eastward trend, as Plate XXVI shows. He took the most direct line possible, and did not waste labour or time laying out a traverse which would take advantage of any ground slightly less unfavourable. Thus, only the dingle to which reference has already been made and the Tack wood ravine by Hergan (see map) were taken into consideration in setting out the Dyke, which presents two long alignments. One was from Mainstone valley to the dingle, the second from the dingle to the head of the ravine. This was not carried to its natural termination on the col which links Hergan Hill to the upland we are now on, for reasons which will be considered later. Both these alignments are direct, the second remarkably so; the maximum deviation appears to be less than 20 yards in a stretch of over 900 yards in which one (small) valley is crossed.

To return to detail: there is evidence to show that the original breadth of the water gap at the Middle Knuck dingle was only 14 ft., but the opening is now much wider, and the construction of the Dyke has created a small marshy flat on the upper side. Beyond the dingle the Dyke forms a well-marked but damaged bank; it is gapped in the neighbourhood of Middle Knuck farm, but its line can easily be recovered; all the older farm buildings are to the E. of it. At the plantation immediately S. of the farm the Dyke is again undamaged; between fields 5 and 6 (rough pasture) it descends a steepish slope to a small hollow down which a rivulet runs.

The gap at the stream is only 28 ft. wide, and the Dyke, crossing a narrow flat (field 7), rises sharply through Eaton's coppice; it is of moderate scale with a well-marked W. ditch; this is ploughed out in field 8. A patch of moorland (enclosure 9) follows, across which the Dyke presents a high narrow ridge as on the N. slope of Kerry Hill (Chapter V, Plate XXII*a*). The overall breadth here is 43 ft., the scarp 15 ft. on the slope.

From the end of field 9 the Dyke, fairly well preserved, descends a gentle slope to the head of Tack wood ravine, and, leaving the alignment which it has followed so closely, swings round the head of the ravine to join up at a right-angle with the Hergan portion. This short link shows three gaps, of which the middle one (that on a parish boundary) may be original.

The Dyke on the W. slope of Hergan Hill is remarkable. It is a massive work (Profile XLV, Fig. 65) and shows a high bank on the counterscarp. It terminates above Tack wood ravine, where the ends of both main and secondary banks are turned through a right angle; the former is then in line with the bank of the portion we have been describing (though a small opening separates them); the latter ends abruptly, as is shown on Plate

XXVI. We can here study the junction of two constructional techniques. This junction is awkward and incomplete; the builders were apparently indifferent, and made no attempt to disguise it (see p. 153 below).

The extent and character of the country over which the different technique (the counterscarp bank) was here employed may now be considered. The Dyke is aligned across the col (1,186 ft.) and then commences a descent following the curve of the Hergan mass on its W. and SW. face (Plate XXVII) along the southerly of the two valleys which define and isolate it, as far as the Newcastle–Mardu road; here the valley floor is crossed, at 818·9 ft. above sea-level, and hereabouts the peculiar feature we are discussing, which

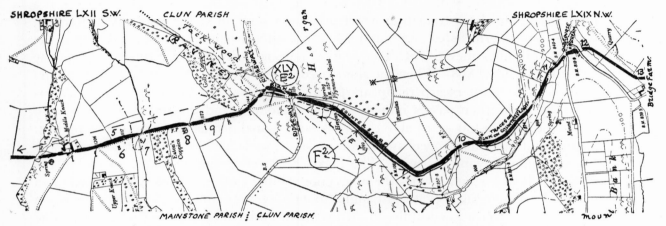

FIG. 54. Middle Knuck to Bridge farm. In Mainstone parish, on the boundary between Mainstone and Clun parishes, and in Clun parish, Shropshire.

A portion of the 6-in. O.S. map reduced to 4 in. to 1 mile. For the significance of the symbols and employed letters, see Fig. 53. (Reproduced from the Ordnance Survey map with the sanction of the Controller of H.M. Stationery Office.)

is less and less marked as we proceed southwards, ends. Viewed in reverse, the Dyke thus constructed traverses a geographical unit; it follows the W. face of a hill ascending to the head of the little valley which defines it, and then, crossing the col and refusing the descent on the further side, ends.

To return to the detailed survey. The Dyke presents a nearly straight alignment across the col and down the slope to Hergan (a cottage holding) and Ffynnon-y-saint, which wells out of the bank. It thus provides an example on a small scale (330 yards) of such alignment on a convex surface rarely seen on the Dyke. The great bank, 23 ft. on the slope at the col, is partly built of material taken from the upper (E.) side. It is gapped by an ancient ridgeway,[1] and near this, at spot-level 1186, by a modern road; down the slope the ditch forms a trackway to the homestead. The Dyke is much damaged near the house, but beyond it is in good condition, smaller than on the col, but as large as it ever is on a

[1] The gap is too wide and has been too much used to permit decision as to whether it is original. But it probably is, for the col provides the only upland line of approach to the Hergan Hill area. Traffic at another nearby point—the angle—has produced a ridged track-way manifestly unrelated to the constructions we are now considering. This packhorse traffic has, moreover, ridged the Dyke at the crossing-place in a curious manner, as is shown in Plate XXVI.

steep slope. Plate XXVII illustrates its character, and, though the lighting (early after-noon) did not emphasize the counterscarp bank, this is clearly seen in the centre. Crossing open pasture fields, on a new alignment direct but not quite straight, the Dyke turns abruptly round the spur seen on the right-hand side of the photograph. The counterscarp bank is maintained until the Dyke descends steeply and directly to cross a small lateral re-entrant (field 10).

As usual in such cases, it is ditched on both sides, while on the narrow flat floor it is a high bank, gapped, with W. ditch. Rising sharply it recovers its commanding position on the W. face of the valley. Here it shows the usual characters for such country—upper berm and lower ditch—with a slight bank on the counterscarp. The slope steepens in a scrubby waste, and by a transition which has been seen on Craig Forda (Chapter IV, p. 61) the upper berm fades away, and the lower ditch becomes the upper berm of the Dyke as it continues its descent. The process here is obscured by a quarry and house ruins (E. of spot-level 868). When the slope become less steep (below the 900-ft. contour) the bank on the counterscarp reappears for a few yards—and for the last time in this stretch. The Dyke then passes into a meadow (field 11), and diagonally across a farm roadway, ending as a low scarp above a brook, all original details of technique being lost.

At this point our valley meets another at an acute angle, also with its little stream; the two streams join, flowing eastward. The Dyke, however, swinging round the end of the spur (Mount Bank) which divides them, ascends the flank of the second valley to its head (near Cefn Bronydd, Fig. 55) at right angles to its previous course; this valley was chosen because it leads, over a low saddle, to a convenient embayment of the Clun valley. The Dyke, in fact, from the Mardu road to the Clun valley clings to the W. slopes of Graig Hill (1,220) as it previously clung to the W. slopes of Hergan; and this alignment gives consistently wide views to the W.

To resume the narrative: the Dyke is carried across the foot of the Mount Bank spur as a high ridge. Its construction blocked the natural course of the northern stream (the pre-Offan channel of which is still apparent), deflecting the waters into its ditch, which is consequently very deep and steep-sided. The present junction of the streams is 100 yards above the original watersmeet. There is no trace of the earthwork on the narrow marshy flat between the Newcastle–Mardu road and the southern stream, but on the farther bank it is clearly visible (in field 12). It passes diagonally up the slope much ploughed down and very straight, and is present in the home-field (no. 13) of Bridge farm as a high rounded ridge with W. ditch, gapped in two places. There is no bank on the counterscarp.

FIGURE 55. *Bridge farm to N. slope of Spoad Hill, in Clun parish, Shropshire*

The bank of the Dyke, extending upwards across rough moorland beyond Bridge farm, is clearly visible, the maintenance of height above the steeply rising valley floor being a notable feature of the layout, as in the Hergan section. In field 14 the Dyke is spread and somewhat shapeless, owing to the wetness of the slope; in the next field (no. 15) it is larger and the W. ditch is well marked. There is a narrow gap in the SW. corner of this field, probably original, which permits the drainage from a boggy patch to ooze through.

In field 16 the Dyke is very massive, and the bank is mainly built up with material from spoil holes on the upper (E.) side. Rough pasture land now gives place to arable, and the Dyke forms a steep balk or linchet between ploughed fields (no. 17). Beyond this, it passes through a grove of pines as a broad rounded bank on the edge of the plateau-like crest of Graig Hill, here overlooking the Clun valley embayment already mentioned; it is built up from spoil holes on the E. side, the lower (W.) ditch being a mere berm. A steep dip—by s of Offa's—follows, the construction of the Dyke on slope and floor being exactly that described on p. 132 (field 10). Passing upwards and on to open downland (enclosure 18),

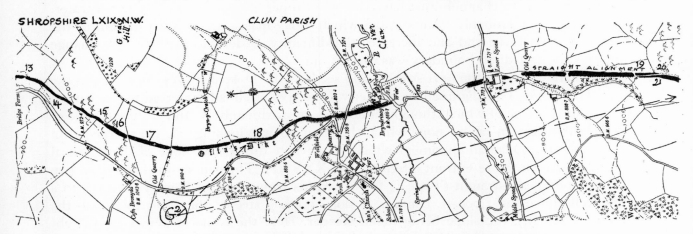

FIG. 55. Bridge farm to N. slope of Spoad Hill, in Clun parish, Shropshire.
A portion of the 6-in. O.S. map reduced to 4 in. to 1 mile. For the significance of the symbols and employed letters, see Fig. 53.
(Reproduced from the Ordnance Survey map with the sanction of the Controller of H.M. Stationery Office.)

the Dyke is seen as a wave on the steep slope, having been levelled at some time not very recent. As one passes on to a swell of the hill at the S. end of this field, the Clun valley opens out, affording magnificent views, and the Dyke is seen ascending its southern slopes (see Plate XXVIII, which shows also, on the left, the Dyke in enclosure 18).

The Dyke (now much more clearly defined) commences its descent, across downland; much of the material is obtained from spoil holes on the E. side, but the W. ditch is present. It passes through an enclosure by BM 803·4 as a well-wooded green ridge with a deep W. ditch, and after a road is crossed it is seen in the home-field of Bryndrinog farm as a magnificent rampart, tree-clad, with W. ditch. The alignment chosen here gives wide views to the W. There is a fragment by the farm buildings, and the remains of the bank are visible in section on the river's edge.

No trace of the earthwork is visible across the alluvial flat of the Clun valley, but when the upland begins again beyond the river it reappears, presenting a broad bank levelled to form a trackway, and a very broad W. ditch. These are lost at Lower Spoad, but reappear in the orchard N. of the 'Old Quarry'.

The layout of the Dyke across the valley is interesting. From the point where the slope eases (the road angle by BM 803·4), an alignment was taken on to the point where the steep slope begins on the other side of the river, by the 'Old Quarry', 850 yards away.

Surviving remains of the Dyke between these points are practically in the same straight line;[1] these remains, moreover, show that it was on a large scale. The nature of the visible frontier across the alluvial flat is something of a problem. From Bryndrinog to spot-level 663 the river Clun was almost certainly the boundary. From spot level 663 to the rising ground where the Dyke reappears a shallow ditch, emptying into the river, is, like the river, approximately in the correct alignment. This ditch appears originally to have been fed by a rivulet which, rising high up on Spoad Hill, passed through Lower Spoad buildings and down the ditch of the Dyke at BM 713·1. Before Lower Spoad was built (seventeenth century?), its channel must have carried at times a heavy volume of storm water. The resultant silt probably formed a fan which today masks the original margin of the alluvium by the Dyke-end and increases the difficulty of determining how the change from Dyke to wet-ditch boundary was carried out.

We may now turn to the next stretch, and see how the Dyke achieves the ascent to the Spoad Hill ridge. The alignment is masterly. The rivulet already referred to has carved out a ravine the line of which, though sinuous, is approximately N. and S.; the E. side of this gave the western-facing slope which the engineer was looking for. He succeeded in securing for the Dyke an alignment which, while very direct, lost none of the practical advantages which the re-entrant offered (Plate XXVIII). The course was laid out in two portions: one dead straight (Type I) for 610 yards from the Old Quarry (800 ft.) to a point well above the 1,000-ft. contour, a slope not too steep;[2] the other thence to the plateau (1,300 ft.), the slope being much steeper. Here the course taken is on a slight curve, following the westward-facing scarp of the dingle up to the point where the latter fades out near the plateau edge (Fig. 56 and Plate XXVIII). The Dyke is a magnificent work from valley floor to crest, and is throughout ditched on the W.

A few details may be added: From the Old Quarry upwards across pasture land, the Dyke is steep-sided and narrow-crested, measuring in two places 24 ft. on the scarp. The most perfectly preserved stretch ends at the gap in field 19. Beyond this gap a track leads on to the bank, partially obscuring its structure; then the crest of the bank forms a hedge boundary between fields 20 and 21, and the (W.) ditch is boggy.

The change of alignment referred to takes place in these fields; the Dyke now climbs more steeply through scrubby and boggy land.

FIGURE 56. *Scotland farm to Llanvair Hill. In Clun and Llanfair Waterdine parishes, Shropshire*

NE. of Scotland farm the re-entrant which we have been following becomes a narrow ravine deeply bitten into the hill-side; the Dyke, on its E. face, is a flat berm or a bank, steep-scarped, with a lower ditch usually small, the whole most impressive: at one point, opposite the farm, the scarp is 29 ft. in length. As the ravine closes up near the crest (Spoad Hill) the Dyke shows characteristic changes, becoming a high ridge with W. ditch,

---

[1] Possibly two alignments meeting at river as at the Camlad (Chapter V, p. 98).

[2] The slight curve in the centre of this straight alignment is due to the shoulder of the hill preventing complete visibility.

and with some evidence of spoil holes on the E. side. Spoad Hill is a level plateau, which commences in the pine-wood by *H* of *H*ill; the Dyke crosses it as a massive and finely preserved bank ditched on the W. There is no evidence of an original gap for the Spoad Hill ridgeway (p. 169), but the modern road may occupy its site. There is a narrow gap at *W* (*W*ell) on the map; here is a marshy hollow, the source of a rivulet which, running E., has determined the curve of the Dyke's alignment. A fine and straight stretch (Type I) follows, 370 yards in length; just S. of BM 1309·4, the scarp of the Dyke measures 24 ft., the overall breadth 63 ft. This stretch ends on the slope of the little valley which divides

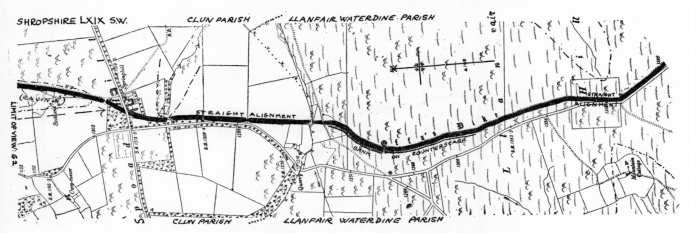

FIG. 56. Scotland farm to Llanvair Hill. In Clun and Llanfair Waterdine parishes, Shropshire.
A portion of the 6-in. O.S. map reduced to 4 in. to 1 mile. For the significance of the symbols and employed letters, see Fig. 53.
(Reproduced from the Ordnance Survey map with the sanction of the Controller of H.M. Stationery Office.)

Spoad Hill and its cultivated fields from the Llanvair Hill moorland. The gap at the brook is as narrow as possible.

The Dyke then breasts the opposing slope of Llanvair Hill; it is massive, and for 700 yards has a bank on the counterscarp; this bank ends at *i* of D*i*ke. There is a gap, which looks modern, at the centre of this stretch. When the level upland (1,350–1,400 ft.) is reached, the Dyke is less massive, but it is a fine structure and singularly perfect. The angle by spot-level 1360 is a key-point on its alignment; the water-parting is here narrow; as the map shows, streams running W. and E. respectively rise a short distance away on either side, and all traffic on these hills was here canalized. The views to the W. from the Dyke bank are hereabouts very limited, and it might have been expected that a course on the edge of the western scarp would have been chosen instead of one on the plateau. An examination of this scarp reveals the cause of its rejection; it is deeply dissected, forming a succession of spurs and re-entrants, and an alignment on its edge would be very sinuous (p. 151).

FIGURE 57. *Llanvair Hill to Brynorgan. In Llanfair Waterdine parish, Shropshire*

After crossing a moorland track by spot-level 1408—the highest point reached by the Dyke in the whole of its course—the ditch becomes wider and flatter than usual for a short distance; then from spot-level 1386 onwards to the end of the moorland, the character present on the N. slope of Llanvair—deep ditch, steep scarp, narrow crest—reappears. The Dyke is in fact very large, a measurement of 29 ft. on the scarp being recorded in one place (Profile xlvi, Fig. 65). A wide stretch of country now opens out, and the Dyke is seen making a gradual descent across agricultural land to a lateral valley of the river Teme; Cwmsanaham Hill, a dark and forbidding mass, on to which it climbs, lies beyond (Fig. 58). The gorge of the Teme near Knighton (Tref-y-Clawdd) and all the greater hills which the frontier line successively crosses—Frydd, Hawthorn, and Herrock—can, moreover, be distinguished on a clear day.

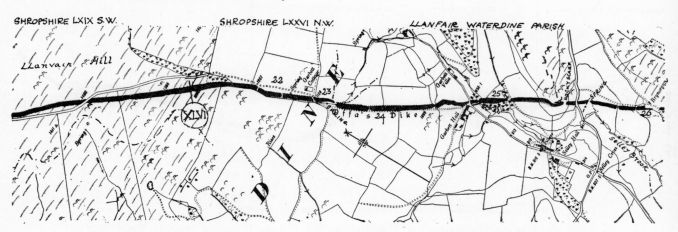

FIG. 57. Llanvair Hill to Brynorgan. In Llanfair Waterdine parish, Shropshire.
A portion of the 6-in. O.S. map reduced to 4 in. to 1 mile. For the significance of the symbols and letters employed, see Fig. 53.
(Reproduced from the Ordnance Survey map with the sanction of the Controller of H.M. Stationery Office.)

The Dyke was aligned from the S. side of Llanvair on to Cwmsanaham Hill, and the maximum deviation from the direct line in this stretch of 1½ miles is only 50 yards. Since a deep valley with intermediate ridges, and much 'dead' ground, is crossed, and there is a descent of over 500 ft. and a rise thereafter of about 450 ft., the accuracy of the layout is remarkable. But the Dyke is nowhere absolutely straight.

Details: the Dyke passes down from the Llanvair moorland into a fir wood, the contours of the mountain side permitting a noble view to the W. In field 22 the earthwork is on a large scale but irregular, the W. ditch being marshy. At the S. corner of this field the Dyke shows a wide gap; in the adjacent meadow (no. 23) it curves sharply to avoid a patch of boggy ground, and has an opening (probably original) for drainage, 10 yards wide; we are here at the head of a small re-entrant facing E. Beyond this opening (in field 24), the Dyke is again constructed on the grand scale, with broad and deep W. ditch, wet in places. In the ill-drained field beyond and below it is less impressive, and immediately to the N. of Garbett Hall it shows a sharp curve designed to avoid a boggy patch; the bank is here much denuded, the ditch a drainage channel and very irregular.

Crossing the Garbett Hall trackway the Dyke is seen above the ravine of the Selley brook as a rounded hump merging into the steep scarp; a knoll seen in the scrub on the opposite scarp is the remains of the Dyke, which reappears in an adjacent enclosure (no. 25) on a fine scale; here it cuts across the nose of the spur which divides the two branches of the Selley. The line thus cleverly maintained in broken country is continued down the easy slope to the second brook and up the opposing hill-side; the gap at the brook is as narrow as possible—being the breadth of the waterway and a ribbon of bog.

The next obstacle is a steep-ended spur, a tongue of high ground separating the valley we are crossing from a broad shallow embayment, part of the same system, which defines the N. end of Cwmsanaham Hill. The Dyke climbs on to this spur and swings round it. The bank is built up from spoil holes on the E.; on either side of the tip of the spur there is a lower (W.) ditch and the scarp is steepened; at the actual tip there is no lower ditch at all. The downward slope from the spur is very steep; a rocky scarp is utilized and the Dyke descends directly to the Selley Cross road and the embayment, presenting a bank of moderate size somewhat gapped, and a W. ditch.

The extent of country described above in so much detail is very small (500 yards from Garbett Hall to the road), but it is deeply dissected, and the Dyke's course and construction most interesting.

From the Selley Cross road the Dyke is seen making a direct but not straight course for Cwmsanaham Hill. It sinks gently to the floor of the embayment; here a well-head is present on the E. side of the line chosen, and the waterflow makes a gap. The Dyke then gradually ascends through pasture fields, forming hedge boundaries. Both bank and (W.) ditch have suffered from the plough, but the scarp is still steep. Crossing field 26 as a high rounded bank with W. ditch, the Dyke is gapped at Brynorgan—probably quarried away.

FIGURE 58. *Cwmsanaham Hill to Panpunton Hill. In Llanfair Waterdine parish, and on the boundary between Llanfair and Stow parishes, Shropshire*

The route up Cwmsanaham Hill is well chosen. It is diagonal, and the objective is the head of the ravine sketch-contoured on the map. This gives the easiest ascent on a very steep slope; there are magnificent views down the valley. We can now see how skilful was the selection of the whole alignment from Llanvair Hill; the eastern-facing slopes by Selley Hall were avoided, and this convenient ascent secured, without sacrifice of straightness.

At the commencement of the ascent the Dyke is a rounded bank of moderate size with W. ditch; there are also spoil holes on the E. side. From the NE. angle of enclosure 27 the scale of the Dyke markedly diminishes and its traces on the hill-side are very faint, being most apparent as the head of the ravine is approached.[1]

As we proceed this reduction of scale is found to be persistent, and is associated with a change of character; it is, therefore, convenient to review the problem it presents before resuming the detailed survey.

From Cwmsanaham to Panpunton Hill (Figs. 58 and 59), a distance of nearly 2 miles, the Dyke is a work so slight in places as to be barely discernible. On Cwmsanaham it is at best the size of a hedgebank; on Panpunton it is occasionally larger. The ditch is con-

---

[1] The Dyke is marked, on this alignment, on the 1833 1-in. O.S. map, sheet 56.

sistently on the E. side on plateaux as well as on slopes. At one point only (on Skyborry spur, Fig. 58) a W. ditch is also present. Sometimes the E. ditch is fairly regular; usually (as on Panpunton Hill) it is but a series of spoil holes. On hill-sides the Dyke shows no trace of the usual lower berm, the steepened scarp fading into the natural slope. The Dyke is frequently very irregular in detail, especially on the Cwmsanaham plateau, where it looks like the irresponsible work of children.

In contrast to the apparently unskilful methods of construction employed, the course of the Dyke is in this stretch skilfully chosen, revealing a competent grasp of the engineering

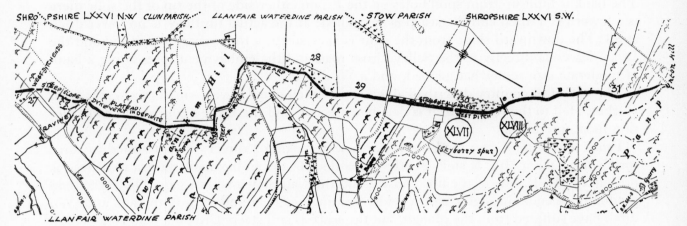

FIG. 58. Cwmsanaham Hill to Panpunton Hill. In Llanfair Waterdine parish, and on the boundary between Llanfair and Stow parishes, Shropshire.

A portion of the 6-in. O.S. map reduced to 4 in. to 1 mile. For the significance of the symbols and letters employed, see Fig. 53.
(Reproduced from the Ordnance Survey map with the sanction of the Controller of H.M. Stationery Office.)

problems involved, and presenting solutions identical with those already studied in more northerly sectors. From the ravine it passes straight across the plateau to the highest point on Cwmsanaham (spot-level 1343), thus avoiding a small re-entrant (cf. Llanvair Hill, p. 136). Swinging around the head of the great *cwm*, it again takes a direct course until descent from Panpunton Hill is necessary, avoiding spur and re-entrant alike.

Reverting to detail: From the head of the ravine (Fig. 58) uphill for 200 yards to the plateau, traces of the Dyke are faint—a ditch, with slight indications of a bank on the W. side (?). A rounded bank (+2 ft.) then appears. In its course (marked by estate boundaries) across the plateau to the head of the next dingle the bank improves a little in size, and beyond this (by the *h* of Cwmsana*h*am) it has a definite E. ditch. At the right angle by spot-level 1343—a remarkable alignment—the bank is broadened and then hollowed out to make a little three-sided enclosure, 3 ×6 ft., like a watchman's post. This is about 25 yards from the edge of the plateau, and does not command the valley. It may be a post-Offan modification for use when a beacon was lit on this hill-top, but it looks original. We turn the corner, and the Dyke now faces S., being on the edge of the plateau overlooking the tremendous gorge of Cwmsanaham, 450 ft. below. It follows the scarp for 90 yards (ditch to N.), then dips sharply down a rocky slope to strike a secondary scarp at a lower level. Though the work is slight, its course here is unmistakable. Passing into a belt of woodland which defines the lower scarp, the Dyke is with difficulty traceable to the head of the *cwm*, but from here to the next wood it forms, on the edge of the steep slope, an irregular low rounded bank. The material was—necessarily—taken from the upper (E.) side, as a ribbon of darker grass bordering the bank shows.

The Dyke is rather larger where it follows the edge of the fir-wood bordering field 28 to a small lateral re-entrant sketch-contoured on the map, which it dips to cross; near the S. end of the wood it again increases in size, being now not much smaller than the lower limit of the normal range, and so continues up to the end of field 29. There are spoil holes on the E. side here; no trace of W. ditch; the alignment is very irregular. The views to the W. hereabouts are magnificent.

The Dyke passes from field 29 across a track into a belt of fir-trees; it is a smallish bank with E. ditch, riddled with rabbit burrows. We are now on a plateau, the neck of Skyborry spur. The Dyke then crosses an open pasture field (no. 30), and along the edge of a pine-wood, being hereabouts straightly aligned (Type I), double-ditched, and about 3 ft. high (see Profile xlvii, Fig. 65). Having crossed the spur, it once more follows a sinuous course on the edge of the upland, forming field boundaries between arable (plateau) and down-land (slope). The E. ditch is ploughed in, and there is no W. ditch; the bank is 2 to 3 ft. in height. At the angle in enclosure 31 the Dyke passes over an outcrop, and the rock-cut E. ditch is 2 to 3 ft. deep.

FIGURE 59. *Panpunton Hill to Frydd. On the boundary between Llanfair parish and Stow parishes, Shropshire, and in Knighton parish, Radnorshire*

The Dyke is now crossing moorland. The bank fades out at the shallow re-entrant by *u* of Panp*u*nton, reappearing on the rising ground beyond. Passing round the steep scarp by the first *l* of Hi*l*l a well-marked E. ditch is seen—irregular, and more a succession of spoil holes than an element of the structure.

This constructional feature is probably significant; it suggests that the Dyke hereabouts was in the mind of its builders a *boundary bank*. The ditch was merely a source of material, and all that was necessary (for reasons to be hereafter considered) was that the *bank* should be sufficiently defined to mark the frontier through what was doubtless forest. Where the Dyke crossed open, probably arable land, on Skyborry spur, material was taken from both sides to ensure clear definition, and here the W. ditch is regular and normal, unlike the E. ditch.

The Dyke becomes very faint on the steep diagonal descent to the 1,000-ft. contour, and seems to merge into a hedge bank. We cannot trace it between this point and the river Teme 400 ft. below. The parish boundary, which has followed it for 1,500 yards, continues on a course through Kinsley wood, which on the map seems likely, but on the ground, having regard to the contours, unlikely.[1] A possible course, which by reason of the lie of the ground and the existence of hedgebanks has much to commend it, follows the W. margin of the Kinsley woodland to Panpunton hamlet; but, as on the former line,

---

[1] Not impossible. The Dyke negotiates the very steep slope of Herrock Hill in a similar direct manner (see p. 148).

traces of a bank in the required direction on the lowland between the Panpunton–Knighton road and the river are absent. Unless documentary evidence is forthcoming, I doubt if the line can be recovered. In Panpunton an intelligent man of middle age told me he had spent many years as a woodman in Kinsley woods and had asked many at what point the Dyke reached the levels, but none knew. Further local inquiries had similar negative results.

Knighton—Tref-y-Clawdd—is situated at the V-junction of the river Teme and the Welcome brook, as Fig. 69 shows. A dominant mass, the Garth Hill, 1,100 ft., divides the one valley from the other; at its foot there is a knoll, the crest of which is some 80 ft.

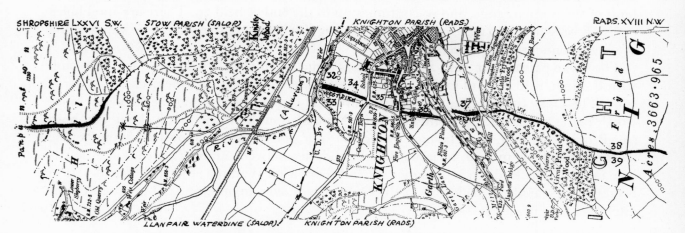

FIG. 59. Panpunton Hill to Frydd. On the boundary between Llanfair and Stow parishes, Shropshire, and in Knighton parish, Radnorshire.

A portion of the 6-in. O.S. map reduced to 4 in. to 1 mile. For the significance of the symbols and letters employed, see Fig. 53. (Reproduced from the Ordnance Survey map with the sanction of the Controller of H.M. Stationery Office.)

above the streams. Along the westward face of this knoll, fronting the Garth Hill, but with an ample glacis, Offa's Dyke is straightly aligned. The old town of Knighton occupies the eastern face of the knoll, the medieval castle being situated on its highest point, between town and Dyke.

The crossing-point of the Teme is similar in geographical character to the crossing-points of the Edenhope and the Mainstone brooks. It is more advantageous in that the line chosen avoids the weakness present in the others—the passage across the foot of an eastward-facing spur; it is less advantageous in that two streams have to be crossed instead of one.

The Dyke, constructed on a noble scale, creates indeed, in the triangle of ground between the streams, a very strong promontory fort, and it is not surprising that a Saxon town should have sprung up within these natural and artificial defences. That we are surveying the defences of a pre-Offan fortress is improbable. The alignment is one that the engineer of the Dyke would naturally choose, and the construction is characteristically Offan (straight stretches[1] with a slight change of direction on the crest line); moreover, the Dyke is similar in scale and alignment for an appreciable distance beyond the Welcome brook, and hence beyond the limits of the hypothetical 'promontory fort'.

[1] Probably Type I: they are much damaged.

The remains of the Dyke at Knighton are threatened by building development, and may be described in some detail. The knoll is steep-scarped where it borders the Teme; on the edge of this the Dyke appears as a high narrow ridge with W. ditch, the line chosen (between enclosures 32 and 33) being a very favourable one, since the ground falls sharply to the W. Rising to a higher level the bank forms a boundary between a meadow (field 34) and the gardens of a row of houses, wherein the W. ditch is obliterated. In field 35 the partly levelled bank is visible, and it continues into the gardens beyond; the adjacent road is on the line of the ditch.

The road junction is the highest point hereabouts and the Dyke changes direction, being visible on the new alignment in the backyard of an adjacent house; in meadow 36 it is a rampart with W. ditch, rounded by cultivation but still of impressive scale. The earthwork is visible as far as Fildas Place, where there is an almost vertical scarp to the dingle formed by the Welcome brook. Beyond the brook is a narrow alluvial flat[1] and a steep slope; the Dyke, necessarily a slight work, ascends this slope diagonally, having a W. ditch; in the meadow above the dingle (field 37), where it recovers its proper alignment, it is as fine as in field 36. Crossing Crydd lane the steep slope begins, and the massive construction characteristic of the Dyke in the valley ends.

Between the valleys of the Teme and the Lugg (5 miles away) is a series of hills running N. and S. and forming a stretch of upland from 1,000 to 1,300 ft. in elevation. The hill flanking the Teme valley, called Frydd, is isolated from the mountain mass to the W. by a re-entrant carved out by a tributary of the Teme; the others, of which Cwmwhitton, Hawthorn, and Furrow hills are the chief, are similarly isolated by a brook in a deep *cwm* flowing S. to join the Lugg, and by the Lugg valley itself. The Dyke passes over the flattened crests of these hills, taking a course which is fairly straight and level, and which avoids the deeply serrated western scarps. The traverse is typical of the Offan engineer in this broken country; the scale and character of the work varies, but is mainly of Cwmsanaham–Panpunton type.

To resume the narrative: the Dyke immediately to the S. of Crydd lane has been destroyed by water-works. It reappears a few yards S. of *MH* on the map, ascending diagonally the W. face of Frydd Hill through woodland; its scale is that of a hedge-bank, and such traces of the ditch as exist are on the E. This character is maintained when the slope eases and the level crest is approached, at the S. end of Great Frydd wood. From here it emerges on to open country—pasture fields. The hedge which divides fields 38 and 39 has been aligned more straightly than the Dyke, the flattened ramp of which is seen beside it.

FIGURE 60. *Frydd to Cwmwhitton Hill. In Knighton Parish and on the boundary between Whitton and Knighton and Whitton and Norton Parishes, Radnorshire*

At the S. corner of field 40 the Dyke is a little larger, and the improved scale (about equal to that on Panpunton Hill) continues in fields 41–42; on the boundary between

---

[1] The Dyke is marked on this flat (the part below the 600-ft. contour) by the O.S. surveyors, but the mound here is probably a silt-fan created by drainage down the ditch.

these fields the Dyke is irregular and spoil holes are seen here and there on the W. side. The end of this field (spot-level 1100) is a crest line and is marked by pine trees; on passing it the Dyke presents a completely altered character, both bank and ditch being on the grand scale. The contrast is dramatic; a patch of scrub separates a bank and *E. ditch* so small that it might easily escape notice from a high rampart and deep *W. ditch*, 60 ft. over all and 28 ft. on the scarp. The difference is graphically shown in the profiles, Fig. 66. That this change—both of scale and character—takes place on a crest line, a spot as easily recognized as the col at Hergan, is significant, and it is most fortunate that the junction

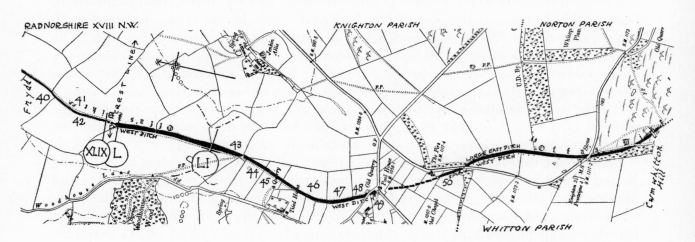

FIG. 60. Frydd to Cwmwhitton Hill. In Knighton parish and on the boundary between Whitton and Knighton and Whitton and Norton parishes, Radnorshire.

A portion of the 6-in. O.S. map reduced to 4 in. to 1 mile. For the significance of the symbols and letters employed, see Fig. 53. (Reproduced from the Ordnance Survey map with the sanction of the Controller of H.M. Stationery Office.)

has escaped serious damage. The stretch from the valley to this point was undoubtedly the work of the Cwmsanaham–Panpunton Hill gang, as the E. ditch shows.

From the crest the Dyke commences a gentle descent to a broad col, where the plateau is narrower than elsewhere. At the lowest point there is an original opening (p. 157). Up to within a few yards of this gap the Dyke is densely wooded. Passing up a gentle slope the Dyke maintains its scale to the end of field 43, where it is gapped; along the level upland, in fields 44, 45, and 46, it is ploughed down, and its original dimensions are uncertain.

The Dyke now swings to the E. to cross the neck which links Frydd to the higher plateaux; the alignment up the slope to Cwmwhitton Hill is direct and very cleverly chosen. The field of view to the W. is ample save for a short stretch S. of the main road (BM 1217·2) at end of Fig. 60, where the Dyke passes behind Cwmwhitton Hill.

Turning again to detail, the Dyke and W. ditch are well preserved on the margin of field 47; the earthwork is on a normal Offan scale, not the tremendous structure we have lately studied. In enclosure 48 it is planted with firs; in the corner of field 49 the ploughed-down bank and W. ditch are clearly visible. Between Pool House and The Firs the Dyke is not marked on the O.S. map[1], but the ploughed-down ridge is just visible in the fields on the line indicated. At the end of field 50 it passes into the rough as a well-marked bank with W. ditch filled with modern rubbish, and reappears on the same alignment in a belt of scrub and fir trees on the farther side of the main road. It is hereabouts a considerable work with a broad shallow E. ditch (spoil trench) and narrow well-defined W. ditch. The level upland is reached N. of the *O* of *Offa*, and from here to the end of Fig. 60 there is a low hummocky bank, much spread, in places seamed with rabbit burrows and occasionally indistinct: ditch uncertain.

FIGURE 61. *Cwmwhitton Hill to Furrow Hill; on the boundary between Whitton and Norton and Whitton and Presteigne Parishes, Radnorshire*

The Dyke now traverses open moorland. It is at first indistinct and then develops as a rounded ridge with a trace of E. ditch. It improves in size as it rises and where it borders

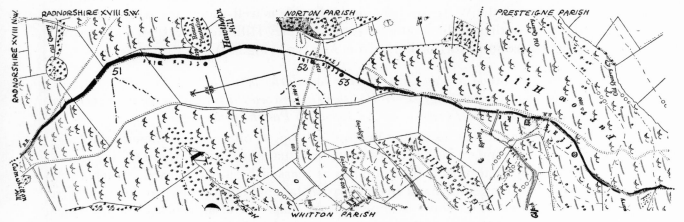

FIG. 61. Cwmwhitton Hill to Furrow Hill. On the boundary between Whitton and Norton and Whitton and Presteigne parishes, Radnorshire.

A portion of the 6-in. O.S. map reduced to 4 in. to 1 mile. For the significance of the symbols and letters employed, see Fig. 53. (Reproduced from the Ordnance Survey map with the sanction of the Controller of H.M. Stationery Office.)

the arable field 51 it is of normal scale with a scarp measuring 13–14 ft., and an E. ditch. Crossing the shallow embayment sketch-contoured on the map the Dyke rises on to the forward (W.) slope of Hawthorn Hill, 1,328 ft. The scale is normal: scarp 20 ft. on slope, overall breadth about 50 ft.; there is a well-marked E. ditch but no trace of one on the W. There never was one here; the corn crop is scanty along the field edge, indicating lack of soil over the rock. The views are magnificent, Kerry Hill and Radnor Forest to the W.; to the S., Newcastle, Herrock, and many other hills, backed by the Black Mountains.

The Dyke can be seen ascending the slope to Newcastle Hill (Castle Ring, Fig. 62) beyond the Lugg valley; it is here in the same alignment as on the downward slope from Hawthorn Hill, and these hills are key points in the layout (see Fig. 69 and p. 125). That the Dyke shows marked deflections from the alignment does not weaken this conclusion; the direct line having been chosen was adhered to as closely as the ground permitted, and

[1] But it is recorded on the 1833 Survey (sheet 56).

when of necessity departed from (as in the Gilfach re-entrant and on the Furrow Hill spur, Fig. 61) was regained as soon as possible.

To return to detail: on the S. slope of Hawthorn Hill the Dyke is ploughed down; we cannot find it in field 52, while in field 53 the bank and E. ditch can just be traced. Passing down a steepish moorland slope it presents a small bank with E. ditch, and this character continues across the head of the Gilfach re-entrant, there being occasional gaps (indicated on the map), and places where the bank alone can be detected. The Dyke is indeed little more than a hedge-bank, as on Frydd. Though small and faint, it is traceable in the heather and bracken on to the Furrow Hill spur and down the farther slope to the end of Fig. 61. The boundary fence is approximately, but not actually, on the line of the Dyke. The ditch, when present, is on the E.

A view rarely seen on the line of the Dyke is afforded by the dip in field 52 where the ridge is narrow, falling away, as the sketch contours show, on both sides. The gaunt and bare hill country to the W. is familiar; on the E. side is well-watered and wooded land, dominated by an outlier of the mountain zone—Wapley Hill, steep-scarped and crowned by a magnificent contour fort of Early Iron Age type (Fig. 69).

FIGURE 62. *Gilfach wood to Pen Offa. On the boundaries between Whitton and Presteigne, and Litton-and-Cascob and Discoed Parishes; in Discoed Parish, on the boundary between Discoed and Evenjobb Parishes, and in Evenjobb Parish, Radnorshire*

There is little doubt that, as on the Furrow hill-top, so on the steep slope to the Lugg valley, the parish boundary is the approximate or actual line of the Dyke. Definite traces, however, are difficult to find. This boundary is marked by a hedge-bank (which being situated on a W.-facing slope has a steep scarp) as far as the SW. corner of field 54; here a slight berm carries on the line—as shown on the map—as far as a rocky outcrop which is the steepest part of the slope. Beyond this point to the road above the river there is no trace whatever, the parish boundary being a hedge with no earth-bank.

In retrospect, we can summarize the character of the Dyke from the Teme valley to the Lugg valley by stating that, apart from a short stretch on either side of an original passage-way on Frydd Hill which is on the grand scale with the usual W. ditch, the whole is of Cwmsanaham type with E. ditch, and mainly subnormal in size.

On the very steep scarp below the road which runs parallel to the river Lugg, the Dyke is large, with W. ditch. There is no trace of it, nor could such be expected, on the narrow marshy flat between foot of scarp and river. Beyond the stream a tributary, the Cascob brook, and a hedge-bank are in the correct alignment. Near the angle of the Cascob the hedge-bank is bordered by a broad W. ditch as shown on the O.S. map, and there is a slight ridge, which may be the ramp of the Dyke, on the E. side of it; but farther to the S. there are no traces on the line provided by the hedge, the Dyke having been completely levelled.[1] It appears in the field above the main road, in the correct alignment, as a high bank with W. ditch, and on this alignment it continues for 180 yards. There is then a

[1] It is marked on this alignment on the 1833 1-in. O.S. Map (sheet 56). Judging by the evidence at either end, it was on a large scale.

slight change of direction; a straight stretch, 570 yards in length, follows, extending uphill to the 900-ft. contour, where the slope steepens. Thus, on valley floor and side alike, Type I alignments seem to have been laid out. The course on the slope is chosen with great skill. It is bordered (as in the Clun valley) on the W. by a dingle down which a brook runs and has a good field of view nearly all the way up.

To resume the narrative: the Dyke from the 600- to the 900-ft. contours is of striking dimensions; it measures 27 ft. on the scarp at several points between fields 55 and 56, while at one point the unusual figure of 32 ft. was reached (see Profile lii, Fig. 66). The

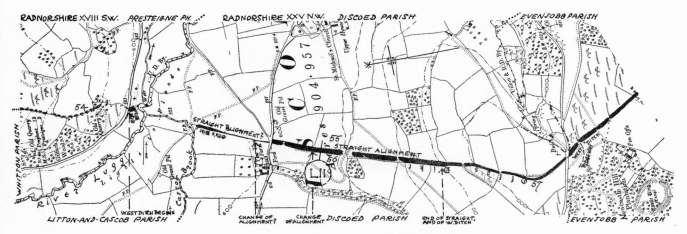

Fig. 62. Gilfach wood to Pen Offa. On the boundaries between Whitton and Presteigne and Litton-and-Cascob and Discoed parishes; in Discoed parish; on the boundary between Discoed and Evenjobb parishes; and in Evenjobb parish, Radnorshire.

A portion of the 6-in. O.S. map reduced to 4 in. to 1 mile. For the significance of the symbols and letters employed, see Fig. 53
(Reproduced from the Ordnance Survey map with the sanction of the Controller of H.M. Stationery Office.)

Dyke is gapped as indicated on the O.S. Survey, where it passes to the E. of a small knoll crowned by a pinewood; beyond this wood the W. ditch is broad enough to be used as a trackway, and the overall breadth of the work is 60 ft. Between the 800- and 900-ft. contours the earthwork is well wooded and its fine scale is maintained; the views to the W. are magnificent. The slope now is at its steepest, the Dyke diminishes in size and becomes sinuous, retaining at first its W. ditch. From the *a* of Off*a* onwards to the crest of the Newcastle Hill spur, where the Dyke changes direction, and thence, on the level, to the road by Bwlch, it is a mere hedge-bank, and no W. ditch is apparent, but there are spoil holes on the E. side. At the angle (field 57) the Dyke is in front (W. of) the hedge-bank and the O.S. map incorrectly records its position.

There can be little doubt but that the transition from the major to the minor scale here, associated with a change from straightness to irregularity, has a physiographical origin; the slope was open cultivated country, the hill-top was forest.

Herrock Hill, the ultimate objective, 2½ miles away, lies SSE. of the spur of Newcastle Hill on which we are standing, but the Evenjobb ravine (Fig. 63) which intervenes was the determining factor governing the layout from the spur. A SE. course was therefore taken on to the head of the ravine; the line just clears a narrow but deep gully opening to the *eastward* by Bwlch, and passes over the forward slope of Hill 1218. The Dyke then follows the steep NW. face of the Evenjobb ravine (Granner wood) to its southern flank; swinging round this flank a new alignment is taken on to the highest point (1,062 ft.) of Burfa Bank. This alignment involves a gradual descent from the 1,000-ft. to the 600-ft. level, which is reached near Burfa farmhouse. The Dyke does not ascend Burfa Bank because the Hindwell brook valley (Fig. 64) has almost immediately to be negotiated, and it is therefore taken in a wide curve round the foot of this steep and isolated hill, gradually descending to valley level. The course of the Dyke across the alluvial flat and up the N. slope of Herrock Hill is direct.

The entire traverse from the Lugg valley to the Hindwell brook valley is thus erratic on plan, but in actual fact the best that could be devised, having regard to the essential conditions which, judging from previous practice, any alignment satisfactory to the engineer had to fulfil. It consistently maintained[1] an ample view to the W., and it avoided the crossing of ravines; the gradients were reasonably easy, and it was possible to lay out the Dyke in straight stretches, which, it may be noted, are here mostly of Type II.

Turning to detail (Fig. 62), the Dyke is on open moorland on the farther side of the Bwlch; it is irregular in alignment, it shows a bank of moderate dimensions (15 ft. scarp) with a W. ditch, and an opening, probably original (p. 158). We now ascend the N. slope of Hill 1218; here the Dyke is a broad, low, rabbit-eroded bank with E. ditch.

FIGURE 63. *Hill 1218 to Burfa. In Evenjobb parish, Radnorshire*

The characters present on the N. slope of Hill 1218 persist into the fir wood and over the SW. face; here the bank is of very moderate size (+3 ft.). Emerging from the fir wood, on the boundary between fields 58–59, a landscape is seen which even in this superb countryside is exceptional. A falling sweep of downland ends abruptly at Granner wood—a dark-green wall, above and beyond which are Herrock, Bradnor, and Hergest hills. On the right, Colva forms the background to a broad lowland patched with colour and light, from which emerge the wooded steeps of Stanner, Old Radnor, and Hanter.

From this viewpoint the immediate objective, the head of the re-entrant, was also visible and the course of the Dyke accordingly corrected. Down the even slope the earth-work is sinuous (Type II), of moderate size, rabbit-eroded, and with no evident ditch—certainly not on the W.

The slope steepens in the rough near the quarries, and here the Dyke is represented by a scarp with a (lower) berm; it points to the former head of the ravine, now quarried away. Beyond a tangle of quarry-roads, mounds, and holes, a broad berm (with no trace of wheel tracks) leads directly to a woodland way, which takes a level line above the 1,000-ft. contour along the whole length of Granner wood. This green way is on a berm with slight traces of a bank on its outer margin, and with a steepened scarp on its inner margin; and, as at Hopyard wood (Chapter IV, p. 54), it has become a pathway. The

---

[1] Save for a few yards by Bwlch, Fig. 62.

Dyke—for this it is without question though not recorded on the modern O.S. map[1]—then swings round the nose of Evenjobb Hill, and leaving the wood for the open country is more clearly defined by a scarp on the hill-side below the berm. This scarp becomes steeper and then a W. ditch appears, as the hill-road to Evenjobb (here a holloway) is approached; the technique is curious and interesting, being the same as that seen on Hergan (p. 130) and other steep diagonal descents (or ascents?).[2] A high bank then makes its appearance near the holloway on the outer edge of the ditch, which here suddenly becomes very broad. It may be a counterscarp bank, part of the Offan structure, but it is

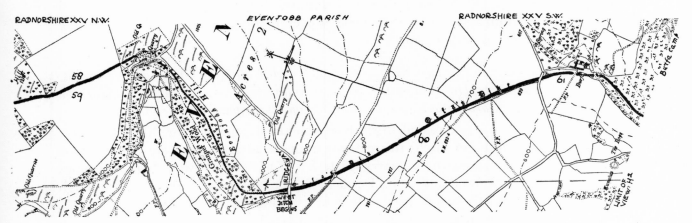

FIG. 63. Hill '1218' to Burfa. In Evenjobb parish, Radnorshire.

A portion of the 6-in. O.S. map reduced to 4 in. to 1 mile. For the significance of the symbols and letters employed, see Fig. 53.
(Reproduced from the Ordnance Survey map with the sanction of the Controller of H.M. Stationery Office.)

unusually massive, even compared with Hergan, and the broad trough-like ditch looks like a quarry. This bank quickly fades into a hedge-bank at its N. end. On the S. side of the holloway the steep scarp of the Dyke is very well marked but the W. ditch is ploughed in, and if there was any bank on its counterscarp it has completely vanished. The holloway certainly represents an ancient route from the upland to the New Radnor plain, a haunt of men from the Early Bronze Age onwards, and, with the Hergan parallel in our minds, it would be unwise to dismiss the counterscarp bank here as definitely later than, or unrelated to, the Dyke.

The Dyke now commences a long easy descent to a second 'Burfa Farm' on a slope trending S. and W., well shown in Plate XXIX; it quickly reacts to the changed conditions and develops a high narrow-crested bank with W. ditch. This bank forms the dividing line between a succession of arable and pasture fields, and is much damaged by agriculture and rabbits. It becomes more massive as one proceeds southwards, and at a point half-way between the 800- and 700-ft. contours measures 24 ft. on the slope—a work distinctly on the major scale. At the S. end of field 60 the W. ditch becomes wet; the Dyke

[1] It is recorded on this alignment on the 1833 1-in. O.S. map (sheet 56).

[2] The query relates to an unknown factor: namely, the direction in which the Dyke alignment was designed in detail, from point to point.

then fronts a green lane and is well wooded. Beyond the *D* of *D*ike this lane passes into the ditch which, as a result of traffic, becomes over-deepened near its junction with the Burfa trackway. The fine scale of the work is fully maintained, and at the *i* of *D*ike, where the ditch is not over-deepened, and the ridge high and narrow, it measures 29 ft. on the scarp.

Crossing the lane the Dyke is present in the homefield of (the second) Burfa Farm (no. 61); it is gapped and damaged, but traceable as a work once massive, up to the barn which adjoins this field. There is an E. ditch and ponds which serve farm purposes and may not be original; no ditch, however, survives on the W. side. The steep and wooded slope of Burfa now confronts us; on it the Dyke is present as a well-defined berm running at the 700-ft. level.

FIGURE 64. *Burfa Bank to Rushock Hill. In Evenjobb and Walton-and-Womaston parishes, Radnorshire; in Lower Harpton parish, on the boundary between, and in, Lower Harpton and Knill parishes, and between Knill and Kington Rural parishes, Herefordshire*

When the Dyke begins to descend Burfa Bank diagonally, making for the valley floor, it is a small ridge with upper ditch; this persists in dense scrub down a steepening slope until we emerge on a trackway by a quarry (Plate XXIX). The earthwork here resembles Offa's Dyke at Hopyard wood and Craig Forda (Chapter IV, pp. 53 and 60), and, though it is not marked on the O.S. maps, no doubt as to its being part of the Dyke can arise.

No trace could be found between the quarry and Knobley brook, and it is uncertain whether the Dyke dipped steeply to the stream, or whether it followed the line of the road to the junction of the Knobley and Hindwell brooks at Ditch Hill bridge.

The first sign of the Dyke on the level arable land is 120 yards beyond the stream;[1] it is very well defined—a broad and high bank measuring 17 ft. on the scarp—with W. ditch, largely ploughed-in or silted up. It is irregular in alignment. There is a broad gap, indicated on the map, and then the Dyke fades out some 20 yards from the bank of a third stream—Riddings brook—which joins the others a short distance to the eastward. Crossing this stream—the county boundary—the Dyke is seen to be a fine work 17 ft. on the scarp on the average, broad as might be expected from the ill-compacted alluvial soil of which it is composed, with original W. ditch[2] largely silted up. All this stretch is well shown on Plate XXIX. A few yards of marsh intervene on which the Dyke is not present; it then, changing direction slightly, ascends the flank of Herrock Hill.

The course of the earthwork on the upland of which this tremendous bastion is an outlier is remarkable. It ascends the exceptionally steep slope directly, a most unusual mode; it passes up the ridge of the north-eastern horn nearly to the crest, and then follows the hill face (at between 1,100 and 1,200 ft.) round to the col which links Herrock Hill to Rushock (Plate XXXI). The view from Herrock over the New Radnor plain and Radnor forest is magnificent, and it provides the best bird's-eye view of the Dyke itself to be seen

---

[1] The O.S. map marks it as present almost on the margin, but nothing exists here today save a hedge and drainage ditch, the alignment of which is not convincing.

[2] A drainage channel on E. side is obviously modern.

anywhere (Plate XXIX); it is as though the builder of the Dyke, before turning his back on the mountains and making for the Hereford plain, selected the most commanding position on the March as the angle of his frontier line, and kept high on it as a gesture of defiance (Plate XXX).

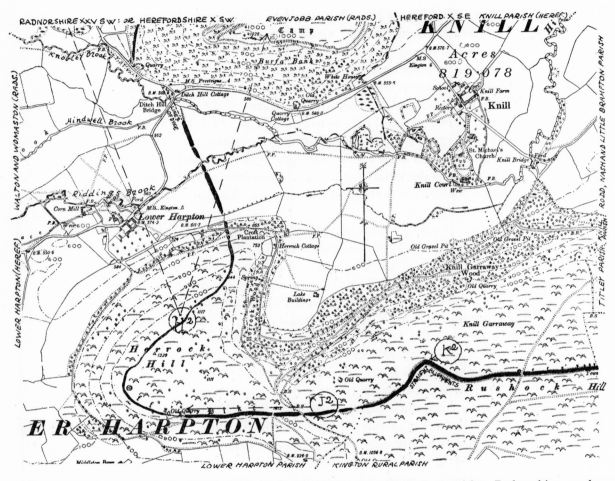

FIG. 64. Burfa Bank to Rushock Hill. In Evenjobb and Walton-and-Womaston parishes, Radnorshire; on the boundary between Lower Harpton and Knill parishes; in Lower Harpton and Knill parishes; and between Knill and Kington Rural parishes, Herefordshire.

A portion of the 6-in. O.S. map reduced to 4 in. to 1 mile. For the significance of the symbols and letters employed, see Fig. 53.

(Reproduced from the Ordnance Survey map with the sanction of the Controller of H.M. Stationery Office.)

Turning to detail: the Dyke is clearly present on the steep slopes in Croft plantation as a rounded bank ditched on both sides, but it is not marked on the O.S. map. On the open hill-side the Dyke, though direct, is irregular. It is a broad (26 ft.) rounded bank with well-marked W. ditch; some spoil has been taken from the E. side also. It becomes smaller as it rises with less definite ditching, and when it turns to the SW. along the face of the hill it presents those changes in profile and construction always met with on steep slopes.

In some places it is a mere berm or shelf; in others there is an upper and a lower ditch. At the outcrop near spot-level 1117 the Dyke cannot in places be traced owing to the weathering of the rocky scarp, and in its passage round the very steep western face of the hill it is hardly visible, the soil having slipped away from the rock. Swinging to the E. the Dyke—a slight berm on the hill-side—passes up the Holywell re-entrant overlooking Bradnor Hill. By the 'Old Quarry'[1] its scale gradually increases, the slope being less steep; it is a bank with lower berm and upper spoil trench. On the saddle by spot-level 1013, where it is gapped, it is a broad bank definitely ditched on the lower slope, now facing S.

The Dyke is now turning its back on the mountains; Rushock Hill is the last considerable stretch of upland to be traversed. Its direction is almost due E., though a SE. course would have, it seems, provided a more direct route to the plain. The alignment was apparently designed to enable the Dyke conveniently to reach the Eywood valley near its head (Chapter VII, p. 175). Given this objective, the course on Rushock, mainly on the flat plateau-like summit, is a reasonable one, giving a sufficient field of view; the only unusual feature is a sharp deviation from the chosen line at one point. The apex of the V thus formed faces Mercia; it is the highest point on the featureless plateau (see p. 153 and Plate XVIIc).

To return to detail: Passing from the col up the slope of Rushock Hill, the Dyke is a considerable bank (Plate XXXI), apparently with an upper ditch only, now occupied by a trackway; on the shoulder of the hill where the track leaves its line there is a definite lower ditch and upper spoil trench. The Dyke is following up to its head a small re-entrant which diverges from the Holywell valley, and it thus maintains right to the plateau of the hill wide visual control to S. and W. Thus, though the E.–W. course is unusual, the layout is normal. On the plateau the Dyke is of normal dimensions and character; it measures 13 ft. on the scarp, is 30 ft. overall, and has a S. ditch.

The approach to, and return from, the angle at spot-level 1245 is carried out by short straight alignments (Type I); the constructional character described above is maintained, the ditch being on the inner side—and thus invisible in Plate XVIIc.

Looking N. and W. the Dyke can be seen on the S. slope of Llanvair Hill, 12 miles away, and the Welsh mountains form the skyline. These are seen for the last time, for when, following the Dyke, one recovers the chosen alignment the Herefordshire plain opens out widely to the E. and S. The alignment on the plateau is direct but irregular, and suggests a forest cover. The Dyke maintains the character and size already described, being indeed singularly uniform on this hill. Numerous large boulders occur in its bank; as similar stones are seen in a modern excavation near by, these are probably 'glacial drift', and derived from the ditch. At the yew trees the plateau begins to narrow and the hill to have a definite ridge. These yews are known as the Three Shepherds: they are visible from all parts of Radnorshire and provide a meeting-point for parish boundaries. Yews are frequently seen on ancient earthworks in S. England, but I had not yet seen such in Wales. At these secular trees the survey was suspended in 1930.

---

[1] Here the Dyke passes out of sight in the photograph, Plate XXXI.

ALIGNMENTS, MAJOR AND MINOR

The major layout has now been described and the actual alignment studied in detail. Here certain features may be summarized and the unity of the design stressed.

In the case of the Unk, and of the Mainstone brook (Plate XXV), the crossing-point chosen is at the point where two valleys meet, and a switchback course across two ravines or valleys is avoided. An essentially similar course is taken in the Teme valley at Knighton. The Lugg valley and the Hindwell brook valley also are crossed at the meeting-place of streams. These parallels are remarkable, and convincing evidence of unity. Again, the technique of the layout of the Dyke in the Clun and the Lugg valleys is identical—a steep spur utilized on the N. side; an easy slope flanked by a lateral ravine on the S. side; advantage taken of river and streams (either natural course, or canalized, *ad hoc*, by the Dyke engineers); direct alignment across the valley from a point high enough up to secure visual control of the whole 'floor'; straight alignment on the S. side.

Long stretches of the Dyke are, as in Denbighshire, aligned with but slight deviation from absolute straightness—e.g. the S. slope of Llanvair Hill, and Evenjobb Hill to Burfa (Plate XXIX). In several cases, as in the Mainstone–Middle Knuck portion (Figs. 53 and 54), at Hergan col (Fig. 54), and especially on the S. side of the Clun valley (Fig. 55 and Plate XXVIII) and the Lugg valley (Fig. 62), the direct line passes over a convex surface. On such places a simple method of cross alignment must have been practised to enable the Dyke to be set out so accurately between mutually invisible points. This is a refinement not previously noticed. The normal method of alignment from crest to crest is very well illustrated in this sector; three crests thus utilized in the neighbourhood of the Lugg valley are indicated by arrows on Fig. 69.

Western-facing slopes are, as usual, skilfully selected and utilized (e.g. Plate XXIX): views to the W. are normal, to E. rare, although the tilt of the country is largely to the E. To this use of W. slopes there is one exception. Where such slopes are deeply indented the Dyke does not zigzag in and out of them but leaves the scarp and takes a straight course across the upland, although the field of view from the Dyke is thus very limited. This striking characteristic is well seen on Llanvair Hill, on Cwmsanaham and Panpunton, and on the Hawthorn Hill–Furrow Hill range.

Generally speaking, one may say of the designer of the Dyke (up to this stage) that (*a*) he sends it straight down small valleys, and (*b*) diagonally down large steep-sided ravines, and that (*c*) he seeks out lateral re-entrants and embayments when crossing main valleys. These characteristics are well exemplified in the Mountain Zone. The little valley S. of Middle Knuck (Fig. 54) illustrates class (*a*), the Mainstone ravine (Fig. 53, Plates XXIV and XXV) class (*b*), the S. side of the Clun valley (Fig. 55 and Plate XXVIII) class (*c*): a rare exception occurs at Herrock (Fig. 64), where a very steep hill is ascended direct.

The three types of alignment analysed in Chapter V are present in the Mountain Zone. Type III, sensitive to the contours of the hills, is, as might be expected, dominant, and can be recognized on every one of the twelve maps: it is well shown on Plate XXXI. Type II is to be seen on Llanvair Hill, near BM 1343·3 (Fig. 56); on Fig. 61 between

Hawthorn and Furrow hills; on Figs. 62 and 63 from Newcastle Hill spur onwards to Burfa farm, and on Fig. 64, Rushock Hill. It is best illustrated in Plate XXV. I find that Types II and III are frequently associated, the sweeping curves of the Dyke which conform to the contours being, in detail, irregular. Nearly the whole of the S. half of the sector, from Cwmsanaham onwards, is of this character; and we may, I think, regard it as having been almost completely forested in the eighth century. Here, the reader will remember, the boundary-bank type of dyke is dominant (see Fig. 69).

(i) *Alignments of Type I*

Alignments of Type I are very limited in extent, but are interesting in distribution. Two are illustrated on Plate XXIV.

N. side of Mainstone ravine (Fig. 53)	Two stretches, 170+160 yards.
Slope, S. side of Clun valley (Fig. 55) . . .	610 yards.
Spoad Hill top (Fig. 56)	370 yards.
Llanvair Hill, angle at spot-level 1360 (Fig. 56) . .	233 yards.
Upper Skyborry spur, Panpunton (Fig. 58) . .	230 yards.
Lugg valley floor (Fig. 62)	Two stretches, *probably* Type I. Watercourse utilized in part. Length (of Dyke only) 300+250 yards.
Slope, S. side of Lugg valley (Fig. 62) . . .	570 yards.
Rushock Hill, right-angled corner (Fig. 64) . .	Three stretches, 40+60+150 yards.

We see that it is probable that there were straight alignments across the Lugg valley floor. The evidence for the Clun valley is similar, but less definite; here the straight alignments seem to have met at the river (Fig. 55). The Dyke goes very directly across a knoll in the Teme valley at Knighton, probably in three straight alignments (Fig. 59). In neither of these latter cases are the existing remains sufficient to justify inclusion in the tabular summary. There is a fourth river valley in the sector, that of the Hindwell brook system; here the alignments are direct but of Type II (Plate XXIX). At the crossing-points chosen by the Dyke engineer, both flanks of the Teme valley and of the Hindwell brook valley are steep, but easy slopes form the south flank of the Clun (Plate XXVIII) and Lugg valleys. Here, then, are situated the most striking examples of straight alignment in the sector. That in a countryside mainly upland the majority of the straight stretches should be found in the very limited valley areas[1] tends to confirm previous conclusions; they indicate the zones in the district most suitable for tillage and dairy farming. The only valley which was apparently not opened up by agriculturists is the least accessible—the Hindwell brook valley. Again, the remarkably abrupt change from straight to sinuous alignment seen at the 900-ft. contour on Figure 62 reveals the Dyke passing from the arable on to the forested uplands. A similar contrast is seen at the Mainstone ravine (p. 127).

Of the few straight stretches on upland plateaux, that at Spoad Hill is particularly interesting; it is adjacent to an ancient ridgeway, and defines the present-day limits, as well (apparently) as the limits over eleven centuries ago, of tilled ground hereabouts

---

[1] Total length of Type I in valleys, 2,060 yards; on hills, 1,083 yards. An additional Type I valley stretch probably exists near Bridge Farm, Clun Parish, Fig. 54.

PLATE XXIV

Offa's Dyke on the N. flank of the Mainstone valley, Salop, from the S., showing straight (Type I) alignments. Taken from point D2, Fig. 53

PLATE XXV

Offa's Dyke on the S. flank of the Mainstone valley, Salop, from the N., showing direct but irregular (Type II) alignments.
Taken from point C2, Fig. 53

PLATE XXVI

NECK OF LAND JOINING HERGAN HILL TO PLATEAU

OFFA'S DYKE

OFFA'S DYKE

MIDDLE KNUCK FARM

OFFA'S DYKE

OFFA'S DYKE

KNUCK BANK

EDENHOPE HILL (BEYOND MAINSTONE) VALLEY

COUNTERSCARP BANK OF OFFA'S DYKE, HERGAN

OFFA'S DYKE AT THE RIGHT ANGLE (RIDGING CAUSED BY TRAFFIC)

TACK WOOD RAVINE

SCARP OF OFFA'S DYKE, HERGAN

Offa's Dyke at Hergan, Salop; showing the bank on the counterscarp, and the right angle where two constructional techniques meet. Taken from point E2, Fig. 54

PLATE XXVII

Offa's Dyke on the W. slope of Hergan Hill, Salop, showing the bank on the counterscarp. Taken from point F2, Fig. 54

PLATE XXVIII

Offa's Dyke crossing the Clun valley. Taken from point G2, Fig. 55

PLATE XXIX

EVEN JOBB

NEWCASTLE HILL AND CASTLE RING

LOWER HARPTON

OFFA'S DYKE

HINDWELL BROOK

OFFA'S DYKE (BY QUARRY)

KNOBLEY BROOK

BURFA BANK

RIDDINGS BROOK

OFFA'S DYKE

LUGG VALLEY (POSITION OF)

BURFA CAMP

Offa's Dyke crossing the eastern margin of the plain of New Radnor. Taken from Herrock Hill, point H2, Fig. 64

PLATE XXX

Herrock Hill: the south-western bastion of the Mercian frontier in the Mountain Zone. Taken from the cross-road, Walton.
The Dyke is indicated by a black line

PLATE XXXI

Offa's Dyke winding along the S. slope of Herrock Hill, looking W. from Rushock Hill, point J2, Fig. 64. The seated figure is on the bank of the Dyke. Cynon brook valley and Stanner Hill occupy the middle distance; beyond is Radnor Forest

PLATE XXXII

A Cross-valley Dyke: Ditch Bank, Llanfihangel Nant Melan, Radnorshire, looking N.

(Fig. 56). This, like the long straight stretches on valley slopes, is of exceptionally large scale.

(ii) *Right-angled corners on the alignment*

A very short straightly-aligned portion of the Dyke at Rushock, Herefordshire, includes a right-angled corner p. 150). Such corners are a novel feature. There are, in addition to that at Rushock, two in this sector, on Cwmsanaham Hill and at Hergan. The angles occur at points well defined geographically: that at Cwmsanaham is at the crest of a dominating hill; at Rushock the highest point on a plateau, while Hergan marks one flank of a narrow col. At Rushock, the Dyke diverges from its course to reach the point in question, and then quickly returns. This divergence suggests an explanation consonant with what we have learnt of the Dyke and its origins. It seems probable that it was agreed by the Powers concerned in the delineation of the frontier that it should here pass over the highest point on the hill. The engineer of the Dyke fulfilled the letter of the law, but did not allow it to interfere more than was absolutely necessary with what he regarded as a suitable alignment. Similarly, the highest point on Cwmsanaham (p. 138) may well have been a fixed point on the frontier agreed upon at the council table. In both these cases the constructional character of the Dyke at the angle is similar to that for some distance on either side.[1]

The Hergan angle (p. 132) represents the junction of two types of construction, and is therefore a more complicated problem. The possibility that we have, in the southern portion, an earlier work (a 'Short Dyke' across a col) incorporated into Offa's Dyke must be rejected. Though situated partly on a col, it is not carried far enough on the N. side to obtain the protected flank which all cross-ridge dykes require: there is a gentle slope between the point where the ends of the two banks return and the steep scarp of the Tack wood ravine. Moreover, the extension, on the other side, of the double-banked construction to the valley foot is consistent with its function as a part of Offa's Dyke, and not with its use as a pre-Offan barrier.

There is, I think, a more acceptable explanation of the facts. There were two gangs at work between Middle Knuck and Hergan. The gang which carried out the Hergan section had its own way of doing things; it finished on the Hergan col as instructed, and left the gang to the north to join up when they got there. For there is, we think, no doubt that the Hergan section was finished first, and that the builder of the northern portion was forced to diverge from what he naturally regarded as the ideal line, in order to link up. The Hergan men were building the Dyke on a westward-facing slope (Plate XXVII), and they continued on this slope to the bitter end. The connexion was the affair of the Middle Knuck gang, not theirs; but they turned their banks through a right angle, and made a neat job before downing tools. Thus we conceive of the Hergan gang working northward from valley to col, and of the Middle Knuck gang working southward to meet them. A reason for the priority given to the Hergan gang will be offered later (p. 169).

---

[1] A third such fixed point may be present on Llanvair Hill (Fig. 56, and p. 126). Here, as at Rushock, but not at Cwmsanaham, straight alignment indicates an open patch in the forest, probably induced by heavy or long-continued traffic of men or cattle.

THE PROFILE OF THE DYKE

Eight profiles are reproduced in two Figures, nos. 65 and 66. Two, nos. xlvi and lii, on Llanvair Hill and in the Lugg valley, are large-scale profiles of normal type, with scarps measuring 29 and over 30 ft., with ditches still, in spite of silting, well over 6 ft. deep, and having overall breadths of 63 and more than 68 ft. respectively. With these may be contrasted typical examples of the 'hedge-bank' dyke with eastern ditch or spoil trench met with for the first time in the survey; nos. xlviii and xlix, measured on hill-tops respectively N. and S. of Knighton. These have scarps measuring 12 and 13 ft., spoil trenches only a few inches to a foot deep, and overall breadths, including the trenches, of 35 and 29 ft. The remarkable and abrupt junction of the 'hedge-bank' and the normal Dyke on a crest line S. of Knighton is illustrated by a sketch plan (Fig. 66) and by profiles taken only 50 yards apart (nos. xlix and l). At one point on Upper Skyborry spur, N. of Knighton, for a few hundred yards only, the hedge-bank type develops a W. ditch, illustrated on Figure 65. It is a straight stretch, and the ground was presumably open. Gradual transitions from the normal to the hedge-bank types can be seen near the Firs, Knighton (Fig. 60), and on Newcastle Hill (Fig. 62).

The second important variation from the normal met with in the Mountain Zone is the bank on the counterscarp. This addition is extensively represented at Hergan; it occurs also in short stretches at three other points (see pp. 128–30 and Fig. 69). The Hergan profile is illustrated (no. xlv) where the counterscarp bank is largest; as will be seen it is a considerable structure, and its presence brings the overall breadth of the work here to an exceptional figure—74 ft. Being on a steepish slope the main bank is in part built up from a spoil trench on the upper (E.) side, but this is not included in the measurements.

Table of Measurements

No. of Profile	Position	Present dimensions of bank (estimated)		Present dimensions of W. ditch (estimated)		Present overall breadth of bank and W. ditch (estimated)
		Height	Breadth	Depth	Breadth	
		ft. in.	ft. in.	ft. in.	ft. in.	ft. in.
XLV	100 yds. N. of spot-level 1186 on W. side of Hergan Hill (Fig. 54)	4 4	31 0	3 8	19 0	50 0 (but adding counterscarp bank = 74 ft.)
XLVI	30 yds. N. of spot-level 1371 at S. end of Llanvair Hill (Fig. 57)	8 0	36 0	6 3	27 0	63 0
XLVII	100 yds. ESE. of farm building, Skyborry Spur (Fig. 58)	3 0	18 2	1 0	11 5	29 7
XLVIII*	200 yds. SE. of no. xlvii (Fig. 58)	2 10	20 0	none	none	†
XLIX*	35 yds. N. of spot-level 1100: ENE. of Woodhouse wood (Fig. 60)	2 0	20 0	none	none	‡
L	50 yds. S. of no. xlix (Fig. 60)	6 6	35 0	4 6	25 4	60 4
LII	240 yds. S. of Yew Tree farm (Fig. 62)	8 4	37 0	6 6	31 6	68 6

* These Profiles show an E. spoil trench.   † Overall breadth with E. spoil trench 35 ft.
‡ Overall breadth with E. spoil trench 29 ft.

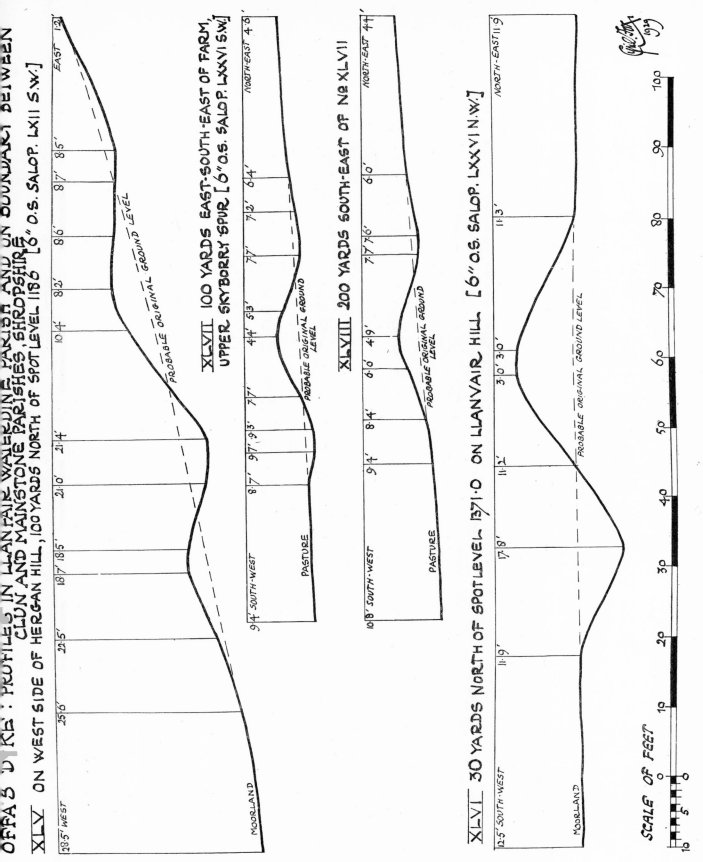

FIG. 65. Profiles XLV, XLVI, XLVII and XLVIII.

OFFA'S DYKE: PROFILES IN KNIGHTON AND DISCOED PARISHES, RADNORSHIRE

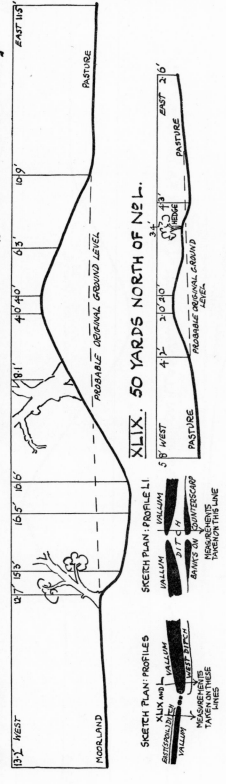

L. 15 YARDS SOUTH OF SPOT LEVEL 1100 NEAR WOODHOUSE WOOD [6"O.S. RADS. XVIII. N.W.]

WEST 13.1' 12.7' 15.3' 16.5' 16.6' 18.1' 4.0' 4.0' 6.3' 10.9' EAST 11.5'

PASTURE

PROBABLE ORIGINAL GROUND LEVEL

MOORLAND

SKETCH PLAN: PROFILES
XLIX AND L.
EAST (SPOIL) DITCH VALLUM WEST DITCH VALLUM
MEASUREMENTS TAKEN ON THESE LINES

SKETCH PLAN: PROFILE LI.
VALLUM
DITCH
VALLUM COUNTERSCARP
BANKS ON MEASUREMENTS TAKEN ON THIS LINE

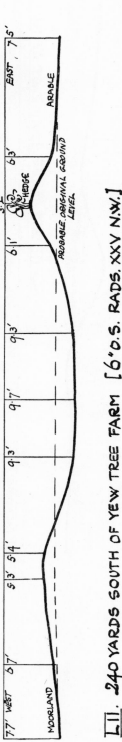

XLIX. 50 YARDS NORTH OF N2 L.

WEST 5.8' 4.1' 2.0' 2.0' 3.4' 4.3' EAST 2.6'

PASTURE

HEDGE

PASTURE

PROBABLE ORIGINAL GROUND LEVEL

LI. SOUTH FLANK OF ORIGINAL OPENING NEAR WOODHOUSE WOOD [6"O.S. RADS. XVIII N.W.]

WEST 7.7' 6.7' 5.3' 5.4' 9.7' 9.3' 9.7' 9.3' 3.2' 6.1' 6.3' EAST 7.5'

MOORLAND

HEDGE

ARABLE

PROBABLE ORIGINAL GROUND LEVEL

LII. 240 YARDS SOUTH OF YEW TREE FARM [6"O.S. RADS. XXV N.W.]

WEST 14.5' 13.8' 18.8' 18.3' 9.7' 2.7' 2.7' 6.4' 10.1' EAST 10.0'

PASTURE

PASTURE

PROBABLE ORIGINAL GROUND LEVEL

SCALE OF FEET
0   5   10
0 10 20 30 40 50 60 70 80 90

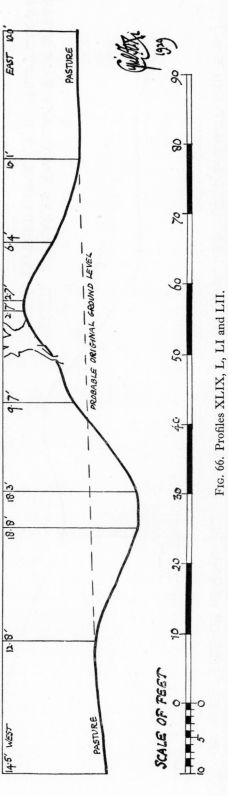

Fig. 66. Profiles XLIX, L, LI and LII.

(i) *Types met with in the zone*

For convenience of reference the types of dyke met with in the Mountain Zone may be classified as follows:

(*a*) *Weak*: Dyke of boundary- or hedge-bank type, with E. ditch.

(*b*) *Normal*: Dyke of normal Offan type with vallum and W. ditch, which, whether intended for defence or no, is essentially defensive according to the principles of warfare in early times.

(*c*) *Reinforced*: Dyke of normal Offan type with W. ditch, but reinforced with a bank on the counterscarp.[1]

One profile, no. li, has not been referred to in this section because it cannot be used for comparative purposes; it is discussed on p. 158.

PASSAGE-WAYS AND GAPS IN THE DYKE

In the main river-valleys of the Mountain Zone, skilful use was made by the engineer of bends in the river, or tributary, perhaps canalized, streams; thus, though gaps existed here in the Dyke considered as an earthwork, as a frontier it was visible and continuous. This is well shown in the Clun valley (Fig. 55) and the Lugg valley (Fig. 62). These adaptations tend to confirm the opinion expressed in Chapter V, p. 86, on the traverse by the Dyke of the Vyrnwy valley.

The survey provides further evidence that gaps necessitated by watercourses were made as narrow as possible. In the valleys of the larger tributaries the planing down of the earthwork by winter floods obscures this characteristic feature, but it is clearly marked at the crossings of streamlets near Middle Knuck (Fig. 54) and Garbett Hall (Fig. 57), and between Spoad and Llanvair Hills (Fig. 56).

Openings for traffic are less numerous in this thinly populated upland country than in the lowlands crossed last year. Some of the hill-ways, anciently important, cross the Dyke by well-worn and broad gaps, as at Hergan (Fig. 54), and these gaps are probably pre-Offan. There are openings, now little used or disused, on Edenhope Hill (p. 128) and Knuck Bank (p. 129), which almost certainly permitted the passage of ancient ridgeways. Two openings which, still surviving substantially as they were made, are definitely part of the original design of the earthwork, will be described here.

The first of these is on Frydd Hill, near Woodhouse wood, S. of Knighton, at about 1,000 ft. above O.D. (Fig. 66 (li)). On either flank the rampart of the Dyke tapers to a point and is bent back so that if projected the ends would meet at an obtuse angle; the gap is narrow, measuring 8·4 ft. on the floor. The terminals are not recurved. The ditch at the opening is unusually broad because its (W.) lip maintains a fairly straight alignment, and so it does not share the reflection of the bank. The ditch is continuous across the opening;[2] its breadth (38 ft.) makes it relatively shallow and traffic dipped to enter and cross it by

---

[1] Descriptions of types (*a*) and (*c*) will be found on pp. 138 and 130–2. It is to be noted that one stretch of 'boundary-bank' type, on Hawthorn Hill, is of normal scale (p. 143).

[2] As at Selattyn Hill—Chapter IV, p. 75.

a slight and narrow cut in the counterscarp. This cut is flanked by low banks which extend for a few yards on either side and then fade out. The Dyke adjacent to the gap on either side is unusually massive (p. 154). The peculiar character of this opening is shown by the sketch plan and the profile on Fig. 66 which reveal the broad ditch, the rampart here bisected near one tip, and therefore very small), and the counterscarp bank. No signs of the ancient trackway which may have passed through[1] it are apparent; on one side (E.) is an arable field, and on the other (W.) moorland. Both are flat, and consequently no holloway, such as would be recognizable today, was formed by traffic.

The second opening is at Newcastle Hill, Discoed (Fig. 62). The bank of the Dyke is here, as in the preceding case, slightly reflected but not recurved or thickened. The (W.) ditch on either side of the opening conforms, and is thus of normal breadth. The original width of the gap measured on the floor was about 5 ft., but a traffic line has at some time been cut into the slope of the bank on one side. A deep trackway (on a slope) leads to the opening from the NW., but cannot readily be traced on flat ground on the E. side of the Dyke; the traffic it at one time carried has been deflected on to the road a few yards to the N. The contours show clearly that the gap is on the line of a hill-way from Radnor forest (Fig. 69), a route now represented by the adjacent hill-road. The Dyke flanking the gap is of moderate dimensions, its scarp measuring 13–15 ft.

It is probable that, as originally designed, Offa's Dyke in the Mountain Zone was, save for stream and traffic gaps, continuous; today it is traceable, or its exact course known, save for a half a mile on the steep S. slope of Panpunton Hill and a few yards on the S. slope of Furrow Hill.

EARTHWORKS ON OR NEAR THE DYKE

Two hill-forts each form a fixed point upon which Offa's Dyke was aligned: one, Castle Ring (Fig. 62), a plateau ring-work on Newcastle Hill; the other, Burfa Camp, a contour hill-fort on Burfa Bank (Figs. 63 and 64), both in Evenjobb Parish, Radnorshire.

Though the Dyke was aligned on the skyline formed by each, it was deflected on to new alignments before the earthworks were reached, leaving Castle Ring 350 yards on the Welsh side, and Burfa Camp 300 yards on the English side, at the nearest points. There is therefore nothing to suggest that to the designer of the Dyke these forts (if both were then in existence) had any significance; the Dyke would probably have been aligned in exactly the same way had they not been present, the hill-tops on which they stand forming in themselves suitable aligning marks.

Of the other earthworks near the Dyke, a 'camp' on Fron Hill, in Clun parish, nearly 1,100 ft. above O.D., is the most interesting. This little fort, 700 yards on the W. side of the Dyke at its nearest point (Fron End, Fig. 55), occupies the tip of a prominent spur facing ESE., and providing extended visual control of the Clun valley (see Plate XXVIII). The defences—a single bank and ditch—across the spur are massive and straightly aligned;

[1] See Fig. 69. The natural crossing-point of an ancient and almost certainly pre-Offan traffic-line is a short distance to the S.

the vallum measures 40 ft. on the slope at one point. Elsewhere on the perimeter the defences are slight. There is, in places, a slight bank on the counterscarp. The original entrance is on the edge of a steep slope at the SW. corner.

'Camp', Upper Knuck, Mainstone, 500 yards from Dyke at nearest point (W. of Upper Knuck, Fig. 54). This is a small 'fort' of promontory type on a valley slope; the flanks of the defences (two weak banks with a ditch between) rest respectively on the steep scarps of a little valley and of a ravine which bites deep into the N. flank thereof. The defences face uphill. It is probably the village site of a pastoral group.

'Camp' on S. slope of Llanvair Hill, L. Waterdine parish, 430 yards NNE. of Dyke at nearest point (spot-level 1257 on Fig. 57). This little enclosure, straight-sided with rounded corners, is in a slight hollow. It is sited for protection from the elements, not from Man, and was probably a cattle enclosure. The defences are a single bank and ditch, very slight. No entrance is apparent.

The position of the more important earthworks is shown on Fig. 69. The Burfa fortress is a characteristic work of a class associated with the Celts of the Early Iron Age, and in such a situation, on the edge of the lowlands, was almost certainly constructed before the Roman conquest of 'Wales'. Two other works of this class lie within easy reach, also on the foothills of the Welsh mountains and to the E. of the Dyke; Wapley and Caer Caradoc. There is none in the highlands W. of the Dyke and it would appear that the hill-town-building Celts either did not penetrate into this country-side or else did not find it worth colonizing. The only 'camps' hereabouts are small plateau or promontory forts such as Fron or the Caerdins[1] (Fig. 69) which appear to belong to a less highly organized culture than the great fortresses. We may perhaps in the future be able to identify them not as Mercian works but as the village sites of Welsh highlanders during the period of Mercian pressure.

Castle Ring alongside the Dyke on Newcastle Hill is, in strength and size, intermediate between the Burfa Hill–Wapley group and the Caerdin–Fron group. Though the type is met with elsewhere in Britain, we have not sufficient evidence to date this example; that it belongs to the Dark Ages is possible.

Certain 'Short Dykes', which can hardly be said to be adjacent to Offa's Dyke but which are of great importance in connexion with it, are discussed on pp. 160 ff.

VARIATION IN CONSTRUCTIONAL METHODS

The Dyke in the sector under investigation presents very varied characters and includes constructional features which have not been previously met with. Portions on the most massive scale alternate with others so inconspicuous as hardly to be recognizable; long stretches in normal (i.e. fairly level) country show no W. ditch, a feature hitherto regarded as the hall-mark of Offan work. Banks on the counterscarp appear and disappear.

[1] One is on the Kerry Ridgeway (Chapter V, p. 114). A second Caerdin, NW. of Fron, also adjacent to an important ridgeway, was also examined in 1929 and found to be a slight work, roughly rectangular with rounded corners, of similar size and character to its namesake, but possessing on the side facing the ridge-way an outer bank and ditch and the earthen base of a 'barbican' or look-out tower (?).

It is evident that the problems of the Dyke must be studied afresh, and conclusions as to its character and history retested and modified if necessary. Fortunately, the Dyke in the Mountain Zone is very well preserved and difficulties due to partial survival seldom arise.

The first problem for determination is that of unity or diversity. Is the Dyke a patch-work of various periods? Do certain portions, the most expensive in labour and time, represent earlier work of a defensive character, the connecting links being supplied by Offa's engineer? To this possibility certain facts seem to supply a definite negative. All parts of the work fit without violence into the major layout, which is governed by con-siderations affecting the whole traverse of over 21 miles. It is unlikely that short works constructed at different times to meet local needs would thus conform. Moreover, the mode of dealing with recurrent obstacles is consistent throughout the sector, and the engineer's choice of a route for the Dyke reveals at all points the same mental processes and expresses the same fundamental principles.

How then are we to reconcile the unity of the Dyke with its diversity of structure, more extreme than in any sector we have hitherto studied? The most promising line of inquiry is geographical—the distribution of the three constructional types (*weak, normal, reinforced*) analysed on p. 157, and their relation to the physiography. Fig. 69 provides the necessary information. It is noticeable that our sector is divided into two halves, in one of which, the northern, the Dyke is usually of *normal* type with occasional *reinforced* portions; the other, the southern, is usually of *weak* type with occasional *normal* portions. In other words, the halves differ in strength, but preserve similar relative differences. Where do these stronger portions occur? In the first place, on ridges as at Edenhope and Mainstone, or on cols or saddles as at Hergan, Frydd, or Newcastle Hill; in the second place in valleys such as those of the Teme and the Lugg. Light is thrown on the significance of this distribution, and of these characters, by an examination of the 'Short Dykes' of the district.

SHORT DYKES—CROSS-RIDGE AND CROSS-VALLEY

In Chapter V (p. 106) the 'Lower Short Ditch', a dyke 2 miles W. of Offa's Dyke, was described and illustrated. This is one of eight similar works, conveniently termed 'Short Dykes', situated in East Radnorshire and its borders, at no great distance from Offa's Dyke. The remaining seven of these were examined during the present season. Fig. 69 shows some of them, revealing the two classes into which they are found naturally to fall. One group consists of dykes bestriding ridges with flanks protected by boggy ground or dingles with precipitous slopes; the other consists of dykes crossing valley floors. They are tabulated and lettered A to H on pp. 167–8.

The cross-ridge dykes within the area, five in number, are thrown across the ridgeways which lead from the central highlands of Wales towards the English midlands. Three span the Kerry ridgeway which descends to the lowlands at Bishops Castle; one a track leading to the Upper Severn valley (Newton–Montgomery area),[1] another (Fig. 67) a track leading

[1] Possibly leading to Rhyd-whiman, the important ford of Montgomery on the Severn.

to the foothills bordering the valley of the Teme. In all the characteristic features, additional to that which defines the group, are a rampart of moderate elevation[1] with a W. ditch; that is, they were built by lowlanders against the hill folk. Two, the Double Deyches S. of Newtown (Fig. 70, D), show in addition a well-marked bank on the counterscarp. Though these two are separated by the boggy hollow in which the river Mule rises, and control divergent hill routes, their general alignment is the same, and their similarity is

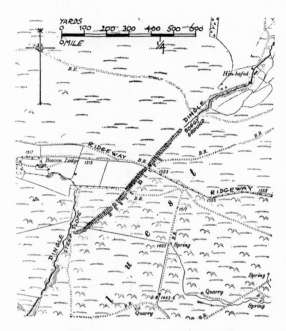

Fig. 67. Cross-ridge Dyke: The Short Ditch on Lan Luest; in Beguildy and Llangunllo parishes, Radnorshire. 6-in. O.S. map, Radnorshire X, NW. and SW.

such that they must be regarded as separate elements of one defensive design, and as being of the same date. Their resemblance to the Hergan section of Offa's Dyke, which lies due E. of them (Fig. 69), is striking. The W. portion of these Deyches, moreover, provides a good example of the use of lateral re-entrants, so familiar on a large scale in Offa's Dyke; it picks up a runlet which has scored a channel in the hill-side, and follows its margin to the main valley—the Mule springheads. The cross-ridge dykes, as a group, show alignments of Types I and III, that is, either straight or conformable to the contour of the country which they traverse.

The cross-valley dykes, three in number, are alike in several respects additional to that which defines their group. All are set out in straight alignments (Type I), thus resembling valley portions of Offa's Dyke (e.g. Vyrnwy–Severn and Camlad, Chapter V, Figs. 35–36 and 40–41), not to mention portions in the zone now under investigation. All have their ditches on the W. and a single bank of considerable dimensions (e.g. Rowe Ditch: at one

---

[1] About equal to an average portion of Offa's Dyke, with scarps 10–18 ft. on the slope.

point, scarp 21 ft., overall breadth 49 ft.). Each is sited at the *western* end of a fertile valley suitable for agriculture and dairying. Wantyn Dyke covers the upper Caebitra valley, Ditch Bank (Plate XXXII) the plain of New Radnor, Rowe Ditch the alluvial flat of the river Arrow between Pembridge and Leominster.

On the flanks of Wantyn Dyke and Ditch Bank, the hills rise steeply to 1,000 ft. and more, and their scarps may be held to have provided sufficient protection against turning

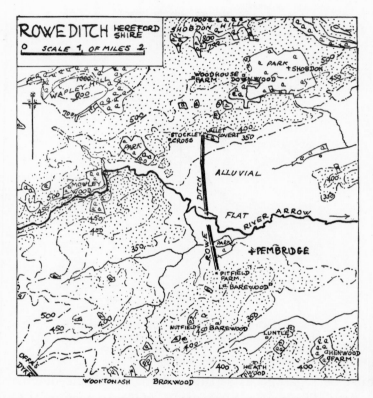

FIG. 68. Cross-valley Dyke: Rowe Ditch, in the Arrow valley, Herefordshire. The dotted areas were probably forest.

movements; both on the N. and S. of Rowe Ditch, on the other hand, the hill slopes are gentle, and the Dyke seems to end in the air. The distribution of farms, hamlets, and trackways, the patches of woodlands, the place-names, and the nature of the subsoil (Old Red Sandstone), however, point to the existence down to the Middle Ages of a broad belt of woodland on the slopes of the Arrow valley hereabouts. Fig. 68 shows Rowe Ditch, the woodland existing today, and the compounds in -wood, -field, and -ley which characterize the local place-names; the induction drawn from these facts is graphically indicated on the map by shading the area held to have been forest. It should be pointed out that Rowe Ditch, in its traverse of the river Arrow, shows a specially close resemblance to Offa's Dyke in its traverse of the Camlad brook valley (Chapter V, p. 99), the engineer of

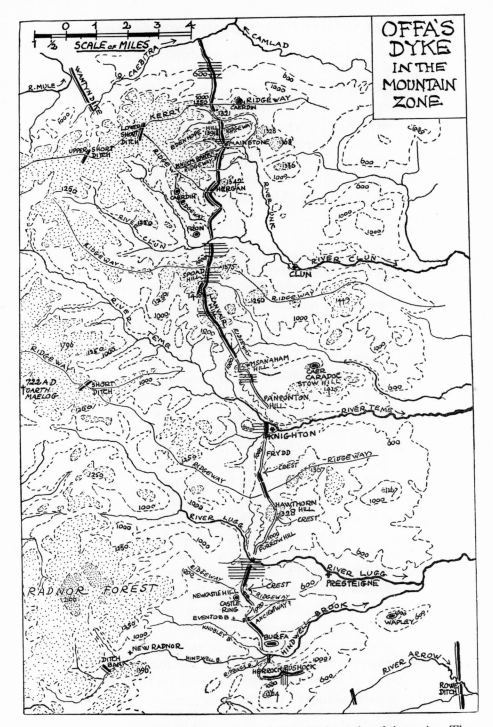

FIG. 69. Structure of Offa's Dyke in relation to the physiography of the region. The more important hill forts, ridgeways, and the Short Ditches within the area are also shown.

Symbols: ‖ = Normal Dyke with W. ditch.   ‖ = Weak Dyke with E. ditch. ‖‖ = Reinforced Dyke with W. ditch. | = Dyke on a steep hill-side where no distinction between types is possible. ≡ = Alignments of Type I (these areas were probably arable fields or meadows in the eighth century).

each having taken a new sighting at the river, resulting in a slight change of direction at the crossing-point.

We are, I think, justified in concluding that the cross-valley dykes were designed to form protective screens immediately in front (west) of agriculturally developed patches of lowland. They are so similar in type and technique that they are most probably of one period: what then is their date? Straight alignment across valley floors being characteristic of Offa's Dyke, and in a further peculiar detail of alignment, identity of technique between one of the cross-valley dykes and Offa's Dyke having been established, we may justifiably ascribe the cross-valley dykes to the Mercians.

Significance of the Short Dykes

The point to which the argument has brought us affords a basis for further advance. Close parallels in technique having been shown to exist between Offa's Dyke and both groups of short dykes, it seems probable that we have in these dykes, whether on the hills or in the valleys, the mark of one school of dyke builders who, at periods which can hardly have been very far apart, were working on them and on Offa's Dyke. The two groups are manifestly complementary. One has its terminals where slopes descend, the other its terminals where slopes ascend. One controls the highland routes of approach from the upland plateaux to the cornlands, meadows, and steadings of the agriculturists; the other provides protection from raiders for the cornlands and farms themselves. Regarding then both groups of short dykes as evidence of the long-continued warfare between the agricultural Mercians and their 'troublesome' neighbours the Welsh highlanders (who perceive their hereditary lands being encroached upon!) are we to regard them as pre-Offan or post-Offan, or as covering both periods? The question cannot yet be definitely answered, but there are weighty considerations pointing to a pre-Offan date. In the first place, most of the short dykes present features suggesting that they are *localized efforts*; the valley dykes protect isolated communities, not the frontier of a state, and the majority of cross-ridge dykes perform a similar function. Only two of the latter, the Double Deyches, control a strategical point, that where the hillways from central Wales are forced by the nature of the country to unite on the watershed between the rivers Ithon and Severn before separating to make for different areas in the lowlands (Plate XXIII). In the second place, they lie both E. and W. of Offa's Dyke; that is, they belong to a period when the frontier was in a state of flux, when Mercian farmers could till as much high-valley country as they could hold, and conversely when—in phases of weakness—the Herefordshire plain itself was much exposed to attack.[1] In brief, the majority represent local effort at defence and consolidation which seems more likely to be pre-Offan than post-Offan. If Sir John E. Lloyd's identification of 'Garthmaelog', where the Welsh gained a victory

[1] If surprise is occasioned by the view that advanced areas such as the New Radnor plain could have been occupied by English farmers in the eighth century and, if so, excluded from Mercian control when the Dyke was made, it may be remarked that an agreed, or a military, frontier may represent withdrawals in certain areas and advances in others, and is not necessarily the exact racial frontier at the time of its formulation. This area is hidated in the Domesday survey and so was in English occupation prior to 1087. On this, see Sir Frank Stenton, *Anglo-Saxon England*, 1943, p. 212, para. 2.

over the Mercians in 722,[1] as being near Llanbister (Rads.) be correct, we are presented with precisely the dated event required by the argument. Llanbister is on the Welsh side— 6 miles W.—of one of the Short Dykes under review. Desultory fighting in advance of consolidation is to have been expected.

These short dykes are not the only running earthworks on the Mercian border: one lies to the W., four (in Montgomeryshire)[2] to the N., of the examples here studied, and there are three to the eastward, in Shropshire.[3]

A sketch-map, Fig. 70, shows the distribution of short dykes on the Welsh borders. They are grouped along that sector of the western frontier of Mercia which is nearest to the centre of the kingdom—the capital, Tamworth—and which was, therefore, the most important from the point of view of the rulers of this State. This sector, moreover, happens to be the most vulnerable. It is where an outlier of the Welsh mountain massif projects like a bastion into the Midlands, providing an easy route for the hillmen into the heart of Mercia, which possesses no natural line of defence hereabouts until the middle valley of the Severn is reached; it is also where the rich lowlands of the Upper Severn, near its junction with the Vyrnwy, are peculiarly liable to attack. From Hereford southward, an admirable frontier (utilized by the Mercians in the Offan period, p. 212 below) is provided by the river Wye, and from the river Vyrnwy northward to the Dee estuary the sharply defined division between lowland and highland formed a convenient and natural boundary, which was reinforced, judging from the character of the lowland soil—glacial drift—by a wide belt of forest.[4]

If then Mercia was to be reasonably safe, this mountain zone, colonizable only to a limited extent by lowland agriculturists, and therefore thinly populated, had to be rendered secure, and the menace of attack on the upper Severn valley dealt with. I suggest that it

[1] *History of Wales*, i, p. 197. The site of the battle is marked on Fig. 69.

[2] There is a number of works in E. Montgomeryshire, the position and character of which, as recorded in the *Inventory* (Royal Commission on Ancient Monuments, Wales, vol. i), suggest that they may belong to the 'short dykes' class as defined in this section, as well as others which manifestly cannot be closely related. The Giant's Grave, no. 337, faces SW., and is evidently a cross-ridge dyke with bank on the counterscarp, belonging to the Double Deyche group (it is marked M on Fig. 70). Of the remainder in the *Inventory*, six, grouped round the Vyrnwy river system, demanded investigation. These are nos. 216, 217, 610, 634, 635, 636. Nos. 634 and 635 were found to face N. and to control a pass leading from the Tanat valley to the Cain valley (O and Q on my map); No. 216 faces N. and controls a pass leading S. from the Vyrnwy valley, near Meifod (N on map); Nos. 217 and 610 deserve detailed study, but do not, I think, belong to the series under consideration. The descriptions in the *Inventory* of all but one of these require correction in detail. No. 636 (P. on map) was not examined, but it is clearly a cross-ridge Dyke facing NW.

[Note (1953): My friend Mr. Noel Jarman, M.A., carried out 'A Field Survey of Some Dykes in East Central Wales' in 1934, his plans being prepared on the same scale as my own for comparative purposes. These dykes are: Pen-y-clawdd Dyke, Llangunllo, Rads.: Shepherds Well Dyke, Radnor Forest; and Cefn-y-Crug Dyke, Radnor Forest. The first was inventoried by the Royal Commission (no. 379): none are recorded on the O.S. maps.

The first controlled traffic from one valley to another *opposite* across the col at their heads—a type not met with in the Mercian system. The second controls 'the only practicable way from W. to E. across the top of Radnor Forest' (1982) while the third 'impedes traffic from S. to N.'; which means 'from England into Wales' —an interesting group. See *Arch. Camb.*, 1935, pp. 279–87.]

[3] These cross-ridge dykes on the Long Mynd were first described by E. S. Cobbold (*Church Stretton*, iii, 1904, pp. 51–55), and are lettered J, K, L, on my map. They are of no great strength but, in my opinion, definitely of 'Mercian' type. I am indebted to Mr. Cobbold for showing them to me, and to Miss L. F. Chitty, F.S.A., for informing me of their existence.

[4] This northern part of the frontier in pre-Offan times was almost certainly protected by Wat's Dyke. See Chapter VIII.

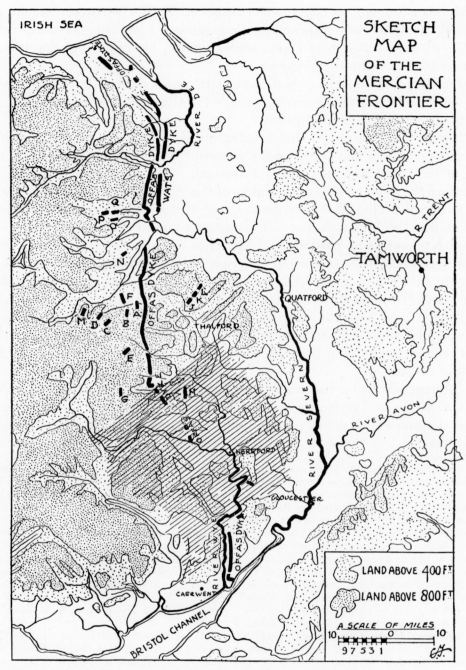

FIG. 70. Sketch map of the Mercian frontier. Offa's Dyke, Wat's Dyke, and the 'Short Dykes' are shown. The latter are lettered A to Q.

is probable that in the cross-ridge, cross-col, or cross-valley dykes scattered over these regions we have evidence of efforts made by the Mercians to control or provide warnings of attacks from the Welsh highlands, and to protect their steadings in its valleys.[1] It also seems likely that all such works will be found to be of the seventh or eighth centuries A.D.

That these efforts were at first unco-ordinated and local can hardly be doubted. Evidences of unifying control and direction are, however, not altogether lacking. The Double Deyches, as we have seen, provide opportunity for effectual scrutiny by 'frontier guards' of a large portion of the traffic from Central Wales into the Midlands. Such Dykes must, I think, belong to a later phase of the development of dyke building than the other cross-ridge dykes studied in this chapter, and it is significant that an adjacent portion of Offa's Dyke (the Hergan section) should resemble them. The Double Deyches then may represent the last phase of the system of localized defence prior to its supersession by an agreed frontier—Offa's Dyke.[2]

List of 'Short' Dykes in East Radnorshire and its Borders

Name and site	Character and length	Alignment	Terminals	Notes and references
	Group I: Cross-ridge Dykes			
Lower Short Ditch (Fig. 69: 'A' on Fig. 70). Across Kerry ridgeway, Mont. and Salop. 1,523 ft. above O.D.	Bank and W. ditch. 800 yds.	In straight stretches	On dingles	See 6-in. O.S. Mont. 44 NE., and *Arch. Camb.*, 1928, p. 43
Upper Short Ditch (Fig. 69: 'B' on Fig. 70). Across Kerry ridgeway, Mont. and Salop. 1,501 ft. above O.D.	Bank and W. ditch. Probably 930 yds.	Follows curve of hill	On dingles	About 330 yds. has been ploughed out. See 6-in. O.S. Mont. 44 SW., and Salop. 61 SW. *Arch. Camb.*, 1901, pp. 291–3

[1] The short dykes lying in front or behind Offa's Dyke in the mountain zone (A to M) mostly face W. or SW., while those in the valley zone (N to Q) mostly face N. or NW. Evidently the highlanders of central Wales were the opponents in the one case, and those of north Wales in the other.

[2] The examination of these Short Dykes suggests that the ancient trackways of Wales in general deserve to be studied with far more care than they have yet received. Moving along those controlled (*ex hypothesi*) by the Mercians in the eighth century, one is conscious that there existed, in the mountain complex of which the area examined forms part, a complete system of intercommunication almost entirely unrelated to that existing today. The alignments of this system are determined by the watersheds. The ways are essentially ridgeways, refusing, except under stress of absolute necessity, to cross any stream—thus, at a high point on the March, where rivers of the importance of the Teme rise, the ancient ways are above their sources, passing at the 1,500-ft. level.

The comparative ease of movement possible on these naturally well-drained crest lines is enhanced by the absence of marked changes in level. For 7 miles the Kerry ridgeway, passing through very broken country, does not change level through more than 100 ft., and this only by gentle gradients.

The inhabitants of Wales were thus provided, by conforming to geographical conditions, with routes which afforded good going and which for the most part were easy to follow, since the greater landmarks of the countryside were permanently in sight, and deflection landed the traveller on steep slopes or in boggy ground. The levels at which men moved on their pastoral activities, for commerce, for war, or amusement, vary, but the normal range in Radnorshire is between 1,000 and 2,000 ft. Thus we may conceive of human activity in early times proceeding along levels 500 to 1,000 ft. above those we use today in the same areas. Indeed, until the nineteenth century, though the Welsh had long occupied the valleys as well as the hills, the hill ways seem normally to have been employed for other than inter-valley traffic.

GROUP I: CROSS-RIDGE DYKES (*continued*)

Name and Site	Character and length	Alignment	Terminals	Notes and references
Double Deyches (*Dyke*) ('C' on Fig. 70). Across Kerry ridgeway, Mont. 1,650 ft. above O.D.	Bank, SW. ditch, and second bank on counterscarp. 630 yds.	Follows curve of hill	On dingle (N.) and marshy flat (S.)	An extension exists (in Rads.) on ridge beyond marshy flat (not examined). See 6-in. O.S. Mont. 43 SE., and Rads. 4 NE. *R.C.A.M.*, Mont. 293, Rads. 86
Double Deyches (*Dyke*) ('D' on Fig. 70). Across Crugyn Bank, Kerry, Mont. *c.* 1,400 ft. above O.D.	Bank, SW. ditch, and second bank on counterscarp. ½ mile	Two nearly straight stretches	On boggy ground and streamlets	Dyke extends 370 yds. on E. beyond limit marked on O.S. map. See 6-in. O.S. Mont. 43 SE. *R.C.A.M.*, Mont. 293
Short Ditch (Figs. 67, 69: 'E' on Fig. 70). Across Lan Lluest, Bugeildy, Rads. 1,523 ft. above O.D.	Bank and NW. ditch. 700 yds.	Straight on plateau, follows curve of hill at either end	On dingles	O.S. map does not carry terminals quite far enough. See 6-in. O.S. Rads. 10 NW. and SW. *R.C.A.M.*, Rads. 85, and Fig. 67 of this book

Group II: CROSS-VALLEY DYKES

Wanten Dyche (*Dyke*) ('F' on Fig. 70, and Fig. 69). Across upper valley of Caebitra, where it interdigitates with the R. Mule, Montgomeryshire	Bank and W. ditch. 2 miles	In straight stretches	On the steep flanks of the valley	Extensions, irregular, on hillside to S.? See 6-in. O.S. Mont. 37 SW., 44 NW. and NE. *Arch. Camb.*, 1901, pp. 279 ff. and *R.C.A.M.*, Mont. p. 58
Ditch Bank ('G' on Fig. 70, Plate XXXII and Fig. 69). Across gorge of Summergil brook SW. of New Radnor, Radnorshire	Bank and slight trace of SW. ditch, no trace of NE. ditch. 400 yds.	Straight	On the steep flanks of the valley	See 6-in. O.S. Rads. 24 SE. *R.C.A.M.*, Rads. 358
Rowe Ditch ('H' on Fig. 70). See also Figs. 68 & 69. Across valley floor of R. Arrow, near Pembridge, Herefordshire	Bank and W. ditch. 2 miles, 300 yds.	In straight stretches	On rising ground on either flank of the valley	N. end in Vallet Covert quite definite: S. end probably Pitfield farm, now 170 yds. N. of farm. See 6-in. O.S. Hereford, 11 SW. and 18 NW.; *V.C.H.*, Hereford, i, p. 25 (terminals incorrectly recorded) and my Fig. 91

THE GENESIS AND PURPOSE OF OFFA'S DYKE IN THE MOUNTAIN ZONE

We can now return to Offa's Dyke (and Fig. 69) with solutions of its outstanding (local) problems in sight. In the first place, the significance of the stronger portions of the Dyke on the hill-tops is apparent. Such are present adjacent to or bestriding every one of the hill- or ridge-ways which pass through the earthwork, ridgeways which in two cases were controlled, farther west, by short dykes. Particular attention may be drawn to those at Edenhope, Knuck Bank, and Hergan, which pass through 'reinforced' portions of the

Dyke; and those at Kerry Hill (Chapter V, Fig. 50) and Spoad Hill, which pass through exceptionally strong portions of the Dyke. Though no ridgeway can today be traced at or near the remaining stretch of reinforced Dyke—that on Llanvair Hill, this seems to be related to the only upland line of approach from the Kerry Hill area to the Stow Hill district, N. of Knighton. It probably, therefore, fulfilled the same purpose as the others. In at least two cases a happy accident—a slight shift, in the course of centuries, taking place in the point of passage of the cross-dyke traffic—has preserved unchanged what can hardly be other than the gap originally left for wayfarer or merchant passing along such trackways. The example on Newcastle Hill is very significant. Here a small piece (170 yards) of normal dyke construction with a gap, an opening, centrally placed, is sandwiched in between stretches of 'boundary-bank' type: this piece lies across the only possible upland traffic line from Radnor Forest to the Presteigne area.

Again, the Dyke is strongly constructed on the floor, or slopes (if gentle), of every main valley which in this region the Dyke crosses. Of special significance for the argument are the Teme and Lugg valleys, where massive portions intervene between stretches of boundary-bank type. Just as the cross-ridge dykes have their counterparts in certain hill-top portions of Offa's Dyke, so the cross-valley dykes have their counterparts in cross-valley portions of Offa's Dyke.

We cannot avoid the conclusion that the engineer has, in this sector, applied familiar principles of Mercian defensive warfare to the construction of the new frontier, joining up (in the southern half) his carefully constructed and important portions by banks of the roughest description—just sufficiently visible to fix the line through what was doubtless forest (pp. 152, 170)—and in the northern half, where the whole work is of a more massive character, reinforcing important points with an extra bank, or making the Dyke at such points unusually large. Emphasizing the continuity of the Mercian military tradition, I would go so far as to say that it is probable that the gang which was employed at the Double Deyches (pp. 161, 164) subsequently built the Hergan section of the Dyke.

Moreover, since there are strong grounds for believing that alignments of Type I are confined to open country, it is significant that the only extensive examples of such in the present sector—on the Clun and Lugg slopes, and Spoad hill-top—are of exceptionally massive construction. This applies also to the remains of the Dyke, presumably straightly aligned, on the floors of these valleys. In them we may assume that the Mercian frontiersman was in the eighth century firmly planted; he had transformed jungle or marsh into cornland and rich pasture for herds. Here the Mercian control of the new frontier in the Mountain Zone, in so far as its bases were economic, was necessarily centred. The great Dyke formed a barrier in front of the fields of these Anglian intruders, men compelled, by the dangers to which they were exposed, to be as familiar with the broad-bladed war axe and the spear as with the plough and the hoe.

We are now in a position to gauge the significance of the difference stressed in the preceding pages between the N. and S. sections of the Dyke in the Mountain Zone. The distribution of the Short Dykes on Fig. 70 shows that the Kerry ridgeway, its outliers and extensions, formed the chief route of raiding highlanders, since nine out of the sixteen dykes on the map (A to D, F, and J to M), are connected with it.[1] Now this is precisely the area occupied by the northern and stronger portion of Offa's Dyke in this Zone. Here the engineer made a work consistently well constructed and frequently very large; farther south the critical portions alone were well made.

Again, we can now understand why Offa's Dyke in this difficult country was pushed so far forward. It bends sharply backward at Herrock Hill to cross the Herefordshire plain, and thus from the geographical point of view a more easterly and therefore easier traverse of the Mountain Zone was possible (Fig. 70). Such a course was not taken because the Mercians were deeply committed by generations of warlike activity (with its corollary, settlement) on this dangerous frontier to a forward line. History has numerous examples of states which, in the name of security, have advanced their boundaries to the breaking point.

Lastly, we seem in this Zone to be, as it were, at the birth of a work of genius; to be studying the great earthwork *in the limited area where it was evolved*, and where by the greatest good luck its condition is sufficiently perfect to permit an exact analysis of its original structure. Here the engineer learned his job: elsewhere he cast off the defects— the mere boundary bank thrown up from a succession of spoil holes—which dim his achievement.

The question must now be asked, can we any longer regard Offa's Dyke merely as a boundary or visible frontier; does not its construction in this Zone point to its being defensive, at all events in the portions on which the engineer's attention was especially concentrated?

Defensive, perhaps, but in the limited sense of an obstacle. That the Dyke was ever *manned*, here or elsewhere, in the way that a hill-fort was manned, I do not believe. It may safely be assumed from the evidence already recorded that when the Dyke was built in this area the greater part of the country traversed by it was forest. There were extended tracts of cultivated land in the valleys, and patches on the hills, and broad open belts, the results of centuries of pastoral activity, flanking the ridgeways. When the traverse of the Dyke had been plotted, the earthwork was built wherever this traverse crossed a clearing or a traffic line. The intervening spaces were filled in later; hence the abrupt contrasts seen at Hergan in the northern sector, and near Woodhouse wood and in the Lugg valley —Newcastle Hill area in the southern. The Dyke crossing these open spaces provided not only a visible frontier, but also a barrier through which lawful passage could only be attained at fixed points; these doubtless were watched by frontier guards. Whether the Dyke was intended to prevent or make more difficult cattle raids is an arguable point. My friend Mr. E. T. Leeds has suggested to me that it might be impossible for raiding hill-men to induce fat Mercian beeves, spoil from the lowlands, to negotiate such a barrier, and that a strong guard on the gaps—passage-ways through the Dyke—would effectually prevent such activities.

[1] My friend Dr. (now Professor) William Rees points out that there are a succession of important fords on the continuation of the Kerry ridgeway route into the lowlands and towards Tamworth, e.g. Halford on the Onny and Quatford on the Severn.

It would be absurd to suppose that all the problems presented by the Dyke in this sector have been solved, when one considers the variety of conditions and forces—political, military, physiographic, economic, financial, social, personal—operating to produce by their interaction the observed effects, and how few, if any, of these forces can be adequately assessed today. The reader may have noticed that certain features in the construction are unexplained, such, for example, as the occurrence of a dyke-bank of *normal* size with *E.* ditch near Hawthorn Hill. Still, I believe that the reasoning is valid, and that the main conclusions are sound; they certainly reduce to order, and render intelligible, a chaos of facts which at one time appeared to me to be intractable.

Offa's Dyke, a comprehensible achievement

The Dyke has hitherto been regarded as without a precursor in its own area, and it thus has been difficult to understand whence came the driving force which brought it into being, and the engineering skill apparent in its construction. The evidence now marshalled in this chapter suggests that the Mercians had devoted much labour and skill to the construction of linear earthworks for the extension, protection, or consolidation of their territory at its most vulnerable points, so that the great Dyke 'extending from sea to sea' may well have been an ideal to which experience had long been leading the rulers of the kingdom. It was not then the novel idea of a vigorous king; but, on the other hand, so great a work could hardly have been completed or even initiated until the Mercian realm came under the control of a man of exceptional competence, energy, and power of organization.

PLATE XXXIII

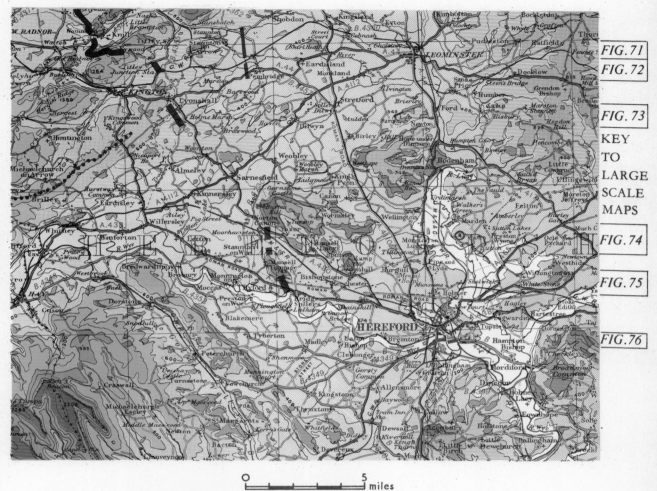

FIG. 71
FIG. 72

FIG. 73

KEY
TO
LARGE
SCALE
MAPS

FIG. 74

FIG. 75

FIG. 76

0   5 miles

Scale ¼ in. to 1 mile

Offa's Dyke in the Wye Valley

(Chapter VII)

(A) In Herefordshire

**The dotted line is a ridgeway, the thin lines Rowe Ditch, Pembridge, and the Row Ditches, Hereford. Sutton Walls, an
Early Iron Age fortress, is also shown**

See pages 173, 174, 181, 182, 203, 206, 221 *n.*, 278, 286

PLATE XXXIV

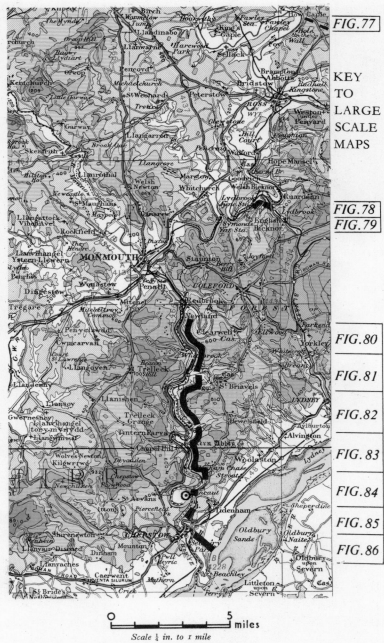

FIG. 77

KEY
TO
LARGE
SCALE
MAPS

FIG. 78
FIG. 79

FIG. 80

FIG. 81

FIG. 82

FIG. 83

FIG. 84

FIG. 85

FIG. 86

0   5 miles

Scale ¼ in. to 1 mile

Offa's Dyke in the Wye Valley

(Chapter VII)

(B) In Gloucestershire
A 'short dyke' at Yatton is shown, and the Lancaut promontory
fort

See pages 173, 174, 182, 278, 286

VII. OFFA'S DYKE IN THE WYE VALLEY— HEREFORDSHIRE AND WEST GLOUCESTERSHIRE (1931)

IN this chapter the record of the course and character of Offa's Dyke is completed. The counties involved are Herefordshire and Gloucestershire, all but a small part of the earthwork being in the Wye valley and the major part closely following the course of that river.

The survey, of course, begins where the field work of 1929 ended, at the 'Three Shepherds'—ancient yew trees on Rushock Hill on the boundary between Lower Harpton and Kington Rural parishes, Herefordshire, 1½ miles south of the Radnorshire border. It ends on Sedbury cliff above the Severn estuary at Sedbury Park in Tidenham parish, Gloucestershire (Frontispiece). The distance as the crow flies is 45 miles, and along the line of the Dyke approximately 60 miles. Of this long distance, however, only 13 miles of dyke are generally recognized and marked on the O.S. map. These known portions are almost entirely in two groups, one in the area between Rushock Hill and the left bank of the Wye at Bridge Sollers above Hereford, the other extending from the left bank of the Wye at Highbury near Redbrook, to the Severn. The gap between these groups measured down the Wye valley is no less than 37 miles, and only in one or two places on this line (near English Bicknor) have any 'accepted' portions of the Dyke been found. Thus there is one large, and several smaller gaps, and these present the major problem with which this report will deal; we must either determine the line of the Dyke, or discuss the reason for its absence, in the districts where its course is unknown or uncertain.

The country traversed in this portion of the survey includes much of exceptional scenic and general interest; it is shown on two maps, Plates XXXIII and XXXIV, comprising the Herefordshire Plain, and the middle and lower valleys of the Wye from Yatton to Chepstow respectively. The point of division is a matter of convenience only.

The western margin of the first map marks the point where the Wye leaves the mountains and enters the Herefordshire Plain—which is mainly drained by this river and its tributaries the Arrow, the Lugg, and the Frome. These and other streams meet to form a wide alluvial flat in the neighbourhood of Hereford, and thus determined the position of a bishop's see and county town. The elevation of the plain is between 400 and 200 ft. above sea-level, the alluvial flat being between 200 and 100 ft. The plain is bounded on the W. by the Welsh mountains—in part by Radnor Forest and its associated uplands, dealt with in Chapter VI; in part by the Black Mountains whose high plateaux and steep escarpments form a magnificent and characteristic landscape SW. of Hereford. It is diversified by outliers of these mountain masses such as Burton Hill (963 ft.) NW. of Hereford, Aconbury (905 ft.) S. of the city, and Seager Hill (886 ft.) W. of it. The course of the river Wye from Brecon Vale, where it issues from the uplands, to Hereford, is ESE.; from Hereford to Yatton it follows a sinuous course, the general direction of which is SSE.

As the second map, Plate XXXIV shows, the Wye from Yatton southward maintains an equally sinuous course to its junction with the Severn, the general direction being slightly W. of S. The valley narrows, and from Goodrich to Chepstow, a distance of some 30 miles, forms a wooded gorge, the continuity of which is extensively broken only at Whitchurch and Monmouth, where, on the right bank, the intrusion of tributary streams or a river forms alluvial flats. This gorge has, extensively on the right bank and locally on the left bank, precipitous rocky scarps and cliffs (Figs. 93, 94). The upland thus trenched by the river forms plateaux or hills on either side, ranging from 500 to over 1,000 ft., the larger mass, known as the Forest of Dean, being on the E. The upland passes by easy stages into the sea plain (Frontispiece), here very narrow, across which the Wye flows to join the Severn.

In descending from Rushock Hill to the Herefordshire plain the Dyke passes on to the Old Red Sandstone, which formation largely occupies the valley of the middle Wye. A few miles S. of Ross the Wye crosses the Carboniferous Limestone; from Bicknor to the neighbourhood of Tintern the river is again on the Old Red Sandstone; from Tintern to Chepstow it once more crosses the Limestone. Thus the rocky limestone scarps and cliffs characteristic of the gorge are of widespread but limited distribution.

As may be gathered from the preceding remarks, the country traversed by the Dyke is of dual character. In Herefordshire, on the Old Red Sandstone, it is rich pastoral land with luxuriant vegetation, varied by parks and, on the hills, woodlands; in Gloucestershire, on the Carboniferous Limestone, it is sheep pasture and commons, with a certain amount of woodland, oak, ash, and yew. The steep slopes bordering the river in whatever formation they occur are extensively wooded.

The extreme range of variation in the level of the Dyke in the northern sector is 936 ft.; it leaves Rushock Hill at 1,136 ft. and reaches the Wye at 200 ft. In the southern sector its highest point is 790 ft. at Hudnalls, in St. Briavels parish; its lowest is only a few feet above sea-level at the W. end of the Tidenham peninsula.

THE COURSE OF THE DYKE

The course of the Dyke is set out on thirteen sections of the 6-inch O.S. map, reduced to 4 inches to 1 mile (Figs. 71–75, 78, and 80–86).[1] The small-scale maps, Plates XXXIII and XXXIV, enable the position of each of these large-scale maps to be found by the reader. An attempt has been made, as usual, by varying the thickness of the line which marks the Dyke, to indicate its varying dimensions.

FIGURE 71. *Rushock Hill to the Eywood brook, in Kington Rural Parish, Herefordshire*

From the 'Three Shepherds' on Rushock Hill the Dyke is of normal dimensions (about 13 ft. on the scarp) and with a S. ditch, for 320 yards. The Dyke then suddenly becomes small (bank 1–2 ft. high) and irregular, and the ditch shifts from S. to N. These

---

[1] Figs. 76, 77, and 79 represent earthworks not definitely forming part of Offa's Dyke. They are included as worthy of consideration.

characters persist for over 150 yards; then the Dyke becomes again clearly defined with well-cut N. ditch, the dimensions being 26 ft. overall and 12 ft. on the scarp, ditch 2 ft. deep. So it continues, on a steepening slope, to the Kennel wood boundary; through the wood it is present as a low rounded bank with N. ditch. In the meadow beyond, the levelled Dyke can be traced nearly to the parish boundary—a small streamlet; there is no sign of it on the ploughland forming the N. flank of the little valley. The level at which it fades out is 810 ft. above O.D. (For the 'Scutch Ditch' in this valley, see p. 177.)

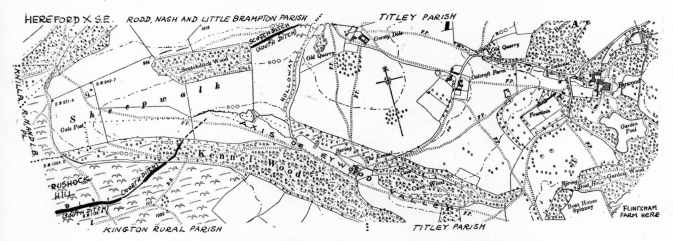

FIG. 71. Rushock Hill to the Eywood brook, in Kington rural parish, Herefordshire.

A portion of the 6-in. O.S. map reduced to 4 in. to 1 mile.
In this and twelve of the following maps a thick black line ■■■■ represents portions of the Dyke clearly visible today; the *degree* of thickness illustrating the relative size of the work at different points in its course. An additional line close to and parallel with the principal one indicates the presence of a bank on the counterscarp. A thick broken line - - - shows that faint traces of the Dyke are present; while a hair line —— represents the approximate alignment of the Dyke where it is now lost, as recorded on the first 1-in. O.S. map, or as indicated by a respectable tradition. A broken hair line — — — represents the probable frontier where the Dyke was not constructed.
Roman numerals in circles point to the exact position where the sectional plan with the corresponding number was made; letters in circles and arrows indicate the approximate position and direction of the camera when the illustration with the corresponding letter was taken. Certain fields and enclosures on the line of the Dyke are identified by arabic numerals.
Sketch contours — · — · — · indicate important natural features on the line of the Dyke not clearly brought out on the Ordnance map.
(Reproduced from the Ordnance Survey map with the sanction of the Controller of H.M. Stationery Office.)

There seems no doubt that the Dyke on Rushock Hill, uniform in size and character, with S. ditch, was constructed by a different gang to that which built the portion with N. ditch on the flank of the Eywood valley. The break in technique is as well-defined as on Frydd (Chapter VI, p. 142). The change takes place where the plateau ends and the Eywood valley begins. It may be surmised that there was, also, a difference in physical conditions—open country above and woodland below.

FIGURE 72. *Flintsham to N. end of Lyonshall Park wood. In Titley and Lyonshall parishes, Herefordshire*

The Dyke reappears near Flintsham farm, about 550 ft. above O.D. in Titley parish, 1⅓ miles as the crow flies from Kennel wood, where we left it. At Flintsham it has recovered its normal N.–S. alignment. It is very well marked—a flattened bank, 50 ft. overall, with broad W. ditch and with a gap in the centre, crossing a small depression trending E. It is aligned on the W. slope of an isolated steep-sided wooded knoll, known as

Berry's wood; the Dyke enters this wood and its bank merges into, its ditch dies into, the slope of the knoll. At its point of disappearance it is undamaged, 36 ft. overall with broad W. ditch. It was quite certainly never constructed on the knoll beyond this point. From the S. side of the knoll an ancient hedge-line leads down to the river Arrow approximately in alignment with the continuation of the Dyke on the farther side of the river. This hedge is mainly on the alluvial flat, but a small portion near the knoll is on a gentle slope, and here faint traces of a levelled bank which cannot be certainly identified with Offa's Dyke are to be seen. Crossing the river, disturbed ground and a mill leat are met with, beyond

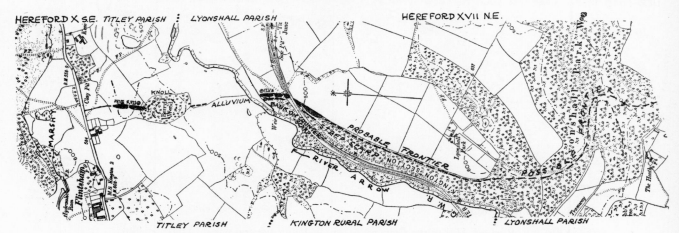

FIG. 72. Flintsham to N. end of Lyonshall Park wood. In Titley and Lyonshall parishes, Herefordshire.
A portion of the 6-in. O.S. map reduced to 4 in. to 1 mile. For the significance of the symbols and letters employed, see Fig. 71.
(Reproduced from the Ordnance Survey map with the sanction of the Controller of H.M. Stationery Office)

which, about 35 yards from the river, a well-preserved portion of the Dyke is seen, extending upwards to the railway embankment. The bank is at first high, the (W.) ditch well defined and narrow; but the bank quickly becomes smaller, the W. ditch broader and flat-floored, and there are traces of a bank on the counterscarp. There is a gap in the centre here. The field is old pasture, and a certain amount of levelling has doubtless taken place. Above and beyond the railway the Dyke is a fine work, presenting a broad flat ditch and counterscarp bank.[1] It is aligned on the point where the river has bitten into the hill forming a steep wooded scarp; it proceeds along the edge of this scarp for a few yards and then ends abruptly, as at Berry's wood. This stretch (of 96 yards) S. of the railway is not marked on the O.S. maps.

The portion of the Dyke here examined, though probably never continuous, certainly was intended to represent a continuous frontier. The gap that exists can be explained: it was occupied by the knoll, a prominent (wooded) landmark, and probably by uncleared jungle thence to the river. The existing dyke structure may be held to have spanned trackways on either side of, and parallel to, the river.

[1] This unusual breadth of ditch associated with the counterscarp bank has been met with before. See Chapter VI, p. 129, lines 38–39. It explains itself as a constructional feature; the spoil for two banks requires a larger ditch than for one.

We may now inquire whether the Dyke was originally thus limited or whether it can be extended in either direction.

At the N. end the 1833 1-in. O.S. map (sheet 56) marks the Dyke northwards up to the Titley–Kington road, thus adding 130 yards to its known length. The alignment is shown on Fig. 72. There is now no trace whatever on the level pasture field which occupies this area, but it may be accepted, as the evidence of this early map is usually reliable. There is no evidence of the Dyke N. of the road on the (disturbed) ground which slopes steeply down to the marshy floor of a brook—the same Eywood brook at which the Kennel wood portion of the Dyke ended.

The intervening ground, the Eywood brook valley, was closely studied. No trace of Offa's Dyke was found. There is, however, an earthwork on the N. flank of this little valley; it is on the steep hill-side E. of Scutchditch wood, and fades out at the re-entrant close by the 'Old Quarry' on the O.S. map. It is not now present in Scutchditch wood, and there is no trace of it on the other side of the re-entrant. The existing structure then is only a little over 200 yards long (see Fig. 71). Its form is that which Offa's Dyke, or any earthwork of defensive type, might take on such a slope—upper bank, steep-scarped: ditch: slight bank on counterscarp.

We can find no reasons which justify the bringing of this isolated fragment of earthwork into the Offa's Dyke system. The hillside is of ancient occupation and cultivation, the boundaries of fields—lynchets—being of striking dimensions. A trackway, in places a holloway and probably prehistoric, which is hereabouts a parish boundary, utilizes the re-entrant as a convenient line of ascent to the plateau. The Scutch Ditch may have had some connexion with this traffic line, as it commands a long stretch of it to the southward.

FIGURE 73. *Lyonshall–Kington road to Holme Marsh, in Lyonshall parish, Herefordshire*

The next known stretch of the Dyke appears to begin near Lyonshall village at 680 ft. above sea-level between fields 4 and 5 on Fig. 73. It is here unmistakable, a high, broad, rounded bank in a plantation, flanked on the W. by a flat ditch, 12–13 ft. broad, full of wet silt into which a stick can be driven for 2 ft. or more. The overall breadth of the work is 50–60 ft. Close inspection shows it to have extended to the NW. along the orchard marked 2; the W. ditch is very plain but the bank is ploughed down. The original termination of the Dyke in this orchard is uncertain; the broad hollow and partly levelled bank now extend to the Kington–Lyonshall road, forming an obtuse angle at the W. corner of the orchard. There is no trace of the Dyke on the opposite side of the road, and it is difficult to see the purpose of this short 'return'. The damage done to the Dyke here by partial levelling makes any discussion as to the genuineness or significance of the 'return' unprofitable. It is sufficient to note that, if it is post-Offan and unconnected with the frontier line, the Dyke ended at the corner of the orchard; for it is not present in the level pasture field marked 1 on the Figure.

The Dyke follows a gentle downward slope between fields 4 and 5, interrupted by one or two cross-tracks and by a small patch of boggy land, on which it was never constructed. The ground then falls somewhat more steeply towards the Curl brook valley and this fall is reflected in the curve which the Dyke takes between the 600- and 500-ft. contours. The broad flat ditch ends at the 600-ft. contour, and the Dyke as it approaches the Lyonshall Drive changes character, the bank being higher and the ditch narrower. At the drive the woodland belt ends; beyond it the Dyke descends an easy slope across pasture fields and has been almost obliterated by cultivation. Near the drive, moreover, recent spoil heaps have covered its remains.

A fine piece of the bank remains at the S. corner of field 6, which shows the scale of the work hereabouts to have been fully equal to that on the hill. The trackway which here

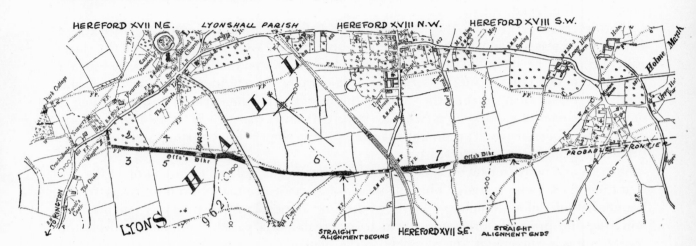

FIG. 73. Lyonshall–Kington road to Holme Marsh, in Lyonshall parish, Herefordshire.
A portion of the 6-in. O.S. map reduced to 4 in. to 1 mile. For the significance of the symbols and letters employed, see Fig. 71.
(Reproduced from the Ordnance Survey map with the sanction of the Controller of H.M. Stationery Office.)

adjoins the Dyke then passes on to the levelled bank, which can best be recognized at B.M. 491·6. It may be noted that the streamlet which rises at Lynhales, and which originally flowed down the natural hollow in field 6, was deflected by the Dyke builders into their ditch and then (as now) reached the Curl brook several hundred yards above its natural point of junction. (For a similar treatment of a mountain stream compare Chapter VI, p. 132, para. 4.)

Between the road adjacent to B.M. 491·6 and the railway the original structure of the Dyke is obscured by an old traffic line and a culverted drainage channel, but beyond the railway the partly levelled bank is clearly visible between pasture fields. For a few yards the streamlet, referred to above, has been carried along the *crest of the bank*, the ancient ditch being seen on the W. side. The streamlet now leaves the bank, which extends as a low broad ridge across pasture field 7 towards the brook. This ridge gets fainter as the valley floor is approached and, for the last 30 yards to the stream, on the alluvium, it is not present. In this stretch, from the plateau to the stream, the fields of view to the W. from the Dyke are good or moderate.

Beyond the brook the ground rises immediately on a gentle slope, and the Dyke is present as a fair-sized bank within a few yards. It quickly develops into a strong work and the W. ditch becomes apparent, though it has evidently been ploughed in. The high and narrow ridge of the bank is being denuded by the trampling of cattle, the crest having been lowered over 1 ft. in places since century-old oaks, which now crown it, were young trees.

The alignment of the Dyke follows uphill a slight depression in the hill-side, thus the field of view to the W. is limited. The Dyke extends beyond the point shown on the O.S. map, ending abruptly precisely on the edge of the plateau; here it is on a magnificent scale, the scarp measuring 21 ft. 7 in., although the ditch is ploughed in.

The general impression given by this Curl brook stretch is that the Dyke was on a grand scale throughout. It was straightly aligned across the valley floor between the points shown on the map, which are close to the 500-ft. contour on either side.

The area intervening between the river Arrow and the Curl brook portions was closely studied. No trace of Offa's Dyke could be found.

FIGURE 74. *Claypits to Garnons Hill: in Yazor and Mansell Gamage parishes, Herefordshire*

The next known stretch of the Dyke begins on the S. flank of Burton Hill below Lady-lift Clump, near Claypits hamlet in Yazor parish. The exact spot is in field 8*a*, half-way between spot-levels 475 and 456·6. Here the Dyke begins abruptly as a very large, broad bank with traces of a W. ditch. It is extensively levelled where it coincides with the Claypits trackway, and also in Upperton farmyard S. of the main road; the W. boundary of the homestead represents its line. The Dyke is present in pasture field 9, this being the first point where it is marked on the 6-in. O.S. map. Here the bank is ploughed down, the W. ditch ploughed in; but since the scarp still measures 13 ft. on the slope, the Dyke must have been built on a large scale hereabouts. Beyond the railway, in a pasture field, the Dyke is covered by a spoil-tip for 25 yards, and is then present, degraded as in field 9, but somewhat smaller. It now becomes a boundary between pasture fields, on a gentle slope towards the Yazor brook: it is at first much damaged, but W. of a pond (where it is gapped), in a grove of oaks, both bank and ditch are fairly perfect and moderate in scale, the scarp measuring 16 ft. at an average point. The Dyke continues down the short slope to the stream, getting smaller, and ends precisely at the edge of the marshy flat, 50 yards from the present course of the brook. It is evident that not one yard of its original length has been lost here.

The Dyke was aligned in two straight stretches from the field near the Claypits to the river, a distance of two-thirds of a mile. It is very well sited, being on a hillside trending to the SW.; it therefore commands wide views to the W.

Beyond Yazor brook the O.S. map is misleading. There is no trace of the Dyke, as indicated on the map, at any point on the hedge line between the stream and Bowmore wood; and where it recommences, on the 400-ft. contour S. of the wood, it is *not* marked on the map. Here it is a tremendous bank, with W. ditch partly ploughed in. It extends to the S., uphill, for 220 yards; the ditch (in field 10) can be traced a little farther than the bank, a few yards of which may have been levelled. It is definitely not present at the S. end of fields 10 and 11. This short isolated piece of Dyke is in alignment with the long stretch on the N. side of Yazor brook. There is, however, no sign of the Dyke along a straight line joining the two terminals. In particular, the low river terrace which, on the S. side, borders the alluvial flat, is continuous and undamaged across this line, conclusive proof that no bank was ever constructed here.

The area between Holme Marsh, where the preceding portion of the Dyke ends, and Claypits, was closely examined. The distance is considerable, 6 miles. Nothing to suggest the recommencement of the Dyke can be seen in the neighbourhood of Holme Marsh.

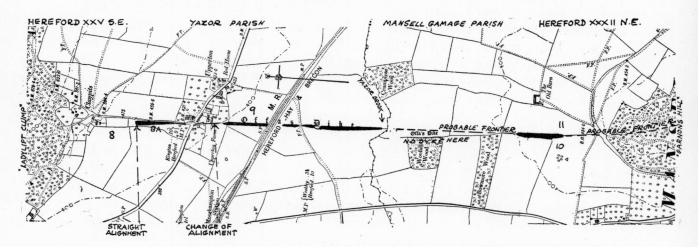

FIG. 74. Claypits to Garnons Hill: in Yazor and Mansell Gamage parishes, Herefordshire.
A portion of the 6-in. O.S. map reduced to 4 in. to 1 mile. For the significance of the symbols and letters employed, see Fig. 71.
(Reproduced from the Ordnance Survey map with the sanction of the Controller of H.M. Stationery Office.)

At Claypits, on the other hand, a large bank close to, parallel with, and extending beyond the Dyke to the N., attracted attention. (This forms the E. boundary to field 8, and its neighbour on the S., on Fig. 74.) It proved to be a lynchet, relic of an ancient field system on which the Dyke was a late intrusion. The intervening area of undulating lowland country, arable pasture, and woodland, was then searched, especially along the watershed shown on Fig. 91, but without result.

FIGURE 75. *Garnons Hill to river Wye: on the boundary between Byford parish and Bishopstone and Bridge Sollers parishes, Herefordshire*

Offa's Dyke is present at the S. margin of the Garnons Hill woodland, at about 450 ft. above O.D., adjacent to 'Old Quarry'; it has a well-defined bank and W. ditch. It is gapped and damaged by quarrying, but as 'The Steps' is approached it becomes larger, higher, and continuous. Between the orchard (enclosure 12) and field 13 the ridge of the Dyke has been ploughed down and the W. ditch extensively ploughed in: the scarp is still steep, and the earthwork was originally very large. It diminishes somewhat in size when Big Oaks wood is entered, but is continuously present, with W. ditch, until the main road is reached. Beyond, the bank fades out on a bluff above the river Wye; its character is obscured by quarrying. The W. ditch here has become a drainage channel and is over-deepened, discharging on the narrow flood-plain of the river.

The alignment of this sector is typical of the Offan frontier. The diagonal course down-hill gives wide views, and falling ground to the W. and the bluff above the Wye are features of tactical importance. It is not certain, owing to levelling and destruction, how the Dyke was aligned, but it seems probable that there were two straight stretches between the Quarry and Big Oaks; from Big Oaks to the river, a distance of 400 yards, it is definitely straight.

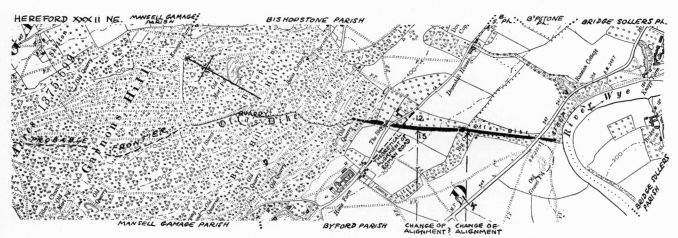

FIG. 75. Garnons Hill to River Wye: on the boundary between Byford parish and Bishopstone and Bridge Sollers parishes, Herefordshire.

A portion of the 6-in. O.S. map reduced to 4 in. to 1 mile. For the significance of the symbols and letters employed, see Fig. 71.
(Reproduced from the Ordnance Survey map with the sanction of the Controller of H.M. Stationery Office.)

The Dyke crossed the Roman road running westward from Kenchester (*Magnis*) near The Steps (Plate XXXIII); the exact spot is not known (pp. 203–4).

The area between the Bowmore wood portion of the Dyke and the 'Old Quarry' on the S. side of Garnons wood, where the Dyke is held to recommence, was closely examined. The O.S. map marks the Dyke as commencing on the crest of Garnons Hill, about 720 ft. above O.D., not on its lower slopes, thus adding 800 yards to the length of the stretch running down to the Wye. Working northwards from the recognized portion by 'Old Quarry', a hedge bank with E. ditch, modern in appearance and forming a parish boundary, is seen to strike steeply up the hill. On reaching the 700-ft. contour it takes a more level course, and is then larger and more like a dyke. Here, however, it seems to be faced with coarse shaly rock (from the ditch) and *at one point passes into and through one of the large shallow quarries with which the hill is pitted.* For the last few yards of its course it is again a small hedge-bank; as a possible portion of Offa's Dyke it comes to an end at a meeting point of parish boundaries, on the crest of the hill. No running earthwork could be found between the termination of this bank and the Bowmore wood sector.

It is not surprising that this stony ridge, though quite clearly a bank formed in comparatively recent times to mark a parish boundary, should have been regarded as Offa's

Dyke, because its course is exactly that which the Dyke might have been expected to take, a point which may prove to be of some significance (see p. 209).

The Middle Wye. Between Bridge Sollers in Herefordshire, and Lydbrook over the county border in Gloucestershire, there are only three short stretches of earthwork which need consideration as possible portions of Offa's Dyke. Of these two, the Row Ditches at Hereford, are well known; the third, a bank near Perrystone Court in Yatton parish, has not previously been recorded. See Plates XXXIII and XXXIV.

FIGURE 76. *The Row[1] Ditches at Hereford*

On the right bank of the Wye, some 300 yards SE. of Wye Bridge, beside the footpath leading to Victoria Bridge, is an earthen bank much damaged and fragmentary, but

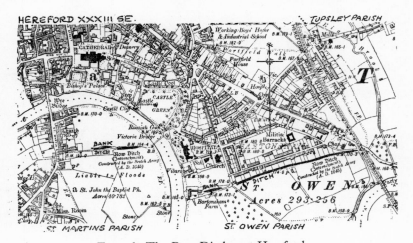

FIG. 76. The Row Ditches at Hereford.

A portion of the 6-in. O.S. map reduced to 4 in. to 1 mile. For the significance of the symbols and letters employed, see Fig. 71.
(Reproduced from the Ordnance Survey map with the sanction of the Controller of H.M. Stationery Office.)

formerly of considerable size. There is evidence that it faced S., and had a broad ditch on this side. It is accredited on the O.S. maps to the Scots army which invested Hereford in A.D. 1645, but is evidently much older.[2] Its position fits in perfectly with that of the medieval city wall and the castle defences on the left bank of the river, and we think that it formed part of a defensive zone covering the river crossing, and that its right flank (now lost) rested on the Wye, immediately W. of Wye Bridge and opposite the medieval defences of the city on that side. It is probably Norman,[3] possibly earlier, but it is unlikely that so extensive a bridge-head defence was needed in Offa's time.

Another earthwork, on the *left* bank of the Wye, near Hereford, also bears the name of Row Ditch. This is first apparent as a low rounded ridge in the garden of Bartonsham

---

[1] For the origin and meaning of the name, see J. G. Wood, *Trans. Woolhope Field Club*, 1901, p. 148.

[2] As Wood properly says; loc. cit., p. 149.

[3] Compare Clawdd Du, the Black Dyke, at Monmouth, which is almost certainly Norman (Fig. 93). It

forms a semicircle on the W. bank of the Monnow, covering the medieval bridge. The ditch, broad like that at Hereford, measures some 35–40 ft., and the bank is 3–6 ft. in height.

farm S. of St. Owen church in the SE. suburb. Here it occupies the edge of the high ground overlooking the broad alluvial flat formed by the river. The road to Bartonsham farm follows the line of its ditch, but at B.M. 178·0 this road turns N., and the ditch is present on the N. boundary of the meadows for some 500 yards. This boundary is the edge of the high ground, and of habitation, and there are slight traces of the bank here and there in the backyards and gardens. Slight evidences of a second bank, on the counterscarp, are probably due to periodical cleansing of the ditch. At B.M. 170·3 the ground to the S. of the alignment rises, the ditch becomes a holloway, and no bank is present. Beyond the railway the earthwork cannot be traced; doubtless it ended on the right bank of the adjacent Eign brook, which ran into the Wye and would have provided a well-protected flank. This curious work is very directly, though apparently not straightly, aligned. Its position suggests that it is defensive; it fronts a loop of the river Wye and its purpose is to cover the ground to the N. (the *Portfield* of Hereford, extensive cultivated land). Its character is consistent with Mercian origin. That it was built by the 'Scots army in 1645' may be at once rejected, and it is not Norman in type. It can hardly be Offa's Dyke; it is improbable that the Welsh should have been in Offa's time permitted to occupy territory on the *left* bank of the Wye immediately adjacent to Hereford. That it was constructed for the defence (on one side) of the town and its 'open' fields at some critical occasion in its early history (let us say between 800 and 1066) seems likely, but there are no facts to go on.[1]

FIGURE 77. *A dyke on S. side of Yatton wood, in Foy parish, Herefordshire*

On the E. side of the main road from Ross to Hereford, E. of Perrystone Court in Foy parish, a broad rounded bank can be seen. This commences at B.M. 509·7 and extends in

an E. direction along the S. margin of Yatton wood, diagonally up a slope facing SW. It ends where the slope eases, as shown in the Figure, being 530 yards in length. The dyke has a S. ditch; near the present main road, where it is largest, it is double-ditched. It is straightly aligned. It is much damaged but was evidently a strong work, equal in scale to a normal portion of Offa's Dyke. Analogy suggested that it was designed to control the approach to the N. along a belt of open land —pastoral or agricultural—on the left bank of the Wye. If so, it was evident that it ought to be present in Perrystone park, W. of Perrystone Court; level ground above the steep scarp of the Wye valley.

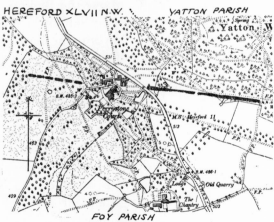

FIG. 77. A 'dyke' at Perrystone Court, in Foy parish, Herefordshire.

A portion of the 6-in. O.S. map reduced to 4 in. to 1 mile. For the significance of the symbols and letters employed, see Fig. 71.
(Reproduced from the Ordnance Survey map with the sanction of the Controller of H.M. Stationery Office.)

[1] These conclusions still seem to me reasonable and probable. But there is an alternative view, based on the similarity of name to Rowe Ditch, Pembridge (p. 162 above), namely, that these Row Ditches are, like it, pre-Offan works, dating perhaps from the establishment of the seventh century bishopric of Hereford by the *Magonsaetan*; see Sir Frank Stenton, *Anglo-Saxon England*, pp. 46–47. (1953).

A bank of considerable size, but almost entirely levelled,[1] was indeed found here; it ends in a grove of oaks on the W. side of the Park, a grove which evidently represents the original limits of the cleared land. The position of the earthwork as now extended is very favourable for defence; it is 500 ft. up, with wide fields of view to the S. and it ends on a rapidly steepening scarp 300 ft. above the river. Its alignment seems to preclude its being part of Offa's Dyke, but it may be regarded as a Magonsaetan work, like Rowe Ditch, Pembridge.[2]

FIGURE 78. *Tumps Hill to Great Collins grove: in the parish of English Bicknor, Gloucester-shire.*

The first point after the Garnons Hill area (Fig. 75) where a well-recognized portion of Offa's Dyke is present, is in English Bicknor parish, over the Gloucestershire border, 27 miles away. On the NE. side of Tumps Hill, overlooking the Wye valley and 200 ft. above O.D., 170 yards SE. of Stowfield House, a high bank begins, the scarp of which still measures (near the *H* of *House*) 16 ft., though the W. ditch, occupied by a trackway, is largely filled in. A roadway recently driven through the Dyke here shows the bank to be over 7 ft. in height and composed of clay and quarried rubble. The Dyke is destroyed where it passes Stowfield House, but immediately beyond it is a high narrow ridge measuring 20 ft. on the scarp. Cut through by the entrance of Stowfield, it changes direction from WNW. to WSW., following the contours of Tumps Hill, and descends the steep slope to Bicknor brook valley, utilizing the W. spur of the hill in a typical Offan manner: both bank and W. ditch are at first very well marked, but are obliterated by a cottage and its garden above the Bicknor road; in the pasture below the road the Dyke is partly levelled, and on the narrow valley floor it is gapped by flood channels and the brook. Rising steeply beyond the brook through a scrubby hanger it regains the 200-ft. contour and the edge of the plateau overlooking the Wye, and ends abruptly just beyond the holloway by *e* of Dyk*e*. Hereabouts it is a rounded bank of moderate size with W. ditch. The valley traverse is straight, but too short to be classed as Type I.

A quarter of a mile farther on, at the SW. corner of field 14, as before on the edge of the scarp which defines the Wye valley, and at the 200-ft. level, the bank of the Dyke reappears, at a point where the plateau is breached by a steep-sided re-entrant. Its course is SW. The Dyke descends to the floor of the re-entrant and, rising on the other side to the plateau level, here represented by a narrow spur, it ends. It is a striking work on the descending slope, a high and broad bank (necessarily) built up from the inner (E.) side; from it there is a magnificent view along the rapidly rising eastern scarp of the Wye valley, here represented by Rosemary Topping. On the floor of the re-entrant the Dyke is a low bank gapped in the centre; beyond, rising through dense scrub, it forms for a

---

[1] The bank can be identified by an oak tree of great age, which is growing on it. This tree is by *F.* of *F.P.* on map.

[2] The place name Yatton (Gate-ton) on the same map may be significant. Cf. *English Place Name Society*, vol. i, pt. 2, p. 29. The dyke may mark the S. boundary of the *Magonsaetan* at a riverside approach road through woodlands. The Forest of Dean mining community to the S. would be their neighbours, a community strongly integrated from early times. (1953).

short distance on the narrow crest a high ridge of limestone rubble. This valley traverse is very direct, but not, on account of the steepness of the slopes, absolutely straight.

These two sections, which in technique of construction and alignment are identical with well-established portions of Offa's Dyke,[1] are linked and extended on the O.S. maps by stretches of doubtful authenticity, which will now be considered.

An ancient and disused holloway ascends steeply from the Wye valley at Lower Lydbrook viaduct to the cottages by *OIN* of *JOIN*T on map 78. At these cottages, bordering it for a few yards, there is a large hedge bank; elsewhere nothing that can be identified

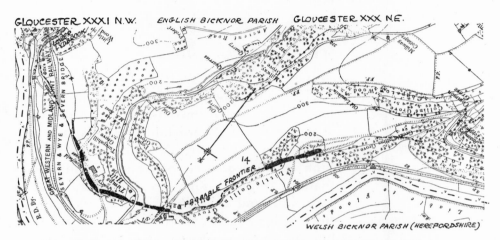

FIG. 78. Tumps Hill to Great Collins grove, in the parish of English Bicknor, Gloucestershire.

A portion of the 6-in. O.S. map reduced to 4 in. to 1 mile. For the significance of the symbols and letters employed, see Fig. 71. (Reproduced from the Ordnance Survey map with the sanction of the Controller of H.M. Stationery Office.

with the Dyke. The holloway originally joined up with the Stowfield House trackway already referred to which follows the ditch of Offa's Dyke, but no trace of an earthwork (other than the hedgebank) is present on its line between the Lydbrook valley and the point where the known stretch of the Dyke begins. The alignment is that which the engineer of Offa's Dyke would choose for a descent to the valley floor, but I cannot feel that there is sufficient evidence to establish it in view of the fact that termination of the Dyke on a plateau is characteristic of the zone to the northward—Herefordshire.[2] There is no trace of the earthwork on the opposite (E.) side of the Lydbrook valley.

Between the two portions under consideration an irregular field boundary is marked 'Offa's Dyke' on the maps. This boundary represents the junction of the plateau and steep river scarp; it is very abrupt and striking, and may be partly artificial—a lynchet. It must be rejected as a constructional part of Offa's Dyke, but can be accepted as part of the frontier alignment (cf. the scarp at Wyegate Hill, p. 87). Beyond the second length of Dyke a broad ridge appears to have been regarded by the Ordnance surveyors as a part

[1] For an explanation of this piece of Dyke, see pp. 213–14 below.

[2] Maclean takes the opposite view: *Trans. Bristol and*

Glos. Arch. Ass. xviii, p. 28. But he is not always reliable; see p. 215 below.

of the earthwork; this, however, is a natural hummock of limestone cresting the river scarp. The berm (by *C* of Great Collins Grove) by which a footpath descends to the floor of the Collins Grove ravine, and the faint trace of a bank which is present for a few yards on the opposite slope, on the well-defined angle of Rosemary Topping hill, require careful consideration. The alignment is that which the Dyke engineers would certainly choose for negotiating this ravine, and this ascent; but the constructions are too slight, having regard to those in the two adjacent re-entrants, to permit us to identify them with any confidence as Offa's Dyke.[1]

From Rosemary Topping southward to Symonds Yat, the scarps fronting the river Wye are very steep or precipitous and the plateau edge forms a natural boundary.

FIG. 79. The earthworks at Symonds Yat, in English Bicknor and West Dean parishes, Gloucestershire.

A portion of the 6-in. O.S. map reduced to 4 in. to 1 mile.

(Reproduced from the Ordnance Survey map with the sanction of the Controller of H.M. Stationery Office.)

FIGURE 79. *The earthworks at Symonds Yat, in English Bicknor and West Dean parishes, Gloucestershire*

The well-known earthworks extending across the neck of the peninsula, formed by a loop of the Wye at Symonds Yat, are popularly attributed to Offa, and may possibly have been utilized by his engineer, since they provide a link between adjacent stretches of cliffs which form a natural frontier. They are, however, older, being the elaborate and characteristic defences of a promontory fort, facing S., of Early Iron Age date. The level flat, here 485 ft. above sea-level, has on either flank precipitous scarps 400 ft. high. The fourfold defences rest on these scarps, the original entrance to the defended area being apparently on the site of the existing—and very ancient—N.–S. road. W. of this road the earthworks are undamaged; E. of it they have suffered and are suffering degradation. The innermost vallum is very fine; it was found to measure 35 ft. on the scarp at a favourable point, with crest about 10 ft. above natural ground level.

FIGURE 80. *Highbury wood to Wyegate Hill, in Newland parish, Gloucestershire*

No trace of the Dyke, or of any earthwork resembling it, exists on the left bank of the Wye between Symonds Yat and Redbrook, a distance, measured along the sinuosities of the valley, of some 10 miles. The slopes on the Mercian side are precipitous from Symonds Yat to Far Hearkening Rock in the N., and very steep from Wyesham to Redbrook in the S., but in the middle zone, the neighbourhood of Monmouth, the slopes are easy and for over 2 miles the valley floor is wide.[2]

S. of Lower Redbrook the ravine, in which flows the tributary stream which gives its name to the hamlet, defines on the E. a long narrow tongue which is parallel to the Wye,

---

[1] Again, see Maclean: op. cit., p. 30.   [2] For Clawdd Du, at Monmouth, see footnote, p. 182.

and is linked to the main plateau at its S. end. On this flat-topped spur, 500 ft. above O.D. and 450 ft. above the Wye, the Dyke reappears. It is a very large work—a broad bank with berm, and (necessarily) with upper (E.) spoil trench, on the edge of the very steep W. slope; at a favourable point it measured (including spoil trench) 76 ft. overall. Its beginning—or ending—S. of the *H* of *H*ighbury, is an original feature; the three elements mentioned above show a slight downward trend and fade into the slope, which here becomes more acute. The continuation to the N. marked on the O.S. map is a comparatively modern work—a stony bank, probably a collapsed dry-stone wall. This does not

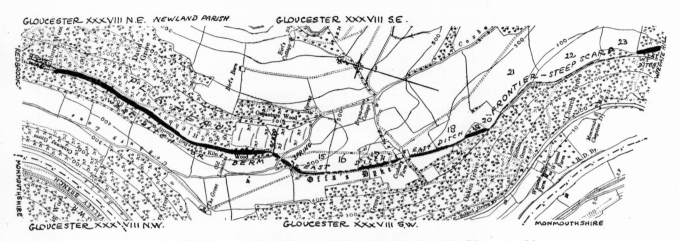

FIG. 80. Highbury wood to Wyegate Hill, in Newland parish, Gloucestershire.
A portion of the 6-in. O.S. map reduced to 4 in. to 1 mile. For the significance of the symbols and letters employed, see Fig. 71.
(Reproduced from the Ordnance Survey map with the sanction of the Controller of H.M. Stationery Office.)

link up with the ridge of the Dyke, but commences on the E. margin of its upper spoil trench. It leaves the scarp, and ends abruptly on the level plateau; it is almost certainly built with material from an adjacent limestone quarry. No trace of the Dyke can, moreover, be seen (on any possible alignment which might have been taken) in the cultivated fields and pastures adjoining Coxbury Lane, W. of the Dyke: easy slopes 200–400 ft. up which separate the steep scarp of the Highbury plateau from the secondary but precipitous scarp at the foot of which the Wye flows.

The sector of Offa's Dyke, then, which begins in this manner at Highbury, extends with but few gaps to the sea at Sedbury.

The profile of the Dyke varies from point to point along the Highbury plateau, the W. edge of which it consistently follows; its form depends on the angle which the scarp makes with the plateau. The undergrowth—which is of recent origin, for Highbury plain was formerly under cultivation—was too dense for the usual method of progression, and the survey was perforce made by incursion at selected points.[1] On it are some of the largest yews which I, familiar with the chalk of S. England, had ever seen. The plateau narrows

[1] Many difficulties have been met with in the survey, but this is the first time that movement along the line of the Dyke was found to be physically impossible without the use of a billhook.

to a ridge at its S. end; here the Dyke is a high rounded bank with no lower berm, the scarp being too steep. It then fades out, but the gap is a narrow one, the steep drop to the easier slope below being partly bridged by a broad rounded bank. This descends through woodland to Coxbury Lane; beyond the lane a bank continues in the same alignment, but is less well marked, there being a holloway on its W. side, and spoil ditch on the E. Its continuity is broken mid-way by boggy ground. A new course is then taken, the Dyke being aligned on the forward (W.) slope of the Coxbury farm knoll. It is only faintly traceable on the S. boundary of fields 15 and 16, but the ridge is well marked in the orchard (enclosure no. 17) as a broad grassy bank with ancient trees: there is certainly no W. ditch. The W. boundary of the homestead is on the line of the Dyke, which reappears on the farther side as a broad, low, lynchet-like bank trending downhill across rough pasture. Still no ditch is evident, but the material for the bank must have come from the E. side. On the SW. side of field 18 the Dyke is represented by a steep scarp; beyond, in Oaken Grove wood (enclosure 19), the limestone reappears and the Dyke, a broad bank ditched on the E., is but little altered. At the S. end of this wood the Dyke strikes the second or lower scarp, here precipitous, which is 400 ft. above O.D. The skill of the layout in this stretch is striking: a steep descent followed by an almost straight alignment on easy gradients for half a mile. The scarp now reached is wooded, while the gentle slope above is occupied by pasture fields; cultivation has accentuated the sharpness of the transit by causing silt to accumulate along the lower edge of the fields, but the Dyke is non-existent.[1] This is proven in the neighbourhood of field 23, where there is no modern boundary to accentuate the division between easy and steep slopes, and no trace of any bank or ditch. The use of the natural scarp here instead of an artificial construction is identical with that at English Bicknor (p. 185).

At the corner of this field (23) the frontier line, now on the 300-ft. contour, leaves the lower limestone scarp. Represented once more by a visible Dyke it commences the ascent of Wyegate Hill; this is here a very large bank built of limestone rubble with lower ditch or berm and upper spoil trench.

FIGURE 81. *Creeping Hill (Wyegate Hill) to Rose Cottage, Hudnalls, in St. Briavels parish, Gloucestershire.*

The Dyke ascends to the 550-ft. level on the shoulder of Wyegate Hill, although within ¼ mile it has to descend to 100 ft. to cross the Mork brook. This curious course reminds us of that on the shoulder of the Long Mountain (Chapter V, p. 117), and seems in this case to be due to a determination on the part of the engineer to maintain wherever possible a commanding alignment above the Wye.

In its diagonal ascent the Dyke maintains for some distance the large scale already described. At the highest level reached—where the slopes are almost precipitous—it is small and much obscured by stone quarries. It then descends; as the slope eases the Dyke is more clearly visible, the lower berm becoming a (W.) ditch. The work is now similar in scale to that seen on the ascent; the sweeping curve of the alignment so noticeable on

[1] The O.S. map is in error in marking the Dyke between fields 20 and 23.

the map is dictated by the contours of the hill-side. Crossing the road the Dyke is present in St. Margaret's Grove as a broad ridge, ditched on the E., and is probably still on the limestone.[1] It ends on boggy ground in which springs rise just above the 100-ft. contour, the extension eastwards to St. Margaret's Well shown on the O.S. maps being a natural river terrace.

The topography of the country hereabouts is interesting. The Mork brook lateral valley, separating Wyegate Hill from the upland known as Hudnalls and St. Briavels Common, which is its next objective, is bifurcate, and a line taken across the intervening

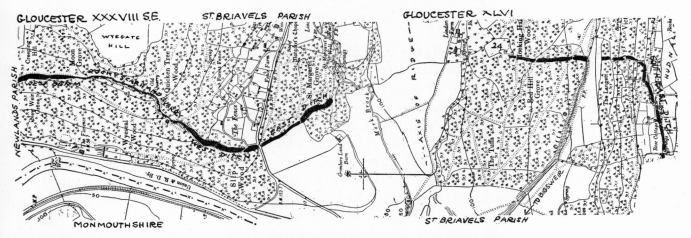

FIG. 81. Creeping Hill (Wyegate Hill) to Rose Cottage, Hudnalls, in St. Briavels parish, Gloucestershire.
A portion of the 6-in. O.S. map reduced to 4 in. to 1 mile. For the significance of the symbols and letters employed, see Fig. 71.
(Reproduced from the Ordnance Survey map with the sanction of the Controller of H.M. Stationery Office.)

ground, a knoll (Lindors Farm) some 400 yards broad, would be the natural one for the Dyke. This knoll, on which the Dyke cannot be found, is isolated from the upland on the E. by Allens Grove, low boggy ground, source of many streamlets, and must in early times have been practically inaccessible. Thus it seems to have been possible, having regard to these natural obstacles, to dispense with the Dyke[2] from St. Margaret's Grove to the base of the St. Briavels upland.

Here, then, at the base of the upland, in Mocking Hazel wood, ½ mile from the St. Margaret Grove termination, the Dyke recommences. The wood is a curious place. Mossy limestone boulders are everywhere strewn in it, and the massive boundary walls of enclosure 24 are formed of them. The Dyke itself commences at the point indicated on the O.S. map as a formless pile of such boulders; it quickly takes shape as a broad rounded

[1] The N. half of this portion was levelled, in part, about 1790. Maclean, loc. cit., p. 21.

[2] The Dyke is marked on the 1833 1-in. O.S. map, sheet 35, as present on the Lindors knoll. But as it is shown also crossing the bog and the Mork brook—places where it never could have existed—we are compelled to reject the evidence. The surveyors seem to have followed Fosbroke; see Maclean, loc. cit., pp. 20–21. The character of the field boundaries, and their alignment, between the known portions of the Dyke here, suggest that they accurately represent the frontier line. This complicates the problem, and is no doubt Fosbroke's justification. (1953.)

bank ditched on both sides, in Red Hill Grove. The absence of the Dyke in the lower (N.) portion of Mocking Hazel wood is difficult to account for, as the boggy ground ends near the Lindors farm springs.

The Dyke has apparently been levelled on the ribbon of open ground N. of Red Hill Grove, but is present in places on the steep scarp beyond, dense with fern and brushwood, which it ascends directly. Having attained the desired elevation (and having passed from the limestone on to the Old Red Sandstone), it turns to follow the easy contours of Hudnall's Hill on its W. side, being visible from point to point in the small enclosures which occupy the upper slopes of this hill. The chosen alignment commands magnificent views over the Wye valley.[1]

FIGURE 82. *Birchfield House, Hudnalls, to Cutts Orchard: in St. Briavels, Hewelsfield, and Woolaston parishes, Gloucestershire*

From the neighbourhood of Birchfield House the Dyke follows the easy slopes of Hudnalls, fronting the Wye for over a mile, maintaining a level course first W. and then S. between 650 and 750 ft., until it is forced to descend the S. slopes of St. Briavels Common to cross the next lateral valley, that of Brockweir. The whole of the hill has been subjected for a long period to small-scale and intensive cultivation, and the Dyke, though its course is hardly ever in doubt, has suffered much damage. Where perfect, it is a bank of moderate size, consistently ditched on the E., and without any trace of W. ditch. It was known to the peasantry as the 'Devil's Rudge' (ridge).[2]

To return to detail: the Dyke is present along field boundaries to the angle of the trackway by 'L.B.'; the cottage on the E. side of this trackway is on the bank. The Dyke is well marked in enclosure 25: destroyed in the garden of Birchfield House: the E. ditch and bank are visible in enclosure 26 beyond. Ill-defined in 'Tank' field, it is well marked in field 27, and present in field 28. Near Megs Folly the roadway is in the ditch and the W. hedge on the bank. For 120 yards it cannot be seen, but in field 29 the bank is present, the road being in the ditch. Almost completely ploughed out in field 30, the E. ditch of the Dyke is in field 31, the bank forming its W. boundary. At the S. end of field 32 the bank forms a very steep scarp; the cottage in field 33 is on the bank. Hence to the S. end of field 34 the bank forms field boundaries and is either revetted with stone or has dry stone walling on it; the E. ditch is traceable in several places.

The Dyke now begins the descent to the Brockweir re-entrant, and the view looking S. down the gorge of the Wye along the line of the frontier to the Severn Sea is magnificent. The Dyke, ploughed down, crosses fields 35 and 36 diagonally; it is ploughed out in field 37. Present in field 38, it is barely visible in fields 39 and 40, very well marked

---

[1] The earthwork marked 'Offa's Dyke' which extends from Red Hill Grove to the riverside near Bigsweir House (Fig. 81) is an ancient traffic way to the Bigsweir river crossing, a holloway for the most of its course. If it be studied—for example—where it crosses the 300- and 100-ft. contours respectively, its nature and origin cannot, we think, be in doubt. There is certainly an artificial bank flanking this holloway in places on the N., but this does not resemble Offa's Dyke. Moreover, the NE. return of the 'Dyke' between the 100- and 50-ft: contours is a field boundary—a lynchet—which can be traced SW. through the gardens of Bigsweir House.

[2] Maclean, loc. cit., p. 26.

with its E. ditch in 41, visible in 42. In the orchard, enclosure 43, it is a broad, low, rounded bank. Levelled for a space, a rise in the cross-roads marks its passage to field 44; here, and in fields 45 and 46, it is visible. There are faint traces in field 47, practically none in 48; a rise in the cross-roads marks its passage to field 49, where it is present, passing down a slight declivity to a marshy flat. Thence it can be traced across a tangle of small enclosures, now waste, to field 50, where it is levelled. Rises in the hedgerows carry it across a lane to enclosure 51, orchard, where it is again present. There is a very sharp descent through scrub to the Brockweir brook; on the narrow floor ('Cutts Orchard') a broad high

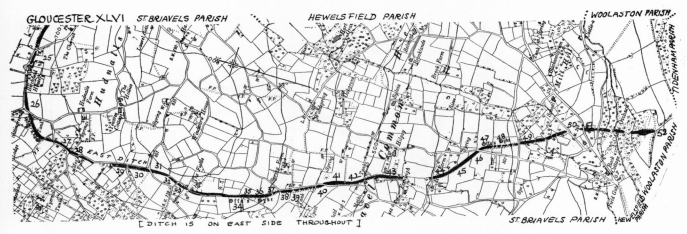

FIG. 82. Birchfield House, Hudnalls, to Cutts Orchard: in St. Briavels, Hewelsfield, and Woolaston parishes, Gloucestershire.

A portion of the 6-in. O.S. map reduced to 4 in. to 1 mile. For the significance of the symbols and letters employed, see Fig. 71.

(Reproduced from the Ordnance Survey map with the sanction of the Controller of H.M. Stationery Office.)

bank is seen revetted with stone walling, which suggests that the Dyke has been at some time enlarged and utilized as a mill dam. The S. flank of the little Brockweir valley is very steep for a few yards, the Dyke being present as a small ridge; directly the slope eases— at about 220 ft. above O.D.—it is for a few yards very large, a broad rounded bank, 66 ft. overall, with well-defined W. ditch, and a spoil ditch on the E. side. It continues, again becoming smaller, across rough pasture to the Madgett Hill–Brockweir trackway, which cuts through it, but it cannot now be traced across the arable field beyond.

FIGURE 83. *Madgett Hill to Worgans wood: in Tidenham parish, Gloucestershire*

Beyond field 52 (where the Dyke is not visible) on the grassy NW. slopes of Madgett Hill, a small low ridge appears with E. ditch and slight W. ditch, ascending as usual diagonally. Above the pasture, at the 500-ft. level, there is a short but steep wooded limestone scarp; the Dyke climbs this and turns SW. along its margin, as a small bank thrown up from the SE. side. Beyond the cross-track it is hardly traceable for a few yards; then a very large bank suddenly appears in the woodland, which, leaving the steep scarp, ascends through Caswell wood to attain the true plateau level, which is hereabouts 600 ft. above

O.D. This high and broad rampart has a deep W. ditch cut in the limestone, and is also—necessarily—built up, to some extent, from the upper (E.) side; the scarp measures 22 ft. 6 in. at an average point. The transition is as striking as that noted near Woodhouse wood in Chapter VI (p. 142). On reaching the plateau edge by Modesgate, the Dyke takes a level course through woodland, following the contours of the hill; it dips slightly to cross a narrow ravine and a brooklet, and is gapped. Beyond, in Lippets Grove, it is a remarkable structure with unusually steep scarp sited exactly on the edge of the plateau; at one point it has a lower berm 10 ft. broad, and a scarp 31 ft. on the slope (Fig. 88, liv).

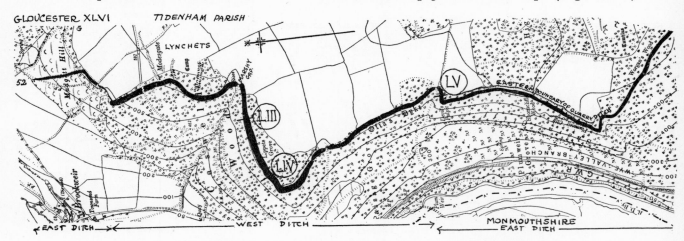

FIG. 83. Madgett Hill to Worgan's wood: in Tidenham parish, Gloucestershire.
A portion of the 6-in. O.S. map reduced to 4 in. to 1 mile. For the significance of the symbols and letters employed, see Fig. 71.
(Reproduced from the Ordnance Survey map with the sanction of the Controller of H.M. Stationery Office.)

Again, at the spur of the hill in Lippets Grove[1] the scarp measures 27 ft. and, though on a steep slope, there is a definite lower ditch 15 ft. across, cleanly cut out of the limestone rock. (This lower ditch is continuous from here onwards for over ½ mile.) No more perfect or impressive stretch of Offa's Dyke exists. If a few trees on the west side were cut down it would look most striking from the right bank of the Wye by Tintern, situated as it is on the crest of very steep and, in places, precipitous slopes, 600 ft. high. The Dyke itself commands magnificent prospects, when gaps in the woodland permit a view over the Wye valley and Wentwood. Old yews and hollies mark its course, the woodland generally being young[2] (see Plates XXXV and XXXVI).

Throughout this Lippets Grove stretch there is a shallow hollow on the upper (E.) side, from which much of the material for the bank was obtained; it is not clearly defined and is in no sense a ditch. The ganger-in-charge dug a lower ditch or berm whenever it was possible.

At the re-entrant near the *e* of Dyk*e* the character of the earthwork again changes; from here to Plumweir Cliff it is a bank, usually broad and flat-topped and without lower berm

[1] The 'Yews head' of the Tidenham Charter (A.D. 956) is the secondary scarp of this spur, above the loop of the river. There are yews still on it (see Plate XXXV).

[2] A colony of wild martagon lilies was flourishing here in 1940–5, A.F.

or ditch, built up from quarries on the E. side with well-defined margins in which lime-stone blocks are still in places lying.[1] These quarries are always shallow and flat-floored, frequently continuous, elsewhere forming isolated pockets: in places they seem too exten-sive for the bulk of the Dyke, and may have been exploited at a later date for dry-walling. The ganger-in-charge of this portion of the Dyke did not trouble about a W. ditch even where the slopes are easy—there is practically no lower ditch to be seen throughout (see Profile lv, Fig. 88).

To return to detail: up to the Devil's Pulpit—a jutting crag of limestone immediately below the line of the Dyke—the earthwork has a high ridge: beyond it is broad and flat like a causeway, on the edge of the very steep scarp. A slight lower berm appears at the 700-ft. contour in Shorncliff wood—*the highest point reached*—but this quickly fades out when the descent begins. Along the border of Shorncliff wood the broad flat-floored quarry can best be studied. The views along this high stretch are commanding, for the river is some 670 ft. directly below us (Plate XXXVI).

In Shorncliff wood the reverse (E.) slope of the Dyke is frequently revetted with dry-stone walling. It is a hedge boundary here, which may account for its renovation.

At the elbow formed by Plumweir Cliff the Dyke makes an acute angle, corresponding exactly with the contour of the precipitous scarp—a curious example of the determination shown by the builders to maintain *complete* visual control of the Wye valley.

A definite change in scale, though not in type, is now manifest, the Dyke becoming smaller immediately S. of the elbow. It crosses the head of the adjacent ravine as a rounded bank behind which is a silt-flat, and makes a steady ascent on an easy slope through Worgan's wood. There is no lower ditch—other than a modern drainage ditch; the bank is of moderate size, the E. quarries at first extensive and continuous, thereafter forming a succession of isolated pockets. At the *d* of Woo*d* (*c.* 630 ft.) descent begins, and the Dyke is decidedly bigger, but still has no W. ditch.

FIGURE 84. *James's Thorns to Broadrock: in Tidenham parish, Gloucestershire*

The Dyke continues to be large as it swings round on an easy slope towards a lateral re-entrant of the combe known as The Slade. There is still no W. ditch, but the E. quarries are well marked. Approaching the re-entrant, a stone wall and old yew trees appear on the Dyke: the hill-side then suddenly becomes very steep, and the Dyke ends. It begins again 70 yards away (at the *O* of Offa) as an enormous bank built up as before from the E. From it there is a good view down and across The Slade, on the opposite flank of which, now cleared of woodland, the Dyke is seen making for the high cliffs of Ban-y-gor.

For a short distance down the slope to the head of The Slade (by the *yke* of D*yke*) the earth-work shows a lower berm. The bank then becomes smaller, crossing the ravine (where there is a young plantation) as a low ridge. It then ascends the slope diagonally, its character by the 'Old Quarry' being a bank of no great size with steep W. scarp. This bank

---

[1] Hence, surely, the term *Stanraewe*—Stone Row—used for the Dyke hereabouts in the Tidenham Charter. See footnote, p. 219.

becomes somewhat larger and traces of an E. quarry ditch develop as the plateau (600 ft.) is regained.

The Dyke now follows the edge of the plateau as far as Dennel Hill (see Plate XXXVII). Up to the spur which defines The Slade on the S., it is of moderate size with an E. quarry ditch, and (in places) a berm on the (W.) side. At the spur there is a definite W. ditch for a yard or two because the Dyke cuts *across* its sharp tip. The Dyke now becomes larger, and is revetted on the inner (E.) side with a modern stone wall. There are quarries, sometimes large as at Devil's Pulpit (p. 193), on this side, and slight traces here and there of a lower (W.) berm or ditch. Then the earthwork, gradually getting smaller, fades out at a

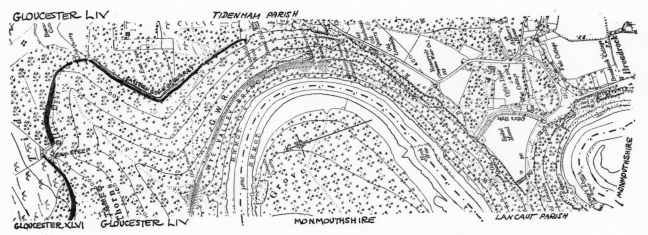

FIG. 84. James' Thorns to Broadrock: in Tidenham parish, Gloucestershire.
A portion of the 6-in. O.S. map reduced to 4 in. to 1 mile. For the significance of the symbols and letters employed, see Fig. 71.
(Reproduced from the Ordnance Survey map with the sanction of the Controller of H.M. Stationery Office.)

rocky scarp at the N. boundary of Dennel Hill House. There is no trace of it in the garden of this or the next house, where the slopes to the Wye, though very steep, are in places climbable; the Dyke may possibly have been destroyed to improve the views. Beyond the gardens the Ban-y-gor cliffs begin, and these extend to the Lancaut peninsula, to which attention may now be directed.

Extending across the level top of this peninsula—formed by a loop of the Wye—from cliff edge to cliff edge, on a curved alignment, is a promontory fort (Plate XXXVII), facing E., and in character similar to but less elaborate than that at Symonds Yat. The defences consist of a main and a secondary bank with corresponding ditches and, in places, a slight bank on the counterscarp of the outer ditch. The former measures 30 ft. on the scarp at one point, and the overall breadth of the whole work is 120 ft. The original entrance was probably at the point where the trackway to Lancaut passes through the defences. Hereabouts there is a famous view of the gorge of the Wye. What is probably a second line of defence made by the people who constructed the fortress is situated on Spital Meend, 300 yards farther W., where the plateau is much narrower. It consists of a bank of moderate size with steep scarp facing E., and definite traces of an E. ditch. The earthwork is complete N. of the trackway to Lancaut, but on the S. of this road it is represented only by isolated hummocks. This work is certainly not Offan, which *never shows a work of military type facing E.* Either it or its greater neighbour may have been adopted by Offa as his boundary; probably the latter, as being the more notable work.

From the Lancaut peninsula high cliffs, or scarps so steep as to be climbed with difficulty, extend to Broadrock (Plates I and XXXVII) and beyond—no trace of the Dyke exists in this zone.

FIGURE 85. *Broadrock to Castleford House in Tidenham parish, Gloucestershire*

Between Lancaut and Chapelhouse wood the plateau level falls from 370 to 200 ft. above O.D. At the wood the cliffs are replaced by steep slopes, varied by rocky outcrops

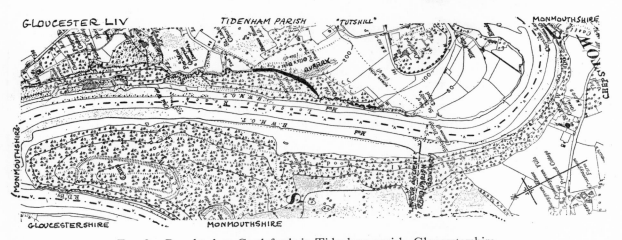

FIG. 85. Broadrock to Castleford: in Tidenham parish, Gloucestershire.
A portion of the 6-in. O.S. map reduced to 4 in. to 1 mile. For the significance of the symbols and letters employed, see Fig. 71.
(Reproduced from the Ordnance Survey map with the sanction of the Controller of H.M. Stationery Office.)

at the 100-ft. level, and so lead by easy gradations to the gentle slopes of Tutshill opposite Chepstow.

The Dyke begins at the 200-ft. contour W. of St. Luke's Church where the cliff ends, as shown on the O.S. maps. It is a bank of moderate size degenerating here and there into a mere accentuation of the angle at the junction of plateau and scarp; a lower berm can in places be traced. It ascends a gentle slope for a short distance, then descends diagonally, making for a cliff edge 100 ft. above the river. For a space, on this descent, the scale of the work increases; the upper (E.) ditch is well marked, as is the lower berm. The Dyke fades out within a few yards of the cliff. It reappears, the size of a hedgebank, on the margin of the rocky scarp a little farther on, following the 50-ft. contour, being most definite where it abuts on the stone wall forming the N. boundary of Castleford home farm. Here it is about $3\frac{1}{2}$ ft. high and 15 ft. broad with E. ditch. No continuation of the Dyke is visible in the strip of woodland SW. of the farm, but this is pocked with small quarries and it may have been destroyed. The purpose of the alignment is however clear:

the Dyke is making for the river bank. Beyond this strip of woodland, on the pastoral slopes almost encircled by the Wye, we have not found the Dyke.[1] There is, moreover, no natural obstacle which could serve as the frontier until the cliff begins again near Wyecliffe House (Fig. 86). On its edge—now modified by quarrying—it may safely be assumed that the frontier, leaving the river bank, recommenced. The area under review, which forms part of Tutshill, has proved a stumbling block to many students of the Dyke, primarily because the O.S. map records a stretch which follows the 200-ft. contour and suggests an alignment on the chord of the arc formed by the river. This piece of 'Dyke' is obviously an old quarry.

It will be observed that the Dyke strikes the river *above* the site of the Roman road from *Glevum*, and the site of the Roman bridge; the almost certain course and position of these are shown on the O.S. map, and on Figure 94.

FIGURE 86. *Tallard's Marsh on the Wye, to Sedbury cliff on the Severn: in Tidenham parish, Gloucestershire*

The tree-clad limestone cliff opposite Chepstow, the base of which is washed by the swift tides of the lower Wye, undoubtedly represents, throughout its length, the Mercian frontier. This cliff declines in height by an even gradient to 50 ft., and then ends abruptly; here the Dyke recommences. The earthwork no longer follows the Wye but cuts across the promontory formed by the confluence of that river and the Severn (see Frontispiece and Fig. 94). On the Severn side of the promontory a cliff of Triassic sandstone ends as abruptly as that of limestone on the Wye side, and provides an equally suitable flank for the frontier dyke (Plate XXXVIII*b*). A straight line between these two points moreover coincides, in the western half, with the southern margin of the plateau which fronts a wide tract of marsh; in the centre there is no *abrupt* fall of the ground but sufficient to give visual control; at the E. end there is marshy ground to the front, of limited but sufficient extent. Thus the engineer's choice is seen to be fully justified. The technique of his layout is interesting. The course, 1,200 yards long, is projected in two straight stretches, to W. and E. respectively of a point E. of Buttington Cottages; the difference in alignment between these stretches is only 4 degrees. The only deviations from straightness are in hollows (e.g. that SE. of Pennsylvania village) invisible from the sighting point or its neighbourhood. The Dyke on this peninsula is of military character in structure as well as in siting, the ditch being consistently on the S. side (Plate XXXVIII*a*).

The Dyke is first visible at the E. end as a hill-side scarp fronting the Tallard marshlands E. of the 'filter beds' (see map). The S. ditch is traceable. Before these 'beds' were made it may have been extended a little farther down the hill, but its limits were set by the re-entrant (marked by a drainage ditch leading SW. into Tallards Marsh) which was

---

[1] At the S. end of this wood a continuous hedge bank or, more accurately, a lynchet, with steep SW. scarp, extends in a curve across the pastures (through the *D* and *p* of St. *D*avids Cha*p*el). The scarp is most clearly marked at its S. termination, near Elm Villa. From Elm Villa the alignment thus indicated would lead to the cliffs by Wyecliffe House. Its position is such as would naturally divide arable from riverside pasture in the Middle Ages. The lynchet passes across, and masks, the line of the Roman road, near St. David's Chapel. There is, however, no indication that this road was trenched at the crossing-point.

formerly a pill or creek, and which is still flooded in part at spring tides. Small boats used to come to the creek as late as seventy years ago, and there was a saw mill where is now the sewage works.[1] That this creek was of importance in Offa's time is rendered probable by the presence, on the defensible knoll which forms the W. flank of the re-entrant, of a small circular earthwork (Fig. 90). This knoll is a spur of the limestone plateau isolated partly by nature and partly by art, and its riverward face is the terminal portion of the Wye cliffs (see p. 204).

To return to the line of the Dyke: its bank, gapped and damaged, is clearly traceable

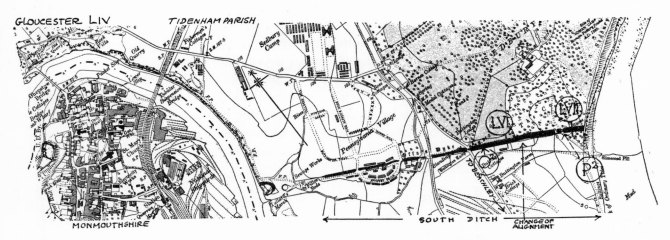

FIG. 86. Tallard's Marsh on the Wye, to Sedbury cliff on the Severn: in Tidenham parish, Gloucestershire.
A portion of the 6-in. O.S. map reduced to 4 in. to 1 mile. For the significance of the symbols and letters employed, see Fig. 71.
(Reproduced from the Ordnance Survey map with the sanction of the Controller of H.M. Stationery Office.)

in front of the houses along the N. side of the Mercian Way, the ditch being occupied first by a trackway and then by the road thus named. The Dyke crosses the little valley beyond the new village, the bank being well marked on the descending slope, obliterated on the floor, and traceable though almost completely levelled on the rising slope beyond the light railway; here the (S.) ditch is very plain and indeed overdeepened. A well-preserved portion of the bank, known as Buttington Tump, survives at the top of the rise, where the road to Beachley passes through the earthwork. It is unusually large, but its S. ditch is filled in. On it is set a standing stone, a roughly shaped mass of conglomerate with stone slabs grouped around its base.

From the lodge gates of Sedbury Park (Frontispiece) to the Severn cliffs the Dyke is little altered, and is on the major scale. Scattered trees line that portion (Plate XXXVIII*a*) included in the Park; here there is a long even slope on the N. side, probably the result of ploughing-down the bank.[2] The S. ditch, though present, is partly filled in. NE. of Buttington Cottages the Dyke bank becomes higher and narrower—more normal (see

[1] Information from old inhabitants.

[2] We do not think that these modifications were introduced during the Civil War (1644), as has been stated. We have seen similar profiles due to agricultural operations frequently in other sectors of the Dyke. But see Ormerod in *Archaeologia*, xxix, pp. 16 and 17.

Profile lvi, Fig. 89). Passing into The Combe (formerly known as Buttington wood),[1] now cleared of timber, the Dyke forms a broad rounded bank ditched on the S.—and with spoil ditch on N., *as is usual on steep slopes.* These ditches become watercourses in wet weather, and are overdeepened near the foot of the slope. On the floor a 20-ft. gap— which, though narrow, is evidently wider than it was originally—admits passage of the brooklet draining the little valley; the Dyke is again gapped close by a modern trackway. On the rising slope the character of the Dyke (Profile lvii) is similar to that on the descending slope; it is sheared off abruptly by the cliff edge, and this termination of Offa's Dyke, 100 ft. above the mean tide level of the Severn Sea, is extraordinarily impressive (Plate XXXVIII*b*). The ground falls steeply to W. and S. as well as vertically to E., thus rendering the position exceptionally dominant; from it practically the whole of the Beachley peninsula is visible, and the eye ranges over wide stretches of sea and land beyond. Memories, extending over six years, of 80 miles of Dyke the alignment of which was governed by one idea—that of visual control of enemy country—flooded the mind, for the place seemed to be to an unusual degree characteristic of the Mercian frontier line as a whole and to evoke the very spirit of its creator. On this now silent and deserted spot, at the southern limit of his Mercian dominion, King Offa ought to be commemorated.

THE ALIGNMENT OF THE DYKE

In the lowlands of N. Herefordshire the Dyke consists mainly of a series of straight alignments (Type I); in Gloucestershire, on the Lower Wye, such alignments rarely occur.

Alignments of Type I
Curl brook valley (Fig. 73 and p. 177), one stretch, 800 yards.
Yazor brook valley (Fig. 74 and p. 179), three stretches, 330, 770, and 220 yards.
Upper Wye valley (Fig. 75 and p. 181), two stretches, 230 and 410 yards.[2]
Sedbury peninsula (Fig. 86 and p. 196), two stretches, 930 and 270 yards.

The total length of Offa's Dyke in the lowlands of N. Herefordshire is 4,670 yards (roughly 2⅔ miles), and of this length 2,740 yards (roughly 1⅔ miles), are in Type I stretches. The interesting fact—which will be studied in its place—thus emerges, that the engineer of the Dyke concentrated his efforts in this area *mainly on ground that was completely cleared.*

The straight alignment in Gloucestershire is most interesting. It is that portion of the Dyke which cuts off the tip of the peninsula between Wye and Severn, fertile lowland country; and Seebohm, in the course of his analysis of King Edwy's Tidenham charter of A.D. 956, suggested that it has been probably driven across the open fields of the adjacent hamlet of Sedbury, then known as Cingestune.[3] Our experience of straight alignments suggests that he was right; and it is interesting that two entirely dissimilar lines of research should produce the same result.

A curious discovery may throw light on the method by which, when necessary, the

---

[1] Ormerod, loc. cit., p. 16.   [3] *The English Village Community*, p. 151.
[2] Possibly a third, by 'The Steps', 300 yards.

Offan engineers laid out their straight alignments. On the S. side of Yazor brook, just above the marshy flat here defined by a low river-terrace, is a flat oval mound raised one foot above the general level, and 10 and 7 yards respectively in long and short diameter. It is exactly in line with the straight stretch of 770 yards on the N. side of the valley. It is quite unlike a burial mound, and seems to be exactly fitted for the base of a lofty aligning mark of timber buttressed by logs. It is placed exactly where such a mark would be needed in forest country (see Fig. 87). Its long axis is at right angles to the course.

The scarcity of straight alignments along the Wye in the southern sector, Highbury–Sedbury, is mainly due to the topography—the Dyke follows the well-defined sinuous and

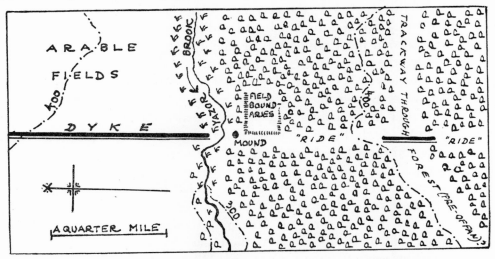

FIG. 87. Aligning mark and ancient field boundaries on the line of Offa's Dyke, in Mansel Gamage parish, Herefordshire. Showing also probable extent of forest and of cleared land in the eighth century.

sometimes deeply indented edge of the plateau (as Plates XXXV and XXXVI), which it only leaves of necessity, to cross deep lateral valleys. The course is based on the engineer's determination to maintain effective visual control of the Wye gorge and to keep as close to the river as possible consistent with the maintenance of height. (Incidentally he is able to utilize existing natural obstacles such as cliffs.) But there are places where straight alignments would seem to have been possible. The most extensive area of this character is the upland mass known as Hudnalls and St. Briavels Common (Fig. 82). The easy contours of this hill would permit of very extended straight alignments; but the course, though in layout admirable, is in execution uncertain and sinuous. That the hill was forest in the eighth century can hardly be doubted by any student of running earthwork who shall examine this Figure with care. The builders were here feeling their way from point to point by sensing the contours, shut out by the tree canopy from a general view.[1] It is equally probable that the valley sides of the Mork brook (St. Margaret's Grove on the N. and Mocking Hazel wood on the S., Fig. 81) had not been cleared of their timber when the frontier was marked out.

[1] See p. 220 (on forest in this area).

THE CHARACTER AND PROFILE OF THE DYKE

Two types of dyke are present on the descent from Rushock Hill, the normal with W. ditch, and the boundary bank with E. ditch. The break in technique is abrupt and two gangs seem to have been at work. This stretch is at the end of the Mountain Zone, wherein these contrasted characters are commonly seen (Chapter VII, p. 174).

In the lowlands of N. Herefordshire the Dyke is everywhere of normal Offan type with W. ditch, and in most places on the major scale, such as one sees at important points farther north. The Dyke at the N. end of the Curl brook valley, and near Bowmore wood in the Yazor valley, may be cited as imposing examples of the work in this region. In one short stretch, S. of the R. Arrow, there is a counterscarp bank, and here, as at Knuck Bank (Chapter VI, p. 129), the ditch is broad and flat-floored. The sector of the Dyke at English Bicknor is also at most points on the major scale; it is of the normal Offan type with W. ditch where the slope of the ground permits.

The Dyke on the lower Wye from Highbury to Sedbury presents most interesting variations, as may be seen from the maps (Figs. 80 to 86), and—in a summarized form—on Fig. 94. This latter figure shows that normal portions with W. ditch alternate with portions having no W. ditch, but E. spoil trenches. This sector provides the most striking stretch of the Dyke on the whole frontier at Caswell wood opposite Tintern Abbey. It is of normal Offan type, $1\frac{1}{5}$ miles in length. Where it ends one can contrast the work of two different gangs, employing entirely different methods. This junction, situated near the Devil's Pulpit, is, as at Woodhouse wood (Figs. 60 and 66, LI), a point well-defined topographically, being the head of a ravine. The gang which built the Dyke with E. spoil trench started well, influenced doubtless by the Caswell wood tradesmen, but their work soon degenerates. This section extends to Dennel Hill and is nearly 2 miles long. Though it is not uniform in scale, and occasionally has a lower berm, it is essentially of one technique, the boundary-bank type of Dyke.

Wherever the Dyke is sufficiently well preserved for accurate observation (as it is on the limestone) the generalization previously made, that where the structure has a W. ditch this is well cut, deep, and well-defined, and that where the material for the bank is obtained from the E. side there is a quarry, a shallow depression, or spoil holes, proves true. To those who built in the former manner the ditch was an essential element of the construction; to those who built in the latter manner only the bank mattered. In the Mountain Zone the E. spoil trench type of Dyke structure was almost invariably weak, of hedge-bank size; but in the Wye valley nearly all the portions of the Dyke similarly constructed are sizable, though they are rarely large.

The types of Dyke met with this year, then, excluding those forms imposed by difficult terrain (which never change), are three in number and may be described as follows:

(*a*) A Bank without W. ditch, with spoil trench (continuous or intermittent) on the E. It is thus of boundary-bank type, but it is usually of normal size.

(*b*) A Bank of normal Offan type with continuous W. ditch (when on a forward slope the W. ditch may be represented by a berm, and some of the upcast is for convenience taken from the E. side also).

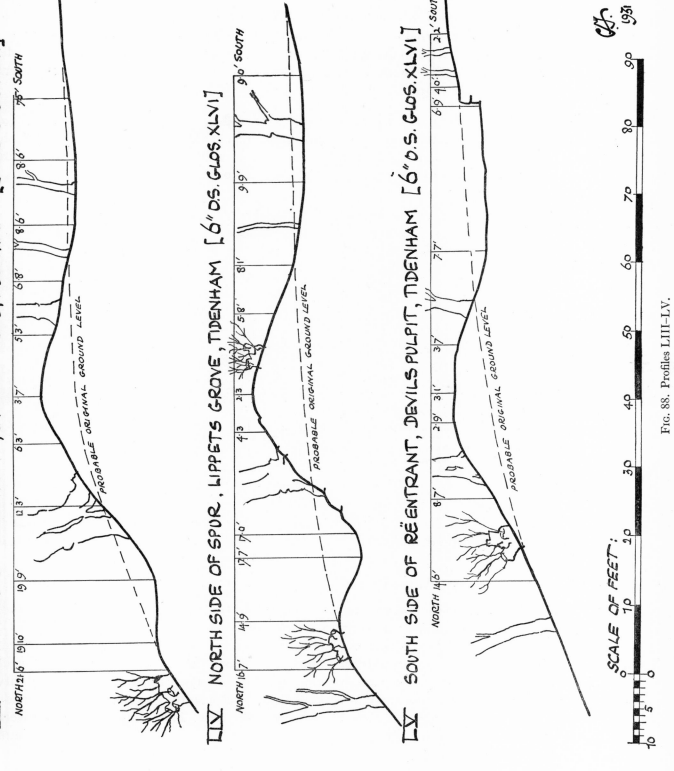

OFFA'S DYKE: PROFILES IN TIDENHAM PARISH, GLOUCESTERSHIRE

LIII SOUTH SIDE OF RE-ENTRANT, CASWELL WOOD, TIDENHAM [6" O.S. GLOS. XLVI]

LIV NORTH SIDE OF SPUR, LIPPETS GROVE, TIDENHAM [6" O.S. GLOS. XLVI]

LV SOUTH SIDE OF RE-ENTRANT, DEVILS PULPIT, TIDENHAM [6" O.S. GLOS. XLVI]

SCALE OF FEET:

Fig. 88. Profiles LIII–LV.

(c) As (b) but reinforced with an additional (small) bank on the outer edge of W. ditch. This ditch, having to provide upcast for two banks, is broader than usual.

Types (b) and (c) we are already familiar with; (a) has appeared before, on this scale, only at Hawthorn Hill (Chapter VI, p. 144). Type (c) only occurs once in the present sectors, by the river Arrow.

Profiles. Five profiles are reproduced on Figs. 88 and 89. One, no. lv, illustrates type (a) at its most imposing manifestation in a limestone area, at the N. end of Tidenham parish. Nos. liii and liv illustrate Type (b) in the same area; and, since the geological structure and terrain are identical, they afford a striking contrast (see pp. 218 f.).

Table of Measurements

No. of section	Position	Present dimensions of bank (estimated)		Present dimensions of W. ditch (estimated)		Present overall breadth of bank and W. ditch (estimated)
		Height	Breadth	Depth	Breadth	
		ft. in.	ft. in.	ft. in.	ft. in.	ft. in.
LIII*	170 yds. S. of re-entrant angle, Caswell wood (Fig. 83)	4 9	37 0	3 0	21 0	58 0
LIV*	100 yds. N. of projecting angle, Lippets Grove (Fig. 83)	7 0	33 0	5 6	20 0	53 0
LV	35 yds. S. of re-entrant angle, Passage Grove (Fig. 83)	5 4	38 0	none	none	†65 0
LVI	180 yds. SE. of Park Gates, Sedbury (Fig. 86)	5 8	35 0	2 0	19 0	54 0
LVII*	40 yds. W. of cliff, Sedbury (Fig. 86) .	4 1	42 0	4 5	25 0	67 0
	Defences on E. side of fortlet, Tallards Marsh (Figs. 86 and 90) . . .	4 0	50 0	4 0	41 0	91 0

* These sections show an E. spoil trench.
† Overall breadth with E. ditch (spoil trench).

The Sedbury profiles, nos. lvi and lvii, illustrate the Dyke constructed on a large scale, but much reduced by denudation.

EARTHWORKS ON OR NEAR OFFA'S DYKE

The earthworks on the line of the Dyke, other than the fort described above, are two in number; the promontory forts (Class A) at Symonds Yat and Lancaut (Plate XXXVII, Figs. 79 and 84), described on pp. 186, 194. The defences of the first of these may have been, and of the second almost certainly were, utilized as part of the frontier by Offa's engineer (cf. Llanymynech hill-fort, Chapter IV, p. 66.) Llanymynech illustrates the probability that these works were brought into service merely because they provided a ready-made bank in the right position from the Mercian point of view. They both face E., and were not modified in any way by the Mercians; no W. ditch was dug within the main vallum in either case.

There are numerous hill-forts (Class B) adjacent to the line of the Dyke and the Wye frontier, but there is no evidence that any of them, save possibly Sutton's Walls, had in the Dark Ages any military significance, or influenced in any way the alignment of the Mercian frontier. They are, however, not without interest, for their distribution suggests that this frontier down to, but excluding the coastal zone, represents a recurrent racial boundary, being then the limit of consolidation in the advance towards the Welsh mountains of the Celts of the Early Iron Age who, in the period immediately preceding the Roman Conquest, built earthworks of this type.

Sutton's Walls is a large contour fort occupying a flattened knoll in Sutton St. Michael parish, 4 miles N. by E. of Hereford. The account in *V.C.H., Hereford*, i, pp. 220–1, is good, but it is incorrect to assume that the artificially steepened scarp which defines the plateau and forms the main element of the defences was originally reinforced with an earth rampart all round. It is associated in legend and story with Offa[1] but excavations carried out in 1950 by Dr. Kathleen Kenyon, F.S.A., yielded, I am informed, no Dark Age finds. The fort is marked on Plate XXXIII.

A few small and weak entrenchments of uncertain origin near the line of the Dyke but unrelated thereto may be dismissed without comment.

We found no trace of a 'camp' at Highbury (Fig. 80) or at Modesgate (Fig. 83); one mentioned in the literature,[2] the other recorded on the O.S. map. At the latter site the Saxon lynchets (cultivation terraces) do not cross the Dyke, but one runs right up to it (p. 219). The lynchet at Yazor, on the other hand (p. 180), seems to belong to a pre-Dyke system and may be of Early Iron Age date.

EXCAVATIONS

Minor excavations were undertaken at two points, one in Herefordshire, the other in Gloucestershire.

(a) *The Steps, Mansel Gamage, Herefordshire*

If Plate XXXIII be examined, it will be seen that straight stretches of the Roman road to the W. from Kenchester (*Magnis*) in the Wye valley survive both on the E. and on the W. of the Dyke. Thus the Dyke must have been constructed across this road. If the point of passage could be located the stratigraphical relation between the two structures could be determined, and valuable evidence obtained of the same order as that from Ffrith (Chapter III, pp. 40 ff.).

Lines were drawn on the 25-in. map in continuation of the alignments of the straight stretches; these intersected at Garnons Home farm, W. of The Steps, the Dyke being crossed as shown on Fig. 75. Since there is hereabouts no apparent topographical reason to account for a deviation from the normal Roman method of constructing roads in

---

[1] Cf. *John Leland's Itinerary*, vol. v, fol. 66, Hearne's ed., 1769.   [2] *Trans. Bristol and G. Arch. Soc.* xviii. 26.

straight alignments, it was thought likely that the road in question would be found on or near to the line thus pencilled on the map; and with the kind permission of Sir John Cotterell, and the co-operation of Mr. G. H. Jack, F.S.A., excavation was undertaken here in the autumn of 1927.

On the theoretical alignment trenches were cut: in the orchard (enclosure 12) and through the bank of the Dyke,[1] also in the pasture field 13. Nothing that could be definitely equated with the road was found; and the complete absence of any traces of the metalling on the *ploughed* fields between the Home farm and enclosure 13 offered no encouragement to further effort. I now consider it likely that the Roman road crossed the Dyke at the same point as the modern road: by 'The Steps'. If so, its structure here has long ago been worn away by traffic, for the road is in a slight hollow.

(b) The fort above Tallard's Marsh, Sedbury, Gloucestershire

The situation and interest of the knoll above Tallards Marsh is referred to on p. 197, and is apparent when Fig. 86 is studied. The defences thereon (Fig. 90) consist of a single bank and a ditch, clearly defined (though lowered by cultivation) on the E., traceable on the N. up to the edge of the cliff, and almost completely eradicated on the S. The profile of the defences, where best preserved—on the line A–B—is seen on Fig. 89; it is here similar in scale to Offa's Dyke. The enclosed area is between one-third and one-half of an acre, and measures about 44 yards from rampart to cliff-edge.[2]

Since this was the only fort on the line of the Dyke which had any claims to be considered as a Mercian work and an integral part of the Offan frontier, it was thought desirable to cut at least one trench across the ditch. Through the kindness of the owner, Mr. Richardson, and of the tenant of the cottage garden, we were permitted to do this on the N. side of the defences near the cliff (the line C–D on plan).

The section thus exposed is seen on Fig. 89. It showed that a natural depression in the limestone extending inwards from the cliff edge had here been utilized as the ditch, the work of man being probably limited to clearing off the overlying humus and clay, since the remains of the rampart (some 18 in. in thickness) showed that it was composed of dirty clay without any limestone blocks. There was found on the *floor* of the ditch the socket of an iron lancehead (9 mm. in greatest diameter, and 35 mm. in length). Though this object is consistent with an Offan date for the earthwork, it does not by any means prove it, for the type is known in Roman and Medieval times as well as in the Dark Ages. A second find illustrated the subsequent history of the site: on 2 ft. of silt which had accumulated since the little fort was deserted, lay a coin of 1806; above this, the ditch contained dirty clay—presumably thrown in when the adjacent rampart was levelled.

WIDE GAPS IN THE DYKE FRONTIER ANALYSED

The problems presented by (A) the gaps in central Herefordshire, and (B) the absence of the Dyke along the middle Wye, will be considered separately in the following pages.

---

[1] The crest of the partially levelled bank was here found to be 6 ft. above natural ground level.

[2] This little fort was probably better preserved in 1842, when Ormerod recognized it: *Archaeologia*, xxix, p. 15.

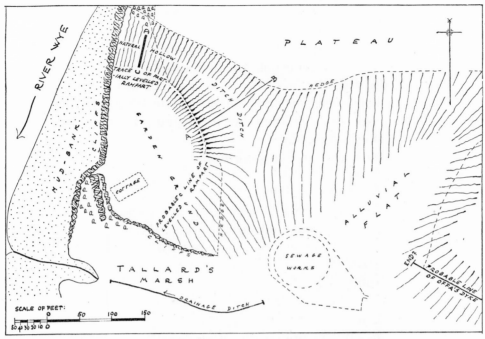

Fig. 90. The fortified spur above Tallard's Marsh (see Fig. 86).

(A) *The frontier from the foot of Rushock Hill to Bridge Sollers on the Wye, in Herefordshire*

It was thought possible that the length of the Dyke in N. Herefordshire, as recorded on the 6-in. O.S. maps, might be materially extended as a result of this investigation, but on balance it has been increased by only 370 yards. Short lengths have been added at Kennel wood, Flintsham, Lyonshall Park wood, Holme Marsh, Claypits, and Bowmore wood, making up 1,300 yards; but against this must be set 930 yards, mainly in Garnons wood, recorded on the maps as Dyke, and here rejected. As a result of these adjustments the four portions[1] of the Dyke in this sector are judged to be respectively $\frac{1}{3}$ mile, $1\frac{1}{12}$ miles, $\frac{3}{4}$ mile, and $\frac{1}{2}$ mile long. They represent little more than a quarter of the distance (13 miles) from the foot of Rushock Hill to the river, measured along their line.[2] The problem of the frontier on the Herefordshire plain is not, however, so difficult as the extent of the gaps would suggest. Firstly, the southern ends of the river Arrow portions, at Berry's wood, and Lyonshall Park wood (p. 176 and Fig. 72), and the southern end of the Curl brook portion, near Holme Marsh (Fig. 73), which are undamaged, show clearly that they were meant to be terminals; we are studying complete entities, not mutilated fragments of more extended works. It is reasonable to suppose that the damaged ends were originally similar; they all

---

[1] Treating the river Arrow and Yazor brook portions as units.

[2] The character of the Dyke in N. Herefordshire, and the spatial relationships, may roughly be stated as follows:

No dyke . . .	$\frac{10}{13}$ of total distance.
Dyke, sinuous (in partially cleared country?) .	$\frac{1}{13}$,, ,,
Dyke, straight (in completely cleared country, arable or meadow?) .	$\frac{2}{13}$,, ,,

suggest this to a greater or lesser degree, corresponding to the extent of the damage they have individually suffered (see pp. 176–8). Secondly, the stretches of dyke are confined to the river valleys which cross the chosen alignment between Rushock Hill and the Wye; that of the Arrow, the Curl brook, the Yazor brook, and in part that of the Wye itself. Thus not only is the distribution of the Dyke fragments, so curious and apparently irrational when examined on an ordinary map (such as Plate XXXIII), capable of explanation when the regional geography is studied, but it is certain that small and inconspicuous portions have not been overlooked, since every river valley is accounted for. In short, *we have the whole construction in this area as Offa made it.*

(i) *The alignment of the Dyke in this area*

The more closely the Dyke in this area is studied the more illuminating does the equation: straight alignment = cultivated land, appear. Across the Curl brook valley (p. 178) the Dyke is straight below the 500 ft. contours only; above this contour on the N. side the land had been partially cleared and the Dyke is sinuous. On the sunny side of Yazor brook and on the sunny side of the Wye straight stretches of the Dyke *begin* about 450 ft. up, obviously the convenient limit for the arable of valley dwellers hereabouts. The contrast between the N. and S. sides of a valley in the eighth century is very striking at Yazor. The ground on the sunless side of the brook, apart from the traffic-way high up the slope, had not been cleared, and the Dyke was therefore not constructed (Figs. 91 and 92), although on the sunny side 1,100 yards of earthwork were necessary. The distaste of the Mercian arable farmers for north-facing slopes has been referred to in a previous Chapter (p. 122), but never has it been so clearly manifested.

(ii) *The cause of the wide gaps in central Herefordshire considered*

Why is the Dyke so intermittent in this area? It is a novel feature in our experience, but is easily explained; *the clue lies in the geology.* On descending Rushock Hill for the Herefordshire plain one passes on to the outcrop of Old Red Sandstone (Fig. 92). This formation provides, in these lowlands, one of the richest soils in the country, a soil which is under natural conditions densely afforested: the 'damp oakwood' of the botanists.[1]

The evidence for uncleared woodland in this area is fourfold:

(*a*) Records: exemplified by the following quotation:

. . . in West Herefordshire the woods were still so dense that in 1233 an order was issued to the Sheriff of Hereford to cause a breach to be made 'through the midst of the woods of Erdelegh (Eardisley), Bromlegh (Brilley) and Witteney (Whitney) between Erdeleg' and Maude Castle, so that it may be safe to pass and repass between the City of Hereford and the said Castle. . . .[2]

(*b*) Existing woods, in their plan and distribution manifestly remnants of an extensive forest.[3]

[1] See C. Fox, *Personality of Britain*, Index, 'oak-wood'.
[2] Robinson, Major S., *The Forests and Woodland*
Areas of Herefordshire, Trans. Woolhope Field Club' 1923, p. 197.
[3] See 1-in. O.S. map, sheet 80.

(*c*) Farm and hamlet-names combined with -wood, showing the existence of woodland, now destroyed, in recent centuries.[1]

(*d*) Earlier compounds in -wood (*wudu*), -ley (*leah*), -field (*feld*), showing that in this area the pre-Domesday settlements were clearings in forest country.[2]

It must be admitted that practically the whole area was forest in Offa's time; then, since intermittent Dyke construction of this sort has not been previously met with, either the forest differs in character from any woodland hitherto occurring on the line of the Dyke, or the policy of the Dyke builder has changed—he is content with less complete definition of the frontier. We think that the former explanation is correct: this soil nourished an unusually luxuriant growth, and dense thickets of thorn and bramble filled the spaces under the tree canopy. Thus the 'damp oakwood' forest was a completely effective natural obstacle, a barrier belt.

The reason for the existence of any Dyke structures at all in the area is indicated by the character and position of the four portions. All lie, as we have seen, in the type of country first cleared by the Saxon settlers—the river valleys; that is why these zones are free from the woodland names so common elsewhere in the area. Thus the explanation of the intermittency which is found in a spurious chronicle, that the Welsh (of Gwent and Glamorgan) destroyed the Dyke, is clearly shown to be a bad guess, formulated after the tradition of the construction of the frontier hereabouts was lost.[3]

Figure 91 illustrates this thesis, and it is interesting to see the lines of attack of these Saxon agriculturists on the forests of western Herefordshire. They pushed up the Arrow valley and its tributaries, the starting-point being doubtless Watling Street;[4] they pushed up the Wye from Hereford[5] along the line of the Roman road, and also, nosing up the lateral valleys to the northward, cleared the lowlands below Burton Hill. Thus this map gives us a likely picture, though in broad outline, of the extent of farmed land—arable and meadow—in this part of Herefordshire in the eighth century. I suspect that we are analysing a process which had been gone through before by the Iron Age Celts primarily in the age of freedom and afterwards during the Roman period; the position of *Magnis* (Kenchester) on the Wye (see map), a tribal centre, lends point to this argument. Thus the forest of the eighth century hereabouts may represent in large measure a reversion to Nature due to the breakdown of civilization in Britain after A.D. 400.

We have given reasons (Chapter VI, p. 164) for believing the Rowe Ditch at Pembridge to be pre-Offan. The zone of open country between Rowe Ditch and Offa's Dyke repre-

---

[1] *Hamlets*: Woodbrook, Kingswood Common, Broxwood, Barewood, Norton Wood, Hen Wood, Hurstway Common. *Farms and Houses*: Welshwood, Winforton wood, Dunwood, Woodbury, Hurstley Wood, The Hurst; also Birches, Woods Eaves.

[2] Sarnsfield, Stockingfield, Devereux Wootton, Woonton Ash, Woodmanton, Eardisley Wootton, Almeley Wootton, Foxley, Wormsley, Darkley, Luntley, Hackley, Mowley, Titley, Ailey, Brilley, Kinley, Kinnersley, Hurstley, Weobley. The same group of compounds occurs in other forest areas in England; cf. *E.P.N.*, Sussex, ii, pp. 550–3.

[3] *Brut-y-Tywysogion*, the Gwentian Chronicle of Caradoc of Llancarvan, entries, A.D. 776 and 784. Ed. Aneurin Owen, *Camb. Arch. Ass.*, 1863.

[4] A N.–S. (Roman) road, which gave them good lateral communications.

[5] The available evidence is in favour of there having been a bishop's see here from about 680. Lloyd, Sir J. E., *Hist. Wales*, i, p. 196, and p. 183, n. 1, above.

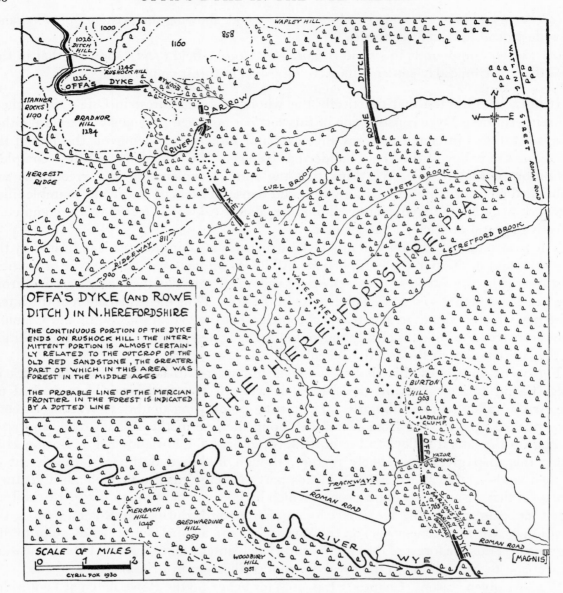

FIG. 91. Offa's Dyke (and Rowe Ditch) in N. Herefordshire: showing probable extent of forest and of cleared land in the eighth century.

sents, then, the extension of the cultivated land in the interval which elapsed between the two constructions.[1]

These agriculturally developed river valleys were in some cases accessible from the west, along ancient routes which the Welsh highlanders were doubtless in the habit of using. The Roman road from the Upper Wye region to *Magnis*, barred by the Dyke, was

---

[1] Another view, that Rowe Ditch (Pembridge) is a principal part of the Offa's Dyke frontier, is negatived on many counts; among them the non-existence of a Dyke bank in the Stretford brook and Tippets brook valleys; see Fig. 91.

PLATE XXXV

The Lower Wye valley below Tintern Abbey. Showing the Dyke on the edge of the scarp from Lippets Grove spur to Shorncliff wood. In the distance is St. Briavels Common. Taken from point M2, Fig. 94, looking NNE.

PLATE XXXVI

The Lower Wye valley at Tintern Abbey. The Dyke follows the crest of the wooded hills (the edge of the scarp) 600 ft. above sea-level. Taken from point L2, Fig. 94, looking ESE.

PLATE XXXVII

OFFA'S DYKE AT DENNEL HILL

DENNEL HILL HOUSE: DYKE INTERMITTED

BOUGHCLIFF

BAN-Y-GOR ROCKS

PROMONTORY FORT, SPITAL MEEND, LANCAUT

BROADROCK CLIFFS — THE SEVERN AND GLOUCESTERSHIRE BEYOND

The Mercian frontier from Dennel Hill to Broadrock forms the background of this picture. The Dyke is intermitted at Dennel Hill House. In the middle distance is Lancaut, and the loop of the Wye. Taken from point N2, Fig. 94, looking ESE.

PLATE XXXVIII

Offa's Dyke at Sedbury park, from the S. The ditch is between the fence and the bank.
Taken from point O2, Fig. 86

b. The end of Offa's Dyke on Sedbury cliffs. Taken from point P2, Fig. 86

doubtless still serviceable, and a well-marked ridgeway leads to the head of the Curl brook valley, the convenience of access of which doubtless accounts for a 'hundred court' being held here in the Middle Ages. The 'reinforced' Dyke in the Arrow valley suggests that an important trackway from the Radnor plain across Bradnor Hill crossed the frontier here (see also Fig. 69). Again, the short stretch of Dyke S. of the Yazor brook was almost certainly thrown across a trackway from the west, a branch, may be, of the Roman route already mentioned. It is too short to have any other significance, and its position on the hill-side is topographically right. It is interesting to observe that the Dyke is always large where the Offan frontier is accessible from the W. This is the case on the N. flank of the Curl brook valley (p. 178), while the scale of the Dyke at The Steps, below Garnons Hill W. of Kenchester (p. 180) must originally have been double that in Big Oaks, a few hundred yards nearer the Wye. Similar effects proceeding from similar causes were noted in Chapter VI (pp. 169–70).

(iii) *The line of the Mercian boundary between the frontier constructions in central Herefordshire*

Our task, now, is to reconstruct the Mercian boundary (the 'notional frontier') between these river valleys, beginning with the gap, 6 miles wide, between the Curl brook and the Yazor portions. It may seem futile to discuss a possible boundary across so wide a gap, but there are two related facts which appear significant. One is that the straight stretch of Dyke across Curl brook, 800 yards long, is aligned on the crest of the southern spur of Burton Hill (Ladylift Clump), 933 ft. above O.D., which is immediately above Claypits, where the Dyke begins again. The other is that this alignment follows almost exactly the watershed trending NW.–SE., which in this area, separates brooks tributary to the Arrow flowing NE. towards Mercia from those tributary to the Wye flowing SW. towards Wales. This watershed is a plateau, here broad, there narrow, 300–400 ft. above O.D.; it is the only alignment in the district which fulfils the requirements on which the Mercian frontier, as represented by Offa's Dyke, has been shown to depend. We can, then, be fairly certain that this watershed was the limit of Mercian territory hereabouts, as shown by the dotted lines on the map, Fig. 91.

From the shoulder of Burton Hill below Ladylift the boundary may have turned S. for a few hundred yards to link up with the Yazor portions of the Dyke. Between these and the Wye valley portion lies Garnons Hill. Here a parish boundary gives a probable indication of the 'notional' frontier, and has been adopted; it is shown on Figs. 74, 75, and 91.

We may now turn to the northern portions. It will be recalled (p. 175) that the Rushock Hill stretch ends on the right bank of the Eywood brook, and when picked up again $1\frac{1}{3}$ miles away is within a few yards of the right bank of the same streamlet. This suggests that the Eywood drainage line—the belt of marsh and jungle through which water meandered—was the boundary. This suggestion is illustrated by a dotted line in Fig. 91. The sinuosity and slightness of the Dyke where it descends into the Eywood valley suggests that this lateral re-entrant was *not cleared* by the Mercians.

The problem of the boundary between the river Arrow and the Curl brook portions is an interesting one. That it followed the edge of the steep wooded scarp which for over half-a-mile flanks the river Arrow on the E., and on which the Dyke was aligned when its construction was intermitted, may be regarded as certain; but nothing further can usefully be said save that, if it submitted to the same conditions as the Dyke itself normally does, it swung round the head of the deep re-entrant in Lyonshall Park wood shown on Fig. 72.

(iv) *The character of the Mercian boundary between these frontier constructions*

What was the nature of the boundary in the forest where there was no Dyke? Did it exist as a visible entity? That it was a frontier line marked by felled trees or a palisade—which when decayed or removed would leave no trace—is possible. But if our assumption —that the absence of the Dyke implies a natural obstacle impassable if left alone—be correct, an artificial barrier seems unnecessary. What *might* be necessary is unhampered *lateral* movement along the frontier; this could be attained by the clearing and main-tenance of a broad ride through the woodlands.[1]

If such rides existed, they might be expected occasionally to be perpetuated on the modern map by the development along them of field and other divisions. It is, for example, not improbable that the parish boundary on Garnon's Hill (Fig. 75) is such a survival. It is an extension of the Dyke, on an alignment which the engineer of the frontier would naturally choose. Again, in the rough pasture field which divides the Yazor brook portion from the Bowmore wood portion of Offa's Dyke, the banks of an ancient field unrelated to the existing system are visible. The W. margin of this field coincides with a line joining the reverse slopes of these dyke constructions. In other words, the field was on the edge of the zone which theoretically had to be kept open. It seems likely that before the frontier in this area lost significance a patch of the forest on the Mercian side was cleared, fenced, and cultivated, the limit being naturally the edge of the open ride. The sketch map, Fig. 87, illustrates this.

It is relevant to notice that the existing portions of the Dyke N. and S. of the river Arrow are linked by a hedge boundary which may in part—but cannot wholly—represent a destroyed piece of the earthwork (Fig. 72).

(v) *Summary*

Having reconstituted the frontier from Rushock Hill to the Wye, we can judge it on its merits as a whole. Topographically, it seems to fail as the best possible alignment in just that part about which doubts were expressed in Chapter VI—between the Hill and the Curl brook portion of the Dyke. Granted the inevitability of the watershed between the latter portion and Burton Hill as the boundary, it would have been more direct and surely more satisfactory from the Mercian point of view to have carried the frontier south-eastward across Bradnor Hill, pointing towards the Curl brook portion. It is possible that the indentation of the frontier at Eywood was imposed by agreement—that the district wherein there grew up the township known as Cingestune (Kington, see Plate XXXIII)

---

[1] In so far as this suggestion is accepted, the idea of a *notional* frontier line of course must be dropped.

was specially reserved in Welsh hands. But it seems more probable, having regard to the small space occupied by the Dyke in the valley of the Arrow that Mercian advance in this valley had not proceeded so far as in the Curl brook valley, and that hereabouts the political frontier accurately mirrors the racial frontier of the eighth century.[1]

The elucidation of the condition of affairs in the Herefordshire plain in the eighth century resolves certain difficulties which historians have felt. That the Wye should here have been the Offan boundary, having regard to the position of Hereford, a Mercian see, on it, and to the proved extension on the right bank of the river of Saxon occupation in the Dark Ages as far as the Dore valley, has seemed highly improbable. But we know now that, though Hereford had probably been in existence in the 7th century, yet *NW. Herefordshire was still nearly all forest in Offa's time*, and so may feel confident that neither the economic bases, nor the manpower, needed for an effective advance beyond the Wye, were present in his time.[2] The *tuns* of the Saxon settlers S. and W. of the Wye in Herefordshire were, we hold, necessarily dependent on post-Offan extensions in population and arable acreage N. of the Wye in the neighbourhood of Hereford. These extensions took place between A.D. 800 and 1100, as shown by the place-names in -ley and -field scattered over those parts of NW. Herefordshire near to the Dyke. Figure 92 shows how widespread the forest-bearing sandstone is in the region.[3]

It will have been noticed that there are several places in N. Herefordshire where the earthwork seems to have been constructed with the express purpose of controlling or blocking a traffic route which crosses it. Gaps for farm traffic and for modern roads are, of course, frequently present, but such rarely show original features. Those most likely to be original are in the Arrow valley, one N. of Berry's Hill, and the other immediately S. of the river.

(B) *The frontier from Bridge Sollers in Herefordshire to Highbury in Gloucestershire, mainly along the middle reaches of the river Wye*

From Bridge Sollers to Highbury, where Offa's Dyke as a continuous frontier recommences, there is only one place where short stretches of the earthwork are present. These, at English Bicknor, are parallel to and overlooking the river Wye.

Now since the Dyke at Bridge Sollers ends on the left bank of the Wye, and since the continuous stretch begins again at Highbury on the steep left flank of the Wye valley, and since an undoubted portion of the Dyke (at English Bicknor) between these two points is similarly situated to the Highbury portion, we may safely conclude that the valley of the Wye is, broadly speaking, the frontier throughout, and that where there is no Dyke the river itself has been utilized as the frontier in precisely the same way as the river

[1] But it should not be overlooked that Berry's Hill in the Arrow valley, on which the Dyke hinges, is like a watch tower: just the sort of key point which the Mercians would seize on (Fig. 72).

[2] Against this new evidence, that relied on by the late Sir John E. Lloyd (*Hist. Wales*, i, pp. 196 and 200 f.) in favour of such pre-Offan extension, cannot, we think, hold. The Welsh counter-pressure was probably, owing to forest conditions, as slight as the English pressure.

[3] A forest barrier has not been suspected here: but the importance of forests (e.g. Selwood and Braden) in the earlier stages of the Saxon advance was well brought out by Green, *Making of England*, ed. 1904, i, pp. 13, 106.

Severn N. of Buttington (Chapter V, Fig. 52). The whole of Erging, then, the Hereford bridgehead apart (?), remained in Welsh hands.

It is remarkable that, though the river was thus for a long distance used as the boundary, it was not so used for the whole distance to the sea. The causes which led to this differential

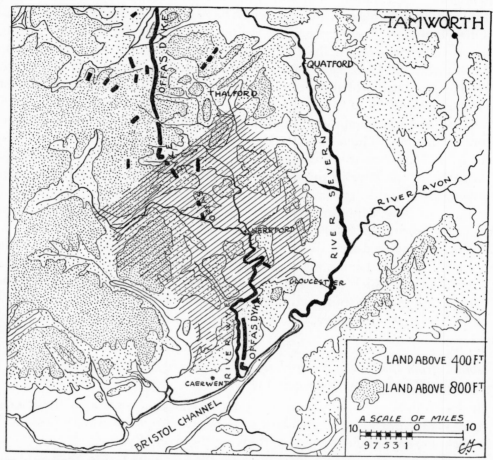

FIG. 92. The southern part of the Mercian frontier. Offa's Dyke and the 'Short Dykes' are shown. The diagonal shading represents the outcrop of the Old Red Sandstone.

treatment by the Mercians seem primarily to be geological. On Fig. 92 the belt of forest-bearing Old Red Sandstone is represented by shading. The reader will see that just as the Dyke as a continuous frontier has been shown to end in N. Herefordshire, where the outcrop of Old Red begins, so the Dyke commences again as a continuous frontier near the point where the Old Red has passed under newer deposits. These newer deposits are members of the Carboniferous System—limestones, sandy clays, and shales—which for the most part provide open or thinly forested country; thus the river Wye is the boundary only so far as it passes through the zone, presumably densely forested and sparsely inhabited by man, Welsh or English.

The junction of Carboniferous Limestone and Old Red Sandstone is not clear-cut. Narrow outcrops of the former approach and even cross the Wye valley, long before the point is reached where the limestone cliffs are the dominant feature of its gorge. The Dyke at English Bicknor is on an outcrop of limestone partly overlaid by clays. Fig. 93 gives

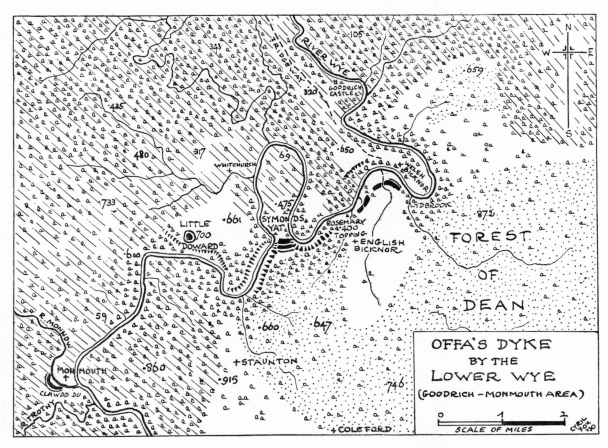

FIG. 93. Offa's Dyke by the Lower Wye. I. At English Bicknor. Cliffs, the Early Iron Age promontory fort at Symonds Yat, the Norman earthwork at Monmouth, and a hill fort are also indicated. Tree symbols, indicating forest, are frequent on the Old Red Sandstone (represented by diagonal shading) and on steep slopes; they occur also on Carboniferous shales and sandstones (represented by dotted areas); and are sparse on the Carboniferous Limestone (unshaded areas).

information essential for consideration of the significance of these isolated portions of the earthwork. Old Red Sandstone deposits (diagonal shading) are mainly but not entirely confined to the Welsh side of the frontier hereabouts. The dotted areas are Forest of Dean sandy clays and shales, the white patches limestone.

The two portions of Offa's Dyke cross two little lateral valleys of the Wye, close to the main stream. Like the valley portions farther north they are complete entities, not mutilated fragments of more extensive constructions. Hedgebanks and holloways between the two banks suggest, just as do similar alignments farther north, that the *frontier* may have been continuous from Lydbrook to Rosemary Topping (see Fig. 78). No Dyke, however, is present in the Staunton area,[1] or in the area N. of Lydbrook, where, as at Bicknor, there is limestone country, presumably open in early times, as now, to the eastward, and it is more reasonable therefore to suppose that the river Wye really was the frontier hereabouts, and that the Dyke structures at English Bicknor were built to deal with a special problem. Here, and here alone in this area, we assume, Anglian settlers had cleared lateral valleys down to the Wye, and access to the cultivated fields had to be controlled. It may be that the ridgeway shown on Fig. 93 led to a pre-Norman crossing place of the Wye near St. Custinin's church, Welsh Bicknor,[2] giving access to the Forest of Dean, and its iron mines.

PRINCIPLES GOVERNING IDENTIFICATION OF OFFA'S DYKE
(WITH SPECIAL REFERENCE TO HEREFORDSHIRE)

Before leaving the forest zone, it should be pointed out that other observers have studied the problem of Offa's Dyke in Herefordshire. Neglecting the adequate study of the existing remains[3] they have concentrated their efforts on searching for, and finding, earthen constructions to fill the gaps. J. G. Wood, in the *V.C.H.*, *Hereford*, goes so far as to assert that he has established the Dyke's 'almost certain course' for some 19 miles along the Middle Wye (vol. i, p. 260). He also describes the course of the Dyke from Rushock Hill to Bridge Sollers, on the assumption that Rowe Ditch formed part of it, recording numerous 'traces' of the earthwork on this line. Such 'traces', both here and on the Middle Wye, consist of a variety of constructions—ditches, silt banks, holloways, causeways, hedgebanks, lanes, field ridges, lynchets, &c. We reject them as affording evidence of the presence of Offa's Dyke.[4] It may be urged, however, that this is unreasonable and un-scientific, since practically every one of these types has been claimed to represent the Dyke in one place or another, in the preceding chapters of this study. This plea requires careful attention, and affords an opportunity for a brief statement of the principles on which the identification of Offa's Dyke has been based.

Running earthworks such as Offa's Dyke are in their normal form, and when unmodi-fied save by the action of time (which operates by lowering the crest of the banks and silting up the ditches), unmistakable. The height or breadth of the bank, the well-defined deep or broad ditch bespeak a work of military character, and none of the constructions or manifestations referred to above can be mistaken for it. But when, as often happens, the bank of Offa's Dyke is ploughed down, and the ditch ploughed in, the Dyke may look like a lynchet; when the bank is levelled inwards and the ditch used as a trackway, the

---

[1] Cf. Maclean, loc. cit., pp. 26 ff.

[2] Llan Custenin-Garth Benni. The ridgeway is shown by Prof. W. Rees, *South Wales and the Border in the XIV Century*, SE. Sheet. An alternative sugges-tion will be found on p. 217, n. 7 below.

[3] e.g. in linking up Rowe Ditch with the Rushock Hill sector, J. G. Wood ignored a considerable stretch of the former lying N. of the point of junction as defined by him (presumably because this stretch is not marked

on the O.S. maps?) *V.C.H.*, *Hereford*, i, p. 259.

[4] At the same time it seems not impossible that in the 20-mile stretch from Hereford to English Bicknor, one or two *short* stretches of unmistakeable Dyke may yet be discovered, thrown across lateral valleys, and brought into existence by similar conditions to those operating at Bicknor. We cannot claim to have searched every field and wood in such areas.

Dyke may resemble a holloway, and so on throughout the list. Again, the small boundary bank into which, in places, the Dyke degenerates cannot constructionally be distinguished from an ancient hedge bank.

What, then, is the touchstone? how can we distinguish the true from the false? The answer is simple. The identification of the Dyke is based on typical portions which retain their original character. Thus *the acceptability of uncharacteristic sectors as veritable portions of the Dyke depends on their being in direct extension of characteristic portions, on an alignment such as the Dyke might be expected to take.* When the gap between two characteristic portions is wide the uncharacteristic manifestations must, to be acceptable, throughout their length follow the alignments which are usual in the case of the Dyke and be continuous. These latter essentials may be illustrated: the Dyke may be represented *for miles* by a boundary bank in nowise differing constructionally from a hedgebank; but ordinary hedgebanks are not continuous for miles, they do not follow tactically sound alignments, nor do they merge at either end in Dyke-banks of military character.

Apart then from ancient literary and traditional identification, to which other standards may in some measure apply, no *isolated* patch of *uncharacteristic* earthwork can be accepted as a portion of Offa's Dyke. Now the identifications which we reject are uncharacteristic, they are not continuous, they are heterogeneous. Thus they are rightly rejected. For in so anciently inhabited a country as Britain there is no difficulty whatever, as can be experimentally demonstrated, in finding here and there some evidence of earthwork—hedgebank, or ditch, or holloway, or lynchet—sufficiently close to any arbitary line one likes to draw on the map. When artificial constructions fail, Nature will help, for the variety of rock structure in the W. of England frequently produces ridges calculated to mislead the unwary. The weaknesses of such 'evidence', when it is studied in the field, are apparent. Some of J. G. Wood's identifications of the Dyke near Ross may be taken as examples. At Park Farm, and at Over Ross, N. of the town of Ross, it is 'plainly to be seen', or 'forms a causeway on the left side of the road'. Now, the road is in a slight hollow at these places, and the slope formed by the junction of natural ground level and holloway is thus identified as the earthwork. The 'deep ditch' at Duxmere, S. of Ross, is an ordinary holloway, and the 'well-developed' bank in Furnace wood is a modern spoil heap.[1] Again, Maclean has recorded a well-marked stretch of 'the Dyke' near Lydbrook, in the right position on the edge of a western-facing scarp and of considerable extent.[2] The bar to its acceptance as part of Offa's Dyke is that it is natural, an unusually hard band of limestone, which has weathered out.

THE SIGNIFICANCE AND CHARACTER OF OFFA'S DYKE BORDERING THE LOWER WYE

Though breaches of continuity in the Dyke occur in the Highbury–Sedbury sector, wherein the actual earthwork totals up to a little over 9 miles in length, it is certain, from

[1] See *V.C.H., Hereford*, i, pp. 260–1. The absence from this record of a map of the supposed trace of the Dyke makes the detection of its errors difficult, and underlines the author's incompetence.

[2] Maclean, loc. cit., p. 29, para. 2.

the character of the terrain at the gaps, that a continuous frontier, utilizing natural obstacles where possible, was designed, and that this frontier was completed. The map of the Lower Wye, Fig. 94, and Plates I and XXXVII, show how the Dyke is linked to limestone cliffs or steep scarps—at Wyegate Hill, at Dennel Hill, and in the Tidenham district—just as it was at Llanymynech in Shropshire (Chapter IV, pp. 65–66). Marshes were also brought into service as natural obstacles at Bigsweir, and earlier constructions at Lancaut.

There is abundant evidence that limestone outcrops were among the most favoured dwelling places of man in Britain. They were well drained and practically free from forest. The outcrop bisected by the Wye and the Mercian frontier is an important one, the larger half of it, measuring 9 miles by 2–4 miles, being in Welsh territory. Centrally situated in this limestone belt was the cantonal town of the Silures, *Venta Silurum* (see Plate XXXIV); and we may reasonably suppose that the population of the belt in Offa's time was still considerable. It afforded on both banks of the river an easy route for traffic, as well as an ideal area for settlement, and the iron of the Forest of Dean probably reached the S. Wales sea-plain by the old Roman road along it. Across this limestone country, then, the Mercians needed a well-defined boundary, and this they obtained; for it may be doubted if, anywhere in these Islands, can be found a historic frontier so adequate, so dominating, as this plateau edge overlooking a swift river in a winding gorge—a gorge which is often narrow and precipitously flanked, in places 600 ft. deep. For those desiring to examine this frontier the right approach is the natural one from the E. across the level upland pastures, near Madgett Hill (Fig. 94) for choice. These fields end at a belt of trees within which is the Dyke; one walks along its bank, and the whole tremendous panorama—Monmouthshire, the Wye and the Severn, the coasts of Gloucestershire and Somerset—is seen down a steep-pitched woodland glade. Alternatively, it can be viewed with equal exhilaration from the Welsh side, as in photographs illustrating this chapter.

The Dyke along the Wye extends farther northward than would appear to be geologically necessary. The limestone belt borders the Wye on the right bank from Chepstow to Tintern only,[1] but the Dyke on the left bank extends some 5 miles beyond Tintern, to Highbury. If a continuous Dyke was needed along this stretch, which fronts wooded hills of Old Red Sandstone formation, it would seem to be equally necessary still farther north, in the Monmouth area. We infer that the proximity of a belt of habitable country in Welsh occupation was not the only reason why a dyke was necessary on the Lower Wye. The clue to the second, and probably the more important reason, is provided by the Tidenham Charter.[2] Tidenham, a large royal manor, occupying the tongue of land between Wye and Severn, was given by King Edwy in A.D. 956 to the monks of Bath Abbey. In its organization, and in the services due from its tenants, it was distinctively English. This is, of course, not surprising when one recalls that the greater part of Tidenham is within Offa's Dyke—the 'dic' of the Charter—in an area that was probably West-Saxon before it was Mercian; it would have then been in English hands for well over 200 years. The manor

---

[1] See marginal note on left side of Fig. 94.
[2] Seebohm, *English Village Community*, p. 148, and *Codex Diplomaticus Aevi Saxonici*, Kemble, 1845, p. 450.

contained, however, two hamlets outside the Dyke. One was Lancaut (Lancawet),[1] which has already been mentioned; the other, unnamed, was in Beachley peninsula (Plate I and Fig. 94). Part of the peninsula was let to *scipwealan*,[2] probably Welsh sailors as the quotation below indicates. There was here, in short, in the tenth century, a little Welsh seaport. In this century these Welshmen were under English control; but does not their presence, coupled with the fact that the Offan frontier was drawn so as to leave the important area occupied by them in Welsh hands, suggest that the Welsh seaport also existed in Offa's time? And why was it left? Not surely for its own sake, but for what it implied. It implied, as Professor William Rees[3] has pointed out, Welsh control of 'the ferry-crossing of the Severn estuary from Aust to Beachley', which under the name of the 'Old Passage' was 'the direct route from the west of England into south-east Wales'. It also seems to imply that the river traffic—the timber trade—on the Wye, which was important in the eleventh century,[4] was also important in the eighth century. Now we begin to see daylight on our problem. The frontier was drawn and the Dyke built on the plateau edge above the Wye mainly because, the trade along the lower reaches of the river being in the hands of the Welsh, it was inconvenient to make the river the political boundary; sailors must be free to land or to moor their boats on either side.[5] Now coastal shipping, right down to medieval times, required free access up to the head of the tidal waters of a river, and Offa's Dyke on the lower Wye had to extend high enough to cover with a reasonable margin the tidal traffic. The high-water mark of ordinary tides, Llandogo, is shown on Fig. 94, but the tide on exceptional occasions reaches Redbrook, *which is under the high plateau where the Dyke ends*.[6] From this point northward, I assume that the peculiar privileges accorded to the Welsh in the tidal reaches ended, and that the river was the boundary. Presumably they could traffic in this zone if they wished, but their liability to English, as well as Welsh, taxes and dues would begin.[7]

[1] It is not yet certain whether the name is Welsh or English. In the Charter of 956 Lancaut had much arable land on the E. side of the Dyke (see *The Church and Parish of Lancaut*, Messrs. Wood, Dobson and Hicks, Trans. Bristol and Glos. Arch. Soc., 58, 1936, pp. 207 ff. I am indebted to Lord Raglan for drawing my attention to this survey). The persistence of Anglo-Saxon parish boundaries through the centuries, illustrated by Dr. G. B. Grundy's studies (*Arch. Journ.* *passim*) makes it likely that the boundaries of A.D. 956 were those of the early eighth century, and that Saxon lands were handed over by Offa to the Welsh, both at Beachley and Lancaut. (1953).

[2] *Cod. Dip.*, loc. cit.: Divisiones et consuetudines in Dyddanhamme: . . . to Cinges tune V hida sind XIII gyrda gafollandes and I hida bufan dic þaet is nu eac gafolland, and þaet utan hamme is gyt sum inland, sum hit is þan scipwealan to gafole gesett. *At Kingston* [now Sedbury] *there are 5 hides including 13 yard lands of rent-paying land, and 1 hide above the Dyke that is now also rent-paying land, and as regards that outside the enclosed land some is still in demesne, some is let out for rent to Welsh shipmen.* I am indebted to Miss A. J.

Robertson, M.A., for advice on the problems of this charter.

[3] *An Historical Atlas of Wales*, 1951, p. 17.

[4] D.B., Gloucestershire, Record Commission, p. 162: 'tantum de navibus in silvam euntibus.' I am indebted to Professor Rees for drawing my attention to this reference. See also An Historical Atlas, *loc. cit.*

[5] Maclean grasped the point about sailors' needs, but he did not follow it up: loc. cit., p. 30.

Sir Joseph Bradney notes that until the nineteenth century most of the 'carrying of merchandise to and from Monmouth was by means of barges'. *Hist. Mon.* ii, p. 219.

[6] Major Frank Phillips, Clerk to the Board of Conservators of the Wye Fishery District, in a letter to my colleague, Mr. Colin Matheson, says: 'sometimes, but on very rare occasions, the effect of the tide, I am told, reaches the tail of the lower Redbrook stream.' Now if the Welsh were granted the river rights 'to the head of the tidal flow,' they would certainly claim the maximum, not the normal.

[7] The Dyke at English Bicknor *may*, I now suggest, represent, not a parallel to the barrier Dykes in

This conclusion reinforces the evidence already collected,[1] suggesting that Offa's frontier was the result of negotiation, a treaty between Welsh and English. Immense labour had to be undertaken by the Mercians in order that the Welsh might have the untrammelled use of their river trade and their seaport. If this interpretation be correct, Offa appears to have been wiser, in thus removing causes of friction, than his successors; for we have seen that by 956—the date of the Charter—the territory outside Offa's Dyke on the left bank of the Wye, adjacent to Tidenham, had been absorbed by the English, doubtless in order that their revenue might benefit from the tolls on the Severn ferry, and Wye river traffic, and on the valuable salmon fisheries.

It is curious that at Redbrook the Dyke begins on the high plateau (Highbury) instead of on the river. Its termination coincides exactly with that of the ancient arable upland, as shown by field boundaries threading the modern woodland. The frontier, represented by a 'ride' through virgin woodlands (p. 210), may have ascended from the river junction at Redbrook, the visible frontier—the Dyke—commencing on the edge of the cultivated lands. It is at least certain that, where first apparent, the Dyke points downhill (fig. 80, and p. 187).

THE SIGNIFICANCE OF THE 'BOUNDARY BANK' DYKE STRUCTURE IN THE LOWER WYE VALLEY

The survey of the Dyke in the centre of the Mercian frontier—the southern half of the Mountain Zone—showed that at all important points it was of normal Offan type with W. ditch, and that the stretches of this type were linked together by less carefully constructed portions of 'boundary-bank' type. 'Important points' were seen to be areas of open country used for cultivation or for traffic. It naturally occurred to me that the curious and puzzling alternation of strong and weak stretches of Dyke in the southern portion, the Highbury–Sedbury sector, might be similarly rationalized. If so, it would not only solve the local problem, but would also bring this sector into close technical relationship with the Mountain Zone sector.

The Highbury–Sedbury sector was therefore studied from this point of view, a start being made on the most interesting portion, that between Madgett Hill and Dennel Hill (Plates XXXV, XXXVI, and XXXVII). Here the Dyke follows the edge of the limestone escarpment, having a cultivable plateau behind and precipitous slopes in front. The geographical and geological conditions seemed to be uniform, and the profound differences in construction which have been described on pp. 191–4 of this work, and summarized in Fig. 94, seemed irrational. It was clear that, if the theory failed here, it was no use attacking the problem of the Dyke structure in this sector on these lines any further. Fortunately, it was recalled that a fine series of lynchets (p. 203) abutted on the northern

Herefordshire, but an isolated extension, northwards, of the Welsh rights to both banks of the river Wye for their carrying trade in timber or (here) iron. The community of interest between the dwellers on either bank was manifest in the fourteenth century, both being called *Bikenor, Bikenore*, by the English. William Rees, *Map of S. Wales and the Border in the †14th Cent.*, SE. Sheet (1953).

[1] Chapter V, pp. 81 ff, and Chapter VI, p. 153.

part of this stretch of earthwork,[1] and that there was a Domesday vill—Modiete—immediately adjacent, represented by the modern farm-house of Madgetts, and by the field-name Modesgate. These lynchets then are memorials of the cultivated lands of this Domesday and pre-Domesday settlement, and *the limits of the normal Offan type of Dyke hereabouts were almost certainly the limits of the common fields of the vill*. In like manner the southern half of this stretch of Dyke, which was almost entirely of boundary-bank type, crossed Tidenham Chase, a forest of the Saxon kings when Tidenham was a royal manor, retained as a forest throughout the Middle Ages. Thus, in this area, the differences in the character of the earthwork can be related to differences in the character of the adjacent countryside in the eighth century.

The initial difficulty then was resolved, and in a manner which suggested that the change from normal Offan type to boundary-bank type of Dyke would be found to mark in every case a change from open fields or pastures to forest or uncultivated country. In respect of five-sevenths of the remaining portions of Dyke of normal Offan type with W. ditch or berm, the available evidence supported this conclusion. Long stretches of the type exist at Highbury, where, on the limestone plateau, there is evidence of the former existence of open fields, and at Sedbury, where straight alignments and the evidence of the Tidenham Charter point to high cultivation in the Dark Ages. The strong portion of Dyke on the S. side of the Brockweir valley (see Fig. 94) was probably a barrier across a narrow open belt, forming a traffic way to the river, of which traces still remain. I can offer no explanation of the shorter stretches of normal Offan type of Dyke which occur on the N. and S. slopes of Wyegate Hill. The sinuous alignment suggests forest.[2]

We may now turn to the examples of Dyke of boundary-bank type other than that adjoining Tidenham Chase. The most important of these are at Coxbury and on the Hudnalls–St. Briavels upland. They are both on the Old Red Sandstone, and therefore likely to have been built in forest; it has already been urged that the uncertain course of the Dyke in the latter area can only be attributed to forest conditions.

We have, then, facts and reliable inductions in respect of the physiography of SW. Gloucestershire in the eighth century, which cover nine-tenths of the course of the Dyke; and these facts and inductions, with one exception (Wyegate Hill), confirm the equations —normal Dyke = open country: boundary-bank Dyke = forest country or 'waste'. Thus, Offa's Dyke in the south of the frontier is seen, in the general technique governing

---

[1] The 'stone-row', or line of stones, of the Tidenham Charter. The relevant boundaries of the Manor in 956 are thus recorded: Of Waegaemuþan to iwes heafdan; of iwes heafdan on stanraewe; of stanraewe on hwitan heal; . . . *Cod. Dip.* iii, appendix CCCCLII. *From Wye-mouth to the Yews Head; from the Yews Head on to the line of stones; from the line of stones on to White corner*. . . . These boundaries have not hitherto been worked out, but they present little difficulty when the significance of 'Yews Head' is realized. It is the limestone spur opposite Tintern Abbey, as seen by a boatman. Cf. St. Abbs Head, and see Plate XXXV, where

the yews, the natural successors to those of a thousand years ago, are visible. The species cannot be exterminated here growing as it does in the deep and narrow clefts of the rock.

[2] Two very small portions of Dyke approximating to normal Offan type occur in the Tidenham Chase area, between Devil's Pulpit (Fig. 83) and the head of The Slade (Fig. 84); (*a*) a look-out point at Shorncliff, the highest on the whole stretch, and (*b*) near the Slade itself where the contours afford easy access to the river. The existence of small patches of open country here is therefore probable.

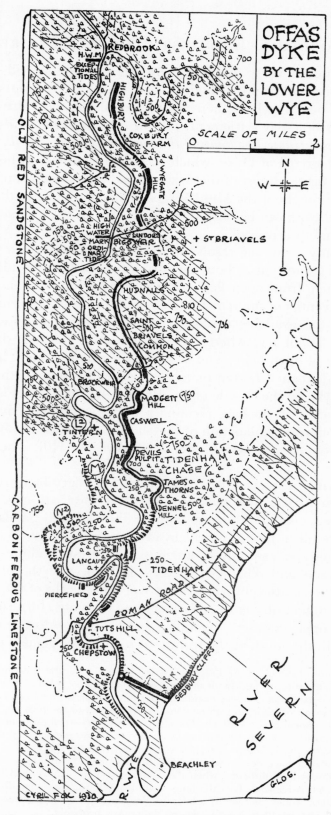

Fig. 94. Offa's Dyke by the Lower Wye. II. From Highbury to Sedbury. The thick black line represents the bank, a thinner line the ditch (or spoil trench). Cliffs, and the promontory fort at Lancaut, are also indicated. Tree symbols, indicating forest, are frequent on steep slopes and on the Old Red Sandstone (diagonal shading), infrequent on Carboniferous Limestone (unshaded areas).

its construction, closely to resemble that part of the earthwork which occupies the central zone of the frontier (Chapter VI).

It may be added that the only difference between the *intermittent* Dyke frontier in N. Herefordshire and the *continuous* Dyke frontier lying to the N. and S. of it respectively is this, that visible links between the strongly constructed portions crossing open country were, in the former case, omitted by reason of the exceptional density of the forest.

THE RELATION OF THE SOUTHERN MERCIAN FRONTIER TO ROMAN ROADS

In the area under consideration in this chapter, from N. Herefordshire to the Severn Estuary, two Roman roads crossing Offa's Dyke have been mentioned. One is the E. and W. road through *Magnis* (Kenchester) in the upper Wye valley; the other the road from *Glevum* (Gloucester) to *Venta Silurum* (Caerwent), which crosses the lower Wye above Chepstow. These are related, the one to the northern group of portions of the Dyke, the other to the southern continuous sector of the earthwork. No Roman road which survives in use, or, indeed, of which the exact course is known, crosses the line of the Offan frontier in the gap, 37 miles broad, between them.[1]

It is here suggested that this is not accidental, but represents a causal relationship. It is obvious that in this southern portion of the frontier the Dyke was built only where it was needed, in areas, that is, which were important in the eighth century. Important areas were those wherein military pressure, or Anglian civil occupation, developed. This advance, whether military or civil, tended to follow Roman roads, because these provided the easiest means of penetration. *Now roads thus used in the Dark Ages tended to survive, being maintained in use for economic as well as military purposes. Roads not so used in the Dark Ages, in country naturally forested, tended to be lost.* Thus, although we know that Roman roads must have existed on the *left bank* of the Middle Wye (e.g. from *Ariconium* and *Glevum* westwards, crossing the Wye at Monmouth), we cannot identify them. They went out of use because the Mercian occupation of this zone was very thin, and when in the Middle Ages the population developed the old ways had long been lost sight of.[2] It is important to notice that the maintenance of Welsh customary tenures in Archenfield, one of the outstanding (and unexplained) facts of early Border history, is due to the absence of Anglian or Saxon pressure on the Middle Wye.[3] The causes of that absence of pressure we believe to be physiographical.

The continued use of the Roman road from *Glevum* to *Venta Silurum* may explain the curious fact that the only place in the entire stretch from Highbury to Sedbury where no

---

[1] See O.S. Map, Roman Britain, 2nd ed., and the small-scale coloured maps illustrating this Chapter.

[2] For an explanation on similar lines of partial survival of Roman roads in East Anglia, see Fox, *Arch. Camb. Reg.*, pp. 288–90. It is relevant to note that the Roman road from Bridge Sollers southwestward to the Dove valley probably survives because it was used by Anglo-Saxon settlers after Offa's time. The spearhead of their advance (Bacton on the right bank of the Dove)

is on its line. See Plate XXXIII, where the road is marked 'Stone Street'. It seems to me that this theory deserves an extended test. If generally true, it should aid the study of the period of the Heptarchy.

[3] The rarity of Early Iron Age hill-forts in this district suggests that the limits of the Anglian advance were determined by geographical factors which had been equally potent in the earlier age.

Dyke *or* natural obstacle is present on the left bank of the Wye is the easy slope opposite Chepstow Castle (Figs. 85 and 94). The Dyke leaves the high ground at Chapelhouse wood, as we have seen, and makes for the river *just above the Roman road crossing*. There is every reason to suppose that the Roman bridge, or a ford, was still in use in the eighth century (the piles are still in the river bed, the Roman road can be traced to the riverside on the left bank, and parish boundaries follow its course on the right bank up the steep slope and for a considerable distance beyond). Now, had the Mercians aligned their frontier across Tutshill, as everyone who has written about the Dyke supposes them to have done, they would have given the Welsh an important bridgehead. They had too much respect for their neighbours to do this. The alignment of the Dyke shows that here, and here only in this southern sector, the Mercians carried their frontier down to the river bank.[1]

COMMENTARY: THE MAJOR PROBLEMS RESOLVED

The major problems connected with the Mercian frontier in the southern stretch of 60 miles, which arise from the fact that Offa's Dyke occupies only some 13 miles of this distance, have been almost completely resolved. The Dyke in Herefordshire and Gloucestershire has been shown to be not the fragmentary remains of a far larger work, but the practically complete structure as Offa left it. The broad gaps are related to a type of country not hitherto met with on the line of the Dyke, namely, dense forest in a rich lowland. Such Dyke structure as exists in this area, which is that of the Old Red Sandstone, is connected with the clearings and cultivated lands of the Mercian settlers. In other words, the Dyke is present in this zone only where Welsh and English were, in the eighth century, actually in contact. The river Wye formed a convenient boundary between the two peoples throughout the greater part of the forest. A ford of the Wye at the Bicknors, near Goodrich, where there is a patch of limestone country on both banks was obviously important to both communities in the eighth century, for a stretch of Dyke covers English Bicknor. In the extreme south, where there are extensive areas of open and habitable country, a nearly continuous stretch of Dyke is present, linked to precipitous cliffs. Here Dyke-structure of normal Offan type gives place to Dyke-structure of boundary-bank type as and when cultivated fields gave place (in the eighth century) to moor or forest; the technique employed by the builders being thus identical with that used farther north, in Radnorshire. A continuous Dyke was needed on the E. bank of the lower Wye, not only because the frontier bisected a zone of fairly intense occupation, but also because the tidal traffic of the river Wye was in Welsh hands.

Again, the Dyke was almost entirely confined to the N. and the S. of the 60 mile stretch under review in this chapter because English pressure was concentrated in these areas; this concentration was related to two of the Roman roads leading into Wales, which were in consequence maintained in partial use during the Dark Ages, and so their courses, in the neighbourhood of the Dyke, are known.

[1] There is no evidence for an eighth century Anglian bridgehead at Strigoil (Chepstow).

Finally, the physiographical and economic conditions shown, by the study of the Dyke, to have been present in the eighth century on the southern portion of the Mercian frontier throw much-needed light on the historical problems of this part of the Welsh March—such as the survival of Welsh customary tenures in Erging (Archenfield)[1]—in the Dark Ages. The southern sectors of Offa's Dyke are among the most difficult to elucidate on the whole frontier, and such success as this chapter describes has been due to the application of experience gained during the previous five years.

[1] For Archenfield, see Sir John E. Lloyd, *Hist. Wales*, i, p. 280. It was known as Ircingafeld in Old English, Sir F. Stenton, op. cit., p. 212.

PLATE XXXIX

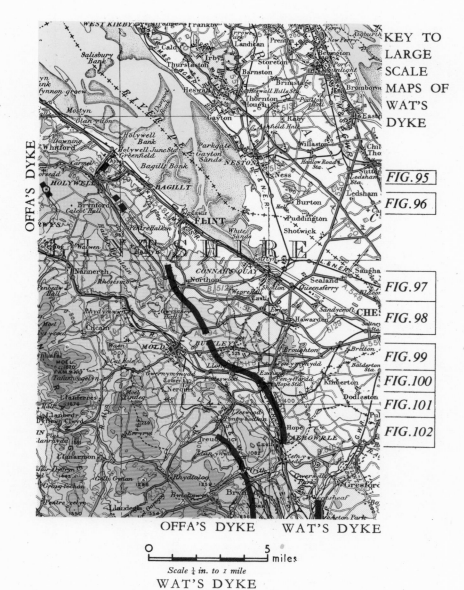

OFFA'S DYKE   WAT'S DYKE

Scale ¼ in. to 1 mile

WAT'S DYKE

Wat's Dyke in Flintshire, Denbighshire, and Shropshire

(Chapter VIII)

(A) The Northern Sectors

The topographical relationship of Offa's Dyke to Wat's Dyke is shown
on the map

See pages 227, 261, 271

PLATE XL

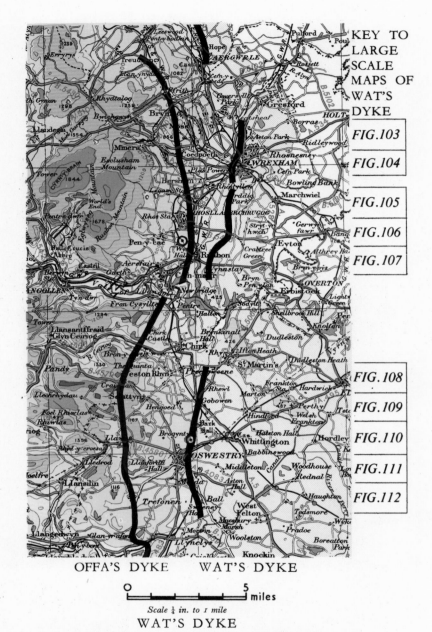

KEY TO
LARGE
SCALE
MAPS OF
WAT'S
DYKE

FIG.103

FIG.104

FIG.105

FIG.106

FIG.107

FIG.108

FIG.109

FIG.110

FIG.111

FIG.112

OFFA'S DYKE   WAT'S DYKE

0   5 miles

Scale ¼ in. to 1 mile

WAT'S DYKE

Wat's Dyke in Flintshire, Denbighshire, and Shropshire

(Chapter VIII)

(B) The Southern Sectors
The topographical relationship of Offa's Dyke to Wat's Dyke is shown
on the map

See pages 227, 260, 261, 271, 286

PART II
WAT'S DYKE

VIII. WAT'S DYKE: FROM THE DEE ESTUARY AT HOLYWELL, FLINTSHIRE, TO MAESBURY, SHROPSHIRE, IN THE BASIN OF THE MIDDLE SEVERN (1934)

WHEN outlining, in 1925,[1] my plans for the investigation of Offa's Dyke, I remarked that 'the investigation of that system of travelling earthworks cannot be considered complete until Wat's Dyke has in like manner been examined, and the relation of the one Dyke to the other considered in all its aspects'.

The travelling earthwork known as Wat's Dyke is generally believed to extend from the estuary of the Dee near Holywell in Flintshire to Maesbury Mill on the Morda, a tributary of the river Vyrnwy in N. Shropshire, a distance, measured along its curved course, of about 38 miles. Throughout the greater part of this distance the Dyke is apparent, but there are broad stretches in respect of which the accuracy of the alignment recorded on the O.S. maps and indicated in the literature is open to doubt, and others where its course, if it exists, is unknown.

INTRODUCTION

The Nomenclature of Wat's Dyke, and its Differentiation from Offa's Dyke

While it will be made clear in this Survey that, on geographical grounds alone, Wat's Dyke is readily and certainly distinguishable from Offa's Dyke, it is proper to point out that the two Dykes have been greatly confused. Ranulf Higden (*c.* 1352) refers to Offa's Dyke as terminating 'between Coleshill and the monastery of Basingwerk' (*inter collem Carbonum et monasterium de Basingwerk*).[2] The author of *Brut y Saeson* (Book of Basingwerk) also refers to Offa's Dyke as terminating 'between the monks house of Dinas Basing and Mynydd y Glo' (*rwng mynachlog ddinas Basing a mynydd y glo*).[3] Clearly it is Wat's Dyke which is here referred to.

Palmer, moreover, notes three farmhouses on Wat's Dyke, called respectively Bryn Offa, Llwyn Offa (Mold Parish, Flints.), and Clawdd Offa (Hope Parish, Flints.); and

---

[1] *Arch. Camb.*, 1926, p. 138.
[2] Polychronicon Ranulfi Higden: Rolls Series, vol. ii, p. 34.

[3] See A. Griscom, *Y Cymmrodor*, xxxv, 1925, pp. 101, 106, and A. N. Palmer, *Y Cymmrodor*, xii, 1897, p. 76.

Edwin Guest states that while, in 1858, he was examining a portion of Wat's Dyke, 'the whole country assured him' that it was Clawdd Offa.[1]

The earliest reference to Wat's Dyke as a distinct structure[2] is apparently in Churchyard's *Worthines of Wales* (1587).

> Within two myles, there is a famous thing,
> Cal'de Offae's dyke, that reacheth farre in length,
> All kind of ware the Danes might thether bring,
> It was free ground, and cal'de the Britaine's strength.
> *Wat's dyke likewise, about the same was set,*
> Betweene which two, both Danes and Britaine's met
> And trafficke still, but passing bounds by sleight,
> The one did take the other pris'ner streight.[3]

Thomas Pennant, however (1810), was the first to describe the Dyke and to define its course. His record is of sufficient importance for full quotation:

A great dike and foss, called *Wat's*, is continued from each side of this post. This work is little known; notwithstanding it is equal in depth, though not in extent, to that of *Offa*. We shall here trace the course of each. *Wat's* can only be discovered on the southern part to *Maesbury* mill, in *Oswestry* parish, where it is lost in morassy ground: from thence it takes a northern direction to *Hen-ddinas*, and by *Pentre'r Clawdd* to *Gobowen*, the site of a small fort, called *Bryn y Castell*, in the parish of *Whittington*: then crosses *Prys Henlle* common, in the parish of *St. Martin*: goes over the *Ceiriog* between *Brynkinallt* and *Pont y Blew* forge, and the DEE below *Nant y Bela*: from whence it passes through *Wynnstay* park, by another *Pentre'r Clawdd*, or township on the ditch, to *Erddig*, the seat of *Philip Yorke, Esq.*, where there was another strong fort on its course: from *Erddig* it goes above *Wrexham*, near *Melin Puleston*, by *Dolydd*, *Maesgwyn*, *Rhos-ddu*, *Croes-oneiras*, *Mr. Shakerley's Gwersyllt*; crosses the *Alyn*, and through the township of *Llai*, to *Rhydin*, in the county of FLINT; above which is *Caer-estyn*, a *British* post: from hence it runs by *Hope* church, along the side of *Molesdale*, which it quits towards the lower part, and turns to *Mynydd Sychdyn*, *Monachlog* near *Northop*, by *Northop* mills, *Bryn-moel*, *Coed y Llys*, *Nant y Flint*, *Cefn y Coed*, through the *Strand fields*, near *Holywell*, to its termination below the abbey of *Basingwork*. I have been thus minute in giving its course, because it is so often confounded with OFFA'S ditch, which attends the former at unequal distances, from five hundred yards to three miles, till the latter is totally lost.[4]

Evidence in favour of this differentiation, and of the antiquity of the name Wat, is given by A. N. Palmer. He says, 'I have been fortunate enough to meet with three documents in which its old Welsh name occurs. In a deed of the year 1431 it is spelled *Clauwdd Wade*, in another of the year 1433 *Claud Wode*, and in Norden's Survey of 1620, *Clawdd Wad*.' He adds, 'It . . . looks as though in the Welsh and English names of Wat's Dyke, we have preserved two forms . . . of the same name, probably Wada, the name perhaps of the Mercian who . . . constructed the Dyke.'[5]

---

[1] *Arch. Camb.*, 1858, p. 338.
[2] Most scholars refuse to admit as authoritative the statement in the Gwentian Brut which *may* refer to Wat's Dyke, to the effect that in 784 Offa laid out a second Dyke nearer to England. *Myvyrian Archaiology of Wales*, 2nd ed., 1870, p. 686.

[3] There is no confirmatory evidence for this statement (2nd Ed., 1776, p. 104).
[4] *Tours* (Rhys's ed., vol. i, pp. 331–2).
[5] Loc. cit., pp. 74–75. Norden's Survey is Harley MS. 3696 in the Brit. Mus. The reference is to folio 60, verso: 'along by the township of Stanstie to a place

The chief contribution made by modern writers to the study of Wat's Dyke is in respect of early documentary sources. Griscom's article in *Y Cymmrodor*[1] is especially noteworthy, though the references to the Dyke are incidental. No detailed field work has hitherto been carried out on any part of the Dyke, and writers subsequent to Pennant add little to the information he gives.

THE COURSE OF THE DYKE

Wat's Dyke, in its course from the Dee estuary to the middle Severn valley, marks the boundary between the lowland of the English Midlands, and the hill country of N. Wales; it follows the line of the palaeozoic outcrop,[2] and crosses three counties, Flintshire, Denbighshire, and N. Shropshire.

It varies in elevation from about 267 to 530 ft. following usually a fairly level course round about 300–400 ft. Its highest point is near Buckley, E. of Mold in Flintshire (Fig. 99), its lowest at Wrexham,[3] Denbighshire (Fig. 104). When it is noted that within two or three miles of the Dyke to the W., elevations of 900 to 1,000 ft. occur, e.g. in the Oswestry area (Selattyn Hill), at Caergwrle (Hope Mountain), and near Northop (Halkyn Mountain), it is manifest that its course is designed to include as much country as lowlanders could conveniently occupy or control.

Changes in level in the country traversed by the frontier are sometimes abrupt. The streams and rivers for the most part run in steepsided ravines and gorges; some of them, parallel to the hill range, have been utilized as elements of the frontier line. These streams are mostly tributary to the Dee, whose valley is crossed by the line of the Dyke NE. of Chirk.

The undulating character of the country in general gives ample scope to the engineer, who desired western-facing alignments. It is almost entirely agricultural, and is but little affected, save by the expansion of the town of Wrexham, by the industrialism of the N. Welsh coalfield. The dingles and ravines are everywhere well-wooded, elsewhere the country-side is open.

Geologically, Pennant sandstones form the underlying rocks throughout the greater part of the course of the Dyke. These are frequently overlaid by glacial drift—boulder clays and gravels—especially in the S. This affects the form of the Dyke, which does not often show the sharply defined profiles seen, for example, on limestone.

The course of the Dyke is recorded from N. to S., as was Offa's Dyke. It is set out on eighteen sections of the 6 in. O.S. map, reduced to 4 in. to 1 mile (Figs. 95–112). The official reference number, or numbers, are indicated on each of them. An attempt has been made by varying the thickness of the line which marks the Dyke, to show its varying dimensions as they exist today. Plates XXXIX and XL, prepared in the same manner as

---

called Clawdd Wad westwards And so along Clawdd Wadd to the brook Gwenfro . . .'. This point, about the builder of the Dyke, is discussed on p. 285 below.

[1] A. Griscom, *Y Cymmrodor*, xxxv, 1925, pp. 97–107.

[2] Fox, *Personality of Britain*, Map B.

[3] Its *line* touches a lower level in the ravine-valley of the Dee; but the Dyke is not present here.

those dealing with Offa's Dyke show the course of Wat's Dyke in relation to upland and lowland, and to Offa's Dyke. They also enable the position of each of the large-scale maps to be found by the reader.

The first point at which a bank and ditch, traditionally and in the literature recognized as Wat's Dyke, is seen is at Holywell. The survey will, therefore, begin at this point.

FIGURE 95.[1] *Holywell area: in Holywell Rural and Urban parishes, Flintshire*

Wat's Dyke was until recently visible as a partially levelled bank with deep W. ditch, 150 yards in length, on high ground east of Holywell, known as the Strand. The construction of a row of cottages has caused the ditch to be filled in for use as a roadway, but traces of the bank still survive. There is now no visible evidence of the Dyke on its traditional line northward from the Strand along Strand Walk, but the alignment of this Walk on to the point where the tiny valley of the Strand becomes a ravine is very suggestive of its former existence.

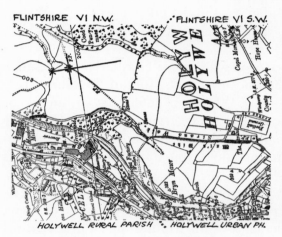

FIG. 95. Holywell area: in Holywell Rural and Urban parishes, Flintshire.

This ravine opens out above Meadow Mills on the flank of the deep trough valley carved out by the Holywell stream; and here a small piece of bank is seen, 21 ft. in breadth, with an over-deepened W. ditch, which is possibly part of the Dyke. It seems to die out in the railway cutting, and beyond this point northward nothing recognizable as Wat's Dyke is to be seen. It is true that railway embankments and cuttings obscure the topography, but the absence of any trace of the Dyke on the grassy knoll S. of Abbey farm makes it almost certain that the structure did not exist in the intervening area. It is, however, reasonably certain that the frontier—apart from any earthwork—extended to the sea; that is to say it terminated close to the little plateau on which Basingwerk Abbey was built. The site is an important one—a flattened spur flanking the Holywell ravine and close to a cliff overlooking the estuary of the Dee.

The name Basingwerk is significant in this connexion. It seems to be compounded with a personal name, Bassa. Complex as the problem of -ing names is, it is reasonably certain that, in this case, the meaning is, *the fort of the people of Bassa*.[2] Pennant records (op. cit. i. 31) that on the SE. side of the site occupied by the abbey, there was a 'vast ditch' (which he identified with Wat's Dyke). This ditch is not now to be seen, but it is presumably obliterated by the railway embankment; linked with the gully on the SW. side, artificial and possibly in part ancient, it might form sufficient protection and entitle the area thus

---

[1] The reduced 6 in. to 1 mile O.S. maps are each so placed on the page that—as in the case of Offa's Dyke —the reader is surveying the earthwork from the Welsh side irrespective of the cardinal points.

[2] English Place-name Society Publications, vol. i, part ii, pp. 42 f. Note on -ing compounds, &c.

isolated to be described as a *weorc* ('work' or fort).[1] King Cenwulf of Mercia, who resumed the Mercian expansion westward, died at Basingwerk in 821.

No Dyke structure is to be expected on the alluvial flat below.

We may now turn to the S., beyond the Strand sector of the Dyke. No trace can now be found, nor has such been recorded, on the high ground E. of Holywell between the Strand and the ravine of the Bagillt brook. A likely alignment is by spot-level 404 and the mill which crowns the highest point hereabouts, down the slope to the head of the dingle by Roft Tob well. This line gives ample visual control to the W. The ground has not been built over, and the absence of any bank or ditch in the area is therefore significant—the Dyke was never constructed here. The portions of the Dyke mapped in Figure 95 may be regarded as part of a design which was never completed, on the analogy of Offa's Dyke in a similar situation (pp. 13 ff. above).

FIGURE 96. *Wern Sirk–Fron Tydyr[2] area: in Holywell Rural parish, Flintshire*

Wat's Dyke reappears, after a break of 1¼ miles, in Wern Sirk wood on the right bank of the Bagillt stream near its source. The E. flank of its little valley, usually a steep scarp, is here an easy slope.

The Dyke begins adjacent to a lateral streamlet and a patch of bog as a very large bluff-ended bank, on a rising slope in a wood, with W. ditch and slight bank on counterscarp (Fig. 113, i). The scarp measures 23–24 ft. The Dyke dies into the hill-side at a cross-hedge, its total length being only 65 yards.

To the N., beyond the lateral streamlet, the bank marked 'Wat's Dyke' on the 6 in. map is a hedge-bank or hedge-scarp at the junction of the arable and meadow, with no features other than those frequently produced by agricultural operations. To the S., on the Wern Sirk moor-land, the line shown as that of the Dyke is merely the well-defined angular junction of plateau and river scarp.

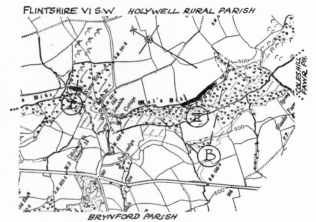

FIG. 96. Wern Sirk–Fron Tydyr area: in Holywell Rural parish, Flintshire.

A road—a deep and ancient holloway—now intervenes, crossing the valley at the hardly discernible watershed between the Bagillt stream, flowing NW., and the Nant-y-Fflint stream, flowing SE.

---

[1] My friend Mr. W. J. Hemp, who as an official of H.M. Office of Works had exceptional opportunities for studying the site, informs me that it is said there used to be a castle there, a stone wall of which was present 100 years ago. He has never seen any traces of the foundations of such a wall. Sherds of Roman pottery are the only objects known from the site suggesting occupation anterior to the foundation of the abbey.

For Cenwulf, see Stenton, *Anglo-Saxon England*, p. 228.

[2] The Editors of *Arch. Camb.* note that the accepted spelling is *Tudur*.

Beyond BM 491·4 and the quarries, the well-defined junction between the cultivated level plateau and the ravine-like valley with its steep and well-wooded sides (illustrated in Plate XLI*b*) is marked as 'Wat's Dyke', but there is nothing artificial about it, save at one point, which requires careful study.

Extending from the *n* of Fro*n* to beyond the *r* of Tydy*r*, a distance of 170 yards, is an artificial construction which cannot be other than the Dyke. The scarp already referred to is steepened and there is a broad berm—the scarp measures at one point 27 ft., the berm 13 ft. across (Fig. 113, ii). Farther on the berm becomes a shallow ditch; then the construction fades out. The scarp of the valley to the S. was very closely examined; I satisfied myself that the only portion of the Dyke in the area is that described above.

The only possible conclusion one can draw is that these two fragments of earthwork represent the N. and S. ends of a stretch of Dyke, designed to cover the 'old road', but never completed. Here, again, the similarity to Offa's Dyke in the N. is striking.

Nant-y-Fflint to the Conwy valley (not figured)

The Nant-y-Fflint valley now becomes broader with gentle and well-cultivated slopes. At one or two places, such as the field boundary (a bank and ditch on the plateau edge) 320 yards due S. of BM 448·2 (6 in. Flints. IX. SE.) the existence of the Dyke may be suspected, but I think the constructions are agricultural in origin. After passing the ford by Windmill Tavern, the western-facing scarp of the Nant becomes steep, the valley a ravine; then the ravine deepens to form a wooded gorge. At its junction with the valley of the Conwy, the gorge opens out; but there is no trace of the Dyke on the pasture fields hereabouts.

The valley of the Conwy was then followed up; it is a wooded ravine which shows no trace of the Dyke until Coed-Llys (p. 226) is reached.[1]

FIGURE 97. *Coed-Llys to Soughton farm: in Northop parish, Flintshire*

At the N. end of Coed-Llys, on the right bank of the stream at its junction with a small tributary, Wat's Dyke recommences, as correctly recorded on the O.S. map. It is a small, low, rounded bank with W. ditch, and it ascends through the wood on a straight alignment (Type I, 380 yards[2]), making for the point where the steep western-facing scarp of the main valley recommences. From Coed-Llys to the cross-track it is a slight bank, with flat lower berm. Thence to the Northop–Holywell road the Dyke (represented by a steep scarp and lower berm or ditch) exactly follows the junction of plateau and valley slope, fading out when this is exceptionally steep.

On the S. side of the road the Dyke reappears, on the edge of a quarry which has destroyed a good deal of it, as a steepened scarp with a broad berm below. It must not be confused with the modern hedge-bank with E. ditch which here crowns it. A little farther on (beyond the patch of woodland on the E. side) it becomes a magnificent work; high

---

[1] The *R.C.A.M.* Flintshire (p. 18, Monument no. 62) is incorrect in stating that the Dyke is present in Coleshill Fawr parish.

[2] For an explanation of this typology, see pp. 119, 264.

bank, deep W. ditch, and (probably) a slight counterscarp bank (over-all breadth 48 ft., scarp 23 ft., see Fig. 113, iii). This scale is maintained along the plateau edge above Coed Uchaf (500 ft. contour), but the Dyke is damaged by a series of lead-mine shafts, which lie mainly along the ditch.

We have reached a watershed: the western-facing scarp dies out, and the Dyke changes direction, following a gentle downward slope and making for a shoulder of land above the Northop brook. This reached, near spot-level 442 above Mynachlog, a fresh alignment is laid out on to the N. slope of Bryn-y-Bal Hill (Figs. 99 and 117), $2\frac{3}{4}$ miles away. The line

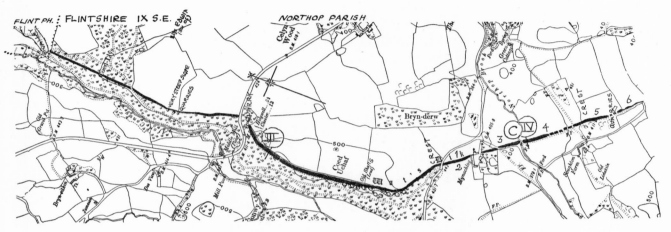

FIG. 97. Coed-Llys to Soughton farm: in Northop parish, Flintshire.

In this and the following fifteen maps a thick black line ▬▬ represents portions of the Dyke clearly visible today; the *degree* of thickness illustrating the relative size of the work at different points in its course. An additional line close to and parallel with the principal one indicates the presence of a bank on the counterscarp. A thick broken line ▬ ▬ ▬ shows that faint traces of the Dyke are present; while a hair line ——— represents the approximate alignment of the Dyke where it is now lost, as recorded on the first 1-in. O.S. map, or as indicated by a respectable tradition. A broken hair line — — — represents the probable frontier where the Dyke was not constructed.
Roman numerals in circles point to the exact position where the sectional plan with the corresponding number was made; letters in circles and arrows indicate the approximate position and direction of the camera when the illustration with the corresponding letter was taken. Certain fields and enclosures on the line of the Dyke are identified by arabic numerals.
Sketch contours — · — · — · indicate important natural features on the line of the Dyke not clearly brought out on the Ordnance map.
A portion of the 6-in. O.S. map reduced to 4 in. to 1 mile.
(Reproduced from the Ordnance Survey map with the sanction of the Controller of H.M. Stationery Office.)

chosen gives a good view to the W. along the greater part of the course, and the Dyke is throughout, except where damaged or destroyed, on an imposing scale.

To return to detail: between fields 1 and 2 the W. ditch of the Dyke is ploughed in; it crosses Mynachlog home pasture as a high scarp, is damaged in the upper part of field 3, but in the lower part reveals the characters normal to a steep descent—a broad, rounded bank, ditched on E. and probably on W. also. The gap at the stream is (as usual in the case of Offa's Dyke) very narrow (about 9 yards), and the Dyke begins again as a high bank with W. ditch (over-all 56 ft., scarp 21 ft., see Fig. 113, iv, and Plate XLIIa). It is partly levelled in field 4, but reappears on the rising slope; it is very fine on the Soughton farm crest (N. end of field 5) but beyond is much damaged by quarrying. The bank then forms the hedge boundary of field 6.

FIGURE 98. *Clawdd-Offa to New Brighton: in Northop parish, and on the boundary between Northop and Mold Rural Parishes, Flintshire*

From spot-level 421 to 'Clawdd-Offa' the Dyke is destroyed to form the road, but here and there traces of ditch and of bank (road causewayed on it) can be discerned. In field 7 the levelled bank and ditch are again clearly seen, and the Dyke survives in patches across the corner of Soughton Hall park. Its W. ditch is a drainage channel by the footpath in field 8, the bank having been spread over the field. The Dyke still survives, ploughed down, in field 9, and can be traced in the adjacent garden. Beyond Fawnog a green lane represents the ditch, and the bank forms the boundary of fields 10 and 11, on the crest of the rise.

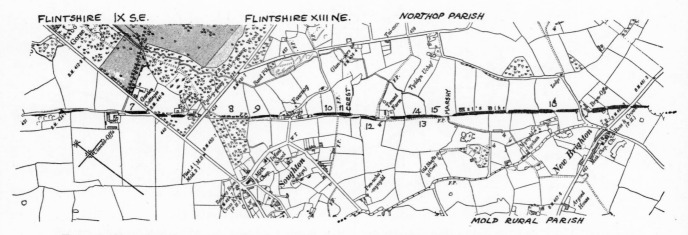

FIG. 98. Clawdd Offa to New Brighton: in Northop parish, and on the boundary between Northop and Mold Rural parishes, Flintshire.

A portion of the 6-in. O.S. map reduced to 4 in. to 1 mile. For the significance of the symbols and letters employed, see Fig. 97. (Reproduced from the Ordnance Survey map with the sanction of the Controller of H.M. Stationery Office.)

The trackway to the farm then passes on to the bank of the Dyke; the W. ditch is plain in field 12. The rounded bank can be seen in the garden of Tenant farm and the field beyond, and the ditch borders the footpath. The bank is undamaged between fields 13, 14, and 15; it fades out in a piece of boggy land, recommencing as a narrow, high ridge. From here to field 16 the Dyke has in many places been damaged by ploughing, the cutting of gaps and the trampling of cattle, and the W. ditch has been ploughed in; but it was originally a very fine work. At the N. end of field 16, a short stretch of the bank is well preserved. Immediately S. of Bryn Offa farm the bank is high and perfect, the W. ditch is a pool; beyond this point it is fairly well preserved, the scarp measuring at one point 21 ft. The clayey soil hereabouts makes the state of preservation very uneven, portions of the bank readily slipping into the ditch. Crossing the road, the Dyke dies away as shown; it never extended any farther. The N. slope of Bryn-y-bal Hill was doubtless impassable woodland.[1]

---

[1] The 1838 1 in. O.S. map marks it on this hill; but this map is untrustworthy so far as the Dyke is concerned.

FIGURE 99. *Bryn-y-ffynnon to Whitehouse farm (and beyond): in Mold Rural parish, Flintshire*

The Dyke faded out (at about 460 ft. above O.D.) on the N. side of the hill; it is present on the S. side, near the crest, in field 17 (at about 530 ft. above O.D.) as a ploughed-down bank. It may have recommenced originally on the crest, now occupied by cottages.

The high bank is visible by the roadside at the new schools, and (much denuded) forms the boundaries of fields down a gentle slope—with a fine view to the W.—to a marshy patch where it dies out. It begins again on rising ground, becoming a good size at the

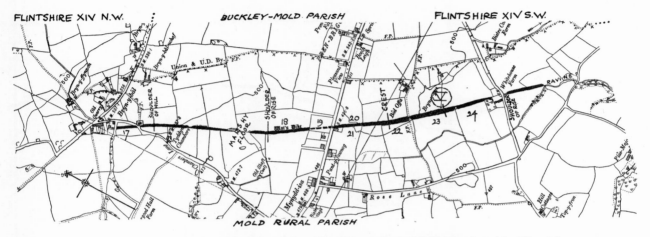

FIG. 99. Bryn-y-ffynnon to Whitehouse farm (and beyond): in Mold Rural parish, Flintshire.
A portion of the 6-in. O.S. map reduced to 4 in. to 1 mile. For the significance of the symbols and letters employed, see Fig. 97.
(Reproduced from the Ordnance Survey map with the sanction of the Controller of H.M. Stationery Office.)

S. end of field 18. It is completely levelled in field 19, but is present, damaged by cattle trampling, between pasture fields 20 and 21. It forms a belt of woodland on the boundary of field 22 and, with its W. ditch, is very well preserved, being on the major scale.

At the highest point (510 ft.) of a gentle rise, near Bod Offa, it changes direction slightly; it is very finely sited hereabouts with wide views to the W. Levelled for a space, it remains untouched in a belt of woodland bordering field 23 (over-all 42 ft., scarp 18 ft., see Fig. 114, v). Its line can easily be traced along field 24; there is an additional (E.) ditch hereabouts, probably a modern drainage ditch.

Gapped beside Whitehouse farm, and quarried on the S. side of the road, the Dyke regains its scale and descends to a tiny ravine, which it strikes at an angle; here it ends, deeply ditched.

From the Bod Offa crest line to Whitehouse farm the Dyke is directly aligned; this direction is maintained to the ravine by 'back' alignment. Thus is seems probable that the entire portion from Bryn-y-ffynnon hill-top was aligned in straight stretches. See Fig. 118, 2.[1]

---

[1] The methods employed in the diagrammatic representations of the Dyke on Fig. 118 are described on p. 264.

FIGURE 100. *Plas Major to Hope Junction: in Mold Rural parish, Flintshire*

The recommencement of the Dyke 400 yards farther down the ravine is most interesting. There is a tiny bank for a few yards bordering the ravine; then a drainage gap; then, leaving the ravine, the Dyke proper begins, a massive rampart, with W. ditch now largely filled in (see Fig. 114, vi). It continues on the same scale, gapped and partially levelled in places, to the Garreg-lwyd farm road by spot-level 336 (Fig. 118, 3); the alignment, in a SE. direction, direct but not dead straight, provides extensive views to the SW. For some distance hereabouts the ditch is perfectly preserved while the bank is ploughed down.

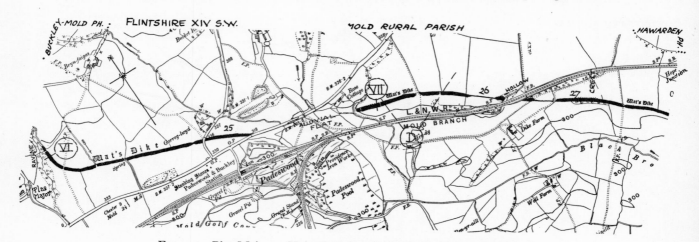

FIG. 100. Plas Major to Hope Junction: in Mold Rural parish, Flintshire.
A portion of the 6-in. O.S. map reduced to 4 in. to 1 mile. For the significance of the symbols and letters employed, see Fig. 97.
(Reproduced from the Ordnance Survey map with the sanction of the Controller of H.M. Stationery Office.)

Crossing the meadow (no. 25) as a broad ploughed-down ridge, and making for the little Black brook valley along a narrowing crest line, the Dyke meets the main road at an acute angle, and is probably incorporated in it for a hundred yards or so.

Intermitted across this valley, where Saxon territory fronted broad marshes now marked by Padeswood pool (Fig. 118, 3) the Dyke recommences on the farther side at a bluff outlined by the 300 ft. contour. Gaining a commanding western-facing slope overlooking a narrow lateral valley, its line is marked by a belt of scrubby oaks (Plate XLIIIa); the ditch is deep and in places boggy, the scarp steep, measuring at one point 24 ft., the overall being 52 ft. (Fig. 114, vii).

The Dyke then dips to cross this second valley, rises on to the flattened spur which separates it from the main Black brook valley (tributary to the Alyn), and thenceforward follows an alignment on its flank which gives wide views to the SW.

To return to the detailed survey: The Dyke is visible though ploughed-down in field 26, and is undamaged where it ends in a spinney by the valley floor and streamlet. Its recommencement is destroyed by the railway, but its ditch is visible in the face of the cutting, and in the pasture field beyond a short section is in its original condition. From here to the next railway crossing (Fig. 101) the Dyke follows as straight a course as possible across undulating country, with a fine field of view to the Welsh mountains, save where it crosses hollows. It has been much denuded by the farmers, and is gapped by drainage channels, but must have been, judging by its scale in field 27, a magnificent work. Here the ploughed-down bank is in the field, while the ditch, in a patch of scrub, is perfect. For the alignment, see Fig. 118, 3.

FIGURE 101. *Rhyd-y-Defaid to Stryt-isaf: in Mold Rural and Hope parishes, Flintshire*

On the rising slope of field 28 the ditch of the Dyke is a drainage channel, the footpath being on the levelled bank. Bordering field 29 the ditch is a holloway. The ditch is well

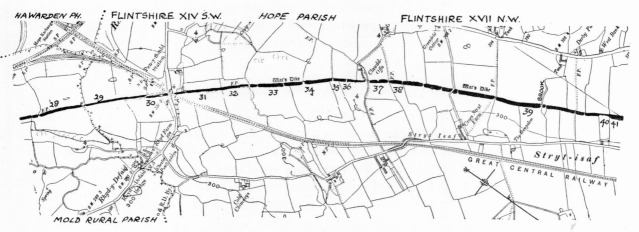

FIG. 101. Rhyd-y-Defaid to Stryt-isaf: in Mold Rural and Hope parishes, Flintshire.

A portion of the 6-in. O.S. map reduced to 4 in. to 1 mile. For the significance of the symbols and letters employed, see Fig. 97.
(Reproduced from the Ordnance Survey map with the sanction of the Controller of H.M. Stationery Office.)

preserved in the SE. corner of field 30, and both ditch and bank are traceable in the gardens on either side of the railway—which here again crosses the line of the Dyke. The country is now level with gentle slopes to the W., and from field 30 onwards for over 900 yards the Dyke is directly aligned (Type II).

In fields 31 and 32 the Dyke has suffered varying degrees of destruction. It then forms the NE. boundary of fields 33 and 34, and is a very fine work, the scarp measuring 20 ft. on the slope in one place—probably a good average for this area. In field 34 there is an opening—a traffic way—12 ft. wide, which looks original; the flanking banks are not recurved.

At Clawdd-Offa the Dyke changes direction, the new alignment bringing it (near Croes Stryt farm) on to the well-defined slopes which flank the important Alyn[1] valley. It follows the course of the river at 350–300 ft. above O.D. for a mile and a half, to Hope (Fig. 102). Its line is direct but not straight, conforming to the relief of the country, and

___

[1] The accepted spelling is *Alun*, but it is confusing to diverge from the Ordnance map which is being so closely followed.

laid out in stretches of Types I and II (Fig. 118, 4 g, h). The views to the W. are consistently fine; the photograph (Plate XLIII*b*) is taken from the Welsh side.

To return to the detailed survey: in fields 35, 36, and 37 the Dyke is much damaged; but a fine and usually fairly perfect stretch on a steepening slope, and with only slight traces of a lower ditch, begins in field 38. It presents the form of a scarp rather than a bank. There are no traces of spoil ditches on the upper (E.) side hereabouts.

The Croes Stryt farm road is a deep holloway, now a drainage channel. At the S. end of field 39 the Dyke is gapped for a water-course; destroyed for a space on the farther side, a small patch reveals its former existence. Then, for a few fields, a sinuous stretch follows of small or moderate size, with W. ditch, considerably damaged; in field 40 (a smallholding) the Dyke has been recently very much cut about. In field 41 the Dyke is full size, and the W. ditch is present; crowned with stubby oaks, the only damage done to its structure of stony clay is that caused by the trampling of cattle. The scarp measures 20 ft. 6 in. at one place in this field.

FIGURE 102. *Pigeon House farm to Caergwrle: in Hope parish, Flintshire*

In field 42 the scarp measures 22 ft., the W. ditch being at its best (Fig. 114, viii); the slope is now easier, and the Dyke recovers its normal character, that of a high bank. As Pigeon House farm is approached, the Dyke becomes clear of woodland and somewhat denuded; it is largely destroyed at the farm, but its course is not in doubt and its ditch (overdeepened) is very well marked on the S. side of the road.

The Dyke now passes to the E. of a low knoll (no field of view, very unusual, see Fig. 118, 4, j, k), and enters a zone of intense occupation or cultivation. It is tree-clad, with broad shallow ditch, bordering field 43. A second knoll intervenes, the Dyke, passing to the E. of it, being with difficulty discernible as the boundary of gardens or, levelled, in a paddock. Across field 44 on the other hand it is clearly apparent, on a descending slope and with a new and more southerly alignment. Its bank, much damaged, then borders the main road and the new Hope by-pass (not marked on the O.S. map) on the W. side, as far as the cross-track beyond the rectory. It is straightly aligned and was on the major scale (Fig. 118, 4, k).

A rise in the hedge at the N. end of field 45 fixes its position; within living memory it followed a course in fields 45 and 45*a* roughly parallel to the new road, curving eastwards into this road in field 46 to avoid a patch of marsh which formerly existed here. My friend Mr. R. W. Jones of Hope points to a thickening of the hedge at the junction of the old and new roads near BM 295·8, as a veritable fragment.[1] The Dyke then rises over the adjacent rocky outcrop—which formed the aligning mark for this stretch—the scarp being quite obvious. Thereafter it follows a curved course along the margin of the alluvial flat of the Alyn (Fig. 118, 4, l). At first it is a fine ridge with ploughed-in W. ditch; as the slope steepens the ridge becomes a scarp (measuring 24 ft. at one point). The W. boundary

---

[1] Mr. Jones watched the destruction of the Dyke here when the new road was built; the track by BM 295·8 was present as a 'pitched way' under it. Good evidence in favour of the view that the builders stopped all but a few selected roads across the frontier.

of Rhydyn farmhouse garden represents this scarp. Beyond the farm track, and directly above the river Alyn, is the base of a rocky hill—Bryn y gaer; a well-cut berm thereon, which is in the right alignment, may represent the Dyke. Whether or no, I have little doubt that it reached the river, and ended, between the 'Old School' and Caergwrle Mill. The so-called 'traces' of the Dyke S. of the Bryn y gaer outcrop in Rhydyn Hall grounds are portions of the (natural) river scarp of the Alyn, or developments of eighteenth century landscape gardening.

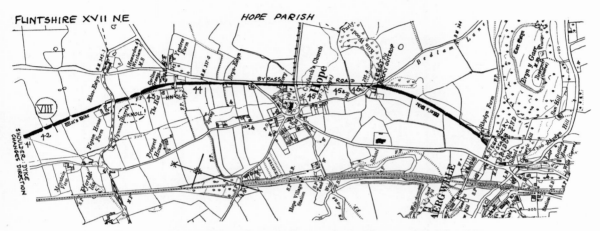

FIG. 102. Pigeon House farm to Caergwrle: in Hope parish, Flintshire.
A portion of the 6-in. O.S. map reduced to 4 in. to 1 mile. For the significance of the symbols and letters employed, see Fig. 97.
(Reproduced from the Ordnance Survey map with the sanction of the Controller of H.M. Stationery Office.)

Bryn y gaer, Caergwrle, to the loop of the Alyn River in Gwersyllt Parish (not figured)

The distance, along the probable line of the frontier, to the next certain stretch of Wat's Dyke is $3\frac{1}{2}$ miles. The intervening zone requires a brief note, especially as the Dyke is marked on the 6 in. O.S. map practically continuously along two-thirds of this distance, from Cefn-y-Bedd to Bryn Alyn.[1] These stretches lie parallel and close to the Alyn river. At every point they have been carefully examined, and nowhere does the evidence on the ground justify the attribution. The river runs usually in a steep-sided ravine with level fields on either flank, the slopes being often wooded. The well-defined junction of plateau and steep slope is a striking but natural feature; it is this junction, on the left bank, which is always seized upon as the Dyke. Occasionally, as is natural enough, a hedge-bank has been made where the arable ends on the edge of the scarp; or the angle of junction of the two planes is emphasized by soil wash, or stones, or field rubbish; but at no point does such a hedge-bank or other artificiality show any trace of Dyke construction. Where the steep scarp is replaced (owing to ancient landslips) by an easy slope, the so-called Dyke is absent; this obviously is just where it would be most definite, were it constructed in this zone.

In short, the Alyn ravine itself represented the frontier in this stretch (see Fig. 117).

[1] Denb. 6 in. O.S., XXI, SE. and XXVIII, NE. In *R.C.A.M.*, Denbighshire, the error is repeated: no. 248, p. 78.

FIGURE 103. *The loop of the Alyn river to the Locomotive Works, Wrexham: in Gwersyllt parish, on the boundary between Gwersyllt and Acton parishes, and in Stansty parish, Denbighshire*

The point made in the preceding paragraphs is well illustrated at the end of the stretch discussed, where the Alyn turns on itself in a hairpin loop and, moving eastward, is of no further service to the frontier makers. This loop is shown on Fig. 103; the narrow spur of upland defined and enclosed by it is occupied by a fine promontory fort (p. 260).

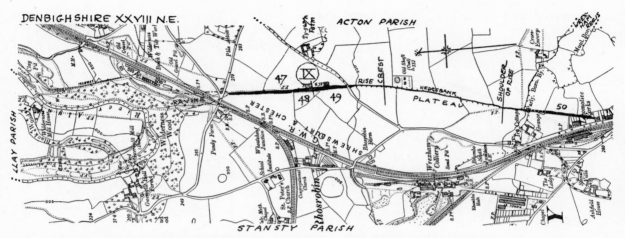

FIG. 103. The loop of the Alyn river to the Locomotive works, Wrexham: in Gwersyllt parish, on the boundary between Gwersyllt and Acton parishes, and in Stansty parish, Denbighshire.
A portion of the 6-in. O.S. map reduced to 4 in. to 1 mile. For the significance of the symbols and letters employed, see Fig. 97.
(Reproduced from the Ordnance Survey map with the sanction of the Controller of H.M. Stationery Office.)

There is no evidence that the W. defences of this fortress, very slight by reason of the steepness of the scarp above the river, were utilized as part of the Dyke frontier; the continuation of the scarp beyond the camp to the S. to the river flat (through *y* of Gwersyllt Mill) is devoid of any trace of artificiality, and the junction of the scarp and plateau in the field to the N. of the fort is marked by a hedge-bank of ordinary agricultural type; moreover, the W. ends of the cross-ditches by *p* of Cam*p* are open and perfect as originally planned.

Wat's Dyke begins again 50 yards to the S. of the 'Y' road junction, near Pandy farm. (From this point northwards to the road, there is a mere hedge-bank.) The construction of the railway obscured the topography, but it is clear that the terminal point is exactly what was the head of a lateral (and doubtless boggy and thickly wooded) ravine opening northward down Wilderness wood to the main river (see Fig. 118, 5, a). From the very beginning, the Dyke was straightly aligned (Type I) to the 300 ft. contour, 620 yards away, and was throughout on a large scale with broad W. ditch; present-day irregularities are due to destruction and levelling.

The Dyke is much damaged by quarrying and by agricultural operations; but the portions of bank or ditch bordering fields 47, 48, and 49 are fine. At one point, the scarp is

19 ft.; at another the ditch is a pond and 21 ft. broad (Fig. 114, ix); at a third the over-all breadth of the work is 52 ft.

Crossing the road, the W. ditch is present for a few yards, the bank quite small; this I take to be the terminal of the straight alignment. Thence onwards, the W. ditch is not seen (nor any E. ditch), and the line of the frontier is taken up by a small hedge-bank (which is a parish boundary) up the little rise, along the crest, and down the other side. Its line is direct, but not straight. There are fine views to the W. hereabouts.

The W. ditch recommences close to the 300 ft. contour (and doubtless the whole Dyke); but the bank is first present in field 50, as a ramp against a wall bordering the footpath. Traces of the earthwork across gardens and waste ground can be found as far as the *W* of *W*orks; from these traces I judge it was built on a large scale.

FIGURE 104. *Rhos Ddu to river Clywedog: in Stansty parish, on the boundary between Broughton-and-Bersham and Wrexham Regis parishes, and in Wrexham Regis parish, Denbighshire*

We now enter the built-up area of Wrexham; the traditional course of the Dyke crosses the main B.R. railway line diagonally, and continues on its W. side past the railway station, across the river Gwenfro and past the workhouse; then, crossing the line again in a similar diagonal manner, the Dyke re-enters comparatively open country at Ruthin road bridge.

The identification of its remains in this area is much assisted by the well-known fact that it here formed the parish boundary of Wrexham Regis on the W.; proof of this is afforded by the survival of undoubted portions of the bank S. of the Regent Street railway bridge, immediately S. of Watery-road railway bridge, and immediately N. of Ruthin-road railway bridge; and by raised banks almost certainly representing the Dyke to the N. of the station. In all these cases, either the remains of the Dyke or the site of its (W.) ditch are coincident with the parish boundary referred to.

The remains of the Dyke S. of Regent Street railway bridge show it to have been a large structure, and that anything should have been left of it in this intensely industrialized area affords grounds for believing it to have been consistently large throughout the stretch.

The ground it crosses is level, apart from the slight dip and rise at the Gwenfro river; and a straight line drawn on the 6 in. map from the foot of Garden Village hill to Ruthin-road bridge passes through every one of the surviving portions. One might thus assume, without further argument, that the Dyke was straightly aligned (Type I) in this sector. But the parish boundary is not dead straight, swinging as much as 15 yards to the E. or W. of the straight line. The Dyke was, however, some 20 yards over-all in this area, and when it lost its function and was dug away the boundary may well have been pushed to one side or other of the ribbon of ground occupied by the work. So I do not regard these deflections as significant.[1]

---

[1] The only *marked* deviation of the parish boundary from the straight line is at the Gwenfro stream; and here we may expect the engineer of the Dyke to have swerved, since the valley floor was invisible from the setting-out point.

We are, therefore, in a position to define the exact course of the Dyke in this zone; to say that it was on the major scale with W. ditch; and that it was laid out on a single alignment (see Fig. 118, 5, b) for over 1 mile.

A note on each of the five surviving segments follows.[1] Near spot-level 285 the Dyke is represented by a piece of ground raised much above the general level. A second similar patch occurs S. of spot-level 278. The adjacent Crispin Lane, which is on the parish boundary, should therefore be on the site of the ditch. This is likely enough.

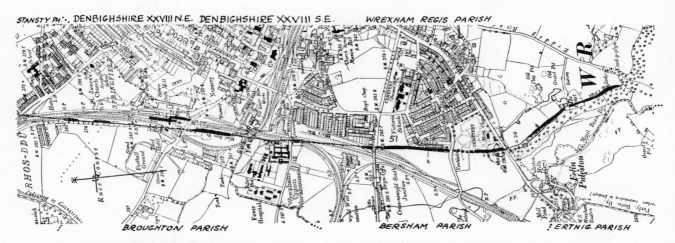

FIG. 104. Rhos Ddu to river Clywedog: in Stansty parish, on the boundary between Broughton-and-Bersham and Wrexham Regis parishes, and in Wrexham Regis parish, Denbighshire.

A portion of the 6-in. O.S. map reduced to 4 in. to 1 mile. For the significance of the symbols and letters employed, see Fig. 97. (Reproduced from the Ordnance Survey map with the sanction of the Controller of H.M. Stationery Office.)

The Dyke S. of the Regent Street bridge is a bulky but now shapeless mass. It is composed of stony gravel, stratified as such a bank should be. The public footpath beyond, then, marks the line of the frontier across the stream—the Gwenfro.

Railway Cottage, Watery-road, is traditionally associated with the Dyke; and in its patch of garden there is visible the reverse slope of the bank. This important fragment fixes the parish boundary hereabouts as having been on the crest of the bank. It follows that the 6 in. O.S. map and the 1838 1-in. O.S. map are in error in indicating the railway siding S. of Watery-road as the Dyke, since this overlaps the above portion. The identification has, indeed, nothing to commend it; there is nothing but a low scarp facing E., made in the railway age! There was no bank here before the siding was built.[2]

The bank in the corner N. of Ruthin-road bridge, though damaged, is undoubtedly the Dyke. It is in line with the stretch beyond the bridge, to which we may now turn.

This stretch extends on an almost identical alignment with the foregoing to the N. end of a little hill 300 ft. above O.D., and 540 yards away. It is slightly sinuous.

[1] I received much help from Mr. Shaw, Permanent Way Inspector, Wrexham District, in dealing with the remains in the area controlled by the railway company: each site was known to him as a portion of the Dyke and was being preserved from further injury as far as possible.

[2] Information from Mr. Shaw.

The long slope of the ploughed-down bank in field 51 and the height of the scarp flanking the footpath indicate the scale of the work here; though the ditch is filled in, the scarp measures 14–15 ft. on the slope. Beyond, the garden walls of the Alexandra Road houses are on the scarp. In recent years the Dyke has been almost completely levelled and the ditch filled in across the (extended) cemetery. It is now best marked on the crest of the hill (300 ft.), where it was certainly very large. The views to the W. are here very fine. Standing on this hill and looking back across the level ground on which the town is built, it was easy to determine how the layout of the Dyke was planned in this area.

The Dyke now swings SE. to follow the western edge of the wooded bluff flanking the Clywedog valley.

Beyond the broad cutting in which the main road runs, no trace of the Dyke is visible for a hundred yards. Then it recommences, very faintly, as a berm-and-scarp notch on the edge of the wooded hanger above the river flat. The scarp steepens: moves back (to the E.) from the margin of the natural slope: develops into a bank: and takes on a (W.) ditch. This device, which permits the presence—however steep the natural slope chosen as the line of the frontier—of a W. berm or ditch, is new to me. It never occurs in Offa's Dyke, the engineer of which would have built his bank from an E. spoil trench. Wat's method avoids this; I have, indeed, seen no traces in Wat's Dyke, save in one short and doubtful sector, of the Offan technique on such terrain.

The Dyke has been destroyed on the site of 'The Court', but its structure has been incorporated into the garden design. It is a magnificent work by the word 'DIKE' on the map; slight bank, scarp, broad ditchlike berm. Where the descent to the valley floor is begun it has been damaged and its further course (if any) is doubtful; there is no trace of it on the alluvial flat of the Clywedog.

FIGURE 105. *Erddig Castle to Middle Sontley: in Erthig parish, on the boundary between Marchwiel and Ruabon parishes, and in Ruabon parish, Denbighshire*

The steep-sided, well-wooded spur, which dominates the other side of the Clywedog valley floor here, is occupied by a castle with unusual constructional features; both 'motte' and 'bailey' are but portions of the flat crest of the spur isolated by enormous quarry-like cross-trenches.

Flanking the motte on the W. at the tip of the spur, overlooking the tributary valley of the Black brook, is a great bank, thrown up from the E., which forms an additional protection for the defenders of the motte (making its dry moat deeper) and must surely be part of the castle. It is almost certainly not, in its present form, Wat's Dyke. This bank, however, fades into a berm or shelf on the hill-side, now a footpath, which is cut through two little spurs, which break the even contour of the steep western-facing hill-side. Landslips obscure the structure, and a quarry cuts into it; beyond the latter, the berm or shelf becomes a broad ditch; then as the W. slope eases, a bank appears. This bank ends on the artificially levelled flat by *E* of *E*rddig park. The sequence of earthwork forms, dependent on terrain, is normal; and wholly, or in part, the structure must be recognized as Wat's Dyke. The Dyke probably existed, but has been destroyed, in the neighbourhood of the house, but traces of both bank and ditch are again present at one point a little farther on, on the edge of the steep, wooded slope above the valley floor, by the rookery. A little farther on again, the steep and regular contour of this river scarp is broken by two small re-entrants. Here, the large and characteristic structure of the Dyke reappears, the intervening spur being cut off by a large bank and ditch (scarp 22 ft., over-all 48 ft.), and the farther spur isolated in a similar manner[1] (see Plates XLIa and XLIIb, also Fig. 115, x).

Beyond the garden of Bryn Goleu and the estate road the Dyke swings southward away from the river scarp and its woodland, entering level cultivated country which gives at

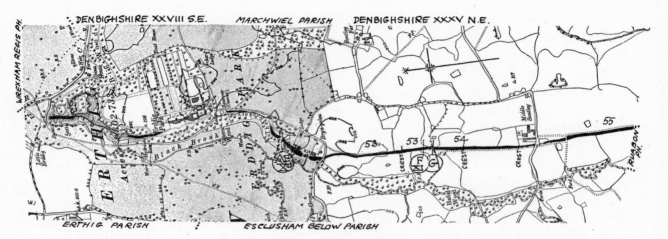

FIG. 105. Erddig Castle to Middle Sontley: in Erthig parish, on the boundary between Marchwiel and Ruabon parishes, and in Ruabon parish, Denbighshire.

A portion of the 6-in. O.S. map reduced to 4 in. to 1 mile. For the significance of the symbols and letters employed, see Fig. 97. (Reproduced from the Ordnance Survey map with the sanction of the Controller of H.M. Stationery Office.)

first little field of view to the W. It has been levelled near Bryn Goleu, but its ditch survives where it swings into a straight alignment.

The stretch thus introduced is interesting. The major alignment was laid across a terrain with very slight variations in level, on to the angle of the Black brook stream by One Oak Cottage and the Black brook bridge, where there is a low knoll; this key point is $1\frac{1}{6}$ miles away (Fig. 106). The ideal alignment was approximately attained by a number of short subsidiary alignments, some dead straight (Type I), others sinuous (Type II); the changes in direction were at minor crestlines (see Fig. 119, 6). The deviation from absolute straightness resulting from this method is found to be surprisingly slight (maximum 70 yards).

To return to the detailed survey. In field 52 the bank is ploughed down, but scarp and ditch survive to show the large scale of the work (Fig. 115, xi, Plate XLIV a and b. In the corner of field 53 the boundary hedge has been placed on the crest of the bank, thus preserving it. Here there is the first slight change in direction.

The crest of the Dyke is within field 54, and the scarp here has the unusual length of

---

[1] The treatment of spurs was similar, though on a very small scale, between Erddig Castle and Erddig House.

31 ft. The alignment is dead straight (not as shown on the O.S. map), from the dip in field 53 to the crest line by Middle Sontley farm. The Dyke goes *through*, not over, the small rise shown on the map half-way along this line (Fig. 119, 6, c).

At the farm the Dyke again visibly changes direction, being aligned on to a low crest at the S. end of field 55. It is direct but not straight. It is practically destroyed for a short distance on either side of the farm road, but traces of the broad ditch remain. The bank is somewhat lowered by agriculture, but long stretches of the ditch remain, wet, silty, and undamaged. At an average point the scarp measured 20 ft. The course of the work is marked by field boundaries and a footpath. The field of view, fair at first, opens out somewhat as the very shallow valley of the Black brook is approached.

From the S. end of field 55 a new alignment (the fourth) is taken on to One Oak Cottage knoll, Black brook bridge; the Dyke is direct but not straight.

FIGURE 106. *Sewage Works to Pentre-clawdd hill: in Ruabon parish, Denbighshire*

As the Black brook bridge is approached, the ditch of the Dyke seems to get smaller, and the bank is not well marked.

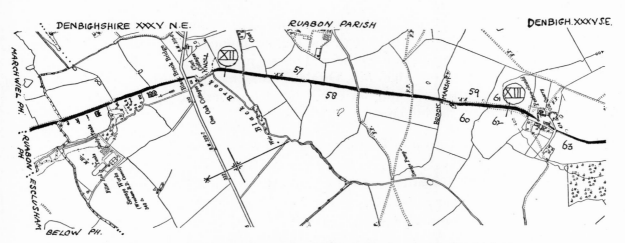

FIG. 106. Sewage works to Pentre-clawdd hill: in Ruabon parish, Denbighshire.
A portion of the 6-in. O.S. map reduced to 4 in. to 1 mile. For the significance of the symbols and letters employed, see Fig. 97.
(Reproduced from the Ordnance Survey map with the sanction of the Controller of H.M. Stationery Office.)

Crossing the Black brook road, the cottage boundary fence is seen to be in the ditch of the Dyke. The bank seems to die into the rounded knoll; it certainly never was constructed on it, the contours being natural, the surface unaltered. The break here may well be due to two gangs having been at work who have not linked up, through bad staff work. The break is very short; 100 yards.

Beyond the knoll is a marshy patch draining into the Black brook. At its farther edge, 310 ft. above O.D., the Dyke begins again on gently rising ground. It was aligned across level ground on to the crest of a well-defined hill (Pentre-clawdd), rising to 474 ft., a mile away. For 1,340 yards the Dyke is dead straight (Type I); then rising off the flat it becomes slightly sinuous (exactly as at Wrexham) and before reaching the aligning mark breaks off on to a new course (see Fig. 119, 7, a).

The scale of the work was large throughout this stretch. In the cultivated ground the Dyke is fairly well preserved, excellently preserved on the Pentre-clawdd hill-slope. There is a W. ditch throughout. The field of view to W. is moderate till this hill is reached, when it becomes very extensive.

To return to detail: In field 56, the Dyke is very large, but flattened and quarried: 66 ft. over-all, 22 ft. on scarp to the wet silt of the W. ditch (see Fig. 115, xii). The irregularities of the hedge in field 57 obscure the directness of the Dyke; there are large patches of undamaged bank here. In this stretch sometimes the bank is ploughed down, sometimes the ditch ploughed in. The broad wet ditch in field 58 is notable. At the foot of the hill an ancient drainage line crosses the frontier and the Dyke fades out for 40 yards. It reappears again between fields 59 and 60 but was a very slight work for 50 yards up the slope. The ditch, however, is broad and wet. The Dyke is well defined and well wooded on the steepish slope between fields 61 and 62; the scarp here measures 17 ft.; the ditch is a muddy bog (Fig. 115, xiii).

The Dyke now changes direction to pass along the forward slope of Pentre-clawdd hill (Plate XLIc). It can be identified at two points across the complex of farm buildings, and recommences in the next field (63), the highest point reached, as a small western-facing scarp; there is no visible ditch here. This slightness of structure on an actual hill crest has many parallels (cf. Hem hill, Offa's Dyke, Chapter V, pp. 97 ff). It may here be due to different gangs working on either side whose linking up was perfunctory, or to dense woodland on the hill crest.

FIGURE 107. *Fron-gôch wood to Wynnstay park: in Ruabon parish, Denbighshire*

The bank quickly develops, and a broad flat ditch appears—broader than is usual in the case of Offa in such a situation—9 ft. on the floor in one place (Fig. 115, xiv). The alignment is determined by the contour of the hill, but the line chosen does not command the hill slope; dead ground is close, though the view is extensive (see Plate XLVa). This occasional character of Wat contrasts with that which would in like case be manifested by Offa. His Dyke always clings to the line of visual control: the shoulder of the hill, the point where the slope steepens. The indifference to dead ground persists down the south-facing slope to the meeting place of tracks by Fron-gôch wood, and is most striking. The Dyke is destroyed at this point, but recommences immediately as a fine straight stretch (Type I) on a gentle downward slope, with good views to the W. impaired by nearby dead ground. This stretch continues to the Ruabon–Overton road, its original continuity broken only by a dingle close to that road. On the whole it is fairly well preserved, particularly in the lower half of the stretch; where best preserved, it is definitely on the major scale, but the W. ditch is noticeably narrow. The best portion of all is in field 65 (Fig. 116, xv, and Plate XLVb); here it ends finely above the dingle which has been dammed in modern times, it is clearly marked, but damaged on the farther side of the dingle.

The Dyke is stated to have crossed Wynnstay park and to have passed in front of the mansion.[1] The record is correct; fortunately it has not been absolutely obliterated. Traces of a broad bank are clearly seen as shown, on slightly rising ground, up to the N. end of the lake. Here is the crest line as seen from Fron-gôch wood, and these traces are, as might be expected, in line with the portion we have just examined. We are thus able to extend the Type I alignment and accurately determine its original limits.

There is no trace whatever beyond this 'false crest' until Wynnstay is passed. Then, on the falling slope with fine views to W., a stretch 90 yards long exists. It is straight as far

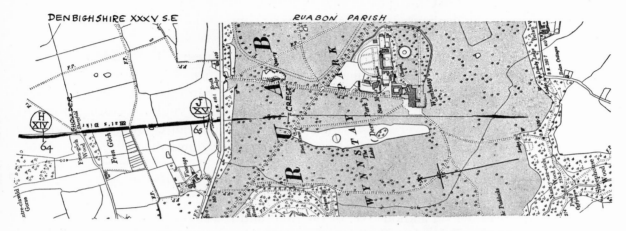

FIG. 107. Fron-gôch wood to Wynnstay Park: in Ruabon parish, Denbighshire.
A portion of the 6-in. O.S. map reduced to 4 in. to 1 mile. For the significance of the symbols and letters employed, see Fig. 97.
(Reproduced from the Ordnance Survey map with the sanction of the Controller of H.M. Stationery Office.)

as could be judged, almost completely levelled, but is 33 ft. broad and 2 ft. high at best, being sufficiently defined to cause the accurate Ordnance surveyors to make a 'tongue' in the 400-ft. contour line where this crosses it. Its filled-in ditch is used as a drainage channel and is piped. Its line projected backwards would run clear of the mansion and meet the portion of the Dyke already described at the 'false crest', and having regard to the tradition, we can with some assurance map the course of the destroyed work across the park from end to end.

I do not think this stretch of the Dyke extended any farther to the S. than the existing traces. Boggy ground, now piped, lies immediately adjacent, then follows a deep and densely wooded ravine opening almost immediately into the river Eitha, itself in a tremendous gorge. This river runs N. and S. and its line may be taken as the frontier; the Dyke is certainly not present on the plateau to the E. of it.

Afon Eitha, the river Dee, the river Ceiriog and Morlas brook (not figured)

From the point where the Dyke ends in Wynnstay park on a plateau 400 ft. above O.D.

[1] Lewis, *Topographical Dictionary of Wales*, 1833, under Ruabon: 'The Dyke, which entered the park near its northern boundary, has been levelled in its course through the grounds.' The 1-in. O.S. map, 1827, sheet 74, marks its line as a parish boundary.

to the point where it begins again at Esgob Mill in St. Martin's parish on a knoll 300 ft. above O.D., is 4 miles as the crow flies. The intervening country, the general level of which is approximately the same, is deeply dissected by the gorge of the Dee and its numerous tributaries which have carved out steep-sided ravines and gorges now, and probably always, densely wooded. Full advantage of the natural obstacle afforded by this system was taken by the Dyke builders, who unquestionably chose courses for the Dyke both N. and S. of the Dee which enabled them to make most use of the tributaries. Thus the frontier (see map, Fig. 117) followed the river Eitha to the Dee; along the Dee to Coed yr Allt, up the river Ceiriog to the watersmeet of the Morlas brook; up to the Morlas brook so long as it ran in a ravine-like channel and its course served—which was, precisely, as far as Esgob Mill.

Though this conclusion seems inevitable, it was not accepted without careful survey of the ground for traces of the Dyke along any possible alignment between the known portions. Such traces do not exist. Those noted on the O.S. map in Rhos-y-llan wood (St. Martin's parish), N. of Esgob Mill, are the now familiar natural angles, resulting from the junction of steep wooded river-scarp with the cultivated plateau country bordering the valley. This angular structure can indeed be traced for miles down the valley, on its flank.

FIGURE 108. *Esgob Mill to Henlle park: in St. Martin's and Whittington parishes, Shropshire*

Esgob farmstead lies on a knoll SW. of the mill, and traces of the Dyke can clearly be seen on the E. side of the farm buildings as a broad, rather shapeless bank extending downhill (under the new railway embankment) to a marshy flat with a sluggish streamlet tributary to the Morlas brook. Intermitted for a few yards, it begins again on rising ground as a grassy bank of moderate size with wet W. ditch.

It might have been expected that the Dyke would have extended to the N. edge of the Esgob knoll, where the Morlas valley becomes ravine-like (cf. Fig. 117). It does not, for reasons hard to envisage today; the dense forest of the river zone probably extended on to the knoll, and it was considered sufficient to carry the Dyke up to the crest and there let it fade out.

The line of the Dyke is preserved across the Shropshire Union canal by a bridge; the ramps of the bridge are the Dyke, but its original character is, of course, impaired. Thence to the cross-roads by Henlle Hall the Dyke bank is in a belt of woodland and is well preserved, but the W. ditch is not so clear. It is on the major scale, directly but not straightly aligned, being on undulating rising ground. The over-all breadth at one point is 56 ft., the scarp at another point 19 ft. although the ditch was here filled in.

Beyond the cross-roads the bank is seen on the margin of field 66, and as a ploughed-down bank in field 67. We have now reached the plateau (400 ft.), having ascended 100 ft. from Preeshenlle bridge. Here there is a gap (probably original) and the Dyke changes direction slightly; it is then straightly aligned (Type I) along level ground for over half a mile, a modern road following its line on the W. side (Fig. 119, 8, c).

The gap and the change of direction coincide with a crest line (compare Offa's Dyke in

Rownal covert, Chapter V, Fig. 42). The Dyke is just traceable in field 68, through the copse beyond, and in the garden of the next house. Both bank and ditch are wooded, and perfect, bordering field 69; here the scarp is difficult to define, measuring at least 21 ft. 8 in., and the over-all is 40 ft. (Fig. 116, xvi). The Dyke is traceable at two points in the adjacent complex of farm buildings (Preeshenlle).

FIG. 108. Esgob Mill to Henlle park: in St. Martin's and Whittington parishes, Shropshire.
A portion of the 6-in. O.S. map reduced to 4 in. to 1 mile. For the significance of the symbols and letters employed, see Fig. 97.
(Reproduced from the Ordnance Survey map with the sanction of the Controller of H.M. Stationery Office.)

FIGURE 109. *Preeshenlle to Pentre-wern (and beyond): in Whittington and Selattyn parishes, Shropshire*

The Dyke appears to have curved round the hummock represented by field 70, on the present line of the road. In field 71 there is a fragment of the bank exceptional in bulk, the road being in the ditch. The Dyke is then interrupted by a cross-road and a farm-croft, but reappears as marked on Fig. 109. Here the half-mile stretch which the evidence shows was dead straight (except in field 70) and on a large scale, ends: on the flank of the little valley of the river Perry (Fig. 119, 8, d). The direction then changes, the Dyke proceeding diagonally down the steepish slope to the stream. It was apparently thrown up from the W. side, and is a striking structure 25 ft. 6 in. on the scarp. The Dyke is obscure on the margin of the valley floor, and a bank has been made across it; but it is well marked, with a W. ditch, S. of *ft* of Sha*ft* to the edge of the stream.

Beyond the stream, the main road 50 yards south of BM 337 is on the bank of the Dyke, being from 2 to 4 ft. above the adjacent field no. 72. On the other hand, the garden of a cottage on the E. of the road by BM 337 is 3 ft. above the road, and this rise may represent the bank. I conclude that the Dyke recommenced on the S. flank of the river Perry in the farmyard of Bryn-y-castell opposite the point where we left it, and passed up the slope past the chapel, converging on the road, which then passed on to its levelled crest.

Traces of the W. ditch are still to be seen in the gardens opposite field 73; the road is now passing off the bank, which reappears, partially levelled, in field 74, near spot-level 353. At the S. end of this field, where the new by-pass road cuts across it, the crest and forward slope of the bank is visible; it is 3 ft. high and very broad. The centre of the filled-in ditch can be discerned, 36 ft. from the road margin; this suggests an original over-all of some 70 ft. for the earthwork, and taking into account the well-marked elevation of the road farther N., suggests that the whole stretch was on the major scale.[1]

The Dyke forms a broad ploughed-down ridge in field 76. It is straightly aligned, and its line when projected exactly coincides with the visible Dyke in field 74; moreover, there

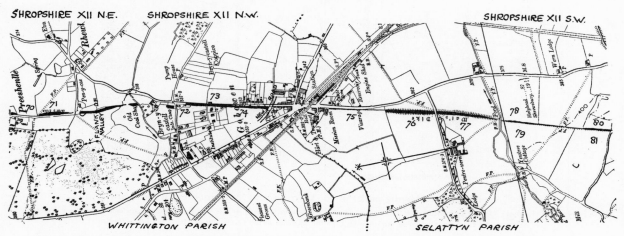

FIG. 109. Preeshenlle to Pentre-wern (and beyond): in Whittington and Selattyn parishes, Shropshire.
A portion of the 6-in. O.S. map reduced to 4 in. to 1 mile. For the significance of the symbols and letters employed, see Fig. 97.
(Reproduced from the Ordnance Survey map with the sanction of the Controller of H.M. Stationery Office.)

are traces on the same line in field 75. Since the ground is level we can deduce its course through Gobowen village with certainty, and we are thus able to recover the entire Gobowen sector of $\frac{3}{4}$ mile, which was almost entirely lost or unrecorded, and to indicate its character (see Fig. 119, 8, e).

In field 77 the direction was changed, but the Dyke having been originally on a small scale here and being now much levelled, the exact point where the change was made is difficult to determine. The earthwork passes across a level flat to the rill; beyond which its presence is doubtful—a slight difference in level between fields 78 and 79 being the only evidence. This difference in level vanishes on the rising (N.) slope beyond; and here it is certain that no Dyke ever existed—the area was probably dense woodland (see Fig. 119, 8, f). On the crest of the rise the Dyke reappears (as a slight work); bank in field 80, ditch in 81.

In sum, we may take it that the change in scale and in direction in field 77 coincided with a change from open country to marshland and then to woodland in which the Dyke was slight and intermittent.

[1] Written in 1931. When revisited in 1932 in order to survey the Dyke in field 74, all the evidence was found to have been destroyed by road widening and reconstruction.

FIGURE 110. *Pentre-clawdd to Oswestry: in Selattyn and Oswestry Urban parishes, Shropshire*

On the next little rise in this undulating country, in field 82, the bank is visible, the ditch being represented by the adjacent holloway. There is then a sharp fall to Pentre-clawdd and its brook, where the traces are very indefinite.

Beyond the brook the ground rises gently; there are ploughed-down traces of a very large bank (situated on a reverse slope); the pond marked on the O.S. map is an enlarged portion of the ditch. As the crest of the rise is approached, the view opens out; the Dyke

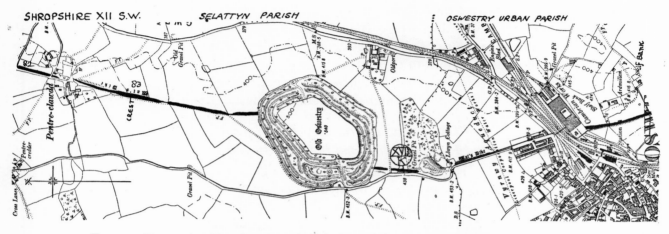

FIG. 110. Pentre-clawdd to Oswestry: in Selattyn and Oswestry Urban parishes, Shropshire.
A portion of the 6-in. O.S. map reduced to 4 in. to 1 mile. For the significance of the symbols and letters employed, see Fig. 97.
(Reproduced from the Ordnance Survey map with the sanction of the Controller of H.M. Stationery Office.)

becomes a very big whale-backed ridge, ditched on W., in field 83. The fortified isolated hill known as Yr Hên Ddinas (Old Oswestry)[1] is separated from this little rise by a shallow dip; the Dyke was on a large scale right up to the point where its bank meets and merges into the lowermost rampart of the fortress, which happens to be a counterscarp bank. The Dyke in this sector has been much reduced by agricultural operations. It is in the same alignment on both sides of the crest (field 83) and may have been laid out from the plateau of Yr Hên Ddinas, which provides a bird's-eye view of the country which the Dyke follows. If Fig. 119, 8, h, be examined it will be seen that such a technique would account for the change in direction at the foot of the hill; this area could not be seen from the top and the course of the Dyke was taken by guess-work.

[1] See W. J. Varley, 'The Hill-forts of the Welsh Marches', *Arch. Journ.*, cv (1948), pp. 50–52. The name 'Old Oswestry' might be thought to give colour to the supposition that this hill-fort was occupied by the Mercians, the existing town of Oswestry representing a movement of the population to a lowland site in more settled times. Professor J. E. Lloyd, whom I consulted on the point, informs me, however, that there is no justification for this view, since the name is modern, arising in all probability as a popular explanation of Yr Hên Ddinas. He notes a parallel in 'Old Carlisle', the local name of the site of the Roman fort of Petrianae; and remarks that such names are on quite a different footing from 'Old Sarum' and the like, where there was a definite transfer from an old site to the new.

The frontier then, we may suppose, followed the outer defences of the ancient fortress, on the W. side; the Dyke begins again on the S. side of the hill on the edge of the lower-most ditch (there being no bank on the counterscarp on this side). *There is no attempt to fill the ditch up in order to link the Dyke bank with the outer vallum of the fortress*; it was, I think, not visualized as a defensive work.

The Dyke is straightly aligned across a slight hollow to the forward slope of the next rise, an outcrop known as Old Gravel Pit Hill; ploughed-down and gapped in the N. of this stretch, it is well preserved in the S. where the scarp measures from 18 to 21 ft. (Fig. 116, xvii, and Plate XLVIa). A considerable portion of the Dyke in the wood must have been destroyed by gravel digging. Above Llwyn Cottage there is a small fragment, as marked on the map. Below the cottage, the ground is now built over; but the height above the road of the front gardens of the houses confirms the record of the 1913 O.S. map.

This road, running downhill to the railway, marks throughout its length the line of the Dyke, a bit of the reverse slope of which is still surviving at spot-level 409·5; and the footbridge across the railway line, though deflected, records a right-of-way along the Dyke.

FIGURE 111. *Oswestry to BM 308·2: in Oswestry Urban parish, on the boundary between Oswestry Urban and Rural parishes, and in Oswestry Rural parish, Shropshire*

From Shelf Bank (in Fig. 110), *c.* 400 ft. above O.D., the Dyke is aligned along the western-facing flank of a shallow valley for over 1,000 yards, to a springhead by Gallows-tree Bank, where this feature ends. The ground is level or gently sloping, and the align-ment offers wide views to the W. The Dyke was on a large or fairly large scale throughout, and is on the whole well preserved.

To return to detail: As far as the cross-road by BM 394·1, the line of the Dyke is marked by a hedge-scarp; thence onward to field 84 by a belt of trees. It is hereabouts revetted, probably in the early nineteenth century, with stone; the W. ditch is extensively ploughed-in. The best-preserved portion is at the SE. corner of field 84. The stone wall forming the E. boundary of the next field, that in which the megalith known as Careg Lwyd formerly stood, is on the bank, the (W.) ditch being fairly well preserved. Beyond this field the Dyke extends downhill to the spring.

The next stretch (to Red House) is obscured by Corporation sewage tanks and ramps. The Dyke is, however, certainly present as a low bank immediately S. of the main road, as shown on the map. A patch of wet ground and a streamlet follows.[1]

Levelled in the garden of Red House, the Dyke reappears as a broad low ridge, directly aligned, running parallel with and on the E. of the road across a dead flat land. At the S. end of field 86 the bank becomes better defined and the (W.) ditch is seen to be broad and flat. These structural characters are probably due to the friable alluvial soil of which the Dyke is built. In the next field (87) the Dyke converges on the road; then traces are present on the E. side of the 'T' road junction at Mile Oak. We are now on a just per-ceptible rise between two drainage systems.

[1] It is possible that the reverse slope of the bank of the Dyke survives in field 85, the stream on the W. side thereof being a sewage ditch and not the original ditch of the earthwork.

A slight bend of the road combined with a slight deflection of the Dyke (Fig. 119, 9, d) now places the latter on the W. of the road; it is present as a hedge-bank bordering field 88; in front is a ditch which becomes broader and deeper as one passes from N. to S. of this field. In field 89 the ditch is filled in; in field 90 the whole work is well marked, the bank being almost wholly in the field. The scale was probably large, as Fig. 116, xviii, shows. The earthwork appears to end at Pentre-coed where the rapid little stream of the Morda makes a sharp angle; but a study of the ground beyond this point discloses a small extension and suggests the possibility of a large one.

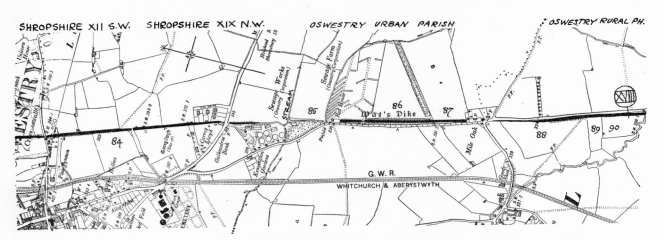

FIG. 111. Oswestry to BM 308·2: in Oswestry Urban parish, on the boundary between Oswestry Urban and Rural parishes, and in Oswestry Rural parish, Shropshire.

A portion of the 6-in. O.S. map reduced to 4 in. to 1 mile. For the significance of the symbols and letters employed, see Fig. 97.
(Reproduced from the Ordnance Survey map with the sanction of the Controller of H.M. Stationery Office.)

FIGURE 112. *Pentre-coed to Newbridge: in Oswestry Rural parish, Shropshire*

In field 91 beyond the apparent termination of the Dyke there are, in the loops of the Morda, several small mounds. These extend for 200 yards in all, and are in line with the Dyke.

The last mound is illustrated in Plate XLVI*b*, on the right of the man with the staff, and is drawn in section in Fig. 116, xix. When the adjacent terrain is examined, it is evident that Wat's Dyke was originally continuous up to this point, and that the Morda then followed a different course along the little alluvial flat which it has created. The intermittency of the Dyke in this last 200 yards then is due to the stream having undermined and washed away the greater part of it. An ancient elm has held the bank together at the point where the photograph was taken.

To this point then, the Dyke certainly extended; here, we may be certain, its alignment first struck the bank of the Morda. That it may have extended much farther as a bank with western ditch into which the Morda was deflected, is a theory which will now be examined.

The Morda stream from Pentre-coed to Newbridge, 1,600 yards, seems to one who follows its course on foot, sinuous; but if it be examined on a map, such as Fig. 112, its course is seen to be unusually straight.

At Newbridge it turns eastward to the farm known as 'Fields', and presents the meanderings normal to a river in a flat land; the same meanderings as it shows N. of Pentre-coed, before making contact with the Dyke.

That the Pentre-coed–Newbridge stretch is in some degree artificially straightened is obvious. It includes two mills—Ball Mill and Maesbury Mill—and it is natural to connect its straightness with them and to regard the new cuts as medieval.

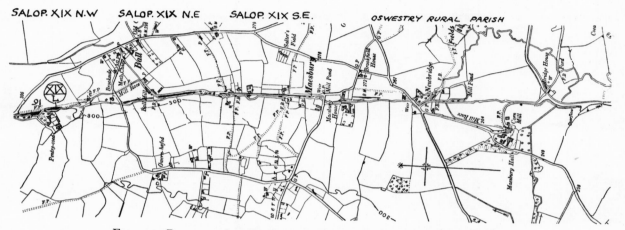

FIG. 112. Pentre-coed to Newbridge: in Oswestry Rural parish, Shropshire.
A portion of the 6-in. O.S. map reduced to 4 in. to 1 mile. For the significance of the symbols and letters employed, see Fig. 97.
(Reproduced from the Ordnance Survey map with the sanction of the Controller of H.M. Stationery Office.)

But there are three facts which suggest that the artificiality is not of medieval origin. The first is, that the straight stretch forms the *overflow channel* of the first of these mills, and the *leat* of the second; that is, the mills seem to bear an accidental relation to the work considered as a piece of engineering. The second is that the material trenched from this straightened stream, which is to be seen here and there on the bank, is always on the E. bank. The stream bed is, in fact, equivalent to the W. ditch of a frontier earthwork, only it happens to have water in it.

The third fact is, that the hummocks of earth, present at various points between that to which it is certain the Dyke extended (by Pentre-coed) and Newbridge Mill, fall readily into place in two successive straight alignments. That is, we appear to have broken remnants of a construction characteristic of Wat's Dyke, and in continuation of it. If so, why is it so incomplete? Let us assume for the sake of argument, that the river Morda was straightened to form the frontier by cutting a new channel—which may have represented the mean of the natural course.[1] The material was thrown out on the E. side, forming a continuous bank. The river was then led into the ditch thus formed, and Wat's

[1] The flatness of the plain through which the Morda runs hereabouts makes it difficult to recover the original course. There are, however, evidences to justify that shown on Fig. 119, 10.

Dyke then possessed the curious feature of running water in the last mile of its straightly aligned course. But, from the moment of completion, the forces of erosion worked ceaselessly to destroy the symmetry of the canalized work, as they worked to destroy the last 200 yards of the normal Dyke at Pentre-coed. Undercutting by the current and landslides in floodtime restored sinuosity to the course of the river, and breached the bank in many places; with the result that, today, after 1,200 years, it is only on a map that the fundamental artificiality of the construction and the unity of the engineering design is recognizable.

This is a plausible case for the high antiquity of the work; but it has elements of weakness. The evidence that a continuous bank was constructed alongside the new channel is slight; it is present in few places, and at no point is it really characteristic. Moreover, in view of the use of natural streams as boundaries elsewhere, it would seem that the unstraightened Morda meandering through the jungle of its alluvial flat would have served quite well as a frontier. From Pentre-coed to the Vyrnwy–Severn valley there was a continuous barrier of marsh, and the southern end of the Dyke (if at Pentre-coed) rested on an effective and extensive obstacle. Thus the canalized extension leads nowhere; and there is no geographical reason why it should have stopped where it did. Bridge House (see Fig. 112) would indeed have been a better termination than Newbridge; and if the map be examined it will be seen that a lane extends the alignment of the straightened Morda over a spur of dry ground on to the margin of the broad alluvial flat beyond (now the canal angle). This curious fact certainly adds to the complexity of the problem, for the lane was never either the Dyke or its ditch.

On the whole, I favour the view that the Dyke ended at Pentre-coed, but do not think that certainty is possible. The first Ordnance map (1827, Sheet 74) marks it to Pentre-coed only, but it is not a reliable authority. The position of the artificial mounds is shown on Fig. 112; the alignment on Fig. 119, 10, e, f. The details are recorded in a footnote.[1]

THE EXISTING PROFILE OF THE DYKE, AND ITS SCALE

The profile of the Dyke was instrumentally determined in twenty places, distributed from end to end of the earthwork. Nineteen of these profiles, many of which have already been referred to, are reproduced, in Figs. 113–16, on the same scale as the Offa's Dyke profiles; they are analysed in the table which follows.

[1] In the field W. of Ball mill-race a low, broad bank is present. A well-marked bank also is present in the wooded belt, between road and stream, below the mill.

The channel hereabouts, cut at the foot of the hillside (the W. edge of the flat) is now very broad and deep; it is manifestly *not* at the lowest point of the valley (which is farther to the E.) and must be artificial.

The original line of the 'new cut', overdeepened by erosion, is preserved opposite F.P. on the map; the stream has cut a new channel to the W. at this point. The road, parallel with the stream, here rises on to a flattened bank—the spoil-heap from the water-way (or the bank of the Dyke). The road remains on or close to the bank for some distance, but the cottage by *M* of *M*aesbury is probably on the bank, the road having swung off it. The mill pool then intervenes; but in the field below the mill traces of a bank reappear, well marked by *B.* of *B.*M., faint elsewhere. No one who examines this field can doubt that the cut, whatever its date or purpose, is artificial or that the spoil was here thrown out on the E. side—but the bank is sprawling, shapeless—not much like Wat's Dyke.

WATS DYKE : PROFILES IN HOLYWELL AND NORTHOP Parishes, FLINTS

I AT WERN SIRK, NEAR HOLYWELL [6" O.S. FLINTS. VI S.W.]

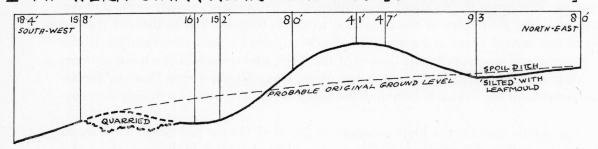

18·4' 15·8' SOUTH-WEST   16·1' 15·2'   8·0'   4·1' 4·7'   9·3   8·6' NORTH-EAST

PROBABLE ORIGINAL GROUND LEVEL

QUARRIED

SPOIL DITCH
'SILTED' WITH LEAFMOULD

II AT FRON TYDYR, NEAR HOLYWELL [6" O.S. FLINTS. VI S.W.]

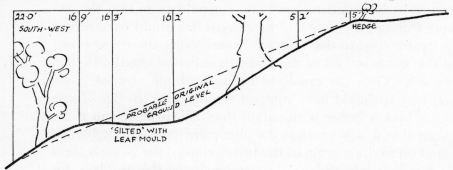

22·0' SOUTH-WEST 16·9' 16·3'   16·2'   5·2'   15·7' HEDGE

PROBABLE ORIGINAL GROUND LEVEL

'SILTED' WITH LEAF MOULD

III 140 YARDS S. OF M[ILE] S[TONE] ON NORTHOP-HOLYWELL RD. [6" O.S. FLINTS. IX. S.E.]

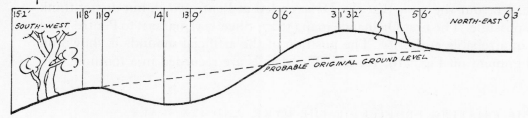

15·2' SOUTH-WEST 11·8' 11·9'   14·1 13·9'   6·6'   3·1' 3·2'   5·6' NORTH-EAST 6·3'

PROBABLE ORIGINAL GROUND LEVEL

IV S. OF FOOTBRIDGE, NORTHOP BROOK, BY SOUGHTON FARM [6" O.S. FLINTS. IX S.E.]

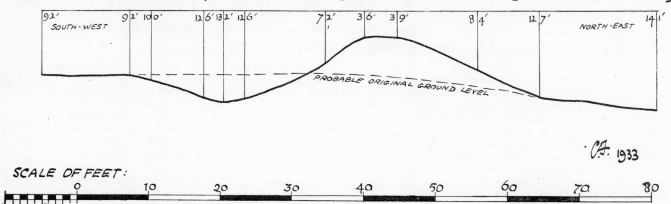

9·2' SOUTH-WEST 9·2' 10·0' 12·6' 13·2' 11·6'   7·2'   3·6' 3·9'   8·4'   12·7' NORTH-EAST 14·1'

PROBABLE ORIGINAL GROUND LEVEL

CF. 1933

SCALE OF FEET :

10 5   0   10   20   30   40   50   60   70   80

FIG. 113. Profiles I–IV.

WATS DYKE: PROFILES IN MOLD RURAL AND HOPE PARISHES, FLINTSHIRE, AND GRESFORD PARISH, DENBIGHSHIRE

V 140 YARDS N.W. OF WHITEHOUSE FARM [6"O.S. FLINTS. XIV S.W.]

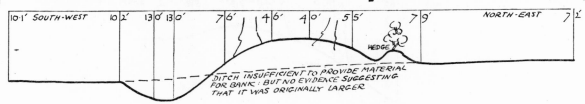

10.1' SOUTH-WEST 10.2' 13.0' 13.0' 7.6' 4.6' 4.0' 5.5' 7.9' NORTH-EAST 7.2'

HEDGE

DITCH INSUFFICIENT TO PROVIDE MATERIAL FOR BANK: BUT NO EVIDENCE SUGGESTING THAT IT WAS ORIGINALLY LARGER

VI 220 YARDS E.N.E. OF PLAS MATOR FARM [6"O.S. FLINTS. XIV S.W.]

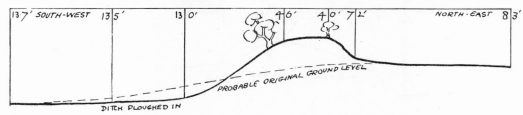

13.7' SOUTH-WEST 13.5' 13.0' 4.6' 4.0' 7.2' NORTH-EAST 8.3'

PROBABLE ORIGINAL GROUND LEVEL

DITCH PLOUGHED IN

VII 180 YARDS S.E. OF ROSE COTTAGE, PADESWOOD [6"O.S. FLINTS. XIV S.W.]

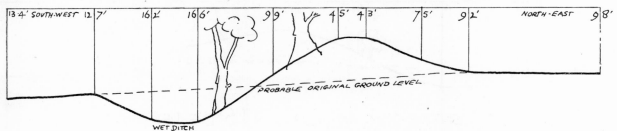

13.4' SOUTH-WEST 12.7' 16.2' 16.6' 9.9' 4.5' 4.3' 7.5' 9.2' NORTH-EAST 9.8'

PROBABLE ORIGINAL GROUND LEVEL

WET DITCH

VIII 220 YARDS N.W. OF PIGEON HOUSE FARM [6"O.S. FLINTS. XXVII N.E.]

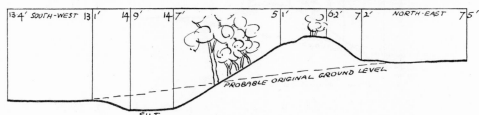

13.4' SOUTH-WEST 13.1' 14.9' 14.7' 5.1' 6.2' 7.2' NORTH-EAST 7.5'

PROBABLE ORIGINAL GROUND LEVEL

SILT

C.H.
1933

IX 170 YARDS W. OF TY GWYN FARM, GRESFORD [6"O.S. DENB. XXVIII N.E.]

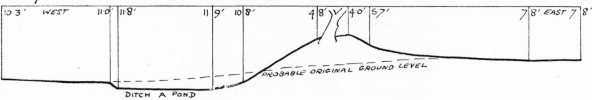

10.3' WEST 11.0' 11.8' 11.9' 10.8' 4.8' 4.0' 5.7' 7.8' EAST 7.8'

PROBABLE ORIGINAL GROUND LEVEL

DITCH A POND

FIG. 114. Profiles V–IX.

WATS DYKE: PROFILES IN ERTHIG AND RUABON Parishes, DENBIGHSHIRE

X. S. OF THE ROOKERY, ERDDIG PARK [6" O.S. DENB. XXVIII S.E.]

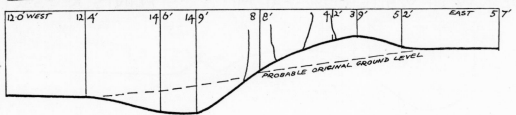

12.0 WEST · 12.4' · 14.6' · 14.9' · 8.8' · 8.1' · 4.2' · 3.9' · 5.2' · EAST · 5.7'

PROBABLE ORIGINAL GROUND LEVEL

XI. 500 YARDS N. OF MIDDLE SONTLEY FARM [6" O.S. DENB. XXXV N.E.]

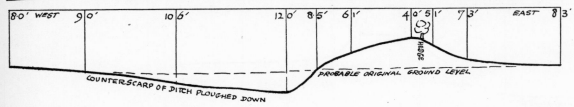

8.0' WEST · 9.0' · 10.6' · 12.0' · 8.5' · 6.1' · 4.0' · 5.1' · 7.3' · EAST · 8.3'

HEDGE

COUNTERSCARP OF DITCH PLOUGHED DOWN

PROBABLE ORIGINAL GROUND LEVEL

XII. S. OF ONE-OAK COTTAGES, BLACK BROOK, RUABON [6" O.S. DENB. XXXV N.E.]

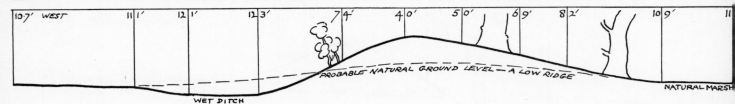

10.7' WEST · 11.1' · 12.1' · 12.3' · 7.4' · 4.0' · 5.0' · 6.9' · 8.2' · 10.9' · 11

PROBABLE NATURAL GROUND LEVEL — A LOW RIDGE

WET DITCH

NATURAL MARSH

XIII. 170 YARDS N.E. OF PENTRE CLAWDD, RUABON [6" O.S. DENB. XXXV N.E.]

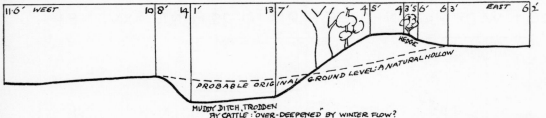

11.6' WEST · 10.8' · 4.1' · 13.7' · 4.5' · 4.3' · 5.6' · 6.3' · EAST · 6.2'

HEDGE

PROBABLE ORIGINAL GROUND LEVEL: A NATURAL HOLLOW

MUDDY DITCH, TRODDEN
BY CATTLE: "OVER-DEEPENED" BY WINTER FLOW?

XIV. 180 YARDS N. OF FRON GOCH WOOD, RUABON [6" O.S. DENB. XXXV S.E.]

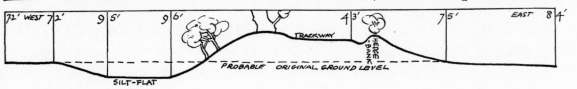

7.2' WEST · 7.2' · 9.5' · 9.6' · 4.3' · 7.5' · EAST · 8.4'

TRACKWAY

HEDGE BANK

PROBABLE ORIGINAL GROUND LEVEL

SILT-FLAT

CH 1933

FIG. 115. Profiles X–XIV.

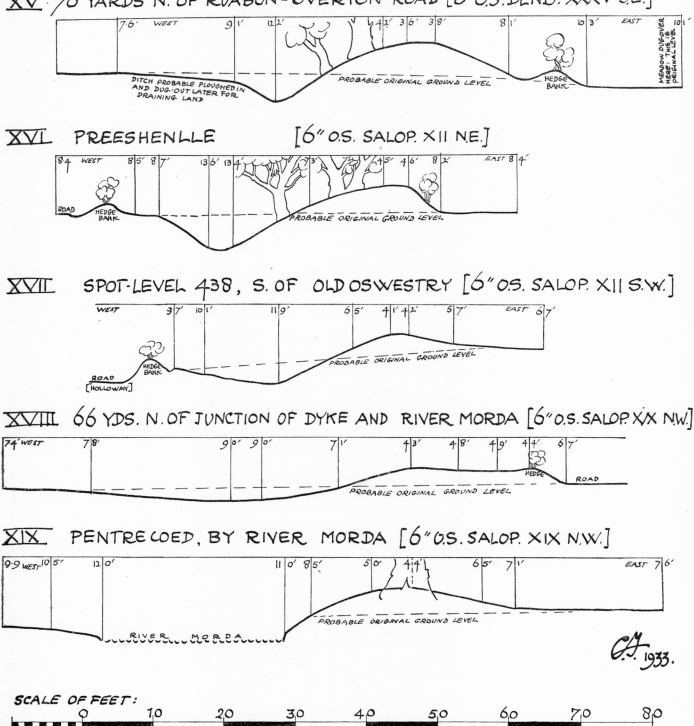

WATS DYKE: PROFILES IN RUABON PARISH, DENBIGHSHIRE, AND IN WHITTINGTON, SELATTYN, AND OSWESTRY RURAL PARISHES, SHROPSHIRE

XV. 70 YARDS N. OF RUABON–OVERTON ROAD [6" O.S. DENB. XXXV S.E.]

DITCH PROBABLE PLOUGHED IN AND DUG-OUT LATER FOR DRAINING LAND

PROBABLE ORIGINAL GROUND LEVEL

HEDGE BANK

MEADOW DUG-OVER HERE: THIS IS ORIGINAL LEVEL

XVI. PREESHENLLE [6" O.S. SALOP. XII N.E.]

ROAD

HEDGE BANK

PROBABLE ORIGINAL GROUND LEVEL

XVII. SPOT-LEVEL 438, S. OF OLD OSWESTRY [6" O.S. SALOP. XII S.W.]

HEDGE BANK

ROAD [HOLLOWAY]

PROBABLE ORIGINAL GROUND LEVEL

XVIII. 66 YDS. N. OF JUNCTION OF DYKE AND RIVER MORDA [6" O.S. SALOP. XX N.W.]

HEDGE

ROAD

PROBABLE ORIGINAL GROUND LEVEL

XIX. PENTRE COED, BY RIVER MORDA [6" O.S. SALOP. XIX N.W.]

RIVER MORDA

PROBABLE ORIGINAL GROUND LEVEL

1933.

SCALE OF FEET:

0   10   20   30   40   50   60   70   80

10   5

Fig. 116. Profiles XV–XIX.

B 3122

Table of Measurements

No. of profile	Position	Present dimensions of bank (estimated)		Present dimensions of W. ditch (estimated)		Present over-all breadth of bank and W. ditch (estimated)	References to photographs
		Height	Breadth	Depth	Breadth		
I.	Wern Sirk	5·6	28·0	3·6	20·0	48·0	
II.	Fron Tydyr	A berm, not measurable					
III.	Northop–Holywell road . .	4·0	24·0	3·9	22·5	46·5	
IV.	Northop brook . . .	5·8	32·0	3·9	24·0	56·0	Plate XLIIa
V.	Whitehouse farm . . .	4·3	26·0(?)	3·0	12·8	38·8(?)	
VI.	Plas Major farm . . .	4·2	21·0	Ploughed in			
VII.	Padeswood	6·4	30·0	4·7	22·6	52·6	Plate XLIIIa
VIII.	Pigeon House farm . .	5·0	23·5	2·8	17·0	40·5	
IX.	Gresford	4·2	25·0	1·8	21·0	46·0	
X.	Erddig	3·4	23·0	3·9	22·0	45·0	Plates XLIa and XLIIb
XI.	Sontley farm . . .	4·5	25·0(?)	2·8	20·0(?)	45·0(?)	Plates XLIVa
XII.	Black brook	4·0	40·0	2·3	25·5	65·5*	and b
XIII.	Pentre-clawdd . . .	4·0	20·0	3·0	21·0	41·0	Plate XLVa
XIV.	Fron-gôch wood . . .	4·3	33·0	2·2	20·4	53·4	
XV.	Ruabon–Overton road . .	4·9	27·0	4·0	20·0(?)	47·0(?)	Plate XLVb
XVI.	Preeshenlle	4·0	20·0	5·0	19·0	39·0	
XVII.	Old Oswestry . . .	3·0	22·0	3·0	20·0	42·0	Plate XLVIa
XVIII.	River Morda (near) . .	2·6	30·0	1·6	30·0(?)	60·0(?)†	
XIX.	River Morda	3·8	30·0	..	..	..	Plate XLVIb

* A natural ridge utilized.   † Built in alluvium, consequently low and broad.

It will be observed that Wat's Dyke has, practically throughout, a considerable bank and a well-made western ditch. Other constructional forms, common in the case of Offa's Dyke, are very rare. A bank of hedge-bank size occurs only on a hill near Wrexham; an E. ditch only on one short, steep slope at Mynachlog; counterscarp banks only for a few yards in the Wern Sirk–Fron Tydyr area and on Coed Uchaf; a spoil ditch on the upper (E.) side only at Wern Sirk (Fig. 113, i).

The rarity of these profiles is such as to make them the exception that proves the rule, which is that Wat's Dyke is constructionally uniform, very much more so than Offa's Dyke.

The country crossed by Wat's Dyke being for the most part lowland, flat or of easy gradients, affords little opportunity for the construction normal in a Dyke following the contour of a steep hill-side—namely, an artificial scarping of the slope with a berm below (as at Fron Tydyr, Fig. 113, ii). On one such slope, S. of Wrexham, Wat's Dyke showed a constructional method never employed on Offa's Dyke (see Fig. 105 and pp. 241–2).[1]

The following Offan types do not occur at all: (a) bank on counterscarp employed on level terrain as an additional obstacle to the main bank;[2] (b) bank on level terrain, ditched on both sides;[3] (c) bank of boundary bank size, ditched on E.[4]

[1] One other possible constructional novelty is the canalization to which reference has just been made.

[2], [3], [4] Chapter V, Fig. 65, Profiles xlv, xlvii, and xlviii; Fig. 66, xlix.

The Dyke being for the most part in cultivated country, few perfect profiles are obtainable. The group of profiles figured, however, contain examples which show the Dyke unaltered save by the slow processes of denudation, and preserving in all probability a close approximation to its original form. Nos. i, iii, iv, vii, x, xvi may be cited in this connexion. These profiles offer no problems; but in places the Dyke, while showing a bulky rampart, has a very small W. ditch, e.g. profiles nos. v, xiv, and xv. No trace of an E. spoil ditch is apparent in these cases; in no. xv a modern reconstruction of the ditch may be surmised, but in the others no such explanation is possible, and the sources of material for the massive banks are not apparent.

The scale of the Dyke is moderate. The essential measurements are set out in the table. There are special reasons to account for the size of the two largest. No. xii (65·5 ft.) is on a natural ridge, which thus provides an abnormally broad bank; no. xviii (60 ft.) is representative of the character of the Dyke on the low flat lands between Red House and the river Morda (Figs. 111–12). This wet soil, mostly alluvium, cannot make a high bank but spreads into a broad low one; the ditch cannot be dug deep, the 'water table' being high, and so is necessarily wide.

Since the limits of variation of the remaining fourteen measurable profiles are 38·8–56·0 ft., and since eleven of these (strung out along the greater part of the Dyke) show a variation within 10 ft. (38·8–48·0 ft.) it can be said that the Dyke is fairly regular in scale from end to end.

The Bank. The extreme range of the estimated height of the bank is 2·6 to 6·4 ft.; eleven profiles show measurements between 4 and 5 ft., which may thus be regarded as normal for the Dyke. The *average* of the two dimensions here studied is as follows:

	Average height of bank	Average over-all of Dyke
Wat's Dyke	18 examples, 4·3 ft.	16 examples, 47·9 ft.
	Compare:	
Offa's Dyke (omitting abnormal forms)	42 examples, 6·3 ft.	34 examples, 58·0 ft.

These figures point to Offa's Dyke being on the average at least half as large again as Wat's Dyke.

EARTHWORKS ON OR NEAR WAT'S DYKE

The following earthworks are on, or close to, Wat's Dyke:

Basingwerk, Flintshire.—This lost earthwork, probably from its name of Mercian origin, situated at the N. end of the Wat's Dyke frontier, is discussed on p. 228.

Llys Edwin, Flintshire.—An early medieval fortress about 500 yards to the E. of the Dyke. If, as is probable, the habitation is of pre-Norman origin,[1] its arable or pasture would extend up to the Afon Conwy; and this would account for the straight alignment

---

[1] Castretone, D.B., as suggested by my friend Mr. T. A. Glenn, I think correctly: *Eduinus tenuit sicut liber homo.*

of the Dyke in Coed Llys—the only straight alignment in the Soughton sector (see Fig. 97).

Caer Estyn, Hope, Flintshire.—A contour hill-fort of normal Early Iron Age type, with bank and ditch (double on the NW. side) of no great strength, occupying the crest of the isolated rocky hill E. of Caergwrle at the base of which the northern sector of the Dyke ends (Fig. 102). Caergwrle Castle occupies the opposite hill on the W.

Promontory Fort in Llay parish, Denbighshire.—The site of this fine fortress above the Alyn river (see p. 238, and Fig. 103) is known as Fox Covert. The main defences, across the neck of the spur, consist of two banks and three ditches, 200 ft. over-all; the outer bank measures 33 ft. on the slope from the ditch floor to crest.

The fort is characteristically Early Iron Age: it may well have been built 700 years, and deserted for 500 years, before Wat's Dyke was thought of. Though the fort was certainly on the line of Wat's frontier, it was not modified in any way to serve as a *constructional* frontier, and there are no authentic stretches of Wat's Dyke anywhere near it. We may suppose that the banks and ditches were enveloped in dense forest and their very existence forgotten.

Erddig Fort, Erthig parish, Denbighshire.—This Norman fortress occupies a similar position to the foregoing, on a spur with steep slopes defined by the junction of the Black brook and the river Clywedog (see Fig. 105). Its relation to the Dyke is described on p. 241. (See *A History of the Country Townships of Wrexham*, A. N. Palmer, 1903, p. 237.)

Yr Hên Ddinas (Old Oswestry) Shropshire.—This magnificent fortress, the outstanding work of Early Iron Age type on the Marches of Wales, occupies an isolated flat-topped hill rising steeply on all sides a hundred feet above the adjacent fields. That this hill forms a cardinal point in the layout of Wat's Dyke is obvious; but there is no evidence that the existence of earlier fortifications had anything to do with its selection. The engineer of the Dyke aligned his work on its highest point (540 ft.) for the same reason that he aligned it on Pentre-clawdd hill (474 ft.); such points gave good visual control. It is probable that the hill was densely wooded in the eighth century, as it is today. (See p. 249, Plate XL, and *Arch. Journ.*, cv, 1950, pp. 50–52.)

To sum up, we have two Early Iron Age forts on the frontier, and a third close to it. When it is remembered that this frontier is 38 miles long, and that the engineer was at pains to include all positions of tactical importance along its line, this number is such as accident might well produce. It is held that none had any military significance when Wat's Dyke was constructed.[1]

Offa's Dyke produces similar coincidences, and provides similar arguments (Chapter VI, p. 158). It is curious that the only constructions which have any claims to *significant* relationship with these Mercian dykes are on the coast; one is 'Basingwerk' at the seaward end of Wat's Dyke, the other is Tallard's ring-work at the southern end of Offa's Dyke[2] on the Wye estuary.

---

[1] This conclusion accords with our general knowledge of Anglo-Saxon military methods. There is no satisfactory evidence that Early Iron Age forts were anywhere reused by them.   [2] Chapter VII, p. 204.

PASSAGE WAYS THROUGH THE DYKE

There are numerous gaps in Wat's Dyke for roads, lanes, and farm tracks; one of the latter is illustrated in Plate XLIV*b*. Though many of these may be original, in only two cases was there any indication of high antiquity.

One in Hope parish, Flintshire, has a very well-defined opening 12 ft. wide, the flanks of which look original (Fig. 101 and p. 235). In the case of the other, near Henlle Hall, Salop (Fig. 108 and p. 246), the position of the opening rather than its character is the important feature. It is on a crest line, as was an opening, probably original, in Offa's Dyke near Montgomery;[1] and it is in a field across which no road or track now runs. The flanks of the opening, like the rest of the earthwork in this field, are ploughed down, and their character lost. But neither at Hope nor at Henlle can a trackway likely to be ancient and running from E. to W. be found today.

THE ALIGNMENT OF THE DYKE

Reference has been made in the course of the preceding narrative to the alignment of the Dyke at various points. Here the main features will be summarized, and their implications followed up.

(i) *The Major Layout*

The frontier represented by Wat's Dyke has been shown to extend from the estuary of the Dee near Holywell to the marshes of the little river Morda, a tributary of the river Vyrnwy; this represents a distance of 38 miles. The Dyke thus has two protected flanks —extensive natural obstacles on which its terminals rest, as Fig. 117 and Plates XXXIX and XL show.

Of these 38 miles, $15\frac{1}{4}$ consist of rivers, for the most part running in ravines; and the map clearly shows that the frontier is cleverly chosen to make the fullest use of such ravines—to reduce, in short, the *constructed* frontier to $22\frac{3}{4}$ miles.[2] The character of these ravines as obstacles—even today—must be experienced to be appreciated. Having spent many days forcing my way along or across them, I can well believe that in the Dark Ages they were regarded as a sufficient line of demarcation, and even (at a pinch) a defensible zone.

The ravines and rivers thus utilized occur at three points along the frontier line; and the Dyke was therefore constructed in three main sectors—which happen to be in three different counties—separated by natural obstacles. These sectors are fairly equal in length.

1. From Nant-y-Fflint to river Alyn (Flintshire), $9\frac{1}{2}$ miles.
2. From river Alyn to river Dee (Denbighshire), 7 miles.
3. From river Dee to river Morda (Shropshire), 6 miles.

---

[1] Chapter V, p. 100.

[2] Minor intermissions: marsh at Padeswood—wood-land near Mold—brooks—rocky outcrops, &c., reduce the actual length of earthwork by $2\frac{1}{4}$ miles to $20\frac{1}{2}$ miles.

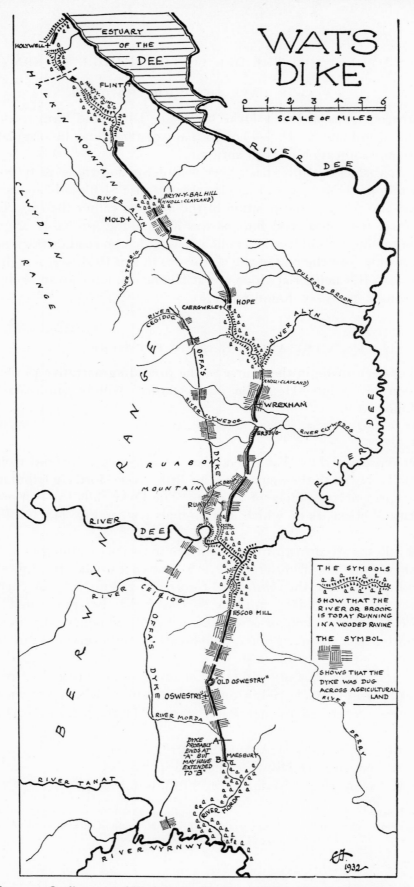

FIG. 117. Outline map of Wat's Dyke. The line of Offa's Dyke is also indicated.

In addition to these extended stretches of Dyke, there are at the northern end the Holywell and Nant-y-Fflint fragments.

The first two of these main sectors are direct but sinuous: as direct as possible having regard to the undulating character of the country, and the desire of the builder to have western-facing slopes, as in the Mold–Hope district; or a river valley on the W. side of the Dyke, as in the Erddig–Ruabon district. The third sector presents two very direct alignments hinging on Old Oswestry, a commanding hill-top.

The straightness of these alignments shows that the general course of the frontier between each natural obstacle was carefully thought out, prior to the consideration of the exact alignment to be followed from point to point. The alignments cover stretches of country which are too extensive, or too undulating to be visualized as a whole; and when we remember that nothing in the nature of a compass or an accurate map was available, the skill and competence of the designer commands our admiration. I say, of the designer; for if there is one induction which any student who surveys the Dyke must inevitably arrive at, it is that the work is a unity, the creation of one mind, the projection of one will.

If Chapter IV of this work, p. 82–83, be referred to, it will be seen that in the course of the Offa's Dyke survey a precisely similar achievement provoked similar comment. The identity of technique in this, the larger aspect of frontier design, between the two works is incontestable. Compare the minor sinuosities coupled with essential directness of the Selattyn–Llanymynech sector of Offa's Dyke with that of the Wrexham–Ruabon sector of Wat's Dyke.

I see no reason to suppose that the existence of the Early Iron Age defences of Old Oswestry, influenced the major alignment: the engineer included the isolated hill, I suggest, because of its tactical importance as a commanding view-point.

Turning to the short sectors at Holywell and at the head of Nant-y-Fflint, it can hardly be doubted that these were constructed to bar access to the coastal flat between Basingwerk and Flint at the only points where natural obstacles were non-existent. In the case of the latter (see Fig. 117) construction was started on either flank of the vulnerable portion but was not carried to the centre—the part that mattered most! At Holywell, only the N. end of the gap is covered by earthwork visible today, or known to have formerly existed; I think that if the Dyke had also been built at the S. end of the gap, it would not have been so completely destroyed as to leave no trace. I therefore consider that the Dyke was left incomplete at both these places. When it is remembered that incompleteness, equally inexplicable on topographical grounds, marks Offa's Dyke in this region, it is legitimate to suggest that—to the Mercians—it was a remote, difficult, and dangerous countryside, and that in the case of both Dykes the constructional and perhaps also military effort involved was too great to be sustained to the end.

The attempted construction of Wat's Dyke hereabouts shows how essential to the Mercians the control of the S. shore of the Dee estuary must have been, presumably as helping to secure the safety of Chester.[1] So narrow a belt of coast-land as that which lies between Fflint—the natural terminal of the Alyn–Nant-y-Fflint stretch of Dyke—and

[1] See Tait in *Flints. Hist. Soc. Publications*, xi, p. 1.

Basingwerk (Holywell) could not have been of much value in itself, and it must have been desperately difficult to hold at this farthest limit of the frontier.

(ii) *The Minor Layout*

One of the chief interests in a survey of this character is to observe the methods whereby, within the limits determined by the major layout, the actual course of the Dyke was planned. It was soon evident that the Dyke was set out in comparatively short stretches: from one rise to another, or from the crest of a ridge to its shoulder, or following the contour of the flank of a valley; and that these stretches were dead straight, fairly straight, or followed a curved course. In brief, the three types of alignment which had previously been met with on Offa's Dyke[1] occur also on Wat's Dyke. These types are:

Type I. Parts of the earthwork which are either demonstrably straight between two mutually visible points, or which were almost certainly so laid out, though now gapped and damaged.

Type II. Parts of the earthwork which between two mutually visible points are sinuous, but which at no point markedly diverge from the straight line.

Type III. Parts of the earthwork which, within the broad limits of general direction, are sensitive to the relief of the countryside.

Type I—the dead straight type—cannot in the case of Wat's Dyke always be distinguished from Type II with such ease as in the case of Offa's Dyke; it seems to me that the technique is not so clearly understood, the application less exact. I found, in drafting this report, that in the many borderline cases it was very difficult to describe in words the extent of inexactitude, or to justify verbally the inclusion of a given sector in one or other group; and was driven to devise a graphic representation, which should enable a reader to judge for himself at a glance the correctness or otherwise of my categories.

The method adopted is shown in Figs. 118 and 119, which include, in ten stretches, practically the whole of the Dyke. The actual course of the earthwork is shown by a dotted line. The theoretical straight alignments to which the actual course of the Dyke conforms exactly (Type I), or approximately (Type II), are shown by thin continuous lines. The points where direction is changed—usually crest lines—are shown by thin lines at right angles to the alignment. The character of the terrain is also indicated: 'level', 'undulating', 'steep slope', and so on.

I believe this graphic method is the only one which enables the layout of a running earthwork to be shown; the explanation of one section will suffice. In Flintshire, between Mynachlog and Bryn-y-bal Hill, the Dyke was directly aligned (Fig. 118, 1). Mynachlog is 442 ft. above sea-level, Bryn-y-bal 556 ft. The country crossed is gently undulating but lower than the terminal points, yielding such spot-levels as 400, 370, 434. The length of Dyke included in this alignment is unusual—2 miles, 370 yards. The Dyke is sinuous, swinging to right and left of a straight line which is the mean; a good example of Type II. The maximum deviations from the straight line are slight, considering the length; 30 yards to the E. at one point, and 35 yards to the W. at another. We can recover the constructional process by examining the topography. A sight was taken from the shoulder of

---

[1] Chapter V, p. 119.

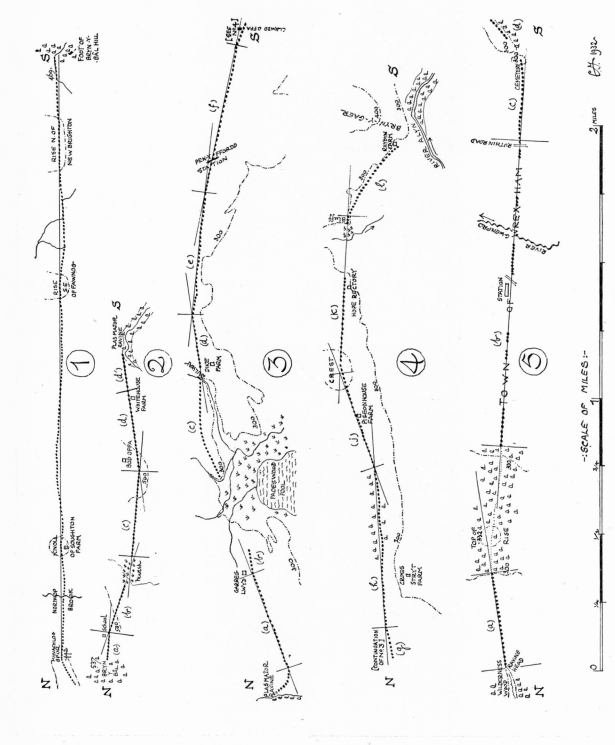

FIG. 118. Analysis, showing how the N. half of Wat's dyke was planned.

Mynachlog on to the first salient feature, the knoll E. of Soughton farm, and a post set up. A similar mark was then set up on the next salient feature, the rise SE. of Fawnog, in a line with the first. Other mark-stakes were placed on the higher ground N. of New Brighton. At these points, the Dyke, when dug, was of course exactly on the straight line; elsewhere exactitude of alignment was neglected.

Tabular List of Straight Alignments

Figure	Diagram	Type I, length	Type II, length	Comments and references
97	..	380 yds.	..	p. 230 of text
97, 98	118, 1	..	2 m. 370 yds.	pp. 231–2 of text
99	2, a	170 yds.	..	..
	b	330 yds.	..	..
	c	550 yds.	..	..
	d, d′	770 yds.	..	p. 233 of text; d and d′ show cross alignment
100	3, a	..	330 yds.	p. 234 of text
	d	..	350 yds.	..
	e	..	780 yds.	Country undulating, deviations may be due to this
101	f	..	970 yds.	..
	4, h	..	1,030 yds.	..
102	j	..	650 yds.	} The Dyke curves at crest to ease the junction of alignments between j and k. The latter is aligned across a marsh on to the next spur: course referred to on p. 237 is not marked here
	k	610 × 50 yds.	..	
103	5, a	620 yds.	..	p. 238 of text
104	b	1 m. 220 yds.	..	p. 239 of text. The longest Type I stretch
	c	..	370 yds.	p. 241 of text
105	119, 6, a–b	360 yds.	..	} p. 242 of text. Change of direction in a slight hollow, not on a crest
	b–c	410 yds.	..	
105–6	119, 6, d	..	570 yds.	p. 243 of text
106	6, e	..	770 yds.	..
	7, a	1,000 yds.	..	} pp. 243–4 of text. Dead straight on flat; sinuous on hill, which was presumably wooded
	..	..	420 yds.	
107	7, b	950 yds.	..	p. 244 of text
	7, c	..	..	Probably Type I but impossible to determine
108	8, a	..	620 yds.	p. 246 of text. On undulating rising ground
	8, b	300 yds.	..	..
108–9	8, c	1,000 yds.	..	p. 247 of text. A slight deviation is due to undulating ground
109	8, e	1,190 yds.	..	p. 248 of text. Though destroyed in Gobowen, type practically certain
109–10	8, f–g	..	..	Dyke too faint or too intermittent to determine types
110	8, h	630 yds.	..	Central portion aligned from hill top. pp. 249–50 of text
	9, a–b	..	..	Probably Type I but too much destroyed for certainty
111	9, c	880 yds.	..	Dyke curves at crest to ease the junction of alignments
	9, 10, d	820 yds.	900 yds.	First half of the alignment (Red House to Mile Oak) is direct, the second (to Pentre-coed) sinuous
	Totals	7 m. 680 yds.	6 m. 1,090 yds.	

The preceding table shows that the total lengths of Type I and Type II alignments are $7\frac{1}{3}$ and $6\frac{2}{3}$ miles respectively out of a total of $20\frac{1}{2}$ miles of constructed (earthwork) frontier. This leaves $6\frac{1}{2}$ miles for Type III. That only one-third of the total length of Dyke should in its alignment be sensitive to the contours of the country is, of course, because the terrain is essentially a lowland one, with few steep slopes or deep re-entrants—these, for the most part being in areas where no Dyke exists. On the other hand, the country over which much of the direct alignment (Types I or II) runs *could* have been traversed by conforming to minor changes of level—that is by Type III methods—if the builders had wished; in short, we observe that the technique of direct alignment was used wherever possible by the engineer of the Dyke.

A comparison of the proportional lengths of each type of alignment in the northern sector of Offa's Dyke is useless, because the physical conditions are so different. The terrain over which Offa's Dyke runs, being in large measure mountainous, markedly undulating, or deeply dissected, Type III alignments necessarily predominate. As a matter of interest, however, the straight stretches of Offa's Dyke on the foothills of the Berwyns parallel to Wat's Dyke are shown on Fig. 117. The straight alignments are related to the valleys; the Cegidog, the Gwenfro–Clywedog, the Dee, the Vyrnwy; but not the Ceiriog, which here runs in a deep trench.

Notes on one or two minor points connected with alignment may close this section.

Changes of direction occur with one exception on crest lines; the exception is near Middle Sontley farm (Fig. 105). Here the Dyke seems to go *through* a small rise, which is the true crest line, rather than over it, changing direction just beyond this rise.

A straight layout over crest lines by means of back alignment occasionally occurs. The best example is at Whitehouse farm (Fig. 99).

Deviation from direct alignment at a crest line, to ease the angle, is a frequent trick. Good examples are: near Hope, Fig. 118, 4; and near Oswestry, Fig. 119, 9.

Gaps necessitated by streams are, as in the case of Offa's Dyke, very narrow, e.g. stream near Mynachlog, Fig. 97.

(iv) *The Relation of the Dyke to Contemporary Agriculture*

In the fifth Chapter on Offa's Dyke[1] arguments were brought forward in favour of equating straight (Type I) alignments with agricultural land—arable or pasture—and sinuous (Type II) alignments with woodland. This interpretation offers no difficulties in the case of Wat's Dyke; indeed, it materially helps us to rationalize the facts. I am convinced that the chief cause of the sinuousness of the Mynachlog sector (Fig. 118, 1) is that the Dyke was dug in wooded country. The salient points where the sighting poles were set up were cleared of woodland, and the Dyke accurately placed; elsewhere the builders avoided the biggest clumps of trees.[2] Across plough or pasture, such as I believe the country shown diagrammatically on Fig. 119, 9, to have been, it was easy to adhere to the straight line at any and all points.

[1] p. 121 ff.
[2] Some of the minor divergences were here due to alignment by guesswork in hollows—Northop brook, for example, is invisible from spot-level 442.

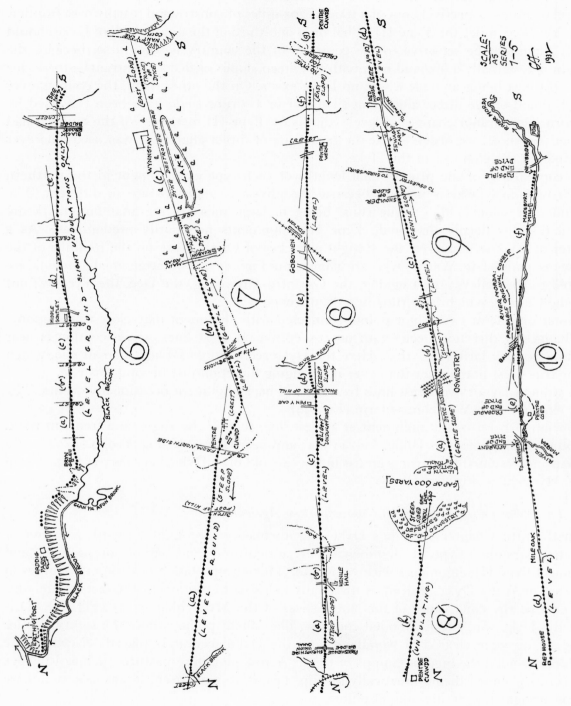

FIG. 119. Analysis, showing how the S. half of Wat's Dyke was planned.

These are two cases where, within a single alignment, a sinuous stretch follows a straight stretch. Between Black brook and Pentre-clawdd (Fig. 119, 7) the straight stretch is on the flat, the sinuous on the slope. This north-facing hill-side is just the place where woodland would survive till a late date. Again, between Red House (Oswestry) and Pentre-coed (Fig. 119, 10), the sinuous stretch is near the marshy jungle of the Morda, which, stretching for many miles, formed the protected southern flank of the Dyke. The land bordering such a marsh might well have been uncleared till a late date.

Accepting the theory that Type I alignments record the exact area of cleared (agricultural) land which existed when the Dyke was built and which it actually crossed, it is of interest to examine the distribution of these open fields, which illustrate the economic conditions along 20 miles of the N. Welsh march in the eighth century. They are shown by a suitable symbol on the diagrammatic map (Fig. 117).

The first point is that the most extensive areas of open fields are near towns of ancient (pre-Norman) foundation—Oswestry, Wrexham; towns not necessarily ancient enough to have grown out of the settlements of the farmers of the Dark Ages who cultivated these lands, but ancient enough to have inherited their arable.

These towns represent, indeed, continuity of cultural tradition on the march. Scholars knowing intimately the history of the region may be able to enlarge my list; Hope village may represent the settlers who cleared the slopes adjacent to the Alyn hereabouts; Ruabon those who tilled the Wynnstay parklands; while Middle Sontley (Fig. 119, 6) may well have been the home of the men who cultivated the ancient fields which lie, as the straight stretches of the Dyke show, immediately to the N. of this homestead. The straight stretch in the Coed Llys woodland (Fig. 97, left), again, may represent a clearing—which has not survived—made by the predecessors of the medieval inhabitants of Llys Edwin.

But the map reveals a feature of still greater interest; it is that the amount of cleared land diminishes as we proceed N. along the Dyke. Though this is fairly obvious, it is well to place it on a statistical basis:

Sector	Length of Dyke actually constructed	Length of Type I alignments	Percentages
North	8 miles, 1,200 yards[1]	1 mile, 1,110 yards	20·3
Middle	6 miles, 370 yards	3 miles, 40 yards	47·8
South	4 miles, 1,600 yards[2]	2 miles, 1,300 yards	55·7

That the cleared land diminishes, implies so much: fewer farms and steadings, denser and more extensive woodland, greater danger to the settler and his flocks and herds from human enemies and wild beasts.

The incompleteness of Wat's Dyke at its northern end, at and near Holywell, has on general grounds been ascribed to the remoteness of this region from the centres of Mercian civilization (p. 263); we can now reinforce that conclusion by observed fact. The fewer farms to which we have referred imply fewer able-bodied men available in a given

[1] Omitting Holywell and Nant-y-Fflint fragments.
[2] Half a mile is omitted in calculating the percentages; the Dyke alignment in this half mile was probably, but not certainly, Type I.

area for communal action; the potential of any human effort would have become progressively less as the end of the frontier was approached.[1]

This conclusion receives striking reinforcement from historical data. Our northern sector bisects the county of Flint; and the Domesday record of this county was subjected to a detailed analysis by the late Professor Tait.[2] He concludes that 'Taking the district as a whole, the impression is left that its thin population and scanty annual return (between £750 and £1,000 on a modern gold standard) must be ascribed rather to its physical features and lack of development than to the effect of past wars and raids'.

A further point of interest arises in this connexion. The three principal sectors of Wat's Dyke (beginning at Coed Llys), northern, middle, and southern, show only three gaps, one as it happens in each sector, other than those necessitated by ravines, marshes, and rivers. These are:

Sector	Place	Character of ground	Character of frontier	Length intermitted (yards)
North . .	Bryn-y-bal, Figs. 98–99	N. slope and crest of a rise	No trace of Dyke nor indication of frontier	820
Middle . .	N. of Wrexham, Fig. 103	N. and S. slopes and crest of a rise	Hedge-bank and parish boundary marks frontier	720
South . .	S. of Pentre-wern, Fig. 109	N. slope and crest of a rise	Hedge marks frontier	200

All these three hills or knolls have easy slopes.

In the case of Offa's Dyke, it was shown that in a given area the N. slopes of hills or rises were the last to be cleared by the Mercian agriculturists,[3] and when these three patches of land on the Wat's Dyke frontier, all wholly or in part of this character, were studied in the field, it seemed probable that the engineers were dealing with forest so dense that a Dyke was held to be unnecessary. This view I see no reason to modify; the

[1] It is assumed that the cleared areas represent, as is almost certainly the case with Offa's Dyke (Chapter VI, p. 169) the efforts of Mercian farmers. The line chosen by the engineers, it is held, represents, roughly, the western limits of their arable and pasture.

It is, of course, possible that the cleared areas represent the activities of an earlier lowland folk, Britons—Welshmen—whose forebears were partially Romanized, who may have stuck to their holdings until Anglian raids gave place to colonization by the organized Mercian state. In either case, the extent of these cleared areas is a fair index of the extent of settled agricultural life in the belt of country crossed by the Dyke at the time it was built.

The argument, again, proceeds on the assumption that the construction of the earthwork was carried out *on a regional basis* by the landowning thanes of each district under the general direction of the King or his nominee—the man who selected the alignment and was responsible for the work. The evidence we possess bearing on the social and political organization of the Anglo-Saxon States suggests that the other method, that of a force like the Roman army which built the German *Limes*, recruited by the State, paid by the State, and continuously employed over a period of years would have been impossible. Much significant though indirect evidence in support of my assumption was obtained when Offa's Dyke was investigated (Chapter VI, p. 152; Chapter VII, p. 200); and an incomplete angle of Wat's Dyke at Black brook (p. 243) may be similarly interpreted.

The question as to whether pressed labour—captives of the Welsh wars—was employed on Wat's Dyke cannot usefully be discussed. We have no evidence.

[2] Flintshire in Domesday Book, *Flints. Hist. Soc.* xi, 1925, pp. 1 ff., esp. p. 7.

[3] Chapter V, p. 122, and Fig. 52.

point of interest in the present connexion is that the longest of these stretches, and the only stretch where the frontier line is completely intermitted, is in the northern sector. This is not, I submit, the operation of pure chance; the facts set out in the table are consistent with those previously adduced, and point to the weakening of human effort, and the greater extent of physical obstacle to that effort, in the northern sector of the frontier.

The essential quality of a true induction is that it should be capable of explaining facts and circumstances unknown when it was formulated. This requirement the theory of the significance of Type I alignments, evolved during the survey of Offa's Dyke, fulfils. It has proved to be the key which opens the door to a complete understanding of the peculiar features of Wat's Dyke, and enables us to visualize the conditions under which it was constructed.

GENERAL CONSIDERATIONS AND SUMMARY

(a) Position

(i) The frontier of which the earthwork known as Wat's Dyke is the outstanding feature extends from the estuary of the Dee at Basingwerk, Flintshire, to the Morda brook, Shropshire, a distance of 38 miles measured along its line. It is roughly parallel to, and from 1,200 yards to $3\frac{1}{2}$ miles to the E. of, the northern sector of Offa's Dyke (Plates XXXIX and XL.)

(ii) The Morda joins the Vyrnwy 8 miles (as the crow flies) S. of the termination of the Dyke, and the Vyrnwy joins the Severn 4 miles below this confluence. Hence the broad valley of the Middle Severn and its greater and lesser tributary forms a natural geographical boundary—and in early times an obstacle difficult to pass—on which the landward end of the Dyke rests.

(iii) The alignment of Wat's Dyke, unlike Offa's Dyke in this area, is wholly in the lowlands (p. 227); it is chosen with great skill to include a number of ravines which are utilized as part of the frontier, thus reducing the length of the artificial frontier line—the Dyke—to $22\frac{3}{4}$ miles, or, excluding minor intermissions, $20\frac{1}{2}$ miles (Fig. 117 and pp. 246, 261).

(iv) Its course is chosen also to give good fields of view to the W.; knolls and rising ground are included wherever possible.

(v) The position of the frontier at the N. end shows the importance which the Mercians attached to the possession of the southern shore of the Dee estuary; the frontier covers only a narrow strip of coast, and must have been difficult to hold (p. 263).

(vi) The distance between Offa's Dyke and Wat's Dyke is never great, and at one point—near Ruabon—is negligible (Plate XLIIIc). As frontiers, however, they represent entirely different concepts: Wat's Dyke presents a visible barrier to the highlanders when they have reached the Lowlands; but Offa's Dyke here controls access to the Lowlands.

(vii) Wat's Dyke is a frontier, a boundary rampart, not a line of defence. In this it resembles Offa's Dyke. Like Offa's Dyke, however, its course was chosen to include defensible positions, according to the tactics of the time; it was designed, like Offa's Dyke, by a man trained in a military tradition (pp. 261–3, and 264).

(b) Character

(viii) Wat's Dyke is uniform in character, a single rampart and a ditch to the W. (pp. 264–7). Considered as an engineering work, it represents a single design and a construction of one period (p. 263).

(ix) The principles governing its alignment and construction are similar to those of Offa's Dyke. It shows the same developed engineering technique, and is a work of the Mercian school of dyke builders. Its similarity to Offa's Dyke may extend to mode of construction—by separate gangs (pp. 243–4).

(x) It differs in minor details of engineering technique from Offa's Dyke. These suffice to reveal another intelligence controlling the work (pp. 241, 264). The differences in technique are not such as to admit of a marked difference in date between the two works.

(xi) The Dyke was never completed. The ramparts preventing uncontrolled access to the coastlands of the Dee between Flint and Basingwerk through gaps in the natural frontier—deep ravines—were only begun. In its incompleteness it resembles Offa's Dyke (pp. 228–30, 263).

(xii) This incompleteness is related to the sparseness of effective occupation of the country N. of Caergwrle—shown by the gradual diminution of agricultural land along the line of the Dyke as it goes northward. The political and military effort involved in its construction faded out in this remote corner of Mercian dominion (pp. 269–71).

(c) Date

(xiii) The prehistoric earthworks on the line of the Dyke had no significance when the Dyke was constructed (p. 280).

(xiv) The extent to which the Dyke forms parish boundaries does not suggest that it had any significance (other than as a recognizable feature of the landscape) when these were allotted (p. 303).

(xv) No objects of any importance bearing on the age of the Dyke are recorded as having been found in its bank or ditch. It crosses, so far as is known, no Roman site, and no deserted occupation site on its line, likely to be of the Dark Ages, has been found or recorded; no excavation work, therefore, has been undertaken by the writer.

(xvi) Since Wat's Dyke shows similar engineering technique to Offa's Dyke, it is a work of the same phase of culture. This renders it very difficult to find direct archaeological evidence bearing on the question—Which is the older?[1]

(xvii) The old name of Wat's Dyke—Wad's or Wada's—that of a hero of Mercian song, associated with Offa in the saga literature, tends to confirm the archaeological evidence as to the similarity in date of the two works (pp. 288–9). It goes, indeed farther, suggesting that both are the work of Offa. But it is improbable that, in one and the same reign, the toilsome labour of creating an earthwork frontier, and then replacing it by another, would have been carried out.

---

[1] In one minor respect, it will be remembered (p. 264), Wat's Dyke showed less engineering skill than Offa's Dyke. The evidence is perhaps subjective and admittedly slight; though it points to this Dyke being the older of the two, I hesitate to use it in this connexion.

(xviii) Since Wat's Dyke approximates in date to Offa's Dyke, and since Offa's Dyke is securely dated between 757 and 796, the permissible limits, archaeologically speaking, and having regard to the point made in the preceding paragraph, would be about 700–50 on the one hand, 800–50 on the other.

In the former case, Wat's Dyke is the first recognizable frontier in the N. of the March of a growing and developing Mercia, which, afterwards constructed a second dyke farther forward in the debatable land; in the latter, it is the second or later frontier of a declining Mercia, unable to hold all its gains, but stable politically and still possessing creative energy.

The indirect archaeological, and the historical evidence, bearing on these two possibilities may now be marshalled.

(xix) The history of Mercia in the post-Offan period (800–50) does not suggest that the above conditions were satisfied, or that the Dyke was likely to have been constructed at that time. King Cenwulf (796–821), an active fighter, who is known to have been campaigning W. of Offa's Dyke in N. Wales, would hardly have withdrawn his frontier in this region; thereafter the rapid decline of Mercia and its conquest by the West Saxons (829) must have rendered great state enterprises impossible.

(xx) In the pre-Offan period, we have the kings Penda (626–55) and Wulfhere (656–75) representing, in Sir John E. Lloyd's view,[1] 'the great age of Mercian territorial expansion', when the country W. of the Severn was conquered and exploited. These kings were followed after an interval by Æthelbald (716–57), the principal English king of his day.[2]

(xxi) Our earlier researches may now be called upon to provide significant probabilities. In addition to Offa's and Wat's Dykes, we have studied a number of Short Dykes, all in the central sector of the Welsh March (Fig. 120).

The distribution 'in depth' of these dykes, illustrating the penetration of Wales,[3] suggests that their construction must have covered a considerable period of time. The earliest may well be of the age of Penda, while one group at least (the Double Deyches) has been held on structural grounds to be the work of the community which afterwards, in this area, built Offa's Dyke (Chapter VI, p. 167). All represent activity in this central sector of the debatable land prior to stabilization.

(xxii) Since Wat's Dyke represents a continuous frontier, it is later in character and probably in date than the majority, if not all, of the Short Dykes. It is not a work of the period of expansion, but is the first effort at precise definition of the limits of conquest. The selection of the northern sector for this effort is, when the extent of forest in the S. is taken into consideration (Fig. 120), easy to understand.

(xxiii) Two lines of induction, then, lead us to the conclusion that Wat's Dyke belongs to the period of Æthelbald, and thus precedes, by not more than one generation, the final

---

[1] *History of Wales*, Vol. I, p. 195.

[2] Lloyd, op. cit., p. 197, and Oman, *England before the Norman Conquest*, p. 331; Sir Frank Stenton, op. cit., pp.202–3.

[3] All, that is, which have as yet been scientifically

studied. At least one such work, the Aberbechan Dykes, Montgomeryshire, faces E., and so represents not Mercian activities, but the adoption by the highlanders of lowland technique in defensive earthwork. *Arch. Camb.*, 1930, pp. 64–65.

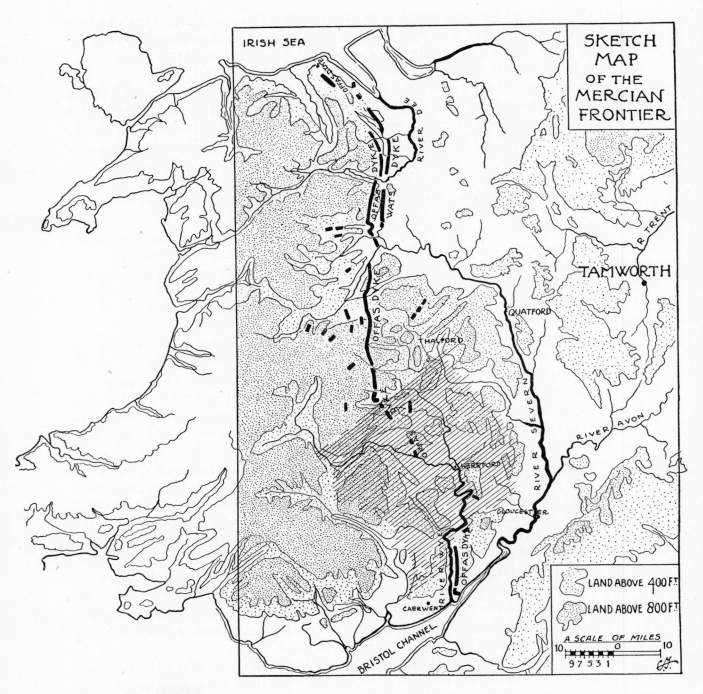

FIG. 120. The frontier Dykes of Wales in the eighth century. Offa's Dyke, Wat's Dyke, and certain cross-ridge and cross-valley Dykes of central Wales are shown. The shaded area represents the outcrop of Old Red Sandstone.

effort to define the whole western frontier of Mercia undertaken by Offa; it may have been still a-building when he came to the throne in 757.[1]

(d) Nomenclature

(xxv) One other question should here be ventilated. Why did 'the whole country assure' Edwin Guest in 1858 that Wat's Dyke was Offa's Dyke? (p. 226 above); and why are there three farmhouse names compounded with 'Offa', on its line?

When the whole of the northern half of these dyke systems are plotted on a modern map such as Fig. 121, it is evident that Wat's Dyke is, in its zone, a much more reasonable frontier against the Welsh than Offa's Dyke, much easier to hold.

From Treuddyn to the sea, 18 miles, only 4 miles of Offa's Dyke is known to exist or to have existed. From Caergwrle, 2 miles only behind the Treuddyn end of the Dyke, Wat's Dyke provides a shorter and continuous frontier of dyke and river gorges to within 2 miles of the sea—14 out of 16 miles.

A switch backward at the Treuddyn–Caergwrle 'hinge' in times of difficulty, from the Offan to the pre-Offan frontier, is likely enough, and the local tradition would thus have had a reasonable foundation in practice.[2]

ACKNOWLEDGEMENTS

Since this printed record completes the research initiated ten years previously, the writer ventures to say that the results justify the policy of the National Museum of Wales and the Board of Celtic Studies of the University of Wales in arranging to give financial support to an approved piece of research over a long period of years. The Editors of *Archaeologia Cambrensis*, in accepting the annual reports [which preceded this collected edition of the survey], did the writer a real service; the preparation of these clarified ideas and indicated the lines on which each successive season's work might most profitably be conducted.

Leave to prosecute our researches was willingly granted by owners and tenants, to whom individually and collectively we expressed our thanks: the special help given by many friends was also recorded in the annual reports referred to.[2]

[1] I have not taken into consideration, in discussing the date of the Dyke, the evidence afforded by Domesday Book as to the extent of hidation in Flintshire. It does not seem safe to draw any conclusions from conditions present in the area 300 years later. See *Flint Hist. Soc. Publications*, xi, p. 1.

[2] These paragraphs were written or rewritten in 1953.

PLATE XLI

a. Wat's Dyke at the Rookery, Erddig park. Taken at point A. Fig. 105

b. An example of the steep-scarped ravines used as a frontier by the builders of Wat's Dyke, at Nant-y-flint, S. of Holywell. The figures are on the edge of the western (Welsh) plateau looking across to the eastern (English) plateau visible above the ravine. Taken from point B, Fig. 96

PLATE XLII

a. Wat's Dyke at Northop brook: the reverse (E.) side. See Profile IV, Fig. 113. Taken from point C, Fig. 97

b. An untouched portion of Wat's Dyke: the Rookery, Erddig park. See Profile X, Fig. 115. Taken at point E, Fig. 105

PLATE XLIII

a. The use of a western-facing slope as a frontier: Wat's Dyke at Padeswood. A line of trees marks the Dyke: the railway is situated on the valley floor. Taken from the opposite side of the little valley—point D, Fig. 100

b. The use of an easy western-facing slope as a frontier: Wat's Dyke on the flank of the Alyn valley. Taken from the western side of the valley at Pen-y-wern, looking across to Croes Stryt farm, Fig. 101

c. View from hill-side near Gardden Hall, N. of Ruabon, where Offa and Wat's Dykes are closest together: looking E. Offa's Dyke is on the line of the houses at foot of hill; Wat's Dyke crosses Pentre Clawdd hill in the middle distance

PLATE XLIV

a. Wat's Dyke near Middle Sontley farm: with W. ditch ploughed in. See Profile XI, Fig. 115. Taken at point F, Fig. 105

b. Wat's Dyke showing gap made for farm traffic. Taken from the shady hollow on the right of photo above, point G, Fig. 105

PLATE XLV

a. Wat's Dyke crossing Pentre Clawdd Hill, looking W. The figure in the foreground is in the ditch; the figure in the middle distance is on the edge of the scarp. The forward slope of the hill is invisible from the alignment chosen. See Profile XII, Fig. 115. Taken at point H, Fig. 107

b. Wat's Dyke immediately N. of Wynnstay park, Ruabon, Denbighshire. There is here only a small W. ditch. See Profile XV, Fig. 116. Taken at point J, Fig. 107

PLATE XLVI

a. Wat's Dyke S. of 'Old Oswestry' hill-fort. See Profile XVII, Fig. 116. Taken at point K, Fig. 110. The hill-fort is situated in the wood in the background

b. The S. end of Wat's Dyke. Fragment of bank adjoining the river Morda near Pentre-coed farm. See Profile XIX, Fig. 116. Taken at point L, Fig. 112

PART III
IX. THE MERCIAN ACHIEVEMENT: A COMMENTARY (1940)[1]

A FRONTIER has been described as a line which you can draw where you like so long as you have force enough, the problem being to ensure respect for your line when you have drawn it. The moderns use concrete, guns, and barbed wire, the ancients constructed a bank and ditch or a wall; but the effectiveness of these devices passes with the will-to-power of the peoples who create them. Offa's Dyke, however, named after an English king of the eighth century, was long recognized both by Welsh and English as their common boundary, and it still has significance. When in 1928 I asked a Montgomeryshire peasant through whose garden the Dyke happens to pass, whether the folk of his hamlet knew what it was or what it meant, his reply though indirect, was not ambiguous: 'You put your head inside the back-door of Bob Jones's cottage there; tell him he was born the wrong side of Offa's Dyke, and see what happens.'

In this Commentary the research detailed in the previous pages on the genesis, nature, and character of the Offan frontier and its predecessors will be summarized, and an attempt made to explain why, though many centuries of rivalry and war between Celt and Saxon followed its creation, the boundary between Welsh and English counties— the Eastern boundary that is of Wales with Monmouthshire—approximates to its line.

OFFA'S DYKE DEFINED

Offa's Dyke consists of a bank of earth, ditched, usually on the W. side but occasionally on both sides. The frontier of which it is the outstanding feature is held to extend from the sea-coast at or near Prestatyn, Flintshire, to the Severn sea at Sedbury cliff, Gloucestershire, completely delimiting the Anglo-Saxon state of Mercia and the Welsh principalities. The distance measured along the line of the Dyke is 149 miles. The length of constructed earthwork is 81 miles; it is fairly continuous in the centre, intermittent elsewhere. At the northern end lengths amounting to some 16 miles in all, though almost certainly included in the scheme, were never constructed; in the centre the river Severn is the boundary for several miles; at the southern end some 47 miles of the frontier consisted of dense forest and a large river along which an artificial line was necessary in certain places only (Fig. 120). The scale of the Dyke varies; a survey taken at some forty different points in its course shows an average height of bank above ground level of over 6 ft., and an over-all breadth for the whole work of nearly 60 ft.[2]

---

[1] When the author was invited by the British Academy to give the Sir John Rhŷs Memorial Lecture in 1940, the western frontier of Mercia in the Dark Ages was chosen as a suitable subject. By permission of the Council, this lecture, altered as necessary, is here reprinted from the *Proceedings*, 1940, pp. 275–300, as a suitable summary of, and commentary on, the survey of both Offa's and Wat's Dykes.

[2] Ch. VIII, p. 259.

ALIGNMENT OF OFFA'S DYKE

The Dyke, broadly speaking, is aligned along the margin of the Welsh uplands. In the N. (Plates VI and XI) it follows the foot-hills of the Clwydian range and the Berwyns; in the centre (Plates XVIII and XXIII) it takes a direct line across the fringe of the high central plateau of Wales in the neighbourhood of Clun and Knighton, reaching up to 1,400 ft. on Spoad Hill, Shropshire; in the S. (Plates XXXIII and XXXIV) it follows the course of the river Wye from its angle by Hereford.

The term 'alignment' in connexion with a travelling earthwork has a dual significance; primarily it concerns the plan and general layout in relation to the main features of the country, secondarily, the mode in which the course is set out and the earthwork constructed from point to point within the directional limits thus determined. We have in short to consider 'major' and 'minor' alignments. The major alignments consist of stretches of Dyke often many miles in length, terminated by a definite change of direction, and appearing practically straight on a small-scale map. These characters can be demonstrated in any sector of the great earthwork; I recall, especially, its trace in the Wrexham–Oswestry district,[1] where the major alignments are 8, 7½, and 12 miles long, with maximal deviations from a dead-straight line of only 280, 300, and 750 yards respectively. The intellectual quality, the eye for country, and the intimate knowledge of the district manifested by the creation of such direct alignments carried out in broken and mountainous country intersected by deep river valleys, without the aid of accurate maps, are remarkable.

Equally direct and equally interesting is the layout of the Dyke across the central March from a point near Montgomery to the Herefordshire plain.[2] The mountain mass here crossed is structurally a high plateau deeply eroded and dissected by drainage lines which run from W. to E. The line of the Dyke is thus across the grain of the country, and the earthwork follows a switchback course; it crosses Llanvair Hill, for example, at 1,408 ft. and the river Lugg at 490 ft. above O.D. Now this layout can be studied from a few salient points—Hem hill, Edenhope, Spoad, and Llanvair hills, Hawthorn and Herrock hills—and there is little doubt that from these the traverse, in which account had to be taken of westward-facing slopes, was outlined by the chief engineer. No finer experience can fall to the lot of the field archaeologist than thus to expose the fundamental technique of a monumental work of thought and ingenuity, hidden from men's minds for a thousand years.

Deviation within such narrow limits as those mentioned above brings the minor alignments into the picture, as important elements of the plan. The policy of the designer, consistently maintained, was to give wherever possible a wide view to the W.; and the study of the use made, to this end, of lateral re-entrants and embayments flanking the greater river valleys which had to be crossed, is a delight to anyone interested in problems of civil engineering—the layout of the Dyke in the Clun valley area (Plate XXVIII) may be here cited. It is probable that the knowledge of such instruments of precision as the

[1] Ch. IV, pp. 79–80, Plate XI.   [2] Ch. VI, p. 152, Plates XVIII and XXIII, also Ch. V, fig. 52.

Romans had was lost in the dark centuries; and we have evidence that the detailed layout of Offa's Dyke was carried out mainly by eye, aided by staves and manual signals. In the case of major and minor alignments alike, changes of direction usually take place on crest lines true or false; absolutely direct alignments are short, from the floor of a valley, it may be, to the shoulder of the hill which flanks it, or from the shoulder to the crest. And when in any minor alignment there is a piece of 'dead' ground, which could not be controlled by staves set up, like the axe-heads of Odysseus, in a line, the trace falters, it is laid out by guess-work, and the inaccuracy of the result is manifested on our Ordnance maps.[1] Only in one place, in the lowlands of Herefordshire, has any indication been obtained of more elaborate methods. On the S. side of Yazor brook, just above a marshy flat here defined by a low river terrace, is an oval flat mound of slight elevation; it is exactly in line with a straight stretch of the Dyke, 770 yards long, on the other side of the valley, and is in an area I believe to have been densely forested, in which the Dyke was never built. It is quite unlike a burial mound and seems exactly fitted to be the base of a lofty wooden structure which should enable the next stretch of Dyke (which is a third of a mile away) to be accurately aligned, as indeed it is.[2]

OFFA'S DYKE AN AGREED FRONTIER

Offa's Dyke marked a boundary, a frontier: it was not a military barrier. But its designer was a man imbued with a military tradition; his frontier was in general a sound piece of work from the point of view of the lowlanders whom he represented, for it gave visual control over foreign territory for the greater part of its length, and it includes tactically strong positions, such as the tremendous bastion of Herrock Hill, Herefordshire, or Selattyn Hill, Shropshire.

The Mercian engineer, however, did not have it all his own way. There are aspects of the chosen alignment which suggest that political considerations were not excluded: that is, the line was not the free choice of a conquering race, but a boundary defined by treaty or agreement between the men of the hills and the men of the lowlands. Two instances for which historical data, likely to be relevant, are available may be cited. The commanding spur N. of the Dee valley above Ruabon on which Pen-y-gardden fort is sited,[3] is excluded, the major alignments of the Dyke hereabouts being conditioned by this exclusion. It may be recalled that about 6 miles to the W. of Gardden is the pillar set up by Concenn (Cyngen) King of Powys,[4] probably in the middle third of the ninth century —he died in 854—to the memory of his great-grandfather Eliseg (*fl.* 765–73); near by we may suppose there was a residence of the Powysian dynasty. That the late eighth-century representative of that House (Brochwel or his son Cadell) should have concentrated his efforts in the field and at the council table to secure a serviceable frontier in such an area is not unlikely.

Again, on the Long Mountain, which forms the eastern flank of the valley of the

[1] Fig. 51 and p. 118–19.
[2] Ch. VII, p. 199.
[3] Ch. IV, p. 52.
[4] References and comment in Ch. IV, p. 81–2.

Severn in Montgomeryshire, the Dyke swings 800 ft. up the western slopes of an upland which was in any case controlled by Mercia; a more direct alignment (affording ample visual control over Welsh territory) would have followed the 400–300-ft. contours.[1] A possible explanation of the deflection is that the ruler of Powys demanded the cultivable, western-facing, lower slopes of the mountain.

A unique, localized deflection should also here be mentioned. On the plateau-like summit of Rushock Hill, Herefordshire, the chosen course of the Dyke gives a sufficient field of view, except at one point where the earthwork turns sharply inwards to pass through the highest point of the hill, 1,245 ft. above O.D., and as sharply returns to its original alignment.[2] I suggest that it was agreed by the Powers concerned in the demarcation of the frontier that it should pass over the crest of the hill; the chief engineer fulfilled the letter of the law, but did not allow it to interfere more than was absolutely necessary with what he regarded as a suitable alignment in the interests of Mercia.

The third instance occurs on the river Wye. No portions of Offa's Dyke, other than a mile-length at English Bicknor, were constructed from the point where it reaches the upper Wye at Bridge Sollers above Hereford, to Redbrook on the lower Wye, a distance of 37 miles.[3] It was built, however, from Redbrook to beyond Tidenham and thence across the tip of the Wye–Severn peninsula, 10 miles of it, in a region where one would suppose it to be least needed! Nowhere in these islands could be found a frontier so adequate, so dominating, as this plateau edge overlooking a swift river in a winding gorge, in places 600 ft. deep (Fig. 94 and Plate XXXVII).[4] I could wish no one better fortune than to see the Dyke thereabouts as I first saw it, approaching from Madgett farm. The ploughed fields end in a belt of trees within which is the Dyke; one climbs its bank and the whole tremendous panorama—Monmouthshire, the Wye, the Severn estuary, and the coasts of Gloucestershire and Somersetshire—comes into view down a steep-pitched woodland glade. Why, then, was the Dyke built here? The reason is implicit, I suggest, in the Tidenham Survey of A.D. 956.[5] Tidenham, a large royal manor occupying the tongue of land between Wye and Severn, was given by King Edwy in that year to the monks of Bath Abbey. In its organization, and in the services due from its tenants, it was distinctively English. This is, of course, not surprising when one recalls that the greater part of Tidenham is within Offa's Dyke—the *dic* of the Survey—in an area that was probably West-Saxon before it was Mercian; it must have then been in English hands for well over 200 years. The manor included the peninsula we have mentioned, part of which was leased to 'foreign' sailors, Welsh surely (*sum hit is þan scipwealan to gafole gesett*). There was here, in short, in the tenth century, a little Welsh landing-place. In this century these Welshmen were under English control; but does not their presence, coupled with the fact that the Offan frontier was drawn so as to leave the important area occupied by them in Welsh hands, suggest that the Welsh landing-place also existed in Offa's time? And

[1] Ch. V, p. 92.
[2] Ch. VI, p. 140.
[3] The bridge-head at Hereford may be Offan: but it is not part of Offa's Dyke (p. 182). See also footnote

no. 1, p. 183.
[4] Ch. VII, p. 219.
[5] F. Seebohm, *English Village Community*, p. 148; K.C.D. iii. 450; B.C.S. 928; Ch. VII, p. 219.

why was it, as well as the left bank of the lower Wye, left outside the frontier? Partly for its own sake, as Professor William Rees has emphasized;[1] the 'landing-place' was the Welsh terminal of the 'Old Passage', the Beachley–Aust ferry which linked SE. Wales with the W. of England. Partly for what it implied. It implied, I suggest, that the river traffic—the timber trade on the Wye, which we know was important in the eleventh century (*tantum de navibus in silvam euntibus*, says Domesday Book)[2] was also important in the eighth century; and we begin to see daylight on our problem. The frontier was drawn and the Dyke built on the plateau edge above the Wye mainly because, the trade along the lower reaches of the river being in the hands of the Welsh, it was inconvenient to make the river the political boundary. Sailors must be free to land or to moor their boats on either bank, and if 'frontier incidents' were to be avoided, the Power which claimed no river rights hereabouts had to align its boundary above the alluvial flats. Furthermore we must remember that coastal shipping in medieval times and later required free access up to the head of the tidal waters of a river, and Offa's Dyke on the lower Wye had to extend far enough north to cover with a reasonable margin the tidal traffic. The high-water mark of ordinary tides is Llandogo, but the tide on exceptional occasions reaches Redbrook; and this village is under the high plateau where the Dyke ends.[3] From this point northward (apart from a possible landing-place at English Bicknor) I suggest that the peculiar privileges accorded to the Welsh in the tidal reaches ended, and that the river was the boundary.[4] Presumably they could traffic in this zone if they wished, but their liability to English, as well as Welsh, taxes and dues would begin.

OFFA'S DYKE A UNITARY WORK

The design of the Dyke, whether in the major or minor stretches, is sufficiently homogeneous to make it certain that it is a work of one period; there is, therefore, nothing inherently improbable in the attribution of the whole work to King Offa of Mercia (A.D. 757–96). This attribution is of dual origin and of respectable antiquity; *Offediche* is mentioned in an English deed of the thirteenth century dealing with land crossed by the Dyke at Rhiston, Salop: and, as everyone knows, the Welsh tradition is recorded in the writings of Asser of St. David's, afterwards Bishop of Sherborne. The relevant passage in his *De rebus gestis Ælfredi* is as follows: . . . *rex nomine Offa qui vallum magnum inter Britanniam atque Merciam de mari usque ad mare facere imperavit*. Asser wrote within a

---

[1] *Historical Atlas of Wales*, 1951, p. 17. For the early importance of Aust, see Lloyd, *Hist. Wales*, i, 175, f. 48.

[2] Domesday Book (Record Commission), i, p. 162.

[3] This immense labour, then, had to be undertaken by the Mercians in order that the Welsh might have the untrammelled use of their seaport and their river trade. If this interpretation be correct, Offa appears to have been wiser, in thus removing causes of friction, than his successors; for we have seen that by 956 the territory outside the Dyke on the left bank of the Wye

had been absorbed by the English, doubtless in order that their revenue might benefit by the tolls on the river traffic.

[4] For comments on the dyke at English Bicknor, see pp. 214 and 218 *n*. The men of Erging may have got their iron from the Forest of Dean miners, by the ridgeway from Welsh Bicknor. The significance of this landing will be, I suggest, exactly the same as that of the greater concession to peaceful relations (1953).

hundred years of King Offa's death, and his position, Welsh birth and training make his testimony weighty.[1]

While it is hardly to be expected that archaeological evidence confirming this attribution could be obtained except by accidental circumstance, it was thought, during the progress of the research, that a useful advance towards certainty would be made if proof of post-Roman date could be obtained. A characteristic stretch of the earthwork traverses Ffrith village in Flintshire where Roman building foundations have long been known; here a section was cut through the bank.[2] Roman rubbish, mostly broken pottery, was found under and in the Dyke, none *on* the Dyke; the excavation thus provided the proof required, for it was built here across a deserted Roman site.

Offa's Dyke is a unitary work: it is proved to be post-Roman in a characteristic sector: I hold therefore that there is now no reason to question the correctness of Bishop Asser's statement. The Dyke, then, is a political document of the first importance fixing the boundary between the most powerful state in England and three smaller Welsh kingdoms —particularly Powys—probably between 784 (the traditional date) and 796.[3]

VARIATIONS IN CONSTRUCTION

I have emphasized the unity of the Dyke, but it is an interesting fact that this unity is limited to design; it does not extend to construction. Several examples may be given. In the mountain zone between the Caebitra brook, Shropshire, and the river Arrow, Herefordshire, the earthwork was built on a massive scale wherever the plotted traverse crossed a clearing or a traffic line (Fig. 69).[4] The intervening spaces were filled in later and less effectively; one may suppose that the maintenance of control over the ridgeways used by the raiding Welsh was of urgent importance, and this governed the works schedule.

In other parts, differences in the scale and character of adjoining portions of the Dyke— as at Caswell wood in the lower Wye valley—suggest that separate gangs were employed (Fig. 94).[5] Sometimes adjacent sectors, though exactly aligned on the same point, do not meet; at other times instructions were misunderstood and the alignments overlap. At Hergan in Shropshire[6] such overlapping ends are joined by a cross-bank; there is no attempt to disguise the error.

ECONOMICS OF CONSTRUCTION

It seems to me probable that the construction of the Dyke by the King of Mercia proceeded in the following manner: the King himself, or a small group of King's thegns closely associated and belonging to the Mercian school of field engineering, planned the work (p. 286 below). The course having been laid down and the dimensions and character in general terms defined, the local economic and social organization of this small Germanic state was utilized. Each land-owning thegn on or near the border was made responsible

---

[1] For the Rhiston deed, Asser's 'Life', and other references in the literature see Appendix I.
[2] Ch. III, pp. 40 ff.
[3] Ch. IV, p. 81. See Sir Frank Stenton, *Anglo-Saxon England*, p. 213.
[4] Ch. VI, p. 161.
[5] Ch. VII, pp. 191–2.
[6] Ch. VI, p. 130.

for a certain length of the Dyke, proportionate to the extent of his estate or resources.[1] I suggest that the other method, a labour force recruited by the State, paid by the State, and continuously employed over a period of years, is, on the evidence we possess of the organization of the states of the Heptarchy, not likely, and it does not fit in with the archaeological evidence. I doubt whether King Offa expended a single *mancus* on labourers, though the taxation which had to be remitted because of the work may have imposed a strain on the royal treasury. Quality, scale, and even the existence of the Dyke then, may have depended on the command of technique and the energy possessed by those in immediate control, landed men and their bailiffs; for supervision, on the evidence available, was not everywhere effective. At the most distant part of the frontier, in Flintshire, Offa's Dyke is consistently of weak boundary-bank character, and remarkably incomplete (p. 287 below). Though quality and scale were thus dependent on inexpert control, the traverse, in meticulous detail, was (the northern portion again excepted) in competent hands.

RELATION OF FIELD, AND FOREST, TO LAYOUT

Appreciation of this fact made the exact layout of the minor alignments, to which reference has already been made, deserving of the closest attention. And it was soon apparent that the straightly aligned stretches were of two types; those in which the Dyke was as straight as a ruler, and those in which slight irregularities or sinuosities, other than those due to dead ground, were frequently apparent.[2] The topographical distribution of those two types having been plotted, it became highly probable that the difference was due, not to differences of technique in the gangs employed, but to different surface conditions. The irregular trace was, it appeared, in forest country, the dead-straight trace in cleared and cultivated areas—the arable or pasture fields of a settled agriculture. A striking example of such a contrast is provided by the Dyke on the cold N.-facing and warm S.-facing slopes respectively of the Mainstone valley in Shropshire.[3] The difficulties of dyke-building in forest country are well shown in another context on the upland in Gloucestershire known as Hudnalls and St. Briavels Common, overlooking the lower Wye (Plate XXXV). The easy contours of this hill would permit of extended straight alignments; but the course, though in layout admirable, is in execution uncertain and sinuous. The builders were, there is little doubt, feeling their way from point to point by sensing the contours, shut out by the tree canopy from a general view.[4]

Another character—intermittency—provided similar information. The Anglians were valley dwellers: and a vivid picture of their activities is provided by the partial construction of Offa's Dyke across the Herefordshire plain from Rushock Hill to the Wye at Bridge Sollers.[5] On descending this hill we pass on to the outcrop of the Old Red Sand-

---

[1] I have in mind the *trinoda necessitas*, in particular the burden known as *burh-bot*. W. H. Stevenson (*Eng. Hist. Rev.* xxix, 1914, p. 689, f. 2) notes that 'the Worcester substitution of *weall-geworc* for *burh-bot* . . . seems to be a survival of a Mercian form, for an original Charter of 836 reads *praeter vallis* (read *valli*) *et pontes* (read *pontis*) *constructionem*'. The explanation of this interesting anomaly may be that half a century of pick-and-shovel work on the frontier had left its mark on legal phraseology in the Mercian State.

[2] Ch. V, p. 119.   [3] Ch. VI, p. 129.
[4] Ch. VII, p. 219.   [5] Ch. VII, p. 208.

stone which provides one of the richest agricultural soils in the country, and one which is under natural conditions densely afforested. The Dyke hereabouts is built in the river valleys only; and each portion long enough for accurate determination is straightly aligned, showing that it was built on cleared land. The Mercians, then, it may be inferred, pushed up the valleys of the Arrow and its tributaries, the starting-point being doubtless Watling Street; they pushed up the Wye from Hereford along the line of this Roman road, and also, nosing up the lateral valleys to the northward, cleared the lowlands below Burton Hill. (I suspect that we are here analysing a process which had been gone through before by the Iron Age Celts primarily in the Age of freedom and afterwards during the Roman period; the position of *Magnis*[1] (Kenchester) on the Wye lends point to the parallel. Thus the forest of the eighth century hereabouts may represent in large measure a reversion to nature due to the breakdown of civilization in Britain after A.D. 400.) It has, then, proved possible on this basis—interpretation of structural character—to create an economic picture of the Welsh March as it was in the eighth century; to obtain a bird's-eye view of the waste and the sown in a ribbon of country some 50 miles long for which we have practically no contemporary economic record.

A reconstruction of the country traversed by the Dyke in the upper Severn valley will indicate the possibilities of the technique (Fig. 52).[2] It is a countryside into which a wedge of Anglian agriculturists might at an early date have forced themselves; and it is noticeable that the straight stretches of Dyke therein occur on land most favourably situated for agriculture. Briefly stated, the condition in the eighth century was as follows: the S. slope of Llanymynech Hill and the area between the Vyrnwy and Severn was arable and meadow land; a narrow belt bordering the Severn near Buttington up to the 300-ft. contour was arable, and above that was woodland; the short straight stretches at the 800–1,000-ft. level in Leighton parish represent, it is probable, not arable but open downland. On the SW. slope of the Long Mountain the rich lands were cultivated up to the 600-ft. contour, the whole area as far as Rownal being, except for Hem Hill, an agricultural countryside. From Rownal to within a thousand yards of Caebitra brook there was thick woodland; thence to this brook was arable. Passing upwards through another belt of woodland the crest of the Mellington Hall spur is reached, whence arable fields and meadows extended to the hamlet of Cwm; from here the Dyke sweeps in a broad arc up the steep slope (pasture and forest) of the Kerry Hill. I do not think anyone would have supposed that out of a purely archaeological survey such results could accrue.

DYKE-BUILDING IN GENERAL: WAT'S DYKE AND THE SHORT DYKES, IN RELATION TO OFFA'S DYKE

One cannot study Offa's Dyke for long without asking—how did the concept of so extensive, so laborious a work arise? One answer is, that this mode of dealing with the

---

[1] The proper form of the nominative is unknown, the name occurring only in the locative.
[2] Ch. V, pp. 120–3.

turbulent hillmen has a long history behind it. In addition to Offa's Dyke, there is, in the N. of the March, Wat's Dyke (Plates XXXIX and XL), and in the centre a series of minor works which can conveniently be grouped under the term 'short dykes'.

Wat's Dyke (Fig. 117) extended from the estuary of the Dee at Basingwerk, Flintshire, to the Morda brook, Shropshire, a distance of 38 miles measured along its line.[1] The space between Offa's Dyke and Wat's Dyke is never great, and at one point—near Ruabon —negligible. As frontiers, however, they represent different ideas—Wat's Dyke presents a visible barrier to the highlanders when they have reached the lowlands; but Offa's Dyke hereabouts, in so far as it was constructed, attempts to control access to the lowlands. Considered as an engineering work, Wat's Dyke represents a single design and a construction of one period. The principles governing its alignment and construction are similar to those of Offa's Dyke. It is, like Offa's Dyke, incomplete near the N. coast. It shows similar engineering technique, and is a work of the Mercian school of dyke-builders.[2] Its similarity to Offa's Dyke may extend to mode of construction—by separate gangs. But it differs in minor details of layout from Offa's Dyke, and these suffice to reveal another intelligence controlling the work; the variations, however, are not such as to admit of a marked difference in date between the two works.

Since Wat's Dyke approximates in date to Offa's Dyke, and since Offa's Dyke is securely dated prior to 796, the permissible limits, archaeologically speaking, would be about 730–60 on the one hand, 800–30 on the other. The history of Mercia in the post-Offan period (800–30) does not suggest that Wat's Dyke was likely to have been constructed at that time. King Cenwulf (796–821), an active fighter, who is known to have been campaigning W. of Offa's Dyke in N. Wales, would hardly have withdrawn his frontier in this region nor would Ceolwulf his brother and successor (821–3) who captured Deganwy;[3] thereafter the decline of Mercia and its conquest by the W. Saxons (829), although independence was regained, will have rendered great state enterprises unlikely.[4]

In the pre-Offan period, we have the kings Penda (632–54) and Wulfhere (657–74) representing 'the great age of Mercian territorial expansion', when country W. of the middle reaches of the Severn was conquered and exploited. These kings were followed after an interval by Æthelbald (716–57), the principal English ruler of his day; and there, it would seem, is the political and archaeological setting for the construction of Wat's Dyke.[5]

We now turn to the 'short dykes', all in the central sector of the Welsh March (Plate XXIII and Fig. 69).[6] Many of them are dug athwart ridgeways leading from the Welsh highlands into the English plain; others are aligned across the heads of fertile valleys. Their distribution in depth (some being on one side, some on the other side of Offa's Dyke) suggest that their construction may have covered a considerable period of time. They differ from both Offa's and Wat's Dykes in being localized efforts; the valley dykes

---

[1] Ch. VIII, p. 227.

[2] The alignment, in minute detail, is analysed in the text (Figs. 118, 119).

[3] Sir Frank Stenton, *Anglo-Saxon England* (1943), p. 228.

[4] Ibid., p. 232.

[5] See pp. 271–5. Stenton (1943) does not refer to this attribution, but considers a date in the '7th or early 8th century' probable, p. 211 note.

[6] Ch. V, p. 113, and Ch. VI, pp. 160 ff.

especially protect isolated farming communities, not the frontiers of a state. They belong to a period, that is, when the frontier was in a state of flux, when Mercian farmers could till as much high-valley country as they could hold, and, conversely, when—in phases of weakness—the Herefordshire plain itself was much exposed to attack. In brief, the majority represent local effort at defence and consolidation.

Then consider their position. They are grouped along that sector of the W. frontier of Mercia which is nearest to the centre of the kingdom—the capital, Tamworth—and which was, therefore, the most important from the point of view of the rulers of this state. This sector, moreover, happens to be the most vulnerable. It is where an outlier of the Welsh mountain massif projects like a bastion into the midlands, providing an easy route for the hillmen into the heart of Mercia, which possesses no natural line of defence hereabouts until the valley of the Severn is reached. I suggest that it is probable that in these cross-ridge, cross-col, or cross-valley dykes we have evidence of efforts made by the Mercians to control or provide warnings of attacks from this difficult country, and to protect their steadings in its valleys. That these efforts were at first both unco-ordinated and local can hardly be doubted. Evidences of unifying control and direction in the most developed and presumably latest of these works are, however, not altogether lacking.

The earliest of the 'short dykes' then may well be of the age of Penda (632–54), while there is reason to hold that the latest were the work of the community which afterwards, in this area, built Offa's Dyke. All represent activity in this central sector of the debatable land prior to stabilization.

The works schedule of this stabilization, Offa's Dyke, can be recovered in broad outline. The 34 miles from the Severn at Buttington, Montgomeryshire, to Rushock Hill, Herefordshire, will have been built first, because it covered the vulnerable Mountain Zone. At its southern terminal, as we have seen, the Dyke represents an agreed alignment, and so peaceful relations with the King of Powys. The frontier, moreover, in the whole of the Zone was laid out in a manner which, judging by the distribution of 'Short Dykes', necessitated some withdrawal on the part of Mercia. The north part of this great stretch fills the lower half of Plate XVIII, the south part the whole of Plate XXIII; the writing of the survey in yearly parts, useful as it was, obscures the Grand Design, which we are now endeavouring to define.

The 25 miles from the Severn at Llanymynech, Shropshire, to Penycoed, Flintshire, set out in three magnificent major alignments, will have been constructed next. Plate XI shows all but 2 miles of these. The Kingdom of Powys must first have been defeated or this long stretch of territory W. of the old frontier (Wat's Dyke, Plate XL) would surely not have been ceded.

The remaining dyke-work is in areas less vital to Mercian security, being farther from the heart of the kingdom, Tamworth. Thirdly, then, will have come the lowland and riverside sectors in Herefordshire and Gloucestershire, fully appraised already, and illustrated in Plates XXXIII and XXXIV.

If, as Sir Frank Stenton holds, the building of the Dyke was compressed into the last few years of the King's life,[1] his energy and organizing power must have operated in some such way as this, the actual work of construction being started by gangs awaiting orders at dozens of points on each of the determined alignments, directly they were staked[2] by the chief engineer.

What of the North Zone? The evidence (Plate VI and Fig. 6) suggests that the course of the Dyke determined by the King from Treuddyn to the sea, 19 miles, was translated into reality from Ysceifiog to Prestatyn, 9 miles, but nowhere else. Its character here— lacking bulk and defensibility—points to exhaustion of both King and people, and it may well be a work of Offa's very last years. He began work at the seaward end of this sector, I suggest, because of the value to Mercian economy of the lead (silver) mines of the Halkyn-Llanasa ridge—whose W. spur is Gop hill—and because it was especially important to control the coastal route from Gwynedd to Chester.[3] If this be so, the reader will say, a better dyke, and more of it, might be expected! The lack of a populous hinterland to supply the labour gangs is a good but partial reason for inadequacy, seeing that Wat's Dyke also was not completed hereabouts. King Offa's death at Rhuddlan, 3 miles W. of his new frontier, however, would better explain the inadequacies of this part of the great work, for it suggests either a breakdown of the peace with Powys, or a failure to come to terms with Gwynedd.[4]

We can now sum up the situation, in a few lines. For a hundred years the Mercians built 'Short Dykes' as and when the circumstances required in the central march ...

... , if one of his sons.

SIGNIFICANCE OF THE NAME 'WAT'

This sequence of events, formulated on archaeological grounds, was reinforced by a piece of evidence of an entirely different order from that which I had hitherto pursued.

[1] 'It probably fell in the latter part' of the period 784–96: *Anglo-Saxon England*, p. 213.

[2] One of the stake-holes, it may be recalled, was found in 1926 under the Dyke at Ffrith, Flintshire.

[3] Edward I built, we know, three of his castles to control this route into Gwynedd, and Offa's second successor, Ceolwulf, raided as far as Deganwy on the Conway, presumably along it, in 822 (1953).

[4] It is not certain to which Power the 'Middle Country' then belonged. Caradog of Gwynedd was 'slain by the English' in 798. Sir John E. Lloyd, *Hist. Wales*, i, p. 237 (1953).

[5] For these Welsh aspects of the frontier problems, see Professor William Rees's *Historical Atlas of Wales*, 1951, Plate 22 and pp. 18–19 (1953).

A. N. Palmer recorded in 1897[1] that he had been 'fortunate enough to meet with three documents in which the old name of Wat's Dyke occurred'. 'In a deed of the year 1431 it is spelled *Clauwdd Wade*, in another of the year 1433 *Claud Wode*, and in Norden's Survey of 1620, *Clawdd Wad*'; he adds: 'It looks as though in the Welsh and English names of Wat's Dyke, we have preserved two forms . . . of the same name, probably Wada, the name perhaps of the Mercian who . . . constructed the Dyke.'

The name Wada was not uncommon among the Anglo-Saxons; it is known historically, and as a place-name compound. But there exists a remarkable record, which suggests that the name Wade for our Dyke had a significance greater than Palmer was aware of.

Walter Map, in *De Nugis Curialium*, written between 1182 and 1193, has a chapter dealing with the deeds of Gado (Wade), a prince of the Vandals. This prince is associated with Offa in a fight with the Romans. One might suppose that this Offa would be king of Angel (in Slesvig), the Uffo of Saxo, ancestor of Offa of Mercia; but Map is careful to note that he is the builder of the 'dyke which still bears his name'.[2] The transfer of the adventure from the shadowy king of Angel of the fourth century to the well-known King of Mercia of the eighth century, his descendant, is not surprising and has close parallels.

In the poem *Widsith*, Wade is a saga hero, ruler of the Hælsingas (*Wada* [*weold*] *Hælsingum*). R. W. Chambers discusses the tale of Wade.[3] He was, perhaps, originally a 'sea-giant' whose name 'lived longer in England than that of any of the old heroes of song, Weland excepted', and Chambers concludes that Wade was 'essentially a helper in time of need'.[4] We have, then, Gado (Wade) a hero of Old English legend, associated with Offa in a saga story current in England in the late twelfth century, and we have, on the Welsh border, the geographically related Dykes of Offa and Wat (or Wade). This can hardly be mere coincidence; it points to a close connexion between the two Dykes, and the association of both, in some way, with the great King of Mercia.

GENESIS OF OFFA'S DYKE

The nature of this association can only be surmised. The presumed builder of Wat's Dyke, Æthelbald, died by violence in 756, and Offa came to the throne after a few months of civil war. The Dyke may then have been still a-building, for at the N. end (p. 229) it was never completed; and it may well have been given by Offa himself the name of the hero associated with his own namesake and ancestor. Thereafter, Offa recasts the frontier, scrapping Wada's Dyke in the process. What an astonishing effort for a small state of farmers and peasants this 80 miles of earthen wall and excavated ditch represented! Whence came the will-power, the drive? We know that sustained communal effort may

---

[1] *Y Cymmrodor*, xii, pp. 74–76. Palmer does not give his sources, but he was a reliable and competent antiquary. With difficulty I found the reference to 'Norden's Survey' which I have quoted verbatim in Ch. VIII, p. 226.

[2] *Cymmrodorion Record Series*, no. 9, 1923, trans. M. R. James, pp. 90–95, especially 91.

[3] *Widsith, A Study in Old English Heroic Legend*, R. W. Chambers, 1912, pp. 95–100.

[4] Kemp Malone (*Widsith*, 1936, pp. 193–4), holds that the name Wada 'seems to have much the same meaning as Breoca' [= breaker (of the shield wall)], 'and refers to prowess in battle'. This would be equally significant from my point of view. The M.E. references to Wade are collected by R. M. Wilson in *Leeds Studies in English*, ii. 15, note 6.

arise from material necessities or derive its source and power from the realm of ideas; the latter is probably the more effective. In this connexion, the apparent intrusion of the Wada-Offa I saga into eighth-century Mercian thought and action provides a clue which seems worth following up, tentatively, for the attention of scholars better equipped than myself.

The achievement of Offa I is recorded in seven famous lines of *Widsith*,[1] which are held to have been composed not later than the seventh century:

> ac Offa geslog   ærest monna
> cniht wesend   cynerica mæst;
> nænig efeneald him   eorlscipe maran
> on orette   ane sweorde:
> merce gemærd   wið Myrgingum
> bi Fifeldore: heoldon forð siþþan
> Engle ond Swæfe,   swa hit Offa geslog.[2]

Now the parallelism to this sequence in the career of Offa II is intriguing. Is it possible that he consciously designed and lived his own saga, based on his great forebear's achievement? The power of the heroic tradition in shaping the lives of noble men is implicit in much of the northern saga literature.[3]

We do not know the age of Offa II when he gained the kingdom of Mercia. The phrase *indolis puer* of the Tredinctun charter (*c.* 757) is probably a translation of some such word as *æðeling*,[4] and is not, therefore, much help. But Offa reigned thirty-nine years and is unlikely to have been very old in 757. Again, only an active campaign and some forcefulness (in the Offa I tradition) could have ousted Beornred within a few months of his assumption of royal power, and Offa II certainly then gained what he made the 'greatest

---

[1] Kemp Malone, op. cit., pp. 203–4.

[2] 'But Offa gained, first of men, by arms the greatest of kingdoms whilst yet a boy; no one of his age [did] greater deeds of valour in battle with his single sword; he drew the boundary against the Myrgingas at Fifeldor. Engle and Swaefe held it afterwards as Offa struck it out' (R. W. Chambers trans.). Fifeldor is on the river Eider in Slesvig.

[3] Compare Kemp Malone's commentary on the Offa I episode in *Widsith*. 'The poet's interest evidently lies, not so much in the deed itself as in the kingdom which was its reward. Or perhaps it is better to say that Offa's precocious prowess in battle would not have struck the poet as important but for its political consequences: it was Offa the builder of a nation . . . who won our poet's admiration.' Op. cit., p. 21.

Mr. Kenneth Sisam, F.B.A., in his *Studies in the History of Old English Literature* (1953) comments (pp. 134–5) on this application of early A.-S. poetry as follows:

'Sir Cyril Fox has suggested that when Offa built Offa's Dyke against the Welsh he had in mind his namesake's fame as a marker of lasting boundaries. This is not fanciful. Beowulf contains plenty of evidence that heroic poetry was much occupied with examples to follow or avoid. The confused *Vitae Duorum Offarum* written in the 12th century at St. Albans in old Mercian territory is evidence that parallels were drawn between the two Offas.'

Mr. Sisam also remarks, in the same connexion, that 'the episode of Offa's continental namesake and ancestor, with a fragment of the Mercian royal genealogy, is loosely inserted in Beowulf (lines 1931–62, C.F.) in a way that is hard to account for unless it was a compliment to his great Mercian namesake'. He considers it likely 'that Mercia had a share in the transmission of Beowulf, and the moulding of it in its extant form'. This view has a history. Cf. R. W. Chambers, *Beowulf*, 1914, p. 94: 'The violent introduction of this episode from the Offa-cycle points probably to an Anglian origin for our poem' (1953).

[4] Birch, *Cartularium Saxonicum*, no. 183, p. 260: 'Grant by Eanberht, Regulus of the Huiccii, and his brothers Uhtred and Aldred, to Milred, Bishop of Worcester of land at Tredingctun or Tredinctun, Co. Worcester, *c.* A.D. 757.' (Offa attests immediately after the persons named above.) I am indebted to Professor Bruce Dickins for the comment in the text.

of kingdoms' according to the ideas of the time; his activity in war was phenomenal. I suggest, then, that Offa's Dyke was intended to parallel Offa I's frontier-making (*merce gemærd* . . .) and that Offa II by such a tremendous effort hoped to achieve an equal result ('heoldon forð siþþan Engle ond Cumbran . . .').[1]

Saxo Grammaticus, who recorded in the twelfth century another version of the Offa I saga, tells us the name of Offa's sword; it was *Skrep*.[2] This emphasizes the *weapon* as forming the very essence of the tradition; and it is a curious fact that a record has come down to us suggesting that Offa II's sword may have been central to *his* story also. '*Ic geann Eadmunde minon breðer* [Edmund Ironside] *þæs swurdes þe Offa cyning ahte*' declares the ætheling Æthelstan in his will (1015).[3] This sword, whether it was the actual weapon of Offa II or the traditional weapon of Offa I, probably came into the possession of the Wessex royal house some 130 years previously, when the 'formal union of Mercia to Wessex' took place.

Widespread appreciation among the Anglo-Saxon aristocracy of a life lived on a heroic model, and of a life's work consciously designed for posterity, would explain the uniqueness of Offa's Dyke; namely that it is the only one of the many works of its class all over Britain to which the name of the builder has been consistently attached.[4]

THE 'BOUNDARY LINE OF CYMRU'

To fulfil the last part of my declared intention in this Commentary I must first compare the political boundary of Wales today—the E. limits of the seven Welsh counties established by the Act of 1538, and of Monmouthshire—with the line of Offa's Dyke. From the coast of the Irish Sea at Prestatyn to Chirk Castle, the boundary (of Flintshire and of Denbighshire) is to the E. of the Dyke. Thence to Presteigne the county boundaries first of Denbigh, then of Montgomery and Radnor, show a fairly close correspondence with the trace of the Dyke. From Presteigne to the neighbourhood of Monmouth county boundaries of Radnor, Brecknock, and Monmouth lie to the west of the ancient frontier; for the greater part of the distance thence to the river Severn the lower Wye is today the boundary as in Offa's time. For two-fifths, then, of the total distance of 149 miles the modern and ancient boundaries closely correspond; for another two-fifths the modern boundary is on the Welsh side of Offa's Dyke, and for the remaining one-fifth on the English side. These fractions and brief descriptions represent a pretty close relationship between Offa's frontier and the modern boundaries, as is seen on the map; all the more

---

[1] I should point out that Miss D. Whitelock (*The Audience of Beowulf*, 1951) is disposed to regard the Widsith evidence as of later date: 'a complimentary reminder that a greater Offa built a greater boundary, Offa's Dyke' (1953).

[2] Saxo's story is conveniently summarized in *Beowulf: An Introduction*, R. W. Chambers, 2nd ed. 1932, pp. 32–33. See also his *Widsith*, pp. 86–87, and 91, f. 2.

[3] Miss D. Whitelock, *Anglo-Saxon Wills*, xx, 1930, p. 58, and note, p. 171.

[4] Professor Bruce Dickins who kindly read this before publication (in 1940), commenting on the theory in general, remarks that Offa II named his son 'Ecgferth' = peace imposed by the sword; and that his own name must have been approved by himself for it is hypocoristic, probably for Osferth. The points made by my friend provide me with valuable support. The *Vitae Duorum Offarum*, again, shows that the two Offas were linked in the popular mind; it is a second-rate authority and does not seem to have any further significance in the present context. For summary and comment see R. W. Chambers, *Widsith*, pp. 88–90, or *Beowulf*, pp. 34–40.

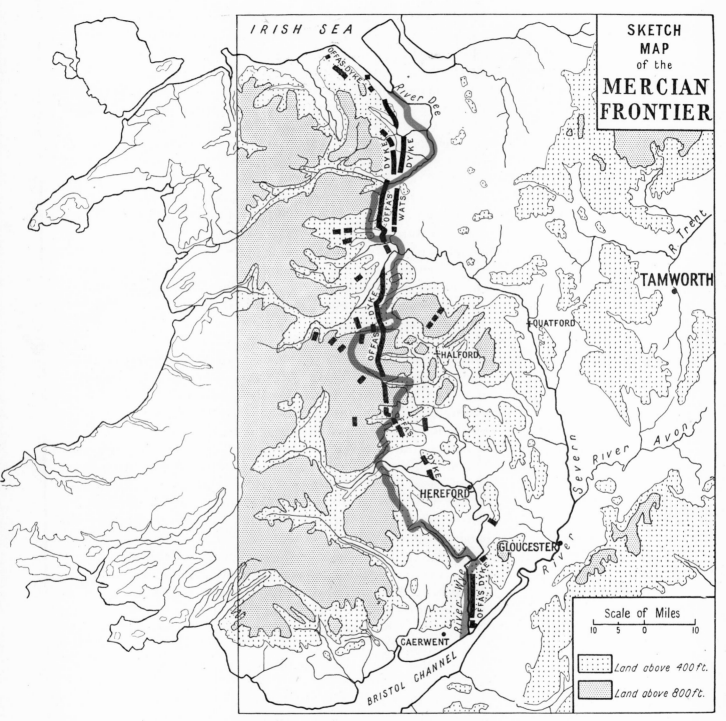

Fig. 121. Offa's Dyke, Wat's Dyke, and other frontier works of Mercia. The black rectangles in the Central March are the 'Short Dykes'. The modern boundary of Wales-and-Monmouthshire is printed in red.

(After *Proc. British Academy*, 1940, opp. p. 300.)

remarkable when it is noted that the two alignments rarely coincide exactly, and that pressure on the Celtic people at one point or another of this long line, whether from Angles, Normans, or Englishmen, from Offa's death in 796 to 1538, a period of over seven centuries, though intermittent was severe.

I venture to attribute the correspondence to natural causes, to which politics have proved unconsciously subservient. Duality of structure is the key to the early history of S. Britain.[1] In the W. are palaeozoic rocks—mainly slates, sandstones, hard and massive limestones: the W. is therefore mountainous. In the E. are secondary and tertiary formations—mainly chalk, gravel, sands, and clays; the E. is therefore a fertile lowland. The change in physical character from one to the other tends to be very abrupt; the palaeozoic outcrop forms in fact a natural frontier. This natural frontier in the part of the island with which we are concerned runs from N. to S. along the Welsh March. The line of the outcrop crosses Flintshire, Denbighshire, and N. Shropshire, thence following the Severn valley to the Bristol Channel. The Mercians never effectively occupied the palaeozoic bastions in N. Wales—the Clwydian Hills and the Berwyns, but in the central and S. march the broken character of the palaeozoic frontier—an upland deeply dissected with fertile intermont valleys—permitted Mercian occupation up to the main Cambrian mountain mass, and to the Wye valley, as we have seen.

I am, of course, aware that subsequent conquests of Wales were far more extensive than the Mercian alignments indicate, and that the limits of these conquests showed little or no correspondence with geological outcrops. This truth suggests that the influence which mountain masses exert on political arrangements does not lie necessarily in the prevention of conquest, but on something much more subtle. It is now accepted as broadly true for the prehistoric and protohistoric periods that in the lowland of Britain new cultures tend to be imposed; that in the highland they tend to be absorbed, transformed, or lost. Wales is a typical highland region, and this cultural elasticity, this stubborn survival of cultural traits, is a marked feature of early Welsh history. The Romans thoroughly conquered 'Wales', but Romanization was only effective in the E. borders and the S. sea-plain. Let us consider a later period of which more is known. The efficiency of the Norman technique of organization and settlement in those regions of Wales where it operated is a commonplace of the textbooks, but there was a great deal of Welsh territory where it was never attempted. The new order was confined to the intermont valleys and the coastal plains, or to the immediate neighbourhood of a fortified post of strategic importance. Only in the more favoured open valleys are Norman settlements found above 400 ft. The high country was left in the hands of the Welsh, whose estates were known as Welshries, being held by customary Welsh tenure and tribute.[2] This was commonsense economics. The life of the highlander is harder than that of the lowlander, and mountainous country requires a special technique for pastoral or agricultural activities; in such techniques the newcomer will be less efficient than the native-born. In Wales he has among other difficulties to

---

[1] See Fox, *Personality of Britain*, 4th ed., Cardiff, 1943, esp. map B, and p. 29.

[2] William Rees, *Handbook to the Historical Map of* *S. Wales and the Border*, 1933, pp. 4 and 14. See also Fox, 'Regional Guides to Ancient Monuments', vol. iv, *South Wales*, 2nd ed., 1950, pp. 24 ff.

combat an unusually heavy rainfall. It is easy to see how in such upland areas native traditions could survive, and furthermore, how the older race, the older customs, and the older language, entrenched in the hills, could in peaceful fashion and by unperceived infiltration reassert their rights and claims in valleys conquered by the sword and settled by English folk, when the sword became rust and the protecting castle a ruin. Such unnoticed pressures, I suggest, shaped the political map of the sixteenth century as it had shaped earlier cultural frontiers.

Offa's Dyke, then, is in our time, among gentle and simple alike, the symbolic frontier[1] —the 'boundary line of Cymru', because there is a natural limit to the territory of a highland people like the Welsh, and the Dyke is the only visible and historic structure which corresponds reasonably well to that fundamental reality: *heoldon forð siþþan Engle ond Cumbran swa hit Offa geslog.*

Valediction

The survey of Offa's Dyke and Wat's Dyke, not to mention the Short Dykes, was certainly a laborious undertaking, both in field and study, and is perhaps tedious to read. But I venture to think that it was worth doing, for other reasons than those indicated in the narrative. It demonstrates the competence, skill, and dogged determination applied through two centuries to the solution of a difficult problem by related groups of Englishmen in the Dark Ages; and the reality and vigour of the Welsh opposition which made such efforts necessary. It also helps us to see, though in blurred outline, one corner of a lost England, the England of the Anglo-Saxon pioneer, adventurer, frontiersman. Here, on the borders of the highland, nature was his enemy as well as man. Densely forested hills, ravines matted with primeval jungle, extensive and impassable marshes environed his ways and conditioned his activities, agricultural and military.

The more closely we have studied the Dykes, the more illuminating, significant, and explicable are their courses and characters. Consequently, the survey illustrates the capacity of archaeology to demonstrate the rationality of its subject matter; to prove that 'any tangle of human facts, patiently unravelled, makes sense'.[2]

[1] As a well-read Welsh friend remarked to me: 'When I refer today to my English neighbours, I often do so naturally in the phrase, "Tu hwnt i Glawdd Offa —beyond Offa's Dyke".'

[2] R. G. Collingwood, apropos of a kindred work— Hadrian's Wall. *J.R.S.* xxi, 1931, pp. 62–63.

APPENDIX I

BIBLIOGRAPHY (1926, 1938)

Arranged in chronological sequences

I. OFFA'S DYKE

A. EARLY AUTHORITIES[1]

Asser, *De Rebus Gestis Aelfredi.*

Simeon of Durham, *Historia regum* (*c.* 1129), Rolls edition, ii. 66.

St. Oswald, Life of, in the Rolls edition of Simeon of Durham, i. 353.

John of Salisbury, *Policraticus* (*c.* 1159), bk. vi, ch. 6.

Giraldus Cambrensis, *Descriptio Kambriae* (1194), bk. ii, ch. 7.

Walter Map, *De Nugis Curialium* (*c.* 1200), dist. ii, cap. 17.

Public Record Office (*MS.* B. 3063) has a (thirteenth century) reference to 'Offediche' in a grant of land in 'Riston', near Chirbury, Salop.

Higden, Ranulf, *Polychronicon* (*c.* 1352), Rolls series, ii. 34–35.

Brut y Saeson, in *Myvyrian Archaiology of Wales* (Denbigh edition, p. 653).

Welsh Laws, Venedotian Code (ii. xvi). Ed. Aneurin Owen, i. 182.

Lewis Glyn Cothi (fifteenth century). *Poetical Works*, ed. 1837, pp. 269–70.

Leland, *The Itinerary in Wales, 1536–9.* Ed. Toulmin Smith, 1906, p. 40.

D. Powel, *Historie of Cambria* (1584), 1811 edition, pp. 16–17.

E. Lhwyd, *Parochialia* (1703) (*Arch. Camb.* Supplement, 1911, iii. 96).

The above records are of varying degrees of interest. The more important, Welsh and English, are quoted and discussed by the following writers:

A. N. Palmer in *Y Cymmrodor*, xii (1897), pp. 66–69.

J. E. Lloyd, later Sir John Lloyd, *A History of Wales* (1911), i, pp. 198–9.

A. Griscom in *Y Cymmrodor*, xxxv (1925), pp. 97–107 (includes a detailed analysis of Welsh sources).

The following should also be consulted:

T. McKenny Hughes, *Archaeologia*, liii (1893), pp. 466–7.

H. L. Jones, *Arch. Camb.*, 1856, pp. 2–5 and 151–4.

J. Earle, ibid., 1857, pp. 201–9.

Thos. Stevens, ibid., 1858, pp. 85–86.

H. S. Milman, ibid., 1860, p. 37.

B. MODERN AUTHORS[2]

Modern study of the Dyke may be said to commence with the antiquary, Thomas Pennant, who published the first edition of his *Tours* in 1783. This list, then, is chronologically arranged.

T. Pennant, *Tours*, 2nd ed., revised by author, 3 vols., 1810, i, pp. 349 ff. Brief topographical account of Offa's and Wat's Dykes. (See also i, p. 31; iii, pp. 200, 219.)

---

[1] I am much indebted to the late Professor Sir John E. Lloyd for assistance in preparing this list.

[2] This bibliography of modern authors contains only papers or books which deal with the Dyke as a whole, or with large portions of it.

S. Lewis, *Topographical Dictionary of Wales*, 1833, 2 vols. Useful notes on the course of the Dyke recorded under the parishes through which it passes.

C. H. Hartshorne, *Salopia Antiqua*, 1841, pp. 181–96. Brief topographical survey of Offa's and Wat's Dykes. Includes a chart showing scale of these and other dykes.

G. Ormerod, 'An Account of Some Ancient Remains, etc.', *Archaeologia*, xxix (1842), pp. 13–17. Description, with map, of the southern portion, chiefly in the neighbourhood of Chepstow.

H. L. Jones, 'Offa's Dyke and Wat's Dyke', *Arch. Camb.*, 1856, pp. 1 ff. A careful survey in broad outline of the whole course, with suggestive comments. The paper contains a note by G. Ormerod supplementing *Archaeologia*, vol. xxix. Supplementary notes to this paper will be found on pp. 151 ff.

Edwin Guest, 'On the Northern Termination of Offa's Dyke', *Arch. Camb.*, 1858, pp. 335 ff.

G. Ormerod, *Strigulensia*. Privately printed. 1861. Contains a chapter on the southern portion of Offa's Dyke, being the substance of the paper previously published in *Archaeologia*, with additions.

W. Trevor Parkins, 'Offa's Dyke', *Arch. Camb.*, 1875, pp. 275 ff. Brief general survey, of little or no value.

T. McKenny Hughes, 'On Offa's Dyke', *Archaeologia*, liii (1893), pp. 465 ff. A valuable analysis of the problems connected with the Dyke.

E. Owen, 'Offa's Dyke', Montgomeryshire Collections, 1896, xxix, pp. 93–111. A brief survey of the problems, with notes on the Llanymynech district.

A. N. Palmer, 'Offa's and Wat's Dyke', *Y Cymmrodor*, xii (1897), pp. 65 ff. Very useful for Denbighshire and Flintshire.

J. E. Lloyd, *A History of Wales*, 1911, pp. 198–201. A brief topographical survey with useful comments.

II. WAT'S DYKE

A. EARLY AUTHORITIES

Higden, Ranulf, *Polychronicon*, *c.* 1352, Rolls Series, ii, p. 34.
Brut y Tywysogion. In *Myvyrian Archaiology of Wales*, 2nd ed., 1870, p. 686.
Churchyard, *Worthines of Wales* (1587), 2nd ed., 1776, p. 104.

B. MODERN AUTHORS

Thomas Pennant, *Tours*, 2nd ed., 3 vols., 1810, i, pp. 31, 349–50.
S. Lewis, *Topographical Dictionary of Wales*, 1833. See under parishes crossed by the Dyke.
H. Longueville Jones, *Arch. Camb.*, 1856, pp. 5–7 and 20–23.
Edwin Guest, ibid., 1858, pp. 335–8.
T. M'Kenny Hughes, *Archaeologia*, vol. 53, Part 2, 1893, pp. 473–4.
A. N. Palmer, *Y Cymmrodor*, vol. xii, 1897, pp. 65–86.
Royal Commission on Ancient Monuments (Wales), vol. ii, *County of Flint*, 1912; vol. iv, *County of Denbigh*, 1914. See Indexes and 'Earthworks' maps.
A. Griscom, *Y Cymmrodor*, vol. xxxv, 1925, pp. 100–3, 106.

III. BIBLIOGRAPHY OF THE AUTHOR'S SURVEY[1]

Offa's Dyke: a field survey:

First Report: 'Offa's Dyke in Northern Flintshire', *Archaeologia Cambrensis*, 1926, pp. 133–79.

Second Report: 'Offa's Dyke from Coed Talwrn (Treuddyn Parish), Flintshire, to Plas Power park (Bersham parish) Denbighshire', ibid., 1927, pp. 232–68.

Third Report: 'Offa's Dyke from Plas Power park, Bersham parish, Denbighshire, to the river

_____
[1] See Preface to this volume, p. xxiii.

Vyrnwy on the boundary between Llanymynech (Shropshire) and Carreghofa (Montgomeryshire) parishes', ibid., 1928, pp. 33–110.

Fourth Report: 'Offa's Dyke in Montgomeryshire', ibid., 1929, pp. 1–60.

Fifth Report: 'Offa's Dyke in the Mountain Zone', ibid., 1930, pp. 1–73.

Sixth Report: 'Offa's Dyke in the Wye Valley', ibid., 1931, pp. 1–74.

'Wat's Dyke: a field survey', ibid., 1934, pp. 205–78.

A brief summary of the work done was published in 1938 in *The Transactions* of the *Yorkshire Society for Celtic Studies* (vol. i, 1937–8), pp. 1–8, and the survey of the Dyke in Herefordshire was reproduced in part in *The Royal Commission on Ancient Monuments, Herefordshire*, vol. iii, pp. xxx–xxxi. *Antiquity*, 1929, pp. 135–54, contains some account of Offa's Dyke with illustrations from the *Archaeologia Cambrensis* papers cited above. The 1940 summary, *Proc. British Academy*, xxvi, pp. 275–300, is largely reproduced in the present reprint.

APPENDIX II

PORTIONS of the Dykes considered to be specially worthy of preservation, and scheduled by the Ancient Monuments Department of H.M. Ministry of Works. The text is that of the submissions made by the author to the Chief Inspector, year by year.

OFFA'S DYKE. CHAPTER III (1927)

A. From spot-level 621 to spot-level 585 on Coed-Talwrn–Llanfynydd road. This road is here on the crest of the Dyke, and widening would destroy the character of the earthwork. Should a wide road be necessary a new alignment should be chosen. See Fig. 11.

B. From Llanfynydd village northward for a distance of 110 yards. Road widening, if undertaken, should be confined to the E. margin; the rampart abuts on the road on the W. side. See Fig. 11.

C. The short portion, 50 yards in length, in the grounds of Ffrith Hall. This is the only fragment adequately representing the original dimensions and character of the Dyke between Llanfynydd and Pen-y-coed farm, a distance of 1 mile 340 yards. See Fig. 12.

D. The Brymbo Hill portion. Fine, and very instructive in its choice of alignment. In the neighbourhood of a growing township, and therefore in danger. See Fig. 12.

E. From Vron farm to the river Gwenfro. An instructive fragment showing method of approach to a ravine. Building operations, judging from the expansion of neighbouring hamlets and townships, may at any time be undertaken here. See Fig. 13.

OFFA'S DYKE. CHAPTER IV (1928)

A. From cross-track S. of 'tank' in Plas Power park to the river Clywedog. A well-preserved portion, presenting an interesting example of 'overdeepening' of the ditch, and showing approach to a ravine on the reverse side of a spur. (See Fig. 18.) Denbighshire, 6-in. O.S. map, XXVIII SW.

B. From scarp on right bank of river Clywedog to embankment, Rhos branch, G.W. Railway. A fine stretch, with a slight change of direction by the mound at Cadwgan Hall. The mound, of unknown origin, but possibly related to the Dyke, should also be scheduled. (See Fig. 18.) Denbighshire, XXVIII SW.

C. From Bronwylfa road to the Pentre-bychan brook. A well-preserved portion, with ancient oaks on the bank. The ditch is very well-marked N. of Pentre-bychan Hall. (See Figs. 18 and 19.) Denbighshire, XXVIII SW.

D. From brick yards of Ruabon brick works to Tatham farm. A finely preserved and very important portion, wooded on the reverse slope of Pen-y-gardden. It is endangered by industrial development. The fort on the hill-top, the existence of which may have determined the course of the Dyke here, should also be preserved. (See Fig. 20.) Denbighshire, XXXV NW.

E. From Tatham bridge to G.W. Railway main line. The portion from the bridge to the grammar school cross-roads has been damaged by road-widening and by extension of the grammar school. The portion thence to the Ruabon–Llangollen road is very well marked, save in the immediate neighbourhood of Tir-y-fron, but is suffering from propinquity to an industrial area. The portion crossing 'The Green' may be threatened by building development. (See Fig. 20.) Denbighshire, XXXV SW.

F. From river Dee to Tan-y-cut. This portion shows the mode of approach to the Dee; the Dyke ends abruptly on the river scarp, revealing an interesting cross-section. (Fig. 21.) Denbighshire, XL NW.

G. From Canal S. of Tan-y-cut to cross-hedge NE. of Wern Cottage. A well-preserved portion in a typical agricultural countryside. (Figs. 21 and 22.) Denbighshire, XL NW.

H. From farm-track E. of Caeau Gwynion to the Little Gate–Glasdir road. A finely preserved portion (See Fig. 22.) Denbighshire, XL NW.

J. From the N. boundary of Chirk park to the lake. A very fine and well-preserved portion, with ancient oaks. (See Fig. 22.) Denbighshire, XL NW.

K. From the S. boundary of Chirk Castle gardens to the 400-ft. contour close to the S. boundary of the park. Very fine, and instructive in its relation to the terrain. (See Figs. 22 and 23.) Denbighshire, XL NW. and XL SW.

L. From the foot-path crossing the Dyke, SW. of Pen-y-Bryn quarry to Careg-y-big farmstead. This stretch of $3\frac{1}{2}$ miles crosses upland pasture or moorland; it is practically complete, for the most part finely preserved, and for many reasons of great importance to students of the earthwork. (Figs. 23 to 25.) Denbighshire, XL SW. and XXXIX SE.; Shropshire, XI NE. and SE.

M. On Baker's Hill. From cross-hedge S. of O of Old Quarry to cross-hedge NNW. of W (Well) on Llawnt–Oswestry road. A very impressive portion of the Dyke on a commanding alignment. (See Fig. 25.) Shropshire, XI SE.

N. On Craig Forda. From the N. end of Race-course wood to the ford N. of Llanforda Mill. A portion remarkable in alignment, and constructionally interesting. (See Figs. 25 to 26.) Shropshire, XII SW. and XI SE.; XIX NW. and XVIII NE.

O. From a point opposite the O to the cross-hedge by the e of Offa's Dyke, SE. of Pentreshannel farm. A perfectly preserved fragment. (See Fig. 26.) Shropshire, XIX NW.

P. From end to end of the field E. of spot-level 654 on the Trefonnen–Treflach road. A perfect fragment, with several unusual features. (See Fig. 27.) Shropshire, XIX SW.

Q. From a point due W. of spot-level 677 to a point due W. of spot-level 668·2 on the main road through Treflach Wood hamlet. A perfect portion, presenting a remarkable alignment in broken country. (See Fig. 27.) Shropshire, XIX SW.

R. On Llynclys Hill. From e of Dyke, at the foot of the scarp, to F of FP, where the bank ends at the cliff face. An interesting moorland section. (See Fig. 27.) Shropshire, XIX SW.

OFFA'S DYKE. CHAPTER VI (1929)

A. From the field numbered 4 on my map (Fig. 35) inclusive to the Severn (Fig. 36), excluding the house and garden known as Hafod Offa and the Llandysilio station area. An interesting succession of straight alignments in flat lowland country. Montgomeryshire XI SW. and XVI NW.

B. From the enclosure numbered 25 to that numbered 29 on my map (Fig. 37), inclusive, i.e. from the by-road to Hope to the centre of Goppas wood. A well-preserved sector including an original gap, an alignment on to a spring-head, and an overdeepened ditch. Montgomeryshire XXIII NE. and SE.

C. The Dyke in Leighton park and woodlands. From Lodge at N. entrance to the park (Fig. 38) to the Old Quarry at the S. end (enclosure numbered 38 in my map, Fig. 40). A very interesting alignment across difficult country. Montgomeryshire XXIII SE., XXIV SW., XXX NE., XXXI NW.

D. From by-road to Nant Cribau to S. end of Nant Cribau park, BM. 436 (Fig. 41). An interesting section which has never been ploughed. Area recently disparked and Dyke damaged by tree cutting. Montgomeryshire XXX NE.

E. From cottage on by-road to Upper Hem to crest of Hem ridge, adjacent to fields numbered 64 and 65 (Fig. 41). An imposing stretch on the W. side of a hill. Montgomeryshire XXX NE. and SE.

F. From Field 77a (Fig. 42) to S. end of Rownal covert. A very fine stretch of the Dyke, on the largest scale, and very well preserved. Montgomeryshire XXX SE.

G. From the Shrewsbury–Montgomery road to a point 300 yards N. of the Lack brook: excluding parts of the Dyke in fields 88–90, and in field 98, on my map (Figs. 42 and 43). A well-preserved and interesting sector sinuous in trace but very direct. Montgomeryshire XXX SE., XXXVII NE.

H. From Brompton bridge to spot-level 617 at Lower Cwm (Figs. 43 and 44). An interesting portion, both sinuous and straight in alignment, including the spur work and finely preserved parts in woodland. Montgomeryshire XXXVIII SW.

I. From the road angle S. of Cwm hamlet (by field 109 on my map, Fig. 44) to the end of the sector, spot-level 1,267. Montgomeryshire XLV NW.

OFFA'S DYKE. CHAPTER VI (1930)

Offa's Dyke in the mountain zone is of exceptional interest and importance. It has therefore been recommended for scheduling from the point where this year's survey begins (near Nuns wood, Fig. 53) to the point where it ends (Three Shepherds on Rushock Hill, Fig. 71), omitting only a few short stretches where the exact line is doubtful, or where the Dyke is badly damaged, or so slight as to be hardly visible.

A. From—and including—Nut wood (Fig. 53) to the river Clun at Bryndrinog (Fig. 55). *Excluding* the valley floors of the river Unk and Mainstone brook (Fig. 53), and the portion (on Fig. 54) from the 900-ft. contour by field 11 to the valley floor where the trackways join near BM 840·4.

B. From the Lower Spoad area, N. of the main road (Fig. 55), to Panpunton Hill (Fig. 58). *Excluding* the steep N. slope of Cwmsanaham Hill from above Brynorgan to the ravine, and the portion bordering the *Cwm* of *Cwm*sanaham on the N. side from the *a* of sc*a*rps to the head of the *cwm* (Fig. 58).

C. The portions in Knighton which form boundaries to fields marked 32, 34, 36, and 37 on Fig. 59.

D. From and including Great Frydd wood on Fig. 59 to Furrow Hill, at the end of Fig. 61. *Excluding* the portion bordering fields 44, 45, 46; that between Pool House and field 50; and that from BM 1217·2 to the end of Fig. 60; also the portion crossing fields 52 and 53 on Fig. 61.

E. The fragment at spot-level 583 (Fig. 62).

F. From road junction by Yew Tree farm (Fig. 62) to the quarry on Burfa Bank (Fig. 64). *Excluding* Granner wood and the quarries at its NE. end, and field 61 by Burfa farm (Fig. 63).

G. From the neighbourhood of Ditch Hill bridge to the 'Yews' on Rushock Hill (Fig. 64).

OFFA'S DYKE. CHAPTER VII (1931)

The small extent of Offa's Dyke from N. Herefordshire to the mouth of the river Wye—some 13 miles —heightens its value as an ancient monument, for on these scattered portions, and on them alone, depends the reconstruction of the historical frontier of the eighth century throughout the entire stretch of 60 miles. It has therefore been scheduled from the point where this year's survey begins (Rushock Hill, Fig. 71) to the point where it ends (Sedbury Cliffs, Fig. 86), omitting only a few short stretches where the exact line is doubtful, or where the Dyke is badly damaged, or so slight as to be hardly visible. The appended list embodies these decisions.

A. From Rushock Hill to Kennel wood inclusive (Fig. 71).

B. The R. Arrow portions as marked on Fig. 72.

C. The Curl brook portion (Fig. 73). *Excluding* the levelled portions on either side of the large fragment in field 6 where the straight alignment begins, up to the Lynhales Drive on the one side and the railway on the other.

D. The Yazor brook portions, as marked on Fig. 74.

E. From N. of 'The Steps' to the river Wye, as marked on Fig. 75.

F. The English Bicknor portions, as marked on Fig. 78. *Excluding* the 'natural' frontier line.

G. From Highbury wood (Fig. 80) to Dennel Hill wood (Fig. 84). *Excluding* the stretches of 'natural' frontier—cliff or scarp—here and there intervening, and also the following: Fig. 80—Dyke bordering field 16; Fig. 82—Dyke from Megs Folly to field 30 inclusive; Dyke on fields 36 to 40 inclusive, and on fields 42, 45, 46, 48.

H. Dyke in Chapelhouse wood (Fig. 85).

I. From filter beds to Sedbury Cliffs (Fig. 86).

WAT'S DYKE. CHAPTER VIII (1934)

Wat's Dyke, having regard to its situation in an agricultural countryside, is singularly complete. This chapter has shown that it is an admirable example of the technique of running earthwork construction, and it is not improbable that now research has been initiated, further discoveries will be made (by historical students) permitting us to place it in its exact historical context. Its importance, then, is likely to increase rather than diminish, and all the characteristic portions should be scheduled by the Ancient Monuments Department of the Office of Works. Much of the Dyke has been destroyed in recent years for housing and road widening, and many stretches, especially those near the two growing towns of Wrexham and Oswestry, are in danger.

A. Fig. 96.—The Wern Sirk and Fron Tydyr portions.

The Northern Sector

B. Fig. 97.—All except partially levelled portion in field 4, and that bordering field 6. Fig. 98.—Portions in fields 7, 10, 11, 14, 15; and thence to road SE. of Bryn Offa. Fig. 99.—All, except in field 19. Fig. 100.—All, except in fields 25, 26, and fragment adjoining railway cutting on S. side. Fig. 101.—All, except in fields 29, 30, 31, 32, and 40. Fig. 102.—From fields 41 to 43 inclusive, and 44, and from BM 295·8 to Rhydyn farm.

The Central Sector

C. Fig. 103.—Portions bordering fields 47, 48, and 49 only. Fig. 104.—Fragment S. of Regent Street railway bridge, and portions S. of Ruabon road, except in garden of 'The Court'. Fig. 105.—All remaining portions in Erddig park, and from fields 53 to 55 inclusive. Fig. 106.—All, except small terminal portion immediately S. of Black brook bridge road, and portions crossing Pentre-clawdd farm complex of buildings. Fig. 107.—From fields 64 to 65 inclusive.

The Southern Sector

D. Fig. 108.—From marsh S. of new railway embankment to road junction E. of Henlle Hall, and portion in field 69. Fig. 109.—Portions from field 71 to river Perry; portion in field 76. Fig. 110.—From *D* of *D*yke S. of Pentre-clawdd farm to Old Oswestry; from Old Oswestry to boundary of Gravel Pit plantation. Fig. 111.—From BM 394·1 to BM 370·1, the portion bordering field 86, and from spot-level 324 to river Morda.

APPENDIX III

OFFA'S DYKE AND WAT'S DYKE AS PARISH OR COUNTY BOUNDARIES

THE extent, absolute and proportionate, to which the Dykes form parish and county boundaries seem to be no greater than might be expected of any earthworks of their prominence, providing as they do visible and convenient limits for administrative units in times subsequent to their functional use as the frontier lines of the Mercian state.

OFFA'S DYKE AND WAT'S DYKE: SUMMARY TABLE OF THE EXTENT OF BOUNDARIES IN RELATION TO TOTAL LENGTH OF THE DYKES

Portion of Dyke	Total length of Dyke	Parish boundaries	County boundaries
I. Offa's Dyke			
N. Flintshire, Ch. II. . . .	6 miles	¾ mile	..
Flintshire and Denbighshire, Ch. III .	5 miles	..	..
Denbighshire and Shropshire, Ch. IV .	22 miles	2 miles 540 yards	3 miles 1,370 yards
Montgomeryshire, Ch. V . . .	15 miles	2,100 yards	3,275 yards
Shropshire, Radnorshire, and Hereford- shire, Ch. VI	21 miles	4 miles 1,330 yards	..
Herefordshire and Gloucestershire, Ch. VII*	13 miles	850 yards	..
II. Wat's Dyke			
Flintshire, Denbighshire, and Shrop- shire	20½ miles	2 miles 1,340 yards	..

* That Offa's Dyke does not form parish or county boundaries anywhere in Gloucestershire is due to its contiguity to the natural boundary formed by the river Wye.

OFFA'S DYKE, DETAILS

Chapter II. Only ¾ mile of the 5-mile stretch whereon the course of the Dyke is exactly or approximately known coincides, or can coincide, with a parish boundary. The short portion in question divides the parish of Llanasa from the parishes of Whitford and Newmarket.

Chapter III. At no point within the sector under investigation does the Dyke form a parish or county boundary.

Chapter IV. In Denbighshire, Offa's Dyke forms the boundary between the parishes of Esclusham Above (Dyke) and Esclusham Below (Dyke) for 1 mile 1,200 yards, and between the SW. angle of Rhosllannerchrugog parish and Ruabon (570 yards); it forms the eastern boundary of Glyn Traian parish for 2 miles 1,430 yards, thus dividing Denbighshire from Shropshire.

In Shropshire, it forms the boundary between Llanyblodwel and Oswestry Rural parishes for a distance of 530 yards. It then, utilizing the western defences of Llanymynech Hill, forms the boundary between Shropshire and Montgomeryshire for a distance of 800 yards; the straight alignment again from the hill to Llanymynech church, a distance of 900 yards, is the boundary between these counties.

The Dyke thus forms parish boundaries for a total distance of 2 miles 540 yards, and county boundaries for 3 miles 1,370 yards, out of a total length, in this section, of some 22 miles.

Chapter V. Offa's Dyke in this sector forms the boundary between the parishes of Llandysilio and Llandrinio for a distance of 1,270 yards (Fig. 35), and between the parishes of Leighton and Trelystan on the slopes of the Long Mountain for about 830 yards (Figs. 38 and 39). The Dyke forms the boundary between Montgomeryshire and Shropshire in the Lymore park region, for a total distance of over 1¾ miles (3,250 yards) (Figs. 41–43). The Montgomery county boundary touches the Dyke at the Devil's Hole (Fig. 41, field 76), and its course across the Dyke at the Kerry Hill ridgeway is deflected by the Dyke in such a manner as to be coincident with it for some 25 yards (Fig. 45 and p. 113). Thus, out of a total length of over 15 miles, 2,100 yards of the Dyke form parish, and 3,275 yards county boundaries.

Chapter VI. Offa's Dyke in this sector forms the boundary in Shropshire between Clun and Mainstone parishes, at the Hergan col, for a distance of 220 yards, and between Stow and Llanfair Waterdine parishes for at least 1,500 yards. In Radnorshire it forms the boundary between Knighton and Whitton parishes for 350 yards, between Whitton and Norton parishes for 2,400 yards, between Whitton and Presteigne parishes for 2,000 yards, between Discoed and Litton-and-Cascob parishes for 230 yards, and between Discoed and Evenjobb parishes at the Newcastle Hill col for 270 yards.

In Herefordshire the Dyke is the boundary between Lower Harpton and Knill parishes for 250 yards, and between Knill and Kington Rural parishes for 1,150 yards.

Thus, of a total length of some 21 miles, 4 miles 1,330 yards of the Dyke form parish boundaries. The Dyke does not, at any point in this sector, form a county boundary.

Chapter VII. Offa's Dyke in this sector forms a parish boundary between Byford and Bishopstone parishes in Herefordshire, for 430 yards, and between Byford and Bridge Sollers parishes, also in Herefordshire, for 420 yards. Thus, of a total length of some 13 miles, only 850 yards of the Dyke form parish boundaries. It does not at any point in this sector form a county boundary.

WAT'S DYKE, DETAILS: AND A COMPARISON WITH OFFA'S DYKE

Chapter VIII. Wat's Dyke now forms a parish boundary:

For 190 yards between Northop and Mold Rural parishes, Flintshire.

For 830 yards between Acton and Stansty parishes; for 1,850 yards between Wrexham Regis and Broughton or Bersham parishes; and for 1,080 yards between Marchwiel and Ruabon parishes, Denbighshire.

For 910 yards between Oswestry Urban and Oswestry Rural parishes, Shropshire.[1]

In all, 2 miles 1,340 yards out of a total length of constructed Dyke of 20½ miles, that is, 13·4 per cent.

The first 1-in. O.S. map, 1827, Sheet 74, marks the line of the Dyke as a parish boundary, in and N. of Wynnstay park, for 1,700 yards; from Preeshenlle bridge to the river Perry, 1 mile 140 yards; and adjacent to the termination of the Dyke at the river Morda, for 270 yards.

If these be included, the total length of parish boundary is 4 miles 1,690 yards, and the percentage 24·4. Offa's Dyke is 81 miles long, and shows 15 miles 225 yards of parish boundaries, that is 18·6 per cent. One-third of this Offan mileage of parish boundaries, 5 miles 1,125 yards, is also a boundary between English and Welsh counties, that is 7 per cent. of the total Dyke length.

I insert these Wat's Dyke figures, and the Offan comparisons, as a record which may save possible future inquirers the trouble of delving for them in the 6-in. maps, or in my papers. But I do not think they have any importance. They show that neither Wat's nor Offa's Dyke had any political significance when the parish and county boundaries were fixed, a fact which no one questions. The percentages, 18 and 24, are close enough to suggest that the same causative factors operate in each. They also are just such as might be expected; the advantage of a visible and recognizable boundary must occasionally override local economic or legal considerations—or it may happen to coincide with them. We should get precisely the same results, I suggest, if the Dykes had been prehistoric.

[1] The P.B. is not in this stretch throughout exactly on the line of the Dyke, having been deflected by the modern road.

INDEX I
(TOPOGRAPHICAL)

Note. Names appearing in Chapter headings or map underlines are not indexed.

INDEX II
(SUBJECT)

Note. Duplication of headings in the *Contents Table* is avoided as far as possible. Neither the Preface nor the Appendixes are indexed herein. Repetitive detail of the course and character of the Dykes is not indexed.

PRINTED IN
GREAT BRITAIN
AT THE
UNIVERSITY PRESS
OXFORD
BY
CHARLES BATEY
PRINTER
TO THE
UNIVERSITY